Bank Recovery and Resolution

International Banking and Finance Law Series

VOLUME 26

Series Editors

Professor Joseph Norton, Professor Ross Buckley and Professor Douglas Arner.

Subjects

Topical issues in international banking and financial services law, such as regulatory responses to the global financial crisis or regulation of alternative investment funds.

Objective & Readership

To provide authoritative analysis of trends and complex subjects for academics, regulators and practitioners involved in international banking and financial services law.

The titles published in this series are listed at the end of this volume.

Bank Recovery and Resolution

Second Edition

Sven Schelo

Wolters Kluwer

Published by:
Kluwer Law International B.V.
PO Box 316
2400 AH Alphen aan den Rijn
The Netherlands
E-mail: international-sales@wolterskluwer.com
Website: lrus.wolterskluwer.com

Sold and distributed by:
Wolters Kluwer Legal & Regulatory U.S.
7201 McKinney Circle
Frederick, MD 21704
United States of America
Email: customer.service@wolterskluwer.com

ISBN 978-94-035-1881-7

e-Book: ISBN 978-94-035-1915-9
web-PDF: ISBN 978-94-035-1924-1

dedicated to Katja
and Richard, Ferdinand, Oskar and August

Table of Contents

Foreword

Banks are complex institutions. The same applies to the restructuring of banks. Since the financial crisis of 2008, enormous efforts have been made worldwide to draft rules to prevent reoccurrence of those events. The Bank Resolution and Recovery Directive is one – if not the most – prominent and novel result of those efforts. It is to be combined with the Single Resolution Mechanism (SRM) and the Resolution Fund. Overall, these new rules stand for a very crucial pillar in the European Banking Union. To understand and keep up to date with all these rules is not easy; those searching for orientation may perceive them as a 'jungle' at first and stay off them, a reaction which is understandable. However, such perception is not advisable as the new rules will likely have a massive impact and are around for good.

Resolution tools like bail-in are– or will be shortly – applicable. The practicability, however, of these rules has not been tested yet (and hopefully will never be). However, in recovery and resolution planning, which has to be undertaken, those rules can be influential – even in times where no crisis is on the horizon. In that way, understanding of a purely hypothetical resolution is important for the recovery and resolution planning and may have an influence on bank structures.

In contrast, when safeness of banks will be looked at with a view of its improvement, their business model must not be forgotten. Banks are important players in our global economy. Lending, deposit taking, payment systems, investment banking and advisory play a crucial role in global economies and capital markets. As financial institutions, banks will only be able to provide these services if they are able to generate sustainable profit. This has to be kept in mind when discussing the safeness of banks. A balanced approach is necessary.

This brings up another topic, which is yet an issue: banks are global players, and the most important financial hubs are located in different jurisdictions, if not continents. However, a full seamless global system of bank recovery and resolution has not been found yet. In a bank crisis, it will therefore be essential that an international understanding of strategy exists – for the sake of the bank, its employees, creditors and, last but not least, the public. Such a strategy is better developed in good times without the high amount of pressure which sometimes occurs in a pending crisis case.

This book aims to put the new rules under the Bank Recovery and Resolution Directive (BRRD) into context, explain and highlight key provisions. It looks at that cross-border wise and intercontinental with a focus on the new European rules. It therefore serves as a point of orientation in a highly complex, legal and practical topic.

Edgar Meister*

* Edgar Meister was Member of the Executive Board of Deutsche Bundesbank for fifteen years responsible for banking supervision and financial stability. Furthermore, he was Chairman of the Banking Supervisory Committee of the European System of Central Banks.

Preface to the Second Edition

Since coming into force of the BRRD and the SRM, various practical examples of bank crisis situations have taken place. Some new forms of dealings have been developed like the so-called precautionary recapitalisation and in some instances the new rules have been applied. Some lessons learnt have gone into a broad revision of the BRRD and SRM-R, which will fully be applicable by the end of 2020. The focus of this revision is MREL and resolution planning and hereby acknowledging that preparedness for resolution is an important factor in making the rules work and in strengthening their credibility. The second edition covers the amended rules as well as practical and other legal developments since the applicability of the new rules. The Swiss overview has been updated by Mariana Wiederkehr.[1] Finally, I would like to thank Aastha Aggarwal for her support with the second edition and Claudia Shah for her help with the manuscript.

Sven Schelo
Frankfurt (am Main), July 2020

1. (née Mariana de Oliveira Leite de Castro).

Preface to the First Edition

Bank restructuring remains and probably will remain a very topical subject. The recent results by the European Central Bank (ECB) in connection with the Asset Quality Review (AQR) and the related stress tests show that many bank balance sheets still contain Non-Performing Loans (NPLs) in significant amounts. One of the challenges going forward will be to find ways to cure or mitigate that problem. The new rules for recovery and resolution can provide additional tools to restructure if no private solution can be found.

Also, many banks – regardless as to how their performance under the AQR has been – will be asked to provide a minimum amount of eligible liabilities (MREL) to create safety buffers in case of a resolution. The exact amount of MREL and its shape and structure will have an important impact on bank balance sheets and – potentially – on its refinancing. This goes along with prudent resolution planning, striking a careful balance between existing bank structures and the need to be 'resolvable' in a worst case. In all this, the interaction between existing and new authorities – be it the national regulators or resolution authorities, the ECB and the Single Resolution Board (SRB) and the European Commission – will yet have to be established.

Therefore, the topic is relevant for the restructuring of existing cases as well as for planning and capital raising going forward.

This book not only focuses on the European legal framework under the BRRD but also looks into the United States (US) and national systems where possible. I would like to thank Mariana de Oliveira Leite de Castro for her support with this book. Her overview of the Swiss system is set out in an own chapter as epilogue. I would also like to thank Mr Edgar Meister for taking the time to provide a foreword to this book and the interesting talks we had on various matters related to the financial markets. Finally, I would like to thank Claudia Schulz for her intense work on looking into and editing the manuscript.

Sven Schelo
Frankfurt (am Main), December 2014

List of Abbreviations

BCBS	Basel Committee on Banking Supervision
AQR	Asset Quality Review
BRRD	Bank Recovery and Resolution Directive
BSR	Bank Separation Regulation
CDS	Credit Default Swaps
CRD	Capital Requirements Directive
CRR	Capital Requirements Regulation
CoCo	Contingent Convertible Bond
DGS	Deposit Guarantee Scheme
EBA	European Banking Authority
ECB	European Central Bank
EDIS	European Deposit Insurance Scheme
EFSF	European Financial Stability Facility
ELA	Emergency Liquidity Assistance
ESM	European Stability Mechanism
ESMA	European Securities and Markets Authority
ESRB	European Systemic Risk Board
ESTER	Euro Short-Term Rate
EURIBOR	Euro Interbank Offered Rate
FDIC	Federal Deposit Insurance Corporation
FMSA	Federal Agency for Financial Market Stabilisation
FINMA	Financial Market Supervisory Authority
FROB	Fondo de Reestructuración Ordenada Bancaria
FSB	Financial Stability Board
GAAP	Generally Accepted Accounting Principles
G-SIB	Global Systemically Important Bank

G-SII	Global Systemically Important Institution
HFSF	Hellenic Financial Stability Fund
IFRIC	International Financial Reporting Interpretations Committee
IMF	International Monetary Fund
IPS	Institutional Protection Scheme
IMREL	Internal Minimum Requirements for Own Funds and Eligible Liabilities
ISDA	International Swaps and Derivatives Association
ITS	Implementing Technical Standards
LAA	Loss Absorption Amount
LIBOR	London Interbank Offered Rate
LREM	Leverage Ratio Exposure Measure
M-MDA	Maximum Distributable Amount
MPE	Multiple Points of Entry
MIS	Management Information System
FMI	Financial Market Infrastructure
MREL	Minimum Requirement for Own Funds and Eligible Liabilities
NPLs	Non-Performing Loans
NCWO	No Creditor Worse-Off
O-SIIs	Other Systemically Important Institutions
RCA	Recapitalisation Amount
RTS	Regulatory Technical Standards
RWA	Risk-Weighted Assets
SFT	Securities Financing Transaction
SIFI	Systemically Important Financial Institution
SOFR	Secured Overnight Financing Rate
SONIA	Sterling Overnight Index Average
SPE	Single Point of Entry
SRB	Single Resolution Board
SRF	Single Resolution Fund
SRM	Single Resolution Mechanism
SRM-R	Single Resolution Mechanism Regulation
SSM	Single Supervisory Mechanism
TLAC	Total Loss Absorbing Capacity
TLOF	Total Liabilities and Own Funds
TREA	Total Risk Exposure Amount

CHAPTER 1

Bank Business

While this book is about the restructuring and resolution of banks, the topic cannot be dealt with and understood adequately without an understanding of the banking business and of the bank's balance sheet.[2] Needless to say, the restructuring and resolution of a bank which is merely organised nationally and which has the traditional deposit taking and lending business is completely different from the restructuring and resolution of an international universal bank with subsidiaries, branches, and representative offices in many countries and which displays complex financial products in its balance sheet. The approaches for each type of institution and the available restructuring, recovery, and resolution tools vary greatly from institution to institution. Therefore, an individual and distinct course of action is necessary. The introduction below is not supposed to be an exhaustive explication, neither of the banking business as a whole nor of the banks' balance sheet. For this purpose, more specialised publications can be taken into consideration.[3]

§1.01 EVOLUTION OF SIZE AND SHAPE OF BANKS

There are hardly any other industries which have changed more dramatically over the last decades than the banking industry. Traditionally, looking at the end of the nineteenth century and the beginning of the twentieth century, most of the institutions were in a traditional depository and lending line of business.[4] Banks would take

2. Ahrend makes a thorough analysis of the link between banking crises and balance sheet contagion.
3. For books with a primary focus on the banking business and the bank's balance sheets from a legal perspective, *see Carnell* et al., The Law of Banking and Financial Institutions; *Mishkin,* The economics of money, banking, and financial markets; *Cranston,* Principles of banking law; *Scharpf/Schaber*, Handbuch Bankbilanz.
4. Davies, Glyn. A history of money: from ancient times to the present day; *Cardiff: University of Wales Press*; pp. 593 et seq. Allen, Franklin/Douglas Gale. Comparing Financial Systems; *MIT Press 2000;* pp. 25 et seq.

deposits from customers, these being individuals or corporates, and would invest those deposits in a prudent and possibly profitable way. Because of the law of large numbers, banks must not have all cash available to repay depositors every day – the likelihood that all depositors will withdraw from their accounts simultaneously at any given day is very small.[5] Hence, only a certain mandatory amount of cash is kept while the remainder is applied elsewhere, i.e. for more profitable purposes. This activity illustrates a very core feature of the banking business, namely the maturity transformation.

As depositors and investments have different schedules for cashing out and depositing or repaying the money, the bank serves as an intermediary to match those needs in an efficient way. While this feature is the main function of the bank and defines its role in the economy, it is also a source of its risk.[6] Banks convert short-term liabilities into long-term assets and vice versa.

The most common way for banks to generate income from deposits taken is to loan them out and earn interests. These loans could vary significantly from consumer loans to real estate or mortgage loans to corporate loans. Of course, this traditional bank business is still alive and still plays a very important role in Europe today. Contemporary institutions pursuing this simpler business model are usually organised as savings banks or smaller regional banks.

However, the banking industry has evolved into much more than that. Instead of financing 'only' national corporates, banks have been financing multinational corporations. Indeed, corporate loans have become larger. But not only the amount has changed also the type of products that are offered has become different. Products developed from ordinary corporate loans be it small or large to more complex loan products like acquisition finance loans involving private equity companies. Product-specific types of lending like large project financings or real estate financing were created. Also, financings related to special situations like debt financing or distressed financing became part of the modern banks' day-to-day operation. Naturally, this led to higher risks. As the number of banks grew, so also did competition. In order to keep up with the evolving market, many institutions have been inclined to reduce the amount of liquid assets to a minimum and lend as much as possible for increased profitability.

Generally, banks have become much more leveraged than non-financial companies because of two main incentives. First, due to contractually fixed interest rates, banks have a higher degree of certainty on the outcome of their assets than industrial corporates do. Industrial corporates, such as commodity manufacturers, are often subject to price fluctuation on both the supply and the sell side. Second, in case of a

5. *Carnell*, p. 45. The authors explain that banks must hence only accumulate a part of such deposits – a so-called fractional reserve – available for cashing out. The matter is not completely undisputed and certain authors fiercely criticise fractional-reserve banking and the validity of the law of large numbers. *See De Soto*, Jesús Huerta. Money, Bank Credit, and Economic Cycle; *Ludwig von Mises Institute. 2nd edition*; p. 115.
6. There may be a risk relating to 'maturity transformation' as the banks' depositors are, at large, individuals with a rather conservative approach to risk-taking. Thus, they are more likely to run and cash out in moments of uncertainty. On the other hand, bankers work as entrepreneurs and often have more appetite for risk. *See McCormick*, p. 19.

liquidity shortage, these banks usually have a prompter access to capital, either in the interbank market or with the central bank.[7]

Already early in the twentieth century, the first signs of the market distortions of a rapidly changing industry started to appear. Much before the Great Depression, the United States's (US's) economy started to face bank failures and bank runs: over five hundred only in 1921.[8] The figures became even higher during and after the 1929 'Black Friday' stock exchange crash: over four thousand banks failed in 1933.[9]

§1.02 CAPITAL MARKET EVOLUTION: INVESTMENT BANKING

The development on the loan side is only a part of this evolution. An even more important evolution, not to call it a 'revolution', occurred over the last decades and is the development in the capital markets. Further away from traditional lending, many banks have offered new financial products closely linked to capital markets like providing or underwriting bonds (debt capital markets) or equity (equity capital markets), especially in connection with initial public offerings. This field of banking activity is referred to as investment banking. Investment banking goes a step further because it is no longer necessarily linked to taking deposits. The investment banking business in the field of initial public offerings is a good example of this. The bank may accept an offering mandate regardless of acting as a depository institution. It is more about finding investors for a certain financial product than converting deposits into loans. In the mandate of an initial public offering, the bank markets the offer, it underwrites the shares for a very short period of time and then immediately places them at an exchange for sale to third-party investors. A roughly analogous mechanic exists for the bond issuance business, where institutions underwrite a certain amount of the bond offering to be then placed to its clients. Other parts of investment banking like mergers and acquisitions (M&A) have a similar strategy, where banks look for adequate potential buyers for a target company and set up structures and processes for the acquisition to take place. These types of products however are even further away from the traditional lending business and are closer to the field of advisory business. Here, banks have started functioning as highly specialised agents, alongside possibly being an interested party in a transaction. In this context, they act as financial intermediaries that reduce transaction costs by way of economies of scale.[10] In short, costs of investment would often be too high for a single investor, say, aiming to purchase one million shares in a certain company. Once a bank ties together a larger group of investors, several (legal, accounting, auditing, regulatory) costs relating to the offering and purchase of those shares can be distributed among the pool of investors.

7. *Carnell*, p. 48.
8. *Alston*, p. 411.
9. Federal Deposit, A History, p. 3.
10. Post-2008 crisis voices allege that such economies of scale can only exist under the premise that the state serves as a continuous backstop for the associated risks. Without the state and the elasticity of law it grants to too-big-to-fail banks in extreme situations, enjoying economies of scale by expanding volume would be unjustified vis-à-vis the humongous and evergrowing uncertainty risk.

Banks also have the expertise, dampening the asymmetric information factor between the corporate and the investor.

Many international and local banks are also active in other areas, such as the brokerage business, where banks buy and sell commercial paper or other intangible investment products. Subject to much controversy and debate in recent years, banks have been quite keen on less customary operations, like selling derivative contracts. Banks are often responsible for keeping these markets liquid and trading with large currency positions (market-making).[11] These types of activities can be seen as investment banking, albeit regulators are still trying to map the flowchart of funds, title and liability in this area. The Bank Recovery and Resolution Directive ('BRRD')[12] is an attempt to solve the 'too big to fail' problem.

Besides the products mentioned above, banks also have critical functions within each economy, the most important one being payment and settlement functions where banks organise payment transfers within each country and across borders.[13] This is one of the engines of an economy and a critical function because the operation of a whole economy depends on effective and punctual payments with regard to salaries, pensions, or payment for deliveries and supplies. In Europe and the US, non-banks are starting to take up this market, and their participation is expected to grow. The facilitation of payment services, as well as the reduction of these costs, was among the

11. A market maker is 'An institution or individual that quotes bid and offer prices for specific stocks or other marketable securities that it holds in inventory (often referred to as "makes a market in"), and is prepared and able to buy or sell those securities at any time on its own account. Note that this is not necessarily the same as a brokerage house, as a broker typically acts as an agent for a customer and charges a commission for helping to consummate a trade with another investor (rather than acting like a market maker who serves as a "principal" by buying or selling from its own inventory of securities). Market makers are normally tasked with providing sufficient liquidity in order to reduce volatility in prices and maintain a "fair and orderly market" for stocks.' FT Lexicon, http://lexicon.ft.com/Term?term = market-maker.
12. Directive 2014/59/EU of the European Parliament and of the Council of 15 May 2014 establishing a framework for the recovery and resolution of credit institutions and investment firms and amending Council Directive 82/891/EEC, and Directives 2001/24/EC, 2002/47/EC, 2004/25/EC, 2005/56/EC, 2007/36/EC, 2011/35/EU, 2012/30/EU and 2013/36/EU, and Regulations (EU) No 1093/2010 and (EU) No 648/2012 and Directive (EU) 2019/879 of the European Parliament and of the Council of 20 May 2019 amending Directive 2014/59/EU as regards the loss-absorbing and recapitalisation capacity of credit institutions and investment firms and Directive 98/26/EC are collectively referred to as 'BRRD'.
13. The term 'critical functions' is defined by Article 2(35) BRRD as activities, services or operations, the discontinuance of which is likely in one or more Member States, to lead to the disruption of services that are essential to the real economy or to disrupt financial stability due to size, market share, external and internal interconnectedness, complexity or cross-border activities of an institution or group, with particular regard to the substitutability of those activities, services and operations. The SRB has further adopted the five relevant economic functions that constitute critical functions as identified by the Financial Stability Board. These are: (i) deposits; (ii) lending; (iii) payment, cash, settlement, clearing, custody; (iv) capital markets; (v) wholesale funding. Details can be found on https://srb.europa.eu/en/content/critical-functions. *See also Dewatripont*, p. 30. Linked to this function, the obviously main risk is operational, as institutions can be beset by information technology malfunctioning or electricity blackouts with major consequences. Data privacy and consumer protection are also top in the pecking order of preoccupation in this scenario.

grounds for the adoption of the Euro.[14] Sometimes, even though the bank is financially unsound, national authorities cannot afford to let the institution fail simply because of its systemic operational relevance. The more systemically important an institution is, the more susceptible it is to cause cascades of failures, a contagion of bank runs and asset implosions. There is, hence, a close connection between the transaction services and the financial intermediation services provided by banks. The extent of that connection has a great impact on the restructuring strategy to be chosen.

In the following sections, some of the typical types of banks shall be shortly described.

§1.03 TYPES OF BANKS

In May 2020, the European Central Bank (hereinafter 'ECB') updated the list of significant supervised entities subject to its single supervision.[15] Among these institutions, mostly commercial banks are found, as well as banking holding companies that include investment banks, mortgage banks, savings banks, building societies, and credit unions. Below are a few words on each of these categories.

[A] Commercial Banks

Commercial banks, sometimes also referred to as universal banks (in case they also do investment banking), are active in the broadest sense of banking business as described above. They offer banking accounts and loans to businesses as well as households.[16] Balance sheet volume sometimes exceeds the amount of a trillion, their product portfolio is widely spread, and the refinancing side is quite diversified. Albeit there are certainly different sizes of commercial banks, given the spread of the product group, those banks are usually among the largest banks in a country and often do play a systemic role for the economy of that country. Sometimes large commercial banks are also global systemically important banks, the so-called G-SIBs,[17] because their failure

14. As per Article 127(2) of the Treaty on the Functioning of the European Union, one of the basic tasks of the European System of Central Banks is 'to promote the smooth operation of payment systems'.
15. ECB. List of Supervised entities. Dated 1 May 2020. https://www.bankingsupervision.europa.eu/ecb/pub/pdf/ssm.listofsupervisedentities202006.en.pdf. Fitch Ratings. Special Report on the Impact of European Banking Union on Banks More to Gain Than Lose, dated September 2013.
16. *Ritter/Silber/Udell*, p. 487. *Cecchetti/Schoenholtz*, p. 327.
17. The international organisations have applied different acronyms with respect to systemically important institutions. The Basel Committee on Banking Supervision refers to 'global systemically important banks (G-SIBs)'. *See* Basel Committee on Banking Supervision, Global systemically important banks updated assessment methodology and the higher loss absorbency requirement, dated July 2013. Available at: http://www.bis.org/publ/bcbs255.pdf. The consolidated version can be found on https://www.bis.org/basel_framework/. The Financial Stability Board refers to 'systemically important financial institutions (SIFIs)'. *See* Financial Stability Board, Policy Measures to Address Systemically Important Financial Institutions, dated 4 November 2011. Available at: http://www.financialstabilityboard.org/publications/r_111104

can have a domino effect on other participants of the financial system even though they might be geographically very distant.

The Basel Committee on Banking Supervision (BCBS) developed a methodology to determine the international relevance of a bank based on a set of indicators, namely size, interconnectedness, and the lack of readily available substitutes or financial institution infrastructure for the services provided, global (cross-jurisdictional) activity and complexity.[18] As mentioned above, the consequences of the failure of a G-SIB can be very disturbing. Therefore, G-SIBs are subject to stricter rules with respect to the composition of their balance sheet. The latest official list includes thirty worldwide spread banks.[19]

[B] Investment Banks

The word 'bank' is sometimes a bit misleading for institutions which are solely active in the field of investment banking. Strictly speaking, for some types of investment banking business, a banking licence is not even required. Nevertheless, many of the large commercial banks are also active in the field of investment banking. Investment banking, as set out above, is or can be defined as searching for or placing products for the benefits of companies and other institutional investors which are looking for investments. It is basically financial intermediation, under which banks bundle different risks.[20] In addition to working for their clients, investment banks often have a significant portion of investment activities on their own account, also known as proprietary trading. Record of such activities is kept in the so-called trading book, which lists the market-related assets such as derivatives and bonds that fall outside the traditional banking customer-related activities.[21] The clients' transactions are registered in the banking book. Hence, the activities that can be found in an investment

bb.pdf. In the European Union legislation, the terms are 'global systemically important institutions (G-SIIs)' and 'other systemically important institutions (O-SIIs)'. *See* Article 131 of Directive 2013/36/EU.

18. Global systemically important banks: updated assessment methodology and the higher loss absorbency requirement, July 2013. Available at: http://www.bis.org/publ/bcbs255.htm.
19. In November 2019, the Financial Stability Board issued an updated list using end-2018 data, with Toronto Dominion being the only new inclusion. Deutsche Bank has moved to a lower bucket, i.e. from Bucket 3 with 2% to Bucket 2 with 1.5%. https://www.fsb.org/wp-content/uploads/P221119-1.pdf.
20. The clear shift in the risk-taking in commercial versus investment banking lies on the fact that loans (typical instruments of the latter) can only be called upon on maturity, while securities can be traded at any time. The commercial bank faces a credit risk of the borrower at the time of vindication and investment banks work around a market risk. *See Gleeson*, pp. 175 et seq.
21. The trading book and the risks relating to it has been at the core of banking regulation since Basel I. Basel II defines it as 'A trading book consists of positions in financial instruments and commodities held either with trading intent or in order to hedge other elements of the trading book. It includes both proprietary positions as well as positions arising from client servicing and market making. To be eligible for trading book capital treatment, financial instruments must either be free of any restrictive covenants on their tradability or able to be hedged completely. In addition, positions should be frequently and accurately valued, and the portfolio should be actively managed.' *See* Bank for International Settlements. Risk-based capital requirements and Boundary between the banking book and the trading book. Dated 15 December 2019. Effective

bank are numerous. They start from underwriting and advising on securities issues and other forms of capital raising, M&A, trading on capital markets and may also include research and private equity investments for the account of corporate clients.[22]

Albeit not strictly legally speaking a bank,[23] investment banks can be domestically and even globally systemically important. This was the Lehman Brothers case, for instance. Lehman Brothers was not a depository bank and hence – at least for the most parts of the group – was not a bank. Nevertheless, Lehman was very active in the lending business globally and provided all sorts of loans. It also was very active in the derivative business and acted as protection buyer and protection seller in many circumstances. Its contractual partners were corporates of all sizes worldwide and other banks. Finally, Lehman was a large broker for the account of clients who bought and sold commercial paper and stocks. Its failure not only led to a strong wave of loss of confidence to the stability of financial institutions but also, due to the complexity of the products that Lehman offered and its strong interconnection with other market players, led to significant losses and exposures around the globe. Hence, not only banks in the narrow meaning of depository banks but also mere 'unlicensed' investments banks, due to their size, complexity of the products and interdependence can have a systemic relevance. Lehman did not have specific settlement functions as it was not a clearing house per se and was not affecting a large amount of payment transactions. However, even without critical functions, bank failure can have a massive effect.

Following the Glass-Steagall Act of 1933, in the US at least, large banks needed to split and divide their investment banking activities from their depository banking activities, albeit under the same brand.[24] Following the enactment of the Gramm-Leach-Bliley Act, which in 1999 repealed the Glass-Steagall Act, the Dodd-Frank Act[25] came as a response to the financial crisis of 2008 and it was the first piece of legislation to once again underline the segregation of depository banking from proprietary trading under the so-called Volcker Rule.[26] This rule restricted US's depository banks from engaging in proprietary trading, so as to cordon risky activities off these institutions.[27]

---

as of 15 December 2019. https://www.bis.org/basel_framework/chapter/RBC/25.htm?inforce=20191215. However, Basel IV will introduce a more objective boundary between banking books and trading books in order to reduce regulatory arbitrage. It will be effective as of 1 January 2022. For a summary of the changes, *see* https://www.bis.org/basel_framework/chapter/RBC/25.htm?inforce=20220101.

22. *See also Financial Times Lexicon* at http://lexicon.ft.com/Term?term=investment-bank.
23. Not all investment banks are depository banks (i.e., have the licence to accept deposits from customers). Also, the investment services industry has gained a quasi-autonomous industry status in the last decades, being the subject of specific regulation as the Markets in Financial Instruments Directive.
24. After that, the regulation of investment services went under the scope of the Securities Exchange Commission.
25. Dodd-Frank Wall Street Reform and Consumer Protection Act, Pub. L. No 111-203, 124 Stat. 1376 (2010) (codified in scattered sections of the US Code). *See Dombalagian*, p. 470.
26. Section 619 (12 U.S.C. section 1851) of the Dodd–Frank Wall Street Reform and Consumer Protection Act.
27. However, the Volcker Rule has been amended by the Federal Deposit Insurance Corporation (FDIC) and the Office of the Comptroller of the Currency (OCC) in 2019. With regard to proprietary trading, the amendments aim to: (i) relax the compliance requirements of the

Other jurisdictions followed the trend. In Germany, according to the *Trennbankengesetz*,[28] those activities also have to be split. In the European regional regulatory level, the Liikanen Review[29] brought up a series of structural changes in the banking industry, including concepts like a liquidation authority, the bail-in recovery tool, adjusted risk-weighting measures and corporate governance practices.[30] Similarly, Vickers Report[31] was adopted in the United Kingdom (UK) and its legislative implementation, although it was expected for 2015, was delayed to 2019 with very clear demarcations. Under the British act, ring-fenced banks (i.e., those which carry out retail depository taking and individual and small business lending) will be banned from trading activities, securities sales and purchase and derivatives trading.[32] For instance, in the UK, ring-fenced banks will be subject to more stringent prudential regulation to ensure their robustness in financial crisis. In this respect, Liikanen Review does not fix tougher standards, allowing discretion for national regulatory authorities. The common ground intertwining Volcker, Vickers and Liikanen is the creation of mechanisms to mitigate the usage of deposits for potentially speculative trading. However, since the three differ in key aspects, a certain degree of regulatory arbitrage will play a role in the future.

Volcker Rule, but at the same time, they impose new compliance requirements on non-US banks; (ii) significantly liberalise changes to the 'trading outside of the United States' exception; and (iii) modify the market-making and underwriting exceptions to the proprietary trading prohibition through changes to the 'reasonably expected near-term demand', thereby allowing banks to presume compliance given that they establish trading desk-level risk limits. The amendment is effective from 1 January 2020, but the banks have until 1 January 2021 to become compliant or voluntarily choose to opt in earlier. *See* Federal Register. Rules and Regulations. 14 November 2019. Vol. 84. No 220. Available at: https://www.occ.treas.gov/news-issuances/federal-register/2019/84fr61974.pdf. Also *see* Securities and Exchange Commission. 17 CFR Parts 200, 240, and 249. Release No 34-87005; File No S7-05-14. RIN 3235-AL45. https://www.sec.gov/rules/final/2019/34-87005.pdf.

28. Gesetz zur Abschirmung von Risiken und zur Planung der Sanierung und Abwicklung von Kreditinstituten und Finanzgruppen dated May 2013. Available at: http://dipbt.bundestag.de/extrakt/ba/WP17/508/50871.html.
29. *See Andenas*, p. 126. *Broome*, 16. *Lastra*, p. 1223.
30. A proposal for Regulation of the European Parliament and of the Council on structural measures improving the resilience of EU credit institutions dated 29 January 2014 was introduced to discuss ring-fencing further. However, on 24 October 2017, the European Commission announced the withdrawal of the legislative proposal for a regulation on structural measures improving the resilience of EU credit institutions (BSR) as there was no foreseeable agreement. The Commission understands that 'the main financial stability rationale of the proposal has in the meantime been addressed by other regulatory measures in the banking sector and most notably the entry into force of the Banking Union's supervisory and resolution arms'. *See* European Union, Withdrawal of Commission proposals (2018/C 233/05). Available at: https://eur-lex.europa.eu/legal-content/en/TXT/?uri=CELEX:52018XC0704(03).
31. The Final Report by the Independent Commission on Banking dated September 2011 and updated in 2013. Available at: https://researchbriefings.files.parliament.uk/documents/SN06171/SN06171.pdf.
32. They will also have to be devised as a separate subsidiary with their own suitably independent board, though common shareholding under the same bank holding company is possible.

[C] Mortgage Bank

Mortgage banks are a type of specialised banks, which focus on real estate lending. They are mostly depository banks. Some of the mortgage banks can become considerably large, particularly when they focus on a particular market sector like commercial real estate financing. The range of products is broad and can start with consumer lending for the acquisition of private homes for individuals to large and specialised lending for the acquisition of real estate portfolios for corporates or funds. These were banks that did not aim directly at liquidity, like the ones investing in bonds and shares.[33]

The refinancing side of those banks can vary. Some of them are in a classical way refinanced mostly by way of taking deposits; others are refinanced by way of issuing bonds, especially covered bonds (*Pfandbriefe*). Those covered bonds were originally a peculiarity of the German market as those bonds provide for a special type of security. Other countries have invented similar systems.[34] A mortgage bank with a *Pfandbrief* licence has to register a certain type of its assets (mostly mortgage loans) into a segregated estate (*Deckungsstock*). This segregated estate serves as security for the covered bonds in case of insolvency of the *Pfandbriefbank*.

The *Pfandbrief* market is subject to special regulation since it is one of the core backbones of refinancing for many local banks at least under the current German regime. For instance, the running of the *Pfandbriefbank* during insolvency proceedings or in a resolution process is separately regulated from other normal banks.

[D] Savings Banks

Savings banks are less focused on certain products, like the mortgage banks, but rather have different characteristics. They are the ultimate depository banks, as their main purpose and tradition is to accept deposits from individuals and sometimes also from big corporates. Their main activity on the product side is to provide loans in all sorts of areas, but typically focused on consumer loans, real estate loans and small corporate loans. Therefore, some of these savings banks can also be considered mortgage banks, depending on the focus of their business.

Historically, savings banks have started in England, in the early nineteenth century, soon spreading to France and The Netherlands.[35] The main characteristic of the savings banks is more about the way they are organised from a corporate structure aspect, both within itself and with each other.

In Germany, the *Sparkassen* are owned by one city or a group of cities within one local community (*Gemeinde*), and they are tied together with each other by way of the

33. *Vliet*, p. 157.
34. Countries like Australia, Iceland, and Slovenia have covered bond system that guarantee segregation of assets registered with the relevant cover register in the case of insolvency of the issuer. For a comparative study of thirty-three jurisdictions, *see* the European Covered Bond Council, at http://www.ecbc.eu/framework/98/Australian_Covered_Bonds.
35. *Davies*, p. 333.

joint guarantee they are taking for each other's liabilities (*Gewährträgerhaftung*).[36] Savings banks (*Sparkassen*), together with private banks (*Privatbanken*) and cooperative banks (*Genossenschaftsbanken*), form the three pillars of the German banking system. Savings banks and cooperative banks have a quite strong focus on the local market, which has proven to be advantageous for these banks during the 2008 financial crisis.[37]

Also, in other places in Europe, especially in Southern Europe like Spain, Portugal, and Greece, the savings banks sector is quite dominant in the banking industry. As a restructuring measure, many of them have merged in the years past the financial crisis for greater efficiency.[38] Such mergers as a strategy for recovery will be dealt with in detail in Chapter 3.

[E] Building Societies

Building societies are very similar to savings banks, though with the essential feature of having their activities restricted to housing finance. This means that customers make deposits with these financial institutions for the sole purpose of investing in housing.[39] As a consequence of such investment, customers have a legal right to obtain loans to finance the construction, the improvement, or the purchase of real property for residential use. Normally, loans can also be made in relation to the acquisition of land where housing units will be built as well as the financing of projects of infrastructure development in residential areas. In most countries, individual savers can deduct the amount of interest paid from their tax assessment basis in total or in part, which makes this type of financing very attractive for the normal taxpayer.

The concept was initially developed in England and, in the late nineteenth century, Germany followed the trend. Nowadays, many banks have a licence to establish building savings accounts on top of their other products, since this has become a quite significant business. In Germany, almost every second household has a building savings contract (*Bausparvertrag*) and the volume of the business exceeds EUR 900 billion countrywide.[40] Given these volumes, some Eastern European economies like Slovakia and the Czech Republic copied the German regulation in the early 1990s. Building societies are still present in England, where they were subject to major restructurings during the 2008 financial crisis.[41] Comparable institutions are also found

36. *Elsas*, p. 30. *Horn*, p. 44.
37. *The Economist*, 2012.
38. For instance, Spanish savings banks. *See* 'Spanish savings banks agree merger as debt crisis bites', BBC News Business, 29 May 2012, http://www.bbc.co.uk/news/business-18246886.
39. *Müssig*, p. 374.
40. According to the German central bank, there were around 26.6 million building savings contracts (*Bausparverträge*) with a total volume of over EUR 903.20 billion in the country in 2019 – https://www.fundresearch.de/Bauen/bausparkassen-diese-anbieter-ueberzeugten-im-test.php.
41. *See* Financial Times, 'UK building society mergers forecast', 28 August 2011. http://www.ft.com/cms/s/0/a905ff18-d18a-11e0-89c0-00144feab49a.html#axzz3JyitCaOP. There have been fifteen mergers and conversions of building societies in the UK between 2007 and 2014,

in France (*Caisse d'épargne-logement*), Italy (*Cassa di risparmio edilizio*), The Netherlands, Spain and Poland.[42]

In order to facilitate cross-border housing lending across Europe, the Commission has commenced studies around this topic in the last decade.[43] There have been attempts to harmonise the regulation, the *European Agreement on a Voluntary Code of Conduct on Pre-Contractual Information for Home Loans*[44] being the most advanced so far. All major European institutions in this field have adhered to this code of conduct.

[F] Credit Unions

These financial institutions are not-for-profit cooperatives created for the promotion of their members, which have the analogous role of a shareholder. They operate under a democratic decision-making system based on the principles of assistance among cooperative members and entrepreneurial responsibility.[45] The customers are deposit makers and - also - often members of the credit unions. Credit unions offer the usual banking services to individuals and small and medium enterprises at affordable prices. They are mainly financed by their own clients, rather than by other financial intermediaries.[46]

Local and regional credit unions may also convene and form larger credit unions and become members thereof. A so-called central body operates as the intragroup financing hub with treasury functions and often as access to the capital markets. This is the case, for instance, of the French bank - Crédit Agricole - formed by a cooperation of thirty-nine local cooperative banks.[47] Similarly, DZ Bank aggregates over one thousand cooperative banks, making it one of the largest financial institutions in Germany.

Credit unions exist all over Europe, with particular relevance in Germany, France, The Netherlands, England, Ireland,[48] and Italy. Over the last years, those cooperative bank structures have proven to be very resilient and successful compared to other organisations.[49] According to Article 45g of BRRD,[50] special rules for meeting

according to the Building Societies Association. https://www.bsa.org.uk/information/consumer-factsheets/general/mergers-and-conversions-(1).

42. *See also*: A European Internal Market for Housing Finance. *Voigtländer et al.*
43. For example, the Commission's White Paper on the Integration of EU Mortgage Credit Markets, available at: https://ec.europa.eu/transparency/regdoc/rep/1/2007/EN/1-2007-807-EN-F1-1.Pdf.
44. *See Hemmetsberger*, p. 160. The text of the Code is available at: https://www.mnb.hu/letoltes/agreement-en-1.pdf.
45. *Thießen*, p. 383.
46. *Berger/Molyneux/Wilson*, p. 554.
47. Credit Agricole Business lines and brands. Available at: https://www.credit-agricole.com/en/business-lines-and-brands/all-brands/credit-agricole.
48. *Katz*, pp. 328-329.
49. *See* DZ Bank financial statements https://www.halfyearreport.dzbank.com/financial-report/key-figures. Also *see* turnover of Crédit Agricole on https://www.credit-agricole.com/en/finance/finance/financial-publications.
50. *See also* Article 12h Single Resolution Mechanism Regulation, i.e. Regulation (EU) No 806/2014 of the European Parliament and of the Council of 15 July 2014 establishing uniform rules and a

the Minimum Requirement for Own Funds and Eligible Liabilities (MREL) requirements may apply to credit institutions permanently affiliated to a central body. Under certain circumstances, the resolution authority may waive MREL requirements for the central body or the affiliated credit institutions which, as the case may be, may reflect the strong integration of the cooperative group.[51]

[G] European Credit Institutions and the Banking Structural Reform

In January 2014, a proposal for a regulation on structural measures improving the resilience of European banks,[52] the so-called Bank Separation Regulation (BSR), came as a response to the Liikanen Report.[53] Specifically, this proposal had addressed the report recommendation to separate proprietary trading[54] and other high-risk trading activities[55] into an autonomous legal entity within a banking group.[56] It aimed at a structural reform relating to systemic risks born by 'too-big-to-save, too-big-to-fail and

uniform procedure for the resolution of credit institutions and certain investment firms in the framework of a Single Resolution Mechanism and a Single Resolution Fund and amending Regulation (EU) No 1093/2010, together with Regulation (EU) 2019/877 of the European Parliament and of the Council of 20 May 2019 amending Regulation (EU) No 806/2014 as regards the loss-absorbing and recapitalisation capacity of credit institutions and investment firms, hereinafter referred to as 'SRM-R'.

51. Such strong integration is also underlined by the solidarity mechanism between the members of the cooperative, e.g. France under Article L. 511-31 of the Monetary and Financial Code.
52. Proposal for a regulation of the European Parliament and of the Council on structural measures improving the resilience of EU credit institutions / COM/2014/043 final – 2014/0020 (COD). The elements of the proposal would be applied to European global systemically important institutions and banks that had total assets amounting to at least EUR 30 billion and trading activities amounting at least to EUR 70 billion or 10% of total assets in the past three years. Also, European banks, parents, subsidiaries, and branches of banks established outside the European Union would be subject to the proposed regulation.
53. *Altvater/Schweinitz*, p. 627.
54. Proposed Regulation 2014/043, under Article 5(4), defined proprietary trading as 'using own capital or borrowed money to take positions of any type of transaction to purchase, sell or otherwise acquire or dispose of any financial instrument or commodities for the sole purpose of making a profit for own account, and without any connection to actual or anticipated client activity or for the purpose of hedging the entity's risk as result of actual or anticipated client activity, through the use of desks, units, divisions or individual traders specifically dedicated to such position taking and profit making, including through dedicated web-based proprietary trading platforms'.
55. High-risk activities include market-making, securitisation, and derivatives. In accordance with Article 5(12) of Proposed Regulation 2014/043, 'market making' means a financial institution's commitment to provide market liquidity on a regular and ongoing basis, by posting two way quotes with regard to a certain financial instrument, or as part of its usual business, by fulfilling orders initiated by clients or in response to clients' requests to trade, but in both cases without being exposed to material market risk.
56. E. Liikanen, Final Report by the High-level Expert Group on Reforming the Structure of the EU Banking Sector dated October 2012. P. 101. In July 2018, the Commission decided to withdraw the proposal as its purpose had in the meantime to a large extent been achieved by other measures. *See* https://ec.europa.eu/info/business-economy-euro/banking-and-finance/financial-supervision-and-risk-management/managing-risks-banks-and-financial-institutions/structural-reform-eu-banking-sector_en.

too-complex-to-resolve'[57] banks. The core rule in this proposal was the prohibition of proprietary trading for global systemically important institutions (G-SIIs).[58] However, the proposal was withdrawn in October 2017 due to lack of agreement between the Member States. It was acknowledged that on the European level, resilience in the banking sector should be pursued by increasing capital requirements, monitoring resilience through stress tests and improving resolvability. Instead, a focus was placed on reviewing the existing rules, leading to a reform of BRRD in June 2019.[59]

[H] Entities Covered by the BRRD

According to Article 1(1) of BRRD,[60] the rules shall apply to the following:

- Credit institutions established in the European Union (EU), i.e. 'undertakings the business of which is to take deposits or other repayable funds from the public and to grant credits for its own account',[61] except for those excluded under Article 1(1) of Directive 2019/878/EU amending Article 2(5) of Directive 2013/36/EU.[62] These can be, for instance, commercial banks, mortgage banks, savings banks, credit unions, and building societies described above.

57. Explanatory Memorandum to the Proposal for a regulation of the European Parliament and of the Council on structural measures improving the resilience of EU credit institutions / COM/2014/043 final - 2014/0020 (COD).
58. Regulation 2014/043 also proposed prohibition on banks from holding units or shares in entities that carry out proprietary trading or in alternative investment funds. However, it allowed trading in Union government bonds (Article 6(2)(b)(ii)).
59. *See* European Union. Withdrawal of Commission proposals (2018/C 233/05). Available at: https://eur-lex.europa.eu/legal-content/en/TXT/?uri=CELEX:52018XC0704(03).
60. The scope of the SRM-R is set in Article 2 thereof.
61. Point (1) of Article 4(1) of Regulation (EU) No 575/2013 of the European Parliament and of the Council of 26 June 2013 on prudential requirements for credit institutions and investment firms and amending Regulation (EU) No 648/2012. Regulation 575/2013 has been amended by Regulation (EU) No 2019/876 of 20 May 2019 as regards the leverage ratio, the net stable funding ratio, requirements for own funds and eligible liabilities, counterparty credit risk, market risk, exposures to central counterparties, exposures to collective investment undertakings, large exposures, reporting and disclosure requirements, and Regulation (EU) No 648/2012. Hereinafter Regulation No 575/2013 and Regulation No 2019/876 will be referred to as 'CRR'. Also, the EBA issued a report and an opinion on 27 November 2014 relating to matters relating to the perimeter of credit institutions, with a view to harmonise the definition of this concept among the Member States and to foster consistency in the Single Rulebook. Documents available at: http://www.eba.europa.eu/-/eba-publishes-an-opinion-on-the-perimeter-of-credit-institutions.
62. They are: (1) access to the activity of investment firms in so far as it is regulated by Directive 2004/65/EU of the European Parliament and of the Council; (2) central banks; (3) post office giro institutions; (4) in Denmark, the 'Eksport Kredit Fonden', the 'Eksport Kredit Fonden A/S', the 'Danmarks Skibskredit A/S' and the KommuneKredit; (5) in Germany, the 'Kreditanstalt für Wiederaufbau', 'Landwirtschaftliche Rentenbank', 'Bremer Aufbau-Bank GmbH', 'Hamburgische Investitions - und Förderbank', 'Investitionsbank Berlin', 'Investitionsbank des Landes Brandenburg', 'Investitionsbank Schleswig-Holstein', 'Investitions - und Förderbank Niedersachsen - NBank', 'Investitions - und Strukturbank Rheinland-Pfalz', 'Landeskreditbank Baden-Württemberg - Förderbank', 'LfA Förderbank Bayern', 'NRW.BANK', 'Saarländische Investitionskreditbank AG', 'Sächsische Aufbaubank - Förderbank', 'Thüringer Aufbaubank', undertakings which are recognised under the 'Wohnungsgemeinnützigkeitsgesetz' as bodies of state housing policy and are not mainly engaged in banking transactions, and undertakings

- Investment firms established in the EU, i.e. legal persons whose regular occupation or business is the provision of one or more investment services to third parties and/or the performance of one or more investment activities on a professional basis, that is subject to the capital requirements of Regulation (EU) No 2019/876, and that is subject to the minimum capital requirement of EUR 750,000. These are mostly the investments banks described above.
- In specific circumstances as described in BRRD, branches of credit institutions and investment firms established outside the EU.
- Financial institutions established in the EU, i.e. undertakings other than credit institutions and investment firms, the principal activity of which is to acquire holdings or to pursue certain financial activities,[63] including holding

recognised under that law as non-profit housing undertakings; (6) in Estonia, the hoiu-laenuühistud, as cooperative undertakings that are recognised under the hoiu-laenuühistu seadus; (7) in Ireland, the Strategic Banking Corporation of Ireland, credit unions and friendly societies; (8) in Greece, the 'Ταμείο Παρακαταθηκών και Δανείων' (Tamio Parakatathikon kai Danion); (9) in Spain, the 'Instituto de Crédito Oficial'; (10) in France, the 'Caisse des dépôts et consignations'; (11) in Croatia, the 'kreditne unije' and the 'Hrvatska banka za obnovu i razvitak'; (12) in Italy, the 'Cassa depositi e prestiti'; (13) in Latvia, the 'krājaizdevu sabiedrības', undertakings that are recognised under the 'krājaizdevu sabiedrību likums' as cooperative undertakings rendering financial services solely to their members; (14) in Lithuania, the 'kredito unijos' other than the 'centrinės kredito unijos'; (15) in Hungary, the 'MFB Magyar Fejlesztési Bank Zártkörűen Működő Részvénytársaság' and the 'Magyar Export-Import Bank Zártkörűen Működő Részvénytársaság'; (16) in Malta, 'The Malta Development Bank'; (17) in The Netherlands, the 'Nederlandse Investeringsbank voor Ontwikkelingslanden NV', the 'NV Noordelijke Ontwikkelingsmaatschappij', the 'NV Limburgs Instituut voor Ontwikkeling en Financiering', the 'Ontwikkelingsmaatschappij Oost-Nederland NV' and kredietunies; (18) in Austria, undertakings recognised as housing associations in the public interest and the 'Österreichische Kontrollbank AG'; (19) in Poland, the 'Spółdzielcze Kasy Oszczędnościowo – Kredytowe' and the 'Bank Gospodarstwa Krajowego'; (20) in Portugal, the 'Caixas Económicas' existing on 1 January 1986 with the exception of those incorporated as limited companies and of the 'Caixa Económica Montepio Geral'; (21) in Slovenia, the 'SID-Slovenska izvozna in razvojna banka, d.d. Ljubljana'; (22) in Finland, the 'Teollisen yhteistyön rahasto Oy/Fonden för industriellt samarbete AB' and the 'Finnvera Oyj/Finnvera Abp'; (23) in Sweden, the 'Svenska Skeppshypotekskassan'; (24) in the United Kingdom, National Savings and Investments (NS&I), CDC Group plc, the Agricultural Mortgage Corporation Ltd, the Crown Agents for overseas governments and administrations, credit unions and municipal banks.

63. As listed in points 2-12 and point 15 of Annex I to Directive 2013/36/EU as amended by Directive 2019/878/EU: '2. Lending including, *inter alia*: consumer credit, credit agreements relating to immovable property, factoring, with or without recourse, financing of commercial transactions (including forfeiting). 3. Financial leasing. 4. Payment services as defined in point (3) of Article 4 of Directive (EU) 2015/2366 of the European Parliament and of the Council. 5. Issuing and administering other means of payment (e.g. travellers' cheques and bankers' drafts) insofar as such activity is not covered by point 4. 6. Guarantees and commitments. 7. Trading for own account or for account of customers in any of the following: (a) money market instruments (cheques, bills, certificates of deposit, etc.); (b) foreign exchange; (c) financial futures and options; (d) exchange and interest-rate instruments; (e) transferable securities. 8. Participation in securities issues and the provision of services relating to such issues. 9. Advice to undertakings on capital structure, industrial strategy and related questions and advice as well as services relating to mergers and the purchase of undertakings. 10. Money broking. 11. Portfolio management and advice. 12. Safekeeping and administration of securities. 15. Issuing electronic money.'

companies, asset management companies, but excluding insurance holding companies.[64]

- Financial holding companies established in the EU, i.e. financial institutions, the subsidiaries of which include at least one credit institution, an investment firm, or a financial institution[65] and their parents.[66] These are often the controlling shareholders of groups forming globally systemically important institutions.

The text of BRRD refers mostly to 'institutions', which include credit institutions and investment firms. In this book, the term 'institution' is applied under the definition of BRRD.

§1.04 PRUDENTIAL REGULATION

There are certain topics that are common to bank restructuring and bank regulation.[67] The questions of why banks are regulated and why legislators decided to create a separate set of rules for their bankruptcy are very important for understanding the regulation of bank recovery and resolution.

The rules of bank recovery and bank resolution are one of the techniques of modern bank regulation. The resolution tools are a form of *ex post* protective regulation, as they are applied after a crisis has occurred. Other parts of modern regulation, such as capital adequacy, are *ex ante* preventive measures of prudential regulation.[68] They are so called because they refer to actions taking place before a crisis occurs, i.e. actions that are supposed to avoid a crisis. Some provisions coming from the resolution sphere like resolution planning and provisions related to MREL do also have the functions as a preventive measure.

[A] Reasons for Regulating

Historically, banks had been regulated for monetary policy purposes. Nowadays, this has changed. Basically, banks are regulated in most jurisdictions for the prime purpose of protecting depositors. Depositors are the fundamental counterparties of banks' commercial activities, and they are not organised to properly monitor complex institutions like banks. Also, it is obviously more efficient to have a single supervisor

64. Article 4(1)(26) of CRR.
65. Point (20) of Article 4(1) CRR.
66. With respect to parent definitions, *see* points (28)–(33) of Article 4(1) of CRR.
67. Banks become insolvent in critical circumstances and research shows that weak political institutions and insufficient investor protection are common factors in countries facing banking crisis. *Perotti*, p. 29.
68. Prudential regulation may be defined as regulation that is 'intended to assure soundness and safety in the banking market by pursuing both objectives: financial stability and consumer protection (referred to as depositor protection). It is concerned with preventive aspects aimed at ensuring financial health and forestalling failures in banking markets. It has two dimensions: at the micro-level, it addresses the solvency and reliability of individual banks, and at the macro-level, it is concerned with the stability of the whole banking system'. *Dragomir*, p. 54.

of a bank instead of supervision by each and every depositor of a bank, as in a 'natural monopoly' so to speak. Hence, this supervision and regulation activity is delegated to a given governmental body (or bodies), usually of the Executive Branch, depending on the political structure of each country.[69]

The rationale behind banking regulation rests on three further pillars. First, systemic risk, being the potential domino effect of one institution's failure onto the other participants via the payments network. Bank recovery and resolution certainly are responding to that reality. Second, the competition within the banking market, ensuring that all participants are acting under equal conditions in a level playing field. Third, the prevention of fraud, money laundering and terrorism. While this may be beneficial to avoiding failures, as shown partly by the Brazilian banking crisis referred to in Chapter 3, it is most effective against problems exogenous to the financial system.[70]

[B] Deposit Insurance

The consumer protection argument sets the ground for the first pillar of banking regulation, i.e. deposit insurance. In the early twentieth century, banks were largely unregulated. However, the Great Depression gave rise to a prominent regulatory trend, especially in the US. The bank runs that took place during this period left many consumers without any funds. As a response to the thousands of bank failures that occurred in the preceding years, the Federal Deposit Insurance Company was created in the US in 1933.[71] Nowadays it has become part of conventional regulatory wisdom, and deposit guarantees are found in Europe as well. Once depositors are certain that they will receive their money back from the 'insurer' (lender of last resort), they are less likely to hasten and call upon deposits in the fear of a crunch.

Deposit guarantee schemes (DGSs) can be compulsory government-implemented or voluntary privately managed. In most countries, DGSs are compulsory for banking institutions.[72] Governments thus have the power to design not only the conditions of the insurance premium but also how the payment will occur if a trigger event occurs. For instance, in Europe, the Directive on Deposit Guarantee Schemes[73] of 1994 was amended in 2014 in order to improve the protection of deposits, maintain depositor confidence, and strengthen safety within the European Banking System.[74] Bank deposits in all Member States shall be guaranteed in the amount up to EUR 100,000 per depositor per institution. The timing for the payment to depositors shall decrease over

69. In very solid review, *Dewatripont* (The Prudential Regulation of Banks, pp. 13 et seq.) argues that banking regulation is analogous to corporate governance under a representation hypothesis. The supervisor and regulator are for depositor what large shareholders and the board of directors are for minority investors.
70. *Cranston*, pp. 66 et seq.
71. *Cranston*, 78.
72. *Schich*, p. 72.
73. Directive 94/19/EC, as recast by Directive 2014/49/EU.
74. European Commission – MEMO/14/296.

time; i.e., currently, depositors may have to wait up to twenty working days until they are able to receive the insured amount.[75]

The financing of the European DGSs shall include a considerable part of *ex ante* funding which shall be collected from banks over a ten-year period. If the *ex ante* funds are insufficient in a financial crisis, the DGS will collect *ex post* contributions from the banking sector. As a last resort, should the private sector contributions be insufficient, alternative funding arrangements such as loans from public or private third parties may be used. There will also be a voluntary mechanism of mutual borrowing between DGSs from different EU countries.[76]

Under BRRD, Member States must enact legislation ensuring an adequate hierarchy of deposits in an insolvency scenario.[77] Thereunder, covered depositors up to EUR 100,000 should have a higher priority in the payment order than uninsured depositors. Deposits above EUR 100,000 by individuals, small - and medium-sized companies have a higher priority than claims by other creditors and shareholders. The Directive, hence, provides a safe harbour to individuals and small enterprises. The European schemes are guaranteed on a regional level, smoothing up the process for depositors in the cross-border insolvency within the EU. In addition to the Deposit Guarantee Scheme Directive (2014/49/EU) and as part of the Banking Union, there are plans to establish a fully integrated European deposit insurance scheme (EDIS) by 2024. The EDIS project is seen to be the third pillar of the Banking Union;[78] however, currently participating Member States have differing views as to the necessity and benefits of such a scheme.[79] A fully integrated European deposit insurance would also provide some additional credibility to deposit protection. The existing system has the weakness that it is only partially prefunded. This means that in a larger bank insolvency, the funding for the deposit protection would come from *ex post* contributions paid by banks in the respective Member States. Depending on the volume of the protection, this can lead to large contributions which, especially in countries with a weaker banking sector can lead to knock-on effects. Those effects can weaken the credibility of the scheme.[80] In this respect, a scheme which is born by a wider group of financial institutions from different Member States like EDIS has more standing and would be even more effective to prevent bank runs which is one of the aims of a deposit

75. According to Proposal for a regulation of the European Parliament and of the Council amending Regulation (EU) 806/2014 in order to establish a European Deposit Insurance Scheme (COM/2015/0586 final- 2015/0270 (COD)) it could change to seven working days.
76. European Commission - MEMO/14/294.
77. Article 108 of BRRD. The Deposit Guarantee Scheme Directive (2014/49/EU) regulates also the limit amount to be paid per depositor per bank, currently at EUR 100,000.
78. *See* European Commission, A European Deposit Insurance Scheme (EDIS) - Frequently Asked Questions, 24 November 2015, https://ec.europa.eu/commission/presscorner/detail/en/MEMO_15_6153.
79. Editors Simon Grima. Pierpaolo Marano. Governance and Regulations' Contemporary Issues. 2018. Vol. 99. Emerald Group Publishing. Page 220 on Germany's hesitation.
80. *See* European Commission, A European Deposit Insurance Scheme (EDIS) - Frequently Asked Questions, 24 November 2015, https://ec.europa.eu/commission/presscorner/detail/en/MEMO_15_6153.

protection scheme.[81] In addition, recent experience with small- or mid-sized banks in a financial crisis showed that the deposit insurance schemes in the EU could benefit from another improvement. While for some small and midsized banks which are not seen to be systemic, insolvency would be an option for a market exit in a severe liquidity or capital crisis. Such insolvency would indeed lead to a call for the deposit protection schemes. However, even in smaller cases, the funding volume which would need to be mobilised on very short notice to cover the depositors could quickly go into double-digit billion amounts. This in turn would, as mentioned, often trigger large *ex post* contributions from other banks,[82] in turn causing a cascade effect or insufficiency of the scheme. Such effects may prevent insolvency as an option. Therefore, it should be evaluated how those *ex post* contributions can be funded other than from contributions from banks in that respective Member State. There is the possibility that the national schemes may lend money to each other;[83] however, this in turn, depends on the ability of the respective national scheme and may show to be cumbersome. As the reimbursement claims of the schemes have a very high ranking in insolvency proceedings (Article 108(1)(b) BRRD), its claims should often be safe, albeit subject to time constraints in insolvency proceedings. Therefore, these reimbursement claims could be taken as security to allow either central bank lending or lending from another source[84] to allow financing of the scheme and open up insolvency as an option.

Some countries, like Switzerland and Germany, also carry out a system of private deposit protection schemes.[85] As required in European regulation since 1994, Germany has put in place a mandatory scheme on top of the voluntary one. Therefore, German banks may enjoy protection both from the European framework and from a private scheme, if they wish to do so.[86]

In international banking, deposit insurance shall combine home-country and host-country arrangements to ensure proper coverage for depositors.[87] In the European regulation,[88] the depositor is covered by the insurance of the country of its bank account. Hence, foreign depositors that held accounts in banks established in Cyprus were protected up to the amount of EUR 100,000.[89] On the other side, the branches of European banks in the other Member States are covered by a home deposit protection regime.[90] Banks with head offices outside the EU shall ensure that deposits in their

81. *See* European Commission, Effects Analysis on the European Deposit Insurance Scheme (EDIS), 11 October 2016, https://ec.europa.eu/info/sites/info/files/161011-edis-effect-analysis_en.pdf.
82. *See* Article 10(8) of Directive 2014/49/EU on those *ex post* contributions.
83. *See* Article 12 of Directive 2014/49/EU.
84. For example, the ESM or SRF.
85. *Kane*, p. 380.
86. *Cariboni*, p. 85.
87. Basel Committee on Banking Supervision, Core Principles for Effective Deposit Insurance Systems: A proposed methodology for compliance assessment, dated December 2010, p. 15. Available at: http://www.bis.org/publ/bcbs192.pdf.
88. *Giovannini*, European Financial Integration, p. 17.
89. *See* FAQ relating to the Financial Assistance for Cyprus prepared by the European Stability Mechanism (updated 18 September 2013) at https://www.esm.europa.eu/sites/default/files/2014-07-28_faq_esm_archived.pdf.
90. *Lastra*, Cross Border, p. 17. *Blair*, p. 776. Article 14 of the Deposit Guarantee Scheme Directive (2014/49/EU).

branches within the EU have a deposit protection coverage that is equivalent to that established in the Deposit Guarantee Scheme Directive (2014/49/EU).[91] An advantage in comparison to other liquidity measures is the fact that the premium is collected *ex ante*, and therefore funded by the bank itself. Differently, state bailouts are funded by taxpayers.[92] The acting of the insured institution must be monitored to avoid moral hazard and, for this reason, deposit insurance acts closely in tandem with banking supervision.[93] The Federal Deposit Insurance Company and the Canadian Deposit Insurance Corporation apply risk-adjusted premiums to shield against high actuarial liabilities.[94]

Deposit insurance is certainly key for the regulation of a bank, but – as any other insurance – it is expected to be pulled out only in the event of an accident. In this case, it may be insolvency or a resolution proceeding, where schemes are required to step in. So, regulation had to go a step further to forestall the occurrence of such banking accident, or bank failures. Also, deposit insurances usually do not cover interbank deposits, which also account for a large portion of a bank's balance sheet and only up to a certain threshold under European directive. Hence, the second principle of bank regulation was identified, the regulation of capital requirements as discussed below.

Under BRRD, DGSs can contribute to a restructuring or resolution. According to Article 109 of BRRD,[95] DGSs have to contribute the amount in cash into the situation which was originally saved by not being able to bail in or partially transfer covered deposits. This ensures that there is no 'windfall' profit for schemes though the non-eligibility of covered deposits for bail-in or comparable measures.

[C] Capital Adequacy

Given the impact of strict regulation on competition and innovation, banks started to pressure the government for deregulation, which then actually occurred during the 1970s and the 1980s of the last century.[96] Yet after the bankruptcy of *Bankhaus Herstatt* in 1974, the close link between the soundness of a bank's balance sheet and the likelihood of its failure became undeniable for supervisory authorities across the globe.[97] Under the pressure to meet strict leverage ratios, banks and financial markets started engineering with both sides of the balance sheet. For instance, off-balance sheet items, such as standby letters of credit, were used and balance sheets became even more leveraged. Once the maximum liability level would be reached, some institutions would start marketing new liabilities that were not accounted for in the capital ratio calculations. In the US regulation, this was the case of standby letters of credit, which were off-balance sheet items. Standby letters of credit did not count as liabilities and, hence, did not negatively affect the leverage ratio. Nonetheless, if such guarantees

91. Article 15 of the Deposit Guarantee Scheme Directive (2014/49/EU).
92. *Schoenmaker*, p. 3.
93. *Carnell/Macey/Miller*, p. 84.
94. *See Ritter*, p. 286 and *Schooner*, p. 65.
95. *See* Article 79 of SRM-R.
96. *Dewatripont*, Prudential, p. 19.
97. *Gleeson*, p. 33.

were indeed called upon due to insolvency of the original borrower, serious losses could be incurred.[98] Hence, the regulation on leverage was not sufficient to capture certain risks and the complexity of the banking activity. Also, institutions could sell parts of a loan portfolio but continue to be subject to certain losses against the buyer. This could happen if the selling institution would undertake indemnity obligations towards the buyer for a part of future losses. As a consequence, the sale proceeds would work to increase the capital of the selling institution, while certain risks would remain within its scope of liability. The regulation was addressing the capital insufficiency risk, while banks pursued a new direction towards contingent liabilities risk with instruments like standby letters of credit.[99]

Already in the early 1980s, central banks and supervisors of the G-10 nations[100] started to think of basic regulatory principles to ensure true effectiveness of bank supervision.[101] A large portion of these principles deals with capital adequacy, i.e. the quantity and quality of the capital instruments expressed in the accounts of the bank's balance sheet. It was a new risk-based approach to the supervision of balance sheets, which appeared to them as the most objective way of ensuring safety and soundness. The result of the ministerial conference was the 1988 Basel Accord, also known as Basel I, which set the path for the modern content of bank regulation.[102] Markets soon developed complex risk management policies and products, which again surpassed the original Basel rules by far. For instance, the original accord did not give credit for hedging instruments such as credit default swaps (CDS), which in practice reduced credit risk in many ways. As a result, the Second Basel Accord, or Basel II,[103] was released in 2004, taking into account these highly advanced risk management methodologies. Basel II is based on three pillars: (1) minimum capital adequacy; (2) supervisory review process, in an internal ratings-based approach of customer exposure and a risk-weighted assessment; and (3) market discipline, expressed in the requirement of disclosure of the banks' financial information publicly. The Basel

98. *Carnell*, pp. 219-220.
99. *See Tarullo*, p. 29.
100. Bank for International Settlements, http://www.bis.org/list/g10publications/index.htm: 'The Group of Ten is made up of eleven industrial countries (Belgium, Canada, France, Germany, Italy, Japan, the Netherlands, Sweden, Switzerland, the United Kingdom and the United States) which consult and co-operate on economic, monetary and financial matters. The Ministers of Finance and central bank Governors of the Group of Ten meet as needed in connection with the meetings of the International Monetary Fund and the World Bank.'
101. *See* the History of the Basel Committee at http://www.bis.org/bcbs/history.htm. The Basel Committee on Banking Supervision was created in 1974 and became a de facto international regulatory body, producing quasi-binding soft law. Its recommendations are very persuasive and most players have adopted them. *See Lastra* (Central Banking), pp. 171-172.
102. Much before 1988, governors had already gathered at the Basel Committee on Banking Supervision to address the fact that the supervision of globally acting institutions, with branches and offices across several jurisdictions, could no longer be hamstrung to national supervisory authorities and central banks. The Basel Concordat, issued in 1975 and amended in 1983, established a framework for supervision of foreign establishments.
103. International Convergence of Capital Measurement and Capital Standards: A Revised Framework. *See Goodhart* on pro-cyclicality. *Ono*, p. 20.

Committee made several reforms in the Basel II texts relating to the trading book and securitisation, the Basel 2.5 package.[104]

The series of bank distresses starting in 2008 showed the Committee that the journey had not yet been completed and put a spotlight (to say the least) on the issue of pro-cyclicality in financial markets regulations and supervisory systems. A revised document containing the lessons learned was released in 2010, the Third Basel Accord.[105] Basel III does not completely replace Basel II, which remains in full force with respect to credit risk and credit risk mitigation, e.g. Basel III amends Basel II particularly with respect to the composition of capital and the calculation of capital requirements. Some details thereof will be discussed in section 1.06 below. The regulatory discussion goes on, but key concepts can be already drawn from the existing regulation. In June 2019, the latest update on these regulation regimes was published. The Basel IV package not only completes the Basel III reforms but also introduces changes in the use of internal models under the internal ratings-based approach which were implemented by Capital Requirements Directive (CRD V)[106] and Capital Requirements Regulation (CRR).[107]

Innovation is the discretionary countercyclical buffer rule, pursuant to which national authorities may require more capital during periods of high credit growth. This in turn restricts the ability of institutions to distribute dividends and other earnings to shareholders and bondholders, while the real advantage therefrom is still uncertain.[108]

The capital adequacy standards gave rise to a whole new series of banking products, to meet compliance of the capital requirements for banks. For instance, the hybrid bond market through which bank refinancing is designed to and products are often tailor-made to meet regulatory requirements in order to be acknowledged as Additional Tier 1 or Tier 2 capital instrument. Similarly, CDS are designed to ease capital requirements related to a certain type of assets.[109]

This all means that the regulatory standards are to a considerable degree already driving the way banks' balance sheets are built.[110] In light of the resolution and

104. *Gleeson*, pp. 242 et seq.
105. A global regulatory framework for more resilient banks and banking systems, as revised in June 2011. In the meantime, the Basel Committee on Banking Supervision also released the Basel 2.5 on the trading book and securitisation.
106. Directive (EU) 2019/878 of 20 May 2019.
107. Regulation (EU) No 575/2013 of the European Parliament and of the Council of 26 June 2013 on prudential requirements for credit institutions and investment firms and amending Regulation (EU) No 648/2012. This has further been amended by Regulation (EU) 2019/876 of the European Parliament and of the Council of 20 May 2019 amending Regulation (EU) No 575/2013 as regards the leverage ratio, the net stable funding ratio, requirements for own funds and eligible liabilities, counterparty credit risk, market risk, exposures to central counterparties, exposures to collective investment undertakings, large exposures, reporting and disclosure requirements, and Regulation (EU) No 648/2012.
108. The effect of this rule has been tested in models. *See Repullo*.
109. Basel Committee on Banking Supervision, Recognising the cost of credit protection purchased, dated March 2013. Available at: http://www.bis.org/publ/bcbs245.htm.
110. Kenadjian, CoCos and Bail-ins, p. 235.

recovery planning, which is becoming more and more present across the world, this trend will eventually increase.

[D] Post-2008 Regulatory Trends

In the financial crisis of 2008, neither banks nor bank regulation has really helped to alleviate the problem. Bank regulation indeed brought about more equity cushions to the balance sheets.[111] Unfortunately, there are still doubts whether these will be sufficient to hinder pro-cyclicality. In future crises, an equity cushion will only effectively work if financial instruments are prudently valued and not overstated in the balance sheet so that risks cannot be appropriately measured. The theory of capital adequacy is currently in search of something more than a mere book-based approach.[112]

Also, in case of a liquidity crisis, like the 2008 one, equity is not a proper cure. This is because capital adequacy relates to the liabilities side of the balance sheet, i.e. how institutions fund themselves. It has less to do with the institutions' liquidity per se. In its true sense, liquidity means 'cash, cash equivalents and other assets (liquid assets) that can be easily converted into cash'.[113] An institution would be illiquid only if it has assets, which bear a positive value but cannot be readily realised. In the emergence of this crisis, many institutions had assets with zero to even negative value – i.e., not 'illiquid' assets, but de facto liabilities. This was the case of subprime mortgage Non-Performing Loans (NPLs), where the break costs of funding could not be charged to the borrower and the security had suffered value depreciation. An apparent liquidity crisis might as a matter of fact sometimes be a solvency crisis.[114] This may also happen with derivatives. With derivatives, there is in one hand, some risk that the derivative contract does lose value so that it is written down to zero. Moreover, there is an additional risk that the value becomes negative and effectively turns into a liability. Hence, the regulation of liquidity has very much to do with the quality of the assets and with their ability to be quickly converted into cash. For this reason, there are also improvements towards liquidity requirements, another important output of the Basel III package.[115]

111. *Alfon* (p. 69) properly notes that capital is not the only buffer against distress. Banks also maintain provisions against defaults. Since these provisions are treated differently from capital both on a tax and on a regulatory standpoint, the decision-making process on these accounting manoeuvres can be intricate.
112. *See Flannery*, p. 21. Also, *Zimmerman* on fair value accounting and the latest financial crisis.
113. FT Lexicon.
114. Since the beginning of the crisis, academics all over the world have progressed towards new angles under which economic policy and regulation should be seen and influenced. For instance, *Sampford* proposes an institutional trust and fiduciary concept linked with reputational and other self-interest incentives. As rooted on Adam Smith's maxim that 'it is not from the benevolence of the butcher, the brewer, or the baker that we expect our dinner, but from their regard to their own self-interest', the author reminds the important role of self-interest in the banks' and bankers' acting when granting NINJA ('No Income, No Jobs, No Assets') loans.
115. *See* Basel Committee on Banking Supervision: Liquidity Coverage Ratio effective as of 15 December 2019.

There is the view that to some extent bank regulation is a technical field, which has at the end of the day helped rather to disguise problems than to diminish them. However, this is not a book about taking sides on whether current capital adequacy is correct or faulty. More exactly, it turns to this subject as an instrument in the bank recovery and resolution process.

§1.05 BANK BALANCE SHEET

An introduction on the balance sheet of a bank is a prerequisite for the analysis of restructuring measures like the bail-in tool or like the bridge bank tool. A bank balance sheet differs from that of an ordinary corporate in various aspects. One aspect is the size of the bank's balance sheets. Even smaller savings banks easily have a balance sheet volume of EUR 20 to EUR 30 billion. As mentioned, large universal banks often exceed balance sheet volumes of EUR 500 billion and even go beyond the trillion euros zone. But the size of the balance sheet is not the only factor that differs compared to a corporate. Also, the complexity of the balance sheet is different from that of an ordinary corporate. As banks have changed from national to international sophisticated institutions, their balance sheets have not only grown but also have become much harder to understand. This is due to the fact that the banks' balance sheets mirror the abstractness of their assets and liabilities.[116] Non-financial firms, as participants of the 'real' economy, own assets that are much easier for non-experts to understand. On the other hand, instead of grains and minerals as stock, a bank has bonds and forward contracts. Another difference relates to the fact that long-term liabilities show up at the top of a company's balance sheet, while short-term liabilities appear at the bottom. The order is reversed in the balance sheet of banks. This may be due to the fact that banks often finance themselves with short-term debt and companies, with long-term equity. *See* Table 1.1 for an example.[117]

Table 1.1 Assets in 100 Millions of Dollars (Numbers with %-Sign Are Percentages of Total Assets)

Cash items			1246.7	10.6%
Securities			2336.8	19.9%
US government and agency	1421.2	12.1%		
Other securities	915.5	7.8%		
Loans			6693.8	57.1%
Commercial and industrial	1320.1	11.3%		
Real estate (including mortgage)	3794.3	32.4%		
Consumer	817.7	7.0%		
Interbank	212.4	1.8%		

116. *See Mishkin*, pp. 225 et seq.
117. Extracted from *Cecchetti*, p. 328.

Other	761.6	6.5%			
Other assets				1439.5	12.3%
Total commercial bank assets	11716.8				
Liabilities in billions of dollars (numbers with % sign are percentages of total liabilities)					
Deposits				7716.1	74.0%
Large time deposits	1886.2		18.1%		
Borrowings				1901.6	18.2%
From banks in the US	256.3		2.5%		
From others	1645.4		15.8%		
Other liabilities				807.8	7.7%
Total commercial bank liabilities	10425.5				
Bank assets – bank liabilities = bank capital	1291.3				

Source: Compiled by author from various sources.

However, there is more to it: balance sheet review does not always give the full picture. Indeed, some sources of credit risk do not appear therein at all. Also committed but unutilised facilities can amount to a very large piece of the banks' accounts but are not always disclosed in the notes to the financial statements.[118] The same can happen with guarantees for financial products. The following pages contain a brief incursion into the assets and liabilities sides of the balance sheet and briefly explain derivatives, as well as international assets and liabilities, given that they also do play an important role in restructurings.

[A] Assets

Looking at the asset side of the balance sheet of a universal bank, the cash position is often distinguished between cash held with other institutions and cash held with central banks. Further categories are claims against other institutions and claims against customers, such as individuals and corporates. The latter is often a larger position as it reflects one of the key businesses of a bank, which is the lending position. In this asset class, these loans are being kept as receivables. Furthermore, institutions, especially universal banks, are investing in bonds and notes, which are issued by public sector borrowers or by private borrowers or other types of securities. A bank often invests in equity, be it equity in other banks or in financial services companies or ordinary corporates. Sometimes, banks hold participation in other group companies, which consequently also are shown up as equity in the balance sheet of the parent company. Groups of affiliate banking entities must usually produce consolidated financial statements. Last but not least, banks hold fixed assets like real estate or certain intellectual property rights, especially with respect to their brand name or other licences. As opposed to non-financial firms, fixed assets normally do not account for a

118. *Gleeson*, p. 7.

significant portion of a bank's balance sheet. Surprisingly, one of the bank's most valuable assets does not appear in its balance sheet even though it bears significant, albeit intangible, value: it is the banking licence, around which many protective internal policies and controls are built and maintained.

The term toxic asset is to some extent a bit of a misleading term.[119] Either assets have the value, which is shown in the balance sheet, or, if they lose value, depreciation has to take place. However, this has nothing to do with the asset being toxic; it is more about the asset losing value. This happens when the current market value of an asset is lower than the face or bookkeeping value, for instance when stock prices plunge in comparison with the price of acquisition by the bank; when there is a downgrading of the rating of a bond constituting a representative portion of the bank's assets; or in the case of NPLs.

One of the most used restructuring techniques with respect to banks was to transfer those so-called toxic assets from the bank to a non-bank institution. The purpose of this was twofold. One purpose was to escape from the regulatory environment of the bank and to allow the asset to be transferred to a non-regulated institution where little or no equity had to be kept for this specific asset. The other simply was the expectation that the value of those assets would increase over time if held and sold at a later stage with a special divestment strategy within that new owner.

There are two aspects to toxic assets which go beyond losing value. First, sometimes they have a negative value because in order to sell them, a negative purchase price has to be paid. Hence, the owner is obliged to invest. Second and more important, there is the core question on the value of derivatives. As mentioned, derivatives may turn from an asset into a liability. If that stadium is reached, it is true to speak of toxic assets as they can seriously damage the bank's balance sheet by not only losing value but also, much worse than that, creating liabilities for the bank.

Any asset write-off leads to a loss, which then in turn leads to a depletion of the capital position. This again may have consequences for the overall equity ratio, which is prescribed by law and the respective regulators. Hence, write-offs are in a double sense expensive: not only do they deplete statutory capital but also they trigger the requirement for additional capital.[120] This can sometimes lead to a vicious circle: assets which need to be brought to the market cannot be sold for a value below book value because the loss would trigger additional capital requirements which the institution cannot afford. Hence, write-offs are avoided for the price of deadlock in the business model and profitability. This is one of the origins of the so-called zombie banks which the asset quality review (AQR) and stress test by the ECB aimed at to identify. However, losses can only be realised if there is capital to absorb them. Otherwise, resolution measures would need to be considered or a state of continuation in a status quo of lethargy will exist.

---

119. A toxic asset may be defined as 'financial assets the value of which has fallen significantly and may fall further, especially as the market for them has frozen. This may be due to hidden risks within the assets becoming visible or due to changes in the external market environment, or both'. FT Lexicon, http://lexicon.ft.com/Term?term = toxic-assets.
120. *Gleeson*, p. 33.

Assets need to be financed, be it by equity, or be it by some form of debt financing. In that sense, the liability side of the balance sheet does not only show the liabilities in the pure sense of the meaning but more broadly the origin of the means with which the asset side is financed.

Comparing a universal bank to a smaller savings bank, the positions on the asset side are not completely identical. A smaller savings bank usually has a much larger percentage of loans to customers while a much lesser proportion of investments in derivatives or participations in affiliates. *See* Table 1.2 with respect to a very broad comparison between the asset side of a universal bank towards a savings bank in continental Europe.

Table 1.2 Balance Sheet Comparison (Approximate Amounts in Billions of EUR)

	Commercial Bank	*Savings Bank*
Total assets	527	34
Cash reserve	13 (2%)	0.032 (0.1%)
Loans to banks	120 (22%)	0.79 (2.3%)
Loans to customers	181 (34%)	18 (52%)
Trading derivatives	111 (21%)	0.21 (0.6%)
Securities (bonds/equities)	35 (6%)	14 (41%)
Total liabilities	510	33
Central bank deposits	-	0.20 (0.6%)
Liabilities to banks	108 (21%)	1.8 (5%)
Liabilities to customers	218 (42%)	21 (63%)
Trading liabilities	118 (23%)	0.21 (0.6%)
Securitised liabilities	34 (6%)	7 (21%)
Subordinated liabilities	10 (2%)	0.6 (1.8%)
Equity	17	0.9

Source: Compiled by author from various sources.

[B] Liabilities

The liability side of the balance sheet encompasses not only liabilities but also equity. This position is of great importance even though equity would not classify as a liability in the accounting and legal sense. Nevertheless, both show the origin of the financing of the various assets that the institution owns.

The liability side of a bank balance sheet shows liabilities to other banks, so-called interbank liabilities, and, of course, liabilities to customers. These would ordinarily be classified as deposits. Within customer deposits, a further distinction can be made. Some of the deposits are only due after a certain period (savings and time deposits), say a period of notice of three months or more. Other deposits are payable immediately upon demand.

It is precisely these deposits payable on demand that are sometimes difficult to classify and to measure liquidity. In a severe crisis, for instance, when it comes to establishing whether a bank is in fact cash flow illiquid each and every due and repayable claim has to be taken up for assessment. However, how shall those deposits payable on demand, i.e. ordinary day-to-day cash deposits on account with the bank, be classified? No bank has the available cash to immediately settle all deposits payable on demand. Therefore, the better view is to only take those deposits into assessment for illiquidity, which have already been called upon, or those that are reasonably expected to be called upon based on experience and comparable cases. Another issue where deposits play a role is the issue of a minimum amount for own funds and eligible liabilities (so-called MREL). Banks will be required under BRRD to maintain a certain, individualised amount of bail-in-able liabilities. However, while deposits, which are not covered, are subject to potential bail-in, they do not count for MREL because they can be terminated without notice.[121] Hence deposits are not reliable enough to be a foreseeable basis for bail-in-able liabilities. Third, deposits are subject to deposit protection – a point that has been and will be explored further.

Further categories on the liability side of the balance sheet can be securitised liabilities, i.e. basically bonds and notes that have been issued by the bank. Bonds can be covered by asset security, but they must not mandatorily. An important kind of covered bond is the German *Pfandbrief*. As mentioned above, claims under such notes are subject to a special security covered bond regime and filed with a special covered bond register. *Pfandbrief*-style securities are insulated from the rest of the banks' liabilities in case of insolvency to guarantee that the security holder will be repaid. Recent examples in the market try to insert covered bonds in a broader sense beyond the *Pfandbrief* market in order to make those types of refinancing more marketable. These are, for instance, the *cedulas hipotecárias* in Spain or the *obligations fonciéres* in France. At the European level, similar types of bonds have been regulated under the Directive on Undertakings for Collective Investments in Transferable Securities and under the Capital Requirement Directive.[122]

Moreover, on the bank's balance sheet liability side, there are subordinated liabilities or other forms of hybrid instruments, which classify as debt at least in civil law legal parameters. Those instruments are called hybrid because they do have elements of equity in them, like the absorption of losses to a certain extent or subordination in the event of insolvency. If certain prerequisites are met, those instruments may to a certain extent classify as regulatory capital (Additional Tier 1 or Tier 2). Hence, it may be very attractive for a bank to refinance itself by means of those instruments rather than by way of classical equity.

121. Article 72a(1)(d) of CRR.
122. *Mastroeni*, p. 49.

Finally, classical equity-like share capital is shown in the balance sheet. The way this share capital is drawn up depends on the legal environment and legal form of incorporation that the institution operates in. A classical stock corporation will draw its equity by way of issuing shares. If it is a bank that is organised by way of a public sector institution, equity will only be available for those shareholders that are classified as public law entities or state enterprises, but not on the capital markets like in the classical stock corporation (e.g., banks, which operate as an *Anstalt des öffentlichen Rechts*). This type of equity is classified as Common Equity Tier 1 capital.

One of the major points and issues in connection with the liability side and bank restructuring is the scope of the resolution tools in connection with the liabilities. For instance, the bridge bank tool provides for certain safeguards in connection with the liability side. Only deposits above EUR 100,000 may be left behind when it comes to transferring liabilities from a failing bank to a bridge bank. Even more rigid safeguards apply to the bail-in tool. Here, a very distinct waterfall of write-downs applies – starting with subordinated debt and ending with senior debt. However, not all types of senior debt are subject to bail-in and the assessment can get quite complicated. There are exceptions for short-term senior debt and for secured senior debt (to the extent that the security is valid) and for deposits, which can only be bailed in above the EUR 100,000 deposit protection scheme threshold. This mechanism will be dealt with in detail in Chapter 6.

[C] Derivatives

Yet one important 'player' of the bank balance sheet is to be mentioned – namely, derivative contracts. The following paragraphs shall only serve as an introduction, as to understand the role of derivatives in the context of bank resolutions.

Derivatives are called derivatives because they always refer to a certain underlying asset, be it a claim from a loan or a piece of stock. There are three main types of very common derivatives found within institutions: interest hedges, foreign exchange hedging contracts, and CDS instruments. Finally, one less commonly seen derivative contract is the equity value hedging instrument.

Derivatives entail two risks, which one does not encounter in other financial instruments:

(i) basis risk, which is the risk of mismatch between the credit risk on the protected asset and the actual protection under the credit derivative; and
(ii) counterparty risk, which is best reflected in the costs that the non-defaulting counterparty in the derivative contract will have to incur to contract new protection, after closing out the derivative with the defaulting counterparty. Different from credit risk, counterparty risk cannot be defined *ex ante*, since it depends greatly on market fluctuations (only the current exposure is known). Also, counterparty risk is bilateral – since a derivative can flow from being in the money to out of the money.

Both margin and netting agreements are fair attempts to tackle counterparty credit risk. A margin agreement limits the potential exposure by means of collateral requirements, once the exposure exceeds a pre-specified threshold. The 'uncovered' counterparty then makes a margin call to request a top-up. The position to market is usually checked on a daily basis. The second type of agreement is more controversial. While closeout netting provisions are beneficial to the hedging counterparties in normal functioning markets,[123] they may be harmful to the system by increasing the contagion and the cascade risks during a financial crisis. Hence, in restructurings, one of the aims often is to avoid triggering such termination combined with closeout netting of derivatives. An attempt to do this is by inserting special rules in the national resolution regimes to delay those all-encompassing netting mechanisms at least for a certain period during which assets are being transferred to a bridge institution.[124] BRRD contains the provisions recommended by the BCBS. Further details of this topic will be discussed below.

[1] Interest Derivatives

Say an institution has made a loan available to a customer, for which the customer has to periodically pay interest rates which can be variable depending on a certain floating reference standard (EURIBOR/ESTER,[125] LIBOR[126]/SONIA[127]/

123. *See* ISDA Research Notes – The Importance of Close-Out Netting by David Mengle, ISDA Head of Research, published on 1 November 2010.
124. Recommendation 9 of the Report and Recommendations of the Cross-border Bank Resolution Group. Basel Committee on Banking Supervision, March 2010.
125. The Euro Interbank Offered Rate, as published by the European Banking Federation. However, from the end of 2021, EURIBOR will no longer be applicable. It will potentially be replaced by Euro short-term rate (ESTER). *See* https://www.ecb.europa.eu/stats/financial_markets_and_interest_rates/euro_short-term_rate/html/index.en.html.
126. The London Interbank Offered Rate, as published by the British Bankers' Association. However, from the end of 2021, LIBOR will no longer be applicable.
127. In the United Kingdom, LIBOR will be replaced by Sterling Overnight Index Average (SONIA). *See* https://www.bankofengland.co.uk/markets/sonia-benchmark. The Bank of England intends to publish a 'SONIA Index' and 'compounded SONIA Period Averages' for certain maturities on a daily basis from the end of July 2020 onwards and has consulted the market on this. The compounded SONIA period averages would in fact be the daily calculated compounded SONIA rate for maturities ending on that date; their publication would relieve market participants of the need to calculate them themselves and would therefore be equivalent to a screen rate. The index, on the other hand, merely facilitates the own calculation of a compounded rate, but has the advantage that it can be used for any chosen maturity. *See* https://www.bankofengland.co.uk/-/media/boe/files/paper/2020/supporting-rfr-transition-by-providing-compounded-sonia.pdf?la=en&hash=2ED72FBB529C17999D3F948A55BD7C6D5F839E62. The Bank of England has further announced that from 1 October 2020, it will: (i) levy a gradually increasing haircut add-on for transactions in the sterling money market ('Sterling Monetary Framework') if the receivables/instruments used as collateral (still) refer to LIBOR, and (ii) gradually no longer accept such receivables/instruments as eligible collateral. *See* https://www.bankofengland.co.uk/markets/market-notices/2020/risk-management-approach-to-collateral-referencing-libor-26-february-2020.

SOFR,[128] etc.) in addition to the spread.[129] Hence, the customer may at some stage end up paying more and at some other points in time pay less interest, depending on the floatation of the referenced standards in the international markets. In order to safeguard the customer as well as its own position in that context, the institution often offers the customer some form of protection in the form of an interest-hedging contract. Under such an agreement, the institution offers the customer a fixed interest rate so that, by this separate (derivative) contract, the customer only has to pay a fixed interest rate compared to the floating interest rates under the loan agreement. The institution would accept a certain fee either as upfront or as a variable for offering this hedging contract. Above this, the institution also starts to share the risk. Now the institution itself may at some stage get less interest under the loan agreement than it has to pay to the customer under the interest hedge agreement. If this occurs, one refers to the hedge as being 'out of the money'.

The bank usually protects itself from this risk by entering into another similar interest hedge agreement with a different player, e.g. another bank or a hedge fund. The bank acts then as a 'protection buyer' seeking protection from that risk from a different external entity. The bank can act as protection seller, as in the original example with the customer seeking protection from floating interest rates, or act as protection buyer where it seeks protection from the risk out of a position where it originally was protection seller. In theory, the bank should therefore net its risk position by entering into similar mirroring hedging contracts. However, sometimes the bank fails to conclude such a mirroring contract or sometimes the respective counterparty cannot afford to pay for the amounts it owes protection. Of course, in the end, if a risk materialises, it is then channelled through to the back-to-back arrangement chains. If the back-to-back counterparty itself has to place the risk out to another

128. In the United States, LIBOR will be replaced by secured overnight financing rate (SOFR). *See* https://www.newyorkfed.org/markets/opolicy/operating_policy_200212. The New York Fed has published 'compounded SOFR averages' and a 'SOFR Index' since 2 March 2020. Compounded SOFR annual interest rates will be made available for any chosen end date; however, not every interest period can be chosen at will, but only 30, 90 or 180 days. The compounded rate for other maturities can be calculated individually using the index. *See* https://www.newyorkfed.org/markets/opolicy/operating_policy_200302.

129. The FT Lexicon gives the following definition of spread: 'Generally, the difference between two prices or interest rates. In stock trading, the difference between the current bid and ask prices for a stock (the bid/ask or bid/offer spread). In futures trading, the price difference between delivery months for the same commodity or asset. In bond trading, the difference between yields of bonds with similar quality and different maturities, or of different quality and the same maturity. In underwriting, the difference between what the issuer receives from the underwriter and what the underwriter receives from the public (underwriting spread).'

For LIBOR-SONIA spread – The Working Group on Sterling Risk-Free Reference Rates published a consultation of credit adjustment spread methodologies for fallbacks in cash products referencing GBP LIBOR. *See* https://www.bankofengland.co.uk/-/media/boe/files/markets/benchmarks/consultation%20on%20credit%20adjustment%20spread%20methodologies%20for%20fallbacks%20in%20cash%20products%20referencing%20gb.

For LIBOR-SOFR spread – the ARRC (the US Working Group with regard to SOFR) deals with the question of how to determine the 'spread' that would have to be added to the new reference interest rate as compensation for the price difference between LIBOR and SOFR; see consultation of 21 January 2020 https://www.newyorkfed.org/medialibrary/Microsites/arrc/files/2020/ARRC_Spread_Adjustment_Consultation.pdf.

institution, it can become a very long chain until the end of the chain is reached where the risk materialises to the ultimate risk-taker. Also, banks do not always micromanage on all and every risk they have taken up in connection with acting as a protection seller. This and the fact that the chain of back-to-back arrangements can be endless in theory - and therefore non-transparent - can make derivatives potentially unpredictable instruments.[130]

When it comes to the balance sheet entries, derivative contracts have by a certain date to be evaluated and taken up either as an asset or as a liability. They show up as an asset if the derivative contract is in the money, i.e. they have a positive value because the amounts received under it are higher than the underlying assets' obligations. They create a liability if it is the other way around.

[2] Foreign Exchange Derivatives

Foreign exchange derivatives work in the same way, whereas here a bank does not sell protection for a variation in interest rates, but for fluctuations of foreign exchange rates. Hence, a customer may seek a contract, under which the bank promises to sell euros against US dollars at a certain fixed rate and a certain date. The derivative contract can develop favourably for the bank if there is an increase in the value of US dollars to euros. In that case, the institution would be in the money with respect to the contract, while otherwise out of the money. As with the interest hedge agreement, also the foreign exchange hedge agreement would usually be mirrored in a back-to-back arrangement with a third party where the institution will then seek protection, i.e. be a protection buyer. Otherwise, the principles are identical.

[3] Credit Default Swaps

With respect to CDS, these have become less common over the last years. Those types of derivatives refer to a specific loan and to the borrower becoming insolvent. In that case, the bank has the right to transfer the loan to a protection seller and cash in the nominal amount of the loan. It is basically an insurance against insolvency of the borrower. If a CDS exists in relation to a banking book asset and the contract fulfils the prerequisites of the regulation, the respective loan amount may be reduced for the purpose of the calculation of the minimum capital required to be withheld.[131] These prerequisites relate to the exposure amount covered by the derivative, the type of borrower and the quality of the protection seller.

Similar rules apply to a hedging agreement with respect to stocks, where a customer seeks to obtain protection with the bank for a decrease of the value of shares of a certain listed company. This can be done by way of entering into an agreement that

130. For an illustrative example of this risk, *see Ritter/Silber/Udell*, pp. 161-162.
131. Article 204(1) of the CRR also includes total return swaps and credit-linked notes to the extent of their cash funding as eligible credit protection (i.e., risk mitigation) instruments.

either the bank is obliged to sell a share for a certain price to the customer or the customer is entitled to sell their share to the bank for a certain price.

In all these circumstances, these contracts can have a value or can be a liability. Depending on the way the contracts (and the markets) develop, they can be found on either side of the balance sheet. The existing sets of accounting principles do treat hedging strategies differently, which adds an extra layer of complexity and may lead to distortions on their full fair value.[132] These derivatives are usually designed according to internationally standardised formats like the International Swaps and Derivatives Association (ISDA) Master Agreement, or other more nationalised types of agreements (e.g., the German *Masterrahmenvertrag für Derivate*[133]). Such master derivative contracts usually serve to link various single contracts with each other.

[4] Derivatives in Restructurings

In bank restructurings, derivatives play an important role. One of the reasons for that is that those contracts are usually governed by international laws, which are not the laws of the jurisdiction where the institution is domiciled. The more crucial point is that frequently a bank runs a book of several thousand, if not tens of thousands, of derivative contracts. Under most of these contracts, upon the occurrence of certain events (e.g., bankruptcy), an automatic closeout netting takes place; i.e., various single contracts are automatically terminated. Consequently, claims under those contracts are set off against each other and the remaining balance becomes immediately due and payable. If all counterparties of a financially distressed institution make use of the closeout netting clause simultaneously, this can very quickly lead to an immense exposure, which the bank would not have otherwise. For this reason, bank resolution regimes contain special measures to deal with that risk: one is, as mentioned to order a period of stay for closeout netting (this complies with US standards); another measure is to completely prohibit any type of termination for the reason of resolution measures.

[D] International Assets and Liabilities

Banks are universal players. Hence, the assets they own are only to a very limited amount located in the country where the institutions are domiciled. Looking at the asset side, a bank may own claims against other banks, which are located in other countries being it within the Eurozone, within EU or beyond these borders. Further, the banks' customers may be spread all over the world. Equity and security positions held by the bank may be spread out as well. Sometimes even a mixture is possible where the

132. For a discussion on the accounting of hedging, *see Gerbhardt.*
133. The International Swaps and Derivatives Association was created in 1985 to harmonise the derivatives' documentation, which gave rise to the rapid expansion of this market around the globe. Today, it has over 900 members, including banks, trading companies, stock exchanges, governments, law firms, insurances companies and accounting firms.

bank holds a loan against a customer in a different jurisdiction and the loan is again governed by the law of a different (third) jurisdiction.

The same applies to the liability side, where creditors of the institution come from different countries and jurisdictions, and the underlying claims may also be governed by different laws. Especially, derivative and other forms of financial contracts are often governed under New York law or English law, completely different from where the institution is situated. This has implications for the applicability and the scope of various resolution tools. For instance, a bridge bank tool - according to which the authorities are empowered to transfer certain assets to a bridge institution - may only be affected if a transfer would also be recognised in the country where the asset is located. The complexity rises even higher when highly regulated jurisdictions are involved, and the transfer requires prior governmental approval. Sometimes, extensive documentation is required, as well as translations, and all these processes can be quite costly and time-consuming. The same applies to liabilities and all types of contracts, especially derivative contracts. As a result, in all these circumstances where resolution tools are to be applied, it has to be assessed where the mature assets, liabilities and contracts are located and which legal regime they are governed by. In the second step, one must then analyse whether the resolution tool will be recognised at all in each given country. Article 55 BRRD therefore provides for the requirement to include contractual recognition clauses in instruments or liabilities that are not governed by the law of a Member State of the EU. Further details of Article 55 BRRD will be dealt with below in Chapter 6.

As a general point, a bank holds not only the assets and liabilities in derivative contracts but also all sorts of other contracts. Though these are not necessarily shown in the bank's balance sheet, they do play an important role in their day-to-day business. These could be employment, rental, information technology (IT) and outsourcing contracts. The IT infrastructure constitutes an asset whose nominal value is much lower than its actual operational value for a bank.

Without a well-functioning IT system, probably no bank today would be able to open in the morning. The management of these licences and systems is a factor that can also be quite relevant in restructurings. Needless to say, when it comes to the applicability of resolution tools, the continuation of the banks business is crucial. In so far as continuation is only possible with those contracts in place, the resolution authority should not only look at the balance sheet of the institution but also look at the contractual situation of the institution. Hence, the authority should make sure those crucial contracts are transferred to a bridge institution and that they are not terminated by way of exercising the bail-in tool.

§1.06 CAPITAL REQUIREMENTS IN EUROPE

As mentioned in section 1.04[C] above, the current internationally valid set of rules on capital adequacy is bundled under the Basel III package, which has been adopted by virtually all relevant jurisdictions of the international financial system.

In the EU, the implementation of Basel III occurred by way of the CRR and the CRD,[134] in force as of January 2014. The fourth Basel Accord was implemented by European legislation on 27 June 2019.[135] These two instruments, commonly known together as the CRD IV package,[136] are crucial to understanding the resolution and recovery tools envisaged in the European regulation. This is particularly true for the bail-in tool, which includes measures that are referenced on ratios and targets for various types of capital instruments.[137] In addition to implementing Basel III, the CRD IV rules govern matters like reliance on external credit ratings,[138] variable remuneration of bank's employees,[139] corporate governance,[140] and sanctions.[141] CRD V intends to address issues raised in relation to the provisions of CRD IV that proved not to be sufficiently clear and have, therefore, been subject to divergent interpretations.

The CRR sets out the core provisions on the quantity and quality of the capital to be maintained by European institutions and defines the types of capital and the guidelines for its calculation. As a regulation, the CRR is directly applicable in the territory of Member States, without the need for transposition into national law. Therefore, it ensures a uniform set of rules applicable to across the EU in the so-called Single Rulebook.[142] The advantages of a regulation are various: (a) it confers increased legal certainty since there is no room for flexibility in the implementation; (b) it reduces regulatory arbitrage; and (c) it reduces information asymmetry by facilitating the comprehension of rules in the market as a whole.[143]

The CRD contains complementary provisions, such as the need for stricter rules for global and other systemically important institutions. For the sake of fair competition and practical comparability of balance sheets among banks under EU supervision, the European Banking Authority (hereinafter 'EBA') has issued several regulatory technical standards (RTS) and implementing technical standards (ITS) relating to the CRD IV rules.[144]

134. Directive 2013/36/EU of 26 June 2013.
135. *See* Basel Committee on Banking Supervision. Basel III: international regulatory framework for banks. https://www.bis.org/bcbs/basel3.htm?m=3%7C14%7C572.
136. Originally, two Directives (2006/48 and 2006/49) governed the matters relating to regulatory capital in the European Union. These Directives have been amended in 2008 (CRD II), in 2009 (CRD III), and in 2010 (CRD IV). The CRD IV package replaces completely the previous amendments. In June 2019, the latest update CRD V was released.
137. *See*, e.g., Article 108(a)(i) of BRRD.
138. *See*, e.g., Article 171(2) of the CRR.
139. *See*, e.g., Article 450 of the CRR.
140. *See*, e.g., Articles 189 et seq. of the CRR.
141. *See* section IV (*Supervisory powers, powers to impose penalties and right of appeal*) of CRD.
142. The European Council minted the term in 2009 in order to refer to the aim of a unified regulatory framework for the EU financial sector that would complete the single market in financial services. http://www.eba.europa.eu/regulation-and-policy/single-rulebook. The European Banking Authority is in the process of updating the rulebook. It has allowed questions related to CRD V, CRR and BRRD to be submitted. *See* https://eba.europa.eu/single-rule-book-qa.
143. Recital (9) of the CRR.
144. An overview of regulatory technical standards and implementing technical standards that have been adopted or are yet to be delivered is found at https://eba.europa.eu/regulation-and-policy/recovery-and-resolution.

Figure 1.1 shows an overview of the various ratio and buffer requirements under the CRD V package. Each will be explained in the following chapters.

Figure 1.1 Capital Ratios and Buffers[145]

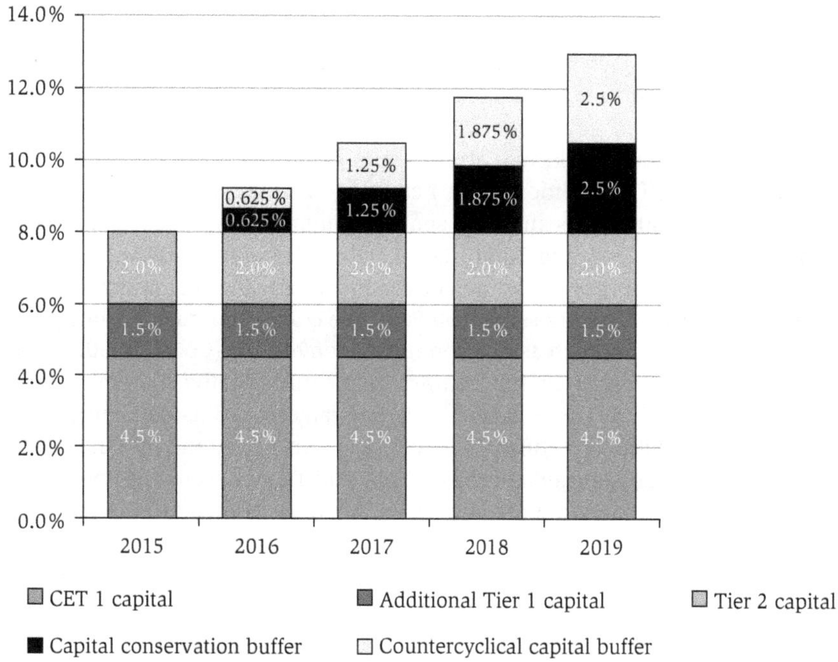

Source: Compiled by author from various sources.

The cornerstone of the CRD V is that banks should always have sufficient equity, or 'own funds' in the European regulation's jargon. Hence, a bank should have sufficient regulatory capital to serve as a buffer and absorb losses in case of its debtors' default. This regime protects creditors and the bank itself. Creditors are protected because the capitalised bank continues to be able to pay its debts even after its own debtors fail to do so. The bank is protected because normally the holders of regulatory capital do not have the same rights as other creditors. For instance, holders of regulatory capital do not have the right to claim compensation or wind up the bank if the capital suffers depreciation or if no payment is made on it.

Under the CRD V, there is a three-tier classification of regulatory capital depending on the quality of such capital. As explained, the amount of capital directly influences the bank's ability to lend and sell products to its customers, i.e. to make a profit. In this context, some types of capital are deemed to be more 'valuable' and allow

145. Accenture, Basel III Handbook, fshttps://fitc-ng.com/vlearning/fvltest/BCAM%20Demo/story_content/external_files/Accenture-Basel-III-Handbook1.pdf.

banks to lend more, in comparison with other types of capital that do not provide a safety cushion for the banks' liabilities. The regulation sets a minimum amount for each type of higher or lower quality capital instrument depending basically on how subordinated such capital is in an insolvency scenario.[146] Regulatory capital is called 'own funds' in the CRR, and it is divided into Common Equity Tier 1, Additional Tier 1 capital, and Tier 2 capital. Common Equity Tier 1 and Additional Tier 1 together form Tier 1 capital.[147]

Common Equity Tier 1[148] capital predominantly consists of common shares issued by the bank and its consolidated subsidiaries and the respective share premiums. Retained earnings, accumulated comprehensive income, other reserves and funds for general banking risk may also account in this category if they are readily available to the bank. The Additional Tier 1 capital[149] includes mainly perpetual deeply subordinated debt instruments and their share premium accounts. Upon non-viability of the issuer, i.e. if the Common Equity Tier 1 ratio falls below 5.125%,[150] Additional Tier 1 capital instruments may be written down or converted into Common Equity Tier 1 instruments by way of two possibilities. First, the conversion may occur by way of contractual arrangements, such as in a contingent convertible (CoCo) bond. Second, a conversion may be ordered in the context of an authoritative bail-in procedure. Instruments that qualify as Tier 2 capital[151] are generally subordinated securities issued by the institution with a maturity of five years or more and no incentive for redemption.[152] The aggregate sum of these Tier 1 and Tier 2 accounts is then adjusted by the deduction of certain amounts, which already have or might in the future affect the real value of the capital.[153]

The sufficient own funds test is diversified by several means. One of them is the actual core capital to assets ratio that a bank is supposed to have.[154] Pursuant to Article 92(2) of the CRR, the following rations apply:

- a common equity Tier 1 capital ratio of 4.5%;
- a Tier 1 capital ratio of 6%;
- an own funds ratio of 8%;[155]

146. Under the CRR, Articles 26-31, banks are required to have EUR 5 million in equity at the time of the initial licensing. From then on, they must keep at all times either this amount or the minimum own funds. Usually, the required own funds fall much above the initial requirement.
147. Article 4 of the CRR.
148. Articles 26-31 of the CRR.
149. Articles 51-55 of the CRR.
150. Article 54 of the CRR.
151. Articles 62-66 of the CRR.
152. Equity has a higher weight as it provides more protection. While still conferring some loss absorption, subordinated debt still counts as part of the bank's total liabilities. As a consequence, it may also contribute to balance sheet insolvency.
153. *Gleeson*, p. 88.
154. There is no undisputedly accepted percentage when it comes to minimum capital. For instance, Huerta de Soto defends a 100% capital reserve in complete repudiation of the law of large numbers.
155. This is in compliance with the Basel III framework. *See Bank for International Settlement*, Basel III, p. 12. The thresholds are significantly higher than those practised before the 2008 crisis and European banks were granted progressive intermediary targets before full compliance was required by January 2019.

- a leverage ratio of 3%.[156]

The amounts of each Common Equity Tier 1, Tier 1 capital, and own funds are measured against the total risk exposure amount (TREA)[157] of the bank in order to calculate the ratios above. The TREA is the sum of risk-weighted exposures (assets) based on adjustments in each risk category.[158] This means that each asset is given a multiple or a risk-weighting factor. The higher the risk, the higher the multiple will be. As one may foresee, a secured loan will have a lower multiple than an unsecured one. Hence, for those assets that are seen to be riskier in terms of losing value, more equity has to be brought up. For those assets, which are to be considered less risky, less equity has to be brought up. In that sense, e.g., in the past, governmental bonds were considered as riskless assets so that for these no equity had to be brought up at all. This meant that in the calculation of the asset side, those assets could be taken out of the equation, while others counted several times. Nowadays, this will depend highly on the country's risk rating.[159] This asset test was in the past further diluted by, for instance, the permission to enter into hedging agreements to mitigate risks. For instance, if certain prerequisites are met, a loan secured by a CDS led to the circumstance that this loan could be set aside for the balance sheet regulatory capital test.[160]

Given the multitude of risks for each type of asset in the non-trading and trading books, e.g. credit risk, position risk, foreign exchange risk and so on, this is a complex task and entails striving over several pages of regulation.[161]

The approach of risk-weighted assets (RWA) is not without criticism: there are views, especially form the US, stating that this differentiated approach helps disguising problems, rather than showing the real liability versus assets ratio. Therefore the 'leverage ratio', measuring liabilities versus assets without risk factors,[162] would be much more adequate to measure risk exposure of banks.[163]

Finally, the CRD V introduced a split of bank's exposures between the non-trading and the trading book.[164] These exposures are usually expected to be kept until maturity and, hence, more subject to credit risk. In the trading book, the exposure will probably exist for a short period of time and is expectedly protected from counterparty failure. Also, trading book exposures are subject to market risk, including variations in interest rates and foreign exchange rates, as well as fluctuations in stock exchange prices of stocks and commodities. All these features contribute to the 'dynamic nature

156. Article 92(1)(d) of the CRR.
157. This is the European equivalent of the 'risk-weighted assets' of the Basel III jargon. Also *see* Article 92(2) CRR, Article 45(2)(a) BRRD and Article 12a(2)(a) SRM-R.
158. Article 92(3) of the CRR. *Gleeson*, p. 104.
159. *Bank for International Settlement*, Quarterly, p. 10.
160. Article 273(5) of the CRR.
161. Namely, the CRD V rules, including the regulatory technical standards and the implementing technical standards.
162. *See* section 1.06[A] below.
163. Vice Chairman of FDIC, *Handelsblatt* 26 October 2014.
164. Recital 59 of the CRR.

of the trading book'.[165] A great portion of losses in the 2008 crisis was found in trading books. In response to this event, Basel and the CRD IV also introduced a set of rules aimed at covering trading book risks. In May 2014, the EBA prepared draft RTS regarding additional valuation adjustments that shall apply to such exposures. The final objective is to achieve 'prudential soundness' with respect to valuation for appropriate maintenance of minimum capital.[166] The requirements for prudent valuation are now to be applied to non-trading book positions as well, as introduced by the CRR.[167]

[A] Leverage Ratio

As recommended by the Basel Committee, an unweighted leverage ratio was created in addition to the usual capital ratios.[168] The ratio shall be calculated by dividing the total Tier 1 capital by the total exposure and be expressed as a percentage (LREM).[169] This is also important for MREL assessment (*see* section 6.02 [A] and [C]). The total exposure shall include all assets on the balance sheet as well as off-balance sheet items.[170] The CRR requires that a G-SII shall maintain a leverage ratio buffer equal to the G-SIIs total exposure measure referred to in Article 429(4) of the CRR multiplied by 50% of the G-SII buffer rate applicable to the G-SII in accordance with Article 131 of Directive 2013/36/EU. A G-SII shall meet the leverage ratio buffer requirement with Tier 1 capital only.[171]

The CRR requires institutions to report this ratio to the competent national authorities.[172] The EBA shall send to the Commission draft ITS on the format and structure for reporting the leverage ratio by the third quarter of 2020.[173] The EBA has

165. EBA, EBA FINAL draft Regulatory Technical Standards on prudent valuation under Article 105(14) of CRR. EBA/RTS/2014/06/rev1. 23 January 2015. P. 6. *See* https://eba.europa.eu/sites/default/documents/files/documents/10180/642449/1d93ef17-d7c5-47a6-bdbc-cfdb2cf1d072/EBA-RTS-2014-06%20RTS%20on%20Prudent%20Valuation.pdf.
166. Article 105 of the CRR.
167. *See* Article 105 of the CRR.
168. Recital 92 of the CRR.
169. Article 429(2) and (3) of the CRR.
170. Article 429(4) of the CRR.
171. Article 92(1a) of the CRR.
172. Article 430(1)(a) of the CRR.
173. Article 430(7) of the CRR; EBA final draft Implementing Technical Standards amending Commission Implementing Regulation (EU) No 680/2014 (ITS on supervisory reporting) with regard to the Leverage Ratio (LR) following the EC's Delegated Act on the LR, p. 14. Available at: https://eba.europa.eu/documents/10180/1113844/EBA-ITS-2015-03+Final+Draft+ITS+amending+ITS+on+LR+Reporting.pdf. *See also* new consultation paper on Draft Implementing Technical Standards on disclosure and reporting of MREL and TLAC issued by EBA on https://eba.europa.eu/sites/default/documents/files/document_library/Publications/Consultations/2020/CP%20on%20ITS%20on%20disclosure%20and%20reporting%20of%20MREL%20and%20TLAC/Consultation%20paper%20on%20the%20ITS%20on%20disclosure%20and%20reporting%20of%20MREL%20and%20TLAC.pdf.

prepared a report entitled 'Report on impact of differences in leverage ratio definitions'.[174] This report defines Group 1 banks as 'internationally active institutions with Tier 1 capital in excess of EUR 3 billion under Basel II' and Group 2 banks as all others.

For the larger institutions in Group 1, the leverage ratio should be lower than for Group 2 institutions. Table 1.3 compares the ratio recommended by the EBA in comparison with the Basel III levels. The leverage also differentiates on the treatment of securities financing transactions (SFTs), depending on the interpretation of the CRR with respect to the accounting treatment of such transactions. The SFT1 column specifies the suggested ratio in case a general accounting treatment is applied, while the SFT2 column refers to a specific treatment for SFTs, which is largely consistent with the Basel regulation.[175]

Table 1.3[176] *Average Leverage Ratios (%) by Group*

	Basel III	*CRR LR SFT 1*	*CRR LR SFT 2*
Group 1	3.3	3.3	3.1
Group 2	3.9	3.9	3.8

[B] Liquidity Ratios

Articles 412 and 413 of the CRR introduced a liquidity coverage requirement and a stable funding requirement respectively. The liquidity coverage shall be measured considering the liquid assets held by institutions and 'the sum of the values of [such liquid assets] which covers the liquidity outflows less the liquidity inflows under stressed conditions'. It is mainly concerned with the short-term net cash position of banks. The thresholds are set out in Article 460(2) of the CRR:

> The liquidity coverage requirement referred to in Article 412 shall be introduced in accordance with the following phasing-in:
>
> (a) 60% of the liquidity coverage requirement in 2015;
> (b) 70% as from 1 January 2016;
> (c) 80% as from 1 January 2017;
> (d) 100% as from 1 January 2018.

The European Commission has enacted a supplement to the CRR with the purpose of regulating and defining liquidity buffer, diversification of assets, liquidity

174. Extracted from the Report on impact of differences in leverage ratio definitions prepared by the EBA. Available at: https://www.eba.europa.eu/documents/10180/534414/EBA+-+Leverage+ratio+analytical+report.pdf.
175. Report on impact of differences in leverage ratio definitions prepared by the EBA, p. 18. Available at: https://www.eba.europa.eu/documents/10180/534414/EBA+-+Leverage+ratio+analytical+report.pdf.
176. Extracted from page 5 Report on impact of differences in leverage ratio definitions prepared by the EBA.

facilities, as well as liquidity outflows and inflows.[177] The liquidity coverage ratio became effective in 2015.

With respect to stable funding, a net stable funding ratio shall attempt to measure the robustness of the funding position over a one-year period.[178] The CRR includes the concept of stable funding but does not specify the method for calculation or the required minimums. Hence, Member States may regulate stable funding requirements while specific EU regulation is discussed.[179] The European net stable funding ratio was proposed by the European Commission in 2016[180] and entered into force on 27 June 2019 by CRR.[181]

[C] Capital Conservation Buffer and Countercyclical Capital Buffer

The CRD created two capital buffers, calculated on top of the minimum own fund requirements, namely the capital conservation buffer and the countercyclical capital buffer.

The capital conservation buffer is intended to ensure that banks 'accumulate, during periods of economic growth, a sufficient capital base to absorb losses in stressed periods'.[182] The countercyclical capital buffer 'should be built up when aggregate growth in credit and other asset classes with a significant impact on the risk profile are judged to be associated with a build-up of system-wide risk, and drawn down during stressed periods'.[183] The latter is calculated on an institution-specific basis and could be waived for some small - and medium-sized investment firms.[184] They have been subject to phase-in thresholds from 2016 up to 2019:[185]

177. For information on the public hearing relating to this empowerment of the Commission to specify the detailed general Liquidity Coverage Requirement for credit institutions, *see* https://eur-lex.europa.eu/legal-content/EN/TXT/PDF/?uri=CELEX:32015R0061 and https://ec.europa.eu/transparency/regdoc/rep/3/2018/EN/C-2018-4404-F1-EN-MAIN-PART-1.PDF.
178. *See* Commission Delegated Regulation (EU) 2015/61 to supplement Regulation (EU) No 575/2013.
179. Article 413(4) of the CRR.
180. Article 510 of the CRR; *See* Report on Net Stable Funding Requirements under Article 510 of the CRR. Available at: https://eba.europa.eu/documents/10180/983359/EBA-Op-2015-22+NSFR+Report.pdf.
181. EBA, Discussion Paper on Defining Liquid Assets in the LCR under the draft CRR. Available at: https://eba.europa.eu/documents/10180/42030/DP-on-defining-liquid-assets-in-the-LCR.pdf.
182. Recital 80 of the CRD.
183. *Ibid.*
184. Article 130(2) of the CRD.
185. Articles 129, 130, and 160 of the CRD.

Timeline	*Capital Conservation Buffer*	*Countercyclical Capital Buffer*
From 1 January 2016 until 31 December 2016	Common Equity Tier 1 capital equal to 0.625% of the total of the risk-weighted exposure amounts	No more than 0.625% of the total of the risk-weighted exposure amounts
From 1 January 2017 until 31 December 2017	Common Equity Tier 1 capital equal to 1.25% of the total of the risk-weighted exposure amounts	No more than 1.25% of the total of the risk-weighted exposure amounts
From 1 January 2018 until 31 December 2018	Common Equity Tier 1 capital equal to 1.875% of the total of the risk-weighted exposure amounts	No more than 1.875% of the total of the risk-weighted exposure amounts
From 1 January 2019	Common Equity Tier 1 capital equal to 2.5% of the total of the risk-weighted exposure amounts	No more than 2.5% of the total of the risk-weighted exposure amounts

If the capital conservation buffer or the countercyclical capital buffer falls below the required minimum, certain payments such as dividends and employee bonuses shall be temporarily prohibited.[186]

[D] Systemic Buffers

Under Article 133 of CRD, Member States may create a systemic risk buffer. The buffer aims at addressing long-term systemic risks which have the potential to have serious negative consequences for the financial system and which are not covered by other rules in the CRD IV package.

This systemic risk buffer shall be of Common Equity Tier 1 capital in the range between 3% and 5% of the exposures to which the buffer applies.[187] The competent authority must obtain the permission of the Commission before implementing rates above 5%.[188]

There is flexibility for each Member State to decide on different buffers for different institutions and to choose if the buffer will apply:

- to all exposures of an institution or to exposures just in the relevant Member State;

186. Articles 129(6), 130(5) and 141(2) and (3) of the CRD.
187. Article 133(11) of the CRD.
188. Article 133(12) of the CRD.

- to exposures in the Member States that set the buffer as well as exposures in third countries or other Member States;
- to exposures of an institution, an individual or consolidated basis;
- to a specific type of institutions or to all supervised institutions; and
- under different settings in the case of G-SIIs and to other systemically important institutions (O-SIIs).

The CRD sets two limits on the discretion of the Member States, which confer reasonability to the buffer requirements:[189]

(1) the systemic risk buffer must not entail disproportionate adverse effects on the whole or parts of the financial system of other Member States or of the Union as a whole forming or creating an obstacle to the functioning of the internal market;
(2) the systemic risk buffer must be reviewed by the competent authority or the designated authority at least every second year.

If a bank does not fulfil the imposed systemic risk buffer, it shall also be prohibited from making certain payments such as dividends and employee bonuses.[190]

[E] Assessment

The exercise of compliance with these ratios and buffers shall be periodically conducted by institutions and reported to the relevant supervisory authority. The ECB has updated their list of significant supervised entities that shall report directly to it from May 2020 on.[191] Suitable regulation has more value when associated with supervision. Hence, the scrutiny must be precise in order to avoid misconceptions or masked figures in banks' financial statements. This is one of the tasks of the Single Supervisory Mechanism (SSM), which is part of the bigger framework establishing the foundations of the European Banking Union. The SSM is complemented by the Single Resolution Mechanism (SRM) and the Single Rulebook. Table 1.4 includes the key dates and events regarding the European Banking Union.

189. Article 133(8) of the CRD.
190. Articles 133(14) and 141(2) and (3) of the CRD.
191. ECB. List of Supervised entities. Dated 1 May 2020. https://www.bankingsupervision.europa.eu/ecb/pub/pdf/ssm.listofsupervisedentities202006.en.pdf.

Table 1.4 Key Dates and Events Regarding the European Banking Union

	SSM	*SRM*	*Single Rulebook*
Legislation	SSM Regulation EBA Regulation	SRM Regulation Intergovernmental Agreement	CRD IV BRRD[192]
Effective date	Effective from 4 November 2014	Effective from 1 January 2016 SRB operational from 1 January 2015	CRD IV effective in Member States' national law from 1 January 2014 Majority of BRRD effective in Member States' national law from 1 January 2015
Summary	ECB to supervise 'significant' Eurozone banks National competent authorities to supervise remainder, subject to ECB power to assume direct supervision EBA responsible for single supervisory handbook	SRB to participate in resolution planning SRB to participate in the resolution decision-making process for cross-border banks using BRRD tools SRF to ensure the viability of restructured banks	CRD IV implements Basel III, including capital/leverage/liquidity requirements BRRD provides bank resolution tools

Source: Compiled by author from various sources.

Even before the start of the SSM, the ECB conducted a comprehensive assessment of over 130 European institutions together with national supervisors. This comprehensive assessment included a supervisory risk assessment, an AQR, and a stress test.[193] The AQR aims at enhancing the transparency of institutions' exposures and risk policies. The stress test measures the institutions' resilience in the event of distress.[194] The assessment started in November 2013 and the results were announced twelve months later. With the results in hand, institutions must decide on at least two issues. First, they must see which findings trigger disclosure obligations and which information will have to be shared with their stakeholders. Second, they will have to verify whether the balance sheet needs improvements. For instance, capital strengthening may be required (i.e., new capital issuance) and/or asset sales (e.g., of risky loans) may have to

192. Modified by the so-called banking package legislation, BRRD, SRM-R and CRR in force since 27 June 2019. SRM-R and BRRD applicable from 28 December 2020 with significant changes especially on MREL as set out below in Chapter 6.
193. *Gstädtner*, Asset Quality, p. 5.
194. ECB. Supervisory Practices Comprehensive Assessment. https://www.ecb.europa.eu/ssm/assessment/html/index.en.html.

be carried out. On the other end, the supervisors shall have sufficient information from the results to determine if signs of the threat of failure are present. The competent supervisor or resolution authority will then ascertain whether intervention measures must be put in place.

CHAPTER 2

Bank Restructuring: What Have We Seen in the Past?

The question of bank restructuring and of bank insolvency has to be differentiated in this very context. In addition, since BRRD came into force, further examples under or around the new regime have been added and will be dealt with in a separate chapter below. In the last hundred years, there have been several large and spectacular bank insolvencies. Some involved bank restructuring attempts, and some did not. In the 1920s, for instance, the US was faced with a number of midsize bank insolvencies. Over four thousand small banks went bankrupt between 1921 and 1929, mostly located in the Midwest and South of the US. Main causes of this massive bank turmoil were an agricultural boom, which led to overly optimistic price forecasts, and an increase of approximately 200% in real estate prices. When that boom stabilised, a bubble burst and the value of the banks' portfolios fell abruptly which led to various collapses.[195] Some studies show synergies between the crisis of the 1930s and the 2008 crisis with the intent of drawing lessons that might be useful in avoiding future crises.[196]

§2.01 EUROPE

Further examples are also helpful for this review, for instance the notorious bank failure that occurred in Europe during the first half of the past century. It was the collapse of the Austrian bank *Creditanstalt,* which had to be urgently restructured by way of a merger with *Bodencreditanstalt* in 1929. *Bodencreditanstalt* was a leading regional bank. Indeed, that very merger only took place because *Bodencreditanstalt* itself suffered severe equity problems and threatened to become bankrupt. The stock

195. *Allen*, p. 111; *Alston*, p. 414; *Baily*, p. 60, *Calomiris*, p. 8; and *Walter*. Federal Deposit Insurance Corporation. The Banking Crises of the 1980s and Early 1990s: Summary and Implications. At: http://www.fdic.gov/bank/historical/history/vol1.html.
196. *See Klein* and *Snowden*.

exchange crash on the other side of the Atlantic and a sequence of mismanagement events are deemed to be the main causes for this failure. Though the merger resulted in combined total assets of approximately USD 250 million (equivalent to about one-sixth of the Austrian Gross Domestic Product (GDP)),[197] the apparent success was not long-lasting. The forced marriage between *Creditanstalt* and *Bodencreditanstalt* could not cure the problem, but only temporarily delay it. Some say it was in fact one of the factors contributing to an even more acute crisis. Shortly thereafter in 1930, *Creditanstalt* went into difficulties again apparently because of the loads of toxic assets and liabilities it had to take upon in the course of the merger. Again, a series of rescue measures were undertaken by governmental intervention through the Austrian Central Bank. Even neighbouring European countries, under fear of contamination through a bank crush of *Creditanstalt*, got involved in the rescue efforts. Those measures only showed interim relief but at the very end could not prevent the ultimate breakdown of *Creditanstalt* in 1931. The bank was nationalised and passed on to several owners over the years, until its final privatisation in 1997, when Bank Austria acquired it from the Austrian government.[198]

A third notable example takes place later on, in the 1970s: the crash of *Bankhaus Herstatt* in Germany. *Bankhaus Herstatt* was not a huge bank but simply a midsize bank. In fact, it probably would not have met the systemic relevance threshold, if this concept (in today's economic and financial meaning) were to be applied to *Bankhaus Herstatt* at that time. Nevertheless, it was a traditional name in the local market. In this case, the troubles arrived because the institution regularly carried out highly speculative transactions on the foreign exchange market. When several of those dangerous trades simultaneously went in the wrong direction, they caused serious losses that could not be covered by *Herstatt's* equity reserves or shareholder contributions.[199] The brusque downturn came as a shock to both the German regulators and the German public. It undeniably brought to light a fact that had ultimately been forgotten by most: even a relatively small bank could cause massive damage by way of frivolous speculation. It also brought to the public's attention another evident situation: there was little to none real supervision on that very institution. The existing supervisory mechanisms did not allow for either the market or the governmental authorities to prevent such a failure. A hard lesson was learned at that moment and it led to fundamental political and market changes. The positive outcome, which arose out of that failure, was the invention of more modern specific bank-related consultation rules under German law. The bank moratorium, for instance, was recognised in a pre-formal insolvency scenario in some legal texts.[200] However, the rules were by far not modern

197. *Lastra* (Cross-Border), p. 352. *Kindleberger*, pp. 225-226.
198. *Lastra* (Cross-Border), pp. 346 et seq.
199. *Hüpkes*, p. 52.
200. The UNCITRAL Model Law on Cross-Border Insolvency sets forth a moratorium and a general stay of creditor's rights against the debtor upon recognition of a foreign insolvency proceeding. *See UNCITRAL*, p. 30. http://www.uncitral.org/pdf/english/texts/insolven/1997-Model-Law-Insol-2013-Guide-Enactment-e.pdf. These principles were transposed into national legislation in the United Kingdom. *Lastra/Chan Ho*, p. 220. Until early 2005, Article 37 of the Swiss Federal Banking Act also included a possibility of moratorium (*Nachlassstundung*). http://www.

enough to cope with the financial crisis of 2008. As mentioned, it was one of the triggering factors of the Basel Accord.

What can be derived from these three short examples is the following: the problems that caused institutions to fail were relatively identical over the last hundred years. Financial markets repeatedly saw an asset valuation bubble driving to expose balance sheets to a certain asset class. Banks are mostly granting loans collateralised by the security of a certain (valuable) asset class, or within a certain (successful) industry sector. Once and if an institution has invested too deeply into a very special asset class that is not properly evaluated due to constantly shifting market distortions, bursting of a bubble eventually translates to severe correction in its balance sheet. This is a recurrent theme in economic history, not long ago observed in Southern Europe, especially in the Spanish banking crisis.

Another well-known recipe for bank failure is a speculative transaction like in the case of *Bankhaus Herstatt*. There are certainly other examples where derivative or other foreign exchange related contracts have led to bank collapses. Some can be found in the 1980s in the US, especially in the Southwest and Northeast where over 1,600 bank failures took place, many of them based on a high volume of speculative activity. Law & Economics explain that the nature of speculation lies partly on incentives that bank shareholders place on management to take on riskier activities.[201,202]

The third reason for bank failure is simply the merger between two distressed institutions or one distressed institution and one healthy candidate, like in the case of *Creditanstalt*. In reality, the merger of two distressed or at least not very economically sound entities cannot lead to a viable solution. Quite the opposite, as one would expect, it induces a worsening of the situation.

In sum, as observed above, bank crises and bank failures have often taken place at the peak of economic cycles, where a given sector's expansion – such as real estate – functions as an incentive to take more risks, by granting more credit and also lending more. Since the profits generated by that sector's expansion do not increase at the same pace as the ever-increasing indebtedness, borrowers start to default their financial obligations. This almost inevitably culminates in banks' failures. Dangerous risk-taking is a core topic of bank failures, which bears a tight correlation with deficiencies in regulation and supervision, as well as deficiencies in the banks' internal controls.

§2.02 EMERGING MARKETS

In emerging market countries, crises can take a different shape. In 1994, the Brazilian government launched a monetary stabilisation plan, *Plano Real*, which made the country's inflation rate drop from monthly 30% to annual 3%.[203] Inflation-related

admin.ch/opc/de/classified-compilation/19340083/200501010000/952.0.pdf. Other countries like Austria, Luxembourg, and France also adopted a debt service moratoria regime. *See Asser*, p. 97.

201. *Carnell/Macey/Miller*, pp. 52-53.
202. *See Dragomir*, p. 313.
203. *See Leitao* on *Plano Real*. Cysne, p. 329.

revenues amounted up to 80% of some banks' revenues and the political adjustment led to over forty bank failures in Brazil.[204] One could say that the inflationary market had been in exponential growth during the decade preceding *Plano Real*. Obviously, this bubble was doomed to burst. Healthy institutions were able to turn inflation-related revenues into services revenues thereafter, but a significant piece of the national financial system – including three major banks – did not survive.[205] Also, this crisis provides good evidence. For instance, a merger has little to no use in those cases where the problem consists of bad-quality assets in the merged entities. Generally, two low-(credit) quality assets do not make a high-quality one. On the other hand, a merger may indeed be helpful if the problem relates to the target's management, and the bidder seeks to replace the former corporate governance structure, or if there are two different types of business so that by way of a merger synergies can be created. There is no one-size-fits-all type of solution, and each existing restructuring technique will be used according to the state of affairs.

§2.03 JAPAN

The Japanese economy faced a bubble during the 1980s,[206] which eventually lead to a banking crisis. The bubble involved an overvaluation of the real estate prices and of the stock market. Some studies show that in the early 1990s, the value of land in Japan was five times higher than in the US.[207] Parallel to that, the Japanese stock market grew exponentially, representing almost half of the global equity market capitalisation in 1989.[208]

In addition to bubbles, other factors are attributed causes of the crisis. These are: a rigid financial regime, slow regulatory response to the bank failures and distress symptoms in the early 1990s, little general public support to tackle with failing institutions, and a lack of disclosure and transparency.[209] As a consequence, 171 banks failed between 1994 and 2003 in Japan.[210]

The tools employed to resolve and recover such banks were quite usual. The *Nippon Credit Bank* was bailed out, and other institutions were subject to arranged mergers, asset separation into a 'bad' bank or temporary nationalisation. The Japanese government instituted a 100% deposit insurance programme and made over USD 200 million available for capital injections into viable banks.[211]

Just like the problems leading to a crisis, the techniques employed to restructure a bank, at least the traditional techniques, are also quite alike. In a brief recap: one of the techniques is the emergency funding by way of loan or guarantee by public and private parties. Another technique is the technique of a facilitated merger, which must

204. *Corazza*, p. 4.
205. *See Corazza*. *Banco Nacional*, *Banco Bamerindus* and *Banco Econômico* were most affected.
206. *Vogel*, pp. 34 et seq.
207. *Stone/Ziemba*, p. 149.
208. *Stone/Ziemba*, p. 149.
209. *Cargill*, p. 38.
210. *Uchida/Udell*, p. 926.
211. *Uchida/Udell*, p. 927.

be well conducted or otherwise will lead to a double failure. The third technique is nationalisation, i.e. the state taking ownership of the institution. The latter is probably the safest haven, as state-owned banking institutions hardly ever become bankrupt. Hence, the following pages briefly discuss and describe the techniques that were illustrated in the examples above, starting with the technique of nationalisation.

§2.04 NATIONALISATION: STATE TAKING OWNERSHIP

The techniques for the state taking ownership can only in theory be very different. On the one hand, a traditional technique could be approached by which the state under the ordinary equity-raising rules becomes the sole shareholder of the institution. For instance, this could happen in the course of an ordinary share purchase or of an ordinary equity-raising process. However, there is no accessible example for such an ordinary equity process in the case of a bank restructuring. This is because, in a bank restructuring scenario, time is of the essence. It will be crucial for the viability of the bank that the government steps in as quickly as possible to rescue the institution. Therefore, equity issuances in the course of bank restructuring by governments always come as extraordinary intervention measures. This very special intervention measure can have different forms, as can be seen below.

In 2008, Germany quickly enacted legislation to accelerate and stabilise the financial markets.[212] The state could take ownership of shares of a bank without adhering to the formalities under the German Stock Corporation Act.[213] In fact, it was even possible to squeeze out minority shareholders without following the formal squeeze-out rules in this Act. In that same year, the newly created mechanisms were applied to the rescue of Hypo Real Estate. Even though the government's approach was heavily debated, the German Federal Supreme Court confirmed it at last.[214] Other countries have passed comparable laws, like the UK, where under the temporary Banking Act 2008, later substituted by the Banking Act 2009, similar rules and wide discretionary powers were delegated to the state. It was under those rules that the British government sought and obtained authorisation to take over a large majority of key banks.[215] Not only in the UK but also in many European jurisdictions as well as in the US, such rules allow governments to assume control over and nationalise banks in critical situations.

These types of rescues, however, have to be differentiated from the resolution tools, like the bridge bank tool. This is another form of the state taking ownership, where part of the businesses of the institution is transferred to a bridge bank held by the government. The bridge bank tool aims at a split of the institution into one viable and

212. The Financial Market Stabilisation Fund Act (*Finanzmarktstabilisierungsfondsgesetz*) and the Act to Accelerate Financial Market Stabilisation (*Finanzmarktstabilisierungsbeschleunigungsgesetz*), each originally dated 17 October 2008.
213. *Aktiengesetz*, dated 6 September 1965, as amended thereafter.
214. *Hüfner*, p. 5. *Kersting*, pp. 282 et seq. *Rumersdorfer*, p. 8.
215. *Chan Ho*, pp. 384 et seq.

systemic part and one non-viable part, which then becomes subject to an ordinary insolvency procedure.

It is valid to stress that the nationalisations described above are likely to avoid any form of creditor loss. Admittedly, they do have an impact on the shareholder's position, as shareholders get deprived of their shares and are subject to compensation. However, the impact usually stops when it comes to further distributing the institution's losses among creditors. Needless to say, the state acquisition is sometimes seen as hostile by existing shareholders, bringing about litigation when they are convinced that their shares have been taken away for token sums. One of the practical examples is the already mentioned Hypo Real Estate case, where minority shareholders initiated several lawsuits. Shareholders also claimed for compensation in the nationalisations of the Northern Rock in England and SNS Reaal in The Netherlands.[216] Therefore, nationalisation does not necessarily mean that shareholders will not get paid anything, but they may (and to a certain extent should) bear a part of the burden. Note that also in this context, there is a difference to the bridge bank tool. In a resolution scenario, this strategy usually does not provide for money to be paid to the shareholders.

Dozens of banks have been nationalised in the last century. Even the German *Abwicklungsanstalten*, the so-called bad banks, are analogous examples for nationalisation, as the *Abwicklungsanstalten* are held by state-owned funds. Though similar, the Spanish bad bank model differs insofar as at least a mixture of private and public investors is sought in the ownership structure of SAREB.[217]

[A] What Is the Common Logic of a Bank Becoming Nationalised?

Clearly, nationalisation per se does not lead to the restructuring of the institution. This will not happen unless the institution is split up by way of a bridge bank tool or is otherwise restructured by way of a bail-in tool or other available means. It is solely the owner who changes fully or to a certain extent. The bank balance sheet and the bank business remain the same. However, through that ownership, the government basically assumes responsibility for the business of the institution and in a de facto manner guarantees the existence of the institution.

The market certainly reacts to this signal, by which confidence in the institution is restored. Obligations and liquidity injections by the government for that institution (and costs for the taxpayer) come naturally as a consequence. To a large extent, this was the reason why bailouts became so unpopular in general public opinion lately.

216. *Steinglass*. Netherlands may need to compensate SNS Reaal shareholders. Financial Times, 12 July 2013. At: http://www.ft.com/intl/cms/s/0/3d826730-eae8-11e2-bfdb-00144feabdc0.html#axzz2o1x5IoNL.

217. SAREB (*Sociedad de Gestión de Activos Procedentes de la Reestructuración Bancaria*) is a private entity created in 2012 to assist in the reconstruction of the Spanish financial sector. It is supposed to supervise and manage the assets of those institutions, which received state aid. The Fund for the Orderly Restructuring of the Banking Sector (*Fondo de reestructuración ordenada bancaria*) holds 45% of SAREB's capital, while the remaining 55% is held by private parties.

However, some authors expressly argue that this type of restructuring, i.e. nationalisation, is the only way to restructure an institution. The examples of Sweden and Norway as successful nationalisations in the Scandinavian crisis of the 1990s[218] are often cited in that context. In the course of that crisis, various banks were taken over by the Swedish government. They were duly supported, and confidence was restored in the marketplace. Following the end of the crisis, the Swedish government was able to sell the shares of those institutions later, to compensate for any investments made and even realise a gain.[219] These arguments are often brought forward when it comes to a nationalisation: the investment will pay out over time, with the adequate confidence restored by way of the nationalisation.[220] Opponents argue that this causes a disruption in the market and results in market discipline being compromised.[221]

§2.05 LIQUIDITY MEASURES

Besides countries taking ownership over institutions, another popular way to restructure banks is simply by providing liquidity through states or state-owned agencies. The manners of providing liquidity are various. One way is the granting of a state guarantee for the institution's obligations. Alternatively, the state may provide loans or a loan-like financing such as silent partnerships or other hybrid instruments. Almost all governments opted for setting up governmental agencies, which would decide or facilitate the decision on whether or not funding would be possible and then actually execute the funding. This was most evident in Europe, where agencies like the German Federal Agency for Financial Market Stabilisation (FMSA), the French *Société de Prise de Participation de l'Etat* (SPPE), the Hellenic Financial Stability Fund (HFSF), or the Spanish *Fondo de Reestructuración Ordenada Bancaria* (FROB) were established. In many cases, also a set of tailor-made rules was set up in order to determine the exact prerequisites and conditions upon which such a funding would be made available.

Such funding would have to be at market conditions (i.e., with interest) in order to not become part of the state aid rules. The same would also apply to nationalisation rules where state aid rules do play a crucial role so as to prevent that nationalisation measures, liquidity or any other support would be seen as forbidden state aid.

218. *Hüpkes*, The Legal Aspects, p. 102.
219. Dougherty. Stopping a Financial Crisis, the Swedish Way. The New York Times, 22 September 2008. At: http://www.nytimes.com/2008/09/23/business/worldbusiness/23krona.html.
220. For example, the bailouts of AIG and Freddie Mac and Fannie Mae were repaid a few years after the governmental takeover. *See* http://www.ft.com/intl/cms/s/0/b649ff9a-97e0-11e1-83f3-00144feabdc0.html#axzz3FaLmgDyV and http://www.ft.com/intl/cms/s/0/ea648d00-47ba-11e3-b1c4-00144feabdc0.html#axzz3FaLmgDyV.
221. For this reason, it is argued that accompanying structural measures, such as reprivatisation upon a specific time frame, must be given in a nationalisation scenario. *See Enoch/Garcia/Sundararajan*, pp. 314 and 326. Stephanou in *Delimatsis/Herger*, p. 217.

[A] ECB and National Central Bank Financings

At the beginning of the 2008 financial crisis, emergency measures by way of nationalisation or state-given liquidity funding were the key measures.[222] However, also central bank financing for distressed institutions played a role. In that context, the ECB has made various instruments available and filled in the financing gap. Interbank financing was a vital element in the liquidity of banks prior to the 2008 financial crisis. As liquidity sources dried up significantly, banks were no longer ready to lend considerable amounts to each other. As a result, the ECB basically had to take on the function and rapidly become the official substitute liquidity provider for regional banks, predominantly by measures carried out by the national central banks. Also, central banks outside Europe, like the Fed and the Bank of Japan,[223] provided large amounts of liquidity to their respective national financial institutions.

Liquidity was mostly provided against the taking of security from the banks that acted as borrowers. Types of acceptable security and the proportion in which each kind of collateral would account were published.[224] As a general rule, security with longer residual maturity would suffer a larger discount, e.g. Eligible security mostly consisted (and still consists) of securities, which the banks themselves would accept against lending, such as asset-backed securities and lower-rated debt instruments.[225] Central European lending to local credit institutions meant that some of the risks on their balance sheets were passed on the ECB and hence also indirectly distributed among Member States. Since all Member States cooperate for the stability of the ECB, the potential default by an institution of one Member State would have an indirect impact on the other members of the European System of Central Banks.

As certain assets became rare, the lending requirements were revised. For instance, bonds denominated in currencies other than euro, but issued and held within the Eurozone could serve as collateral for overnight liquidity facilities.[226] In some of the Southern European states, especially in the case of Greece, Portugal and Ireland, exceptional waivers of the usual requirements were granted in order to make liquidity financings possible under the European Financial Stability Facility (EFSF) programme. National central banks were also authorised to grant at their sole discretion emergency liquidity lines to banks that were temporarily illiquid but still solvent. Under the Emergency Liquidity Assistance (ELA), national central banks practically functioned as lender of last resort for some credit institutions. According to the ELA's rules of procedure, the relevant national central bank must communicate each operation to the ECB, which assesses the suitability of the operation and has the power to restrict it

222. *See Hofmann*.
223. A list of loans is available at: http://www.boj.or.jp/en/announcements/release_2009/fsky0903a.htm/ (Provision of Subordinated Loans to Banks. Bank of Japan. 17 March 2009).
224. ECB. The Implementation of Monetary Policy in the Euro Area, pp. 46 et seq. Available at: http://www.ecb.europa.eu/pub/pdf/other/gendoc2011en.pdf.
225. ECB. Implementation, pp. 72-73.
226. ECB. The Implementation of Monetary Policy in the Euro Area, p. 81. Available at: http://www.ecb.europa.eu/pub/pdf/other/gendoc2011en.pdf.

where appropriate.[227] Under the ELA, national central banks bear the risk and lend directly to the relevant financial institution. The risk of systemic contagion has been the key justification for providing emergency assistance. However, going forward, the increasing concerns relate to the moral hazard as side effects of these liquidity measures. Regulators fear that they send a distorted signal to the market. This brief study of emergency liquidity facilities illustrates a quite common dilemma confronted by state authorities when dealing under the high-pressure environment of bank restructurings. Sometimes, decisions of great magnitude must be taken without sufficient information and in a very tight time frame. All that is left is a choice between the lesser of two evils – in this case, the systemic contagion risk or the moral hazard risk.[228]

[B] European Stability Mechanism: 'Common Backstop'

A final and new source for relief of bank illiquidity and distress is the role of the European Stability Mechanism (ESM). The ESM was set up by the Eurozone Member States to provide funding to the Eurozone countries in distress in July 2011.[229] It has an immense lending capacity of up to EUR 700 billion, comparable even to the International Monetary Fund (IMF).[230] Significant funds have been advanced to Cyprus and Spain, and a large portion thereof was deliberately used to support the local institutions, either by way of equity or by way of debt.

The first state to receive support by the ESM was Spain. In December 2012, a drawdown of almost EUR 40 billion was made. The largest part of this money was given to BFA-Bankia (the resulting entity of the merged *cajas*), Catalunya Caixa, NGC Banco and Banco de Valencia through the *FROB* and a smaller quantity was contributed into SAREB. Hence, in this case, the direct borrower responsible for the repayment of the loan is the Spanish government, not the credit institutions themselves.[231]

227. ECB. Procedures on emergency liquidity assistance, underlying the Governing Council's role pursuant to Article 14.4 of the Statute of the European System of Central Banks and the European Central Bank with regard to the provision of ELA to individual credit institutions, dated 17 October 2013; and the Guideline on Financial Assistance for the Recapitalisation of Financial Institutions.

228. *Olivares-Caminal* in *LaBrosse/Olivares-Caminal/Singh*, pp. 224-226. *LaBrosse /Singh* in *LaBrosse/Olivares-Caminal/Singh*, pp. 13 et seq.

229. Treaty Establishing the European Stability Mechanism. Available at: https://www.esm.europa.eu/sites/default/files/20150203_-_esm_treaty_-_en_1.pdf. *See also* https://ec.europa.eu/economy_finance/articles/financial_operations/2011-07-11-esm-treaty_en.htm.

230. As of October 2013, the International Monetary Fund's forward commitment capacity was about EUR 300,000 billion. FACTSHEET – Where the IMF Gets Its Money, dated 19 November 2013. At: http://www.imf.org/external/np/exr/facts/finfac.htm. According to the Treaty Establishing the European Stability Mechanism, the European Stability Mechanism shall work in cooperation with the International Monetary Fund.

231. European Stability Mechanism. FAQ Financial Assistance Spain. At:https://www.esm.europa.eu/sites/default/files/2014-07-28_faq_esm_archived.pdf, section F. International Monetary Fund, Spain: Financial Sector Reform – Third Progress Report, dated July 2013. IMF Country Report No 13/205.

The ESM gave further support to Cyprus in early 2013 in the amount of approximately EUR 10 billion, 10% of which was advanced by the IMF.[232] The prevailing purpose was to re-establish the local financial sector and to provide Cypriot banks with sufficient funding for their restructurings. Nonetheless, Laiki and Bank of Cyprus had to go into resolution. As part of the resolution, Laiki was split into two parts, i.e. one entity holding all uninsured deposits (this entity will be eventually wound down in a bankruptcy procedure) and a second entity including all insured deposits to be transferred to Bank of Cyprus together with certain assets and liabilities.[233] The rescue measures package included the first official bail-in measure in Europe, since, part of the losses was shared with larger creditors. As a consequence, Cyprus imposed a 47.5% haircut on all deposits above EUR 100,000.[234]

Before the ESM became fully operational in October 2012, Greece, Ireland,[235] and Portugal received aid under the EFSF. This Facility was created as a temporary solution in May 2010. It no longer grants new financings and the administration of the outstanding loans has been taken over by the ESM.[236]

In Greece, the total disbursement by the EFSF was about EUR 50 million. The Greek private bank rescue fund (HFSF) was capitalised with funds to help the local banking sector and acted as a guarantor under the facility agreement between Greece and the EFSF. In particular, the four systemic banks (Alpha Bank, National Bank of Greece, Eurobank and Piraeus Bank) were initially recapitalised in 2013, following the Greek government's debt restructuring. The HFSF contributed EUR 25.5 billion to all four systemic banks, with the resulting holding of total capital ranging from 81% to 95% in each bank.[237]

Note that direct support from the ESM to the banks was not possible until recently, because the European institutions basically wished the governments to be their contractual partners rather than the banks.[238] However, governments did not want to bear the responsibility for national banks, which had operations spread across

232. European Stability Mechanism. FAQ Financial Assistance Cyprus. At: https://www.esm.europa.eu/sites/default/files/2014-07-28_faq_esm_archived.pdf, section G.
233. *See* Central Bank of Cyprus website for Resolution Programme for Laiki Bank on https://www.centralbank.cy/en/announcements/30-03-2013.
234. *Smits*, p. 138.
235. Ireland has successfully exited the EFSF programme on 8 December 2013.
236. European Financial Stability Facility. FAQ on the European Financial Stability Facility. At: https://www.esm.europa.eu/sites/default/files/2014-07-28_faq_esm_archived.pdf, section B.
237. The total share capital increase amount for the four banks was EUR 28.5 billion including the participation of the private sector (exceeding 10%) which amounted to EUR 3.1 billion. At HFSF. Report of the Fund's activities for the period of January-June 2013. http://www.hfsf.gr/files/HFSF_activities_Jan_2013_Jun_2013_en.pdf. In 2014, the second recapitalisation of the four systemic banks took place with the participation of the private sector only, thus resulting in HFSF's holdings dilution. At: HFSF. Report of the Fund's activities for the period of January-June 2014. http://www.hfsf.gr/files/HFSF_Activities_Report_January_June_2014_en.pdf.
238. European Stability Mechanism. FAQ on the main features of the future ESM direct bank recapitalisation instrument. At: https://www.esm.europa.eu/sites/default/files/2014-07-28_faq_esm_archived.pdf, section E.

several jurisdictions.[239] Hence, a direct recapitalisation instrument of credit institutions was finally agreed. As of June 2014, the ESM is able to provide funding to systemically relevant banks in distress directly up to an amount of EUR 60 billion.[240] Key conditions are:[241]

(i) the bank cannot attract sufficient capital from private sources;
(ii) the relevant Member State is unable to recapitalise the bank by itself nor via indirect recapitalisation of the ESM;
(iii) a contribution to loss absorption and recapitalisation equal to an amount not less than 8 % of the total liabilities including own funds;
(iv) a contribution of the resolution financing agreement of 5 % of the total liabilities including own funds;
(v) all unsecured, non-preferred liabilities, other than eligible deposits have been written down or converted in full;
(vi) the relevant Member State invests alongside the ESM. Financial assistance to institutions shall take the form of a direct loan.[242]

Until as of today, the direct recapitalisation tool has not been used. Instead, the SRF has been built up (*see also* Chapter 5 section 5.22[B] below). However, on 4 December 2019, the ESM members agreed in principle on a reform of the ESM Treaty according to which a so-called 'common backstop' will be established latest by 1 January 2024.[243] Under the common backstop, the ESM will be able to lend an amount of up to EUR 68 billion to the SRF to increase its ability to provide sufficient liquidity in large bank resolution processes.[244] Therefore, the ESM could become increasingly

239. *See* information by the European Commission's Directorate General for Economic and Financial Affairs available at: http://ec.europa.eu/economy_finance/assistance_eu_ms/greek_loan_facility/ 'The release of each disbursement to Greece must be approved by both the Eurogroup and the IMF's Executive Board. Prior to this decision, the European Commission, the European Central Bank and the International Monetary Fund staff conduct joint review missions to Greece in order to monitor compliance with the terms and conditions of the programme.' Similarly also to Spain, available at: http://ec.europa.eu/economy_finance/assistance_eu_ms/spain/index_en.htm.
240. Statement by the President of the Eurogroup regarding the ESM direct recapitalisation instrument dated 10 June 2014. Available at: https://www.consilium.europa.eu/media/28065/143163.pdf.
241. *See* European Stability Mechanism. Guideline on Financial Assistance for the Direct Recapitalisation of Institutions. 8 December 2014. https://www.esm.europa.eu/sites/default/files/20141208_guideline_on_financial_assistance_for_the_direct_recapitalisation_of_institutions.pdf.
242. Frequently Asked Questions on the European Stability Mechanism (ESM). Available at: https://www.esm.europa.eu/sites/default/files/2014-07-28_faq_esm_archived.pdf and Guideline on Financial Assistance for the Recapitalisation of Financial Institutions. Available at: https://www.esm.europa.eu/sites/default/files/20141208_guideline_on_financial_assistance_for_the_direct_recapitalisation_of_institutions.pdf.
243. For proposed reforms and revisions, *see* European Stability Mechanism. Explainer on ESM Reform and Revisions to the ESM Treaty. 24 June 2019. https://www.esm.europa.eu/press-releases/explainer-esm-reform-and-revisions-esm-treaty. The revised ESM Treaty will come into force once it has been ratified by all nineteen ESM Member States. This involves approval in the parliaments of all Member States. The ratification process will start following the signature of the agreement amending the ESM Treaty.
244. *See* Reform Explainer on https://www.esm.europa.eu/about-esm/esm-treaty-reform-explainer.

important in the context of bank restructuring and bank resolution. In BRRD, any type of resolution measure, be it the bridge bank or the bail-in tool, will need resolution financing that goes along with it.

[C] State Support in the 2008 Crisis

Table 2.1 shows some examples of liquidity measures in various European jurisdictions. As one may see, most of the data that has been officially confirmed and made publicly available relates to state aid. Though it is known that the private sector also played a role in the restructuring of many banks during the 2008 crisis, it is hard to measure the extent of their participation. A large number of financiers of the recovered banks continue on the global level, and the list also includes the IMF, which took part, for instance, in the restructuring of Cypriot banks, as an indirect lender and a pillar of the 'Troika'.

It is worth mentioning that – as revealed by the table data – most governments opted for capital increases and guarantees, with not as many tradition loans. The capital injections were most often aimed at curing liquidity, but many led to the acquisition of a large portion of the banks' voting share capital, i.e. at least partial nationalisation of these banks.

The review of the European bank restructurings under the recent financial crisis strengthens the case for a supranational approach to the matter. Almost every rescued bank had a multijurisdictional reach and highly intertwined businesses, which could not be reviewed with the eyes of an insulated national authority. Accordingly, all sorts of state aid, including liquidity measures, had to be approved by the European Commission.[245] The support of a bank could only happen upon presentation of a comprehensive restructuring plan, consolidating subsidiaries and relevant affiliated entities. In order to cope with pressing time constraints, the Commission has often granted temporary approval subject to the delivery of a plan as a condition subsequent. There are various cases under analysis still today, particularly involving German and Greek banks.

Table 2.1 State-Funded Liquidity Measures (Approximate Amounts in Billions of EUR[246])

	Capital Injections	*Guarantees*
Österreichische Volksbanken (*Austria*)	1.25	3
Dexia (*Belgium, France and Luxembourg*)	5.2	100

245. *Boudghene*, pp. 29 et seq. European Commission, Memorandum of 13 December 2013 – State aid: Overview of decisions and on-going in-depth investigations in the context of the financial crisis.
246. *Source*: State Aid Register – European Commission. Updated as of April 2019.

	Capital Injections	*Guarantees*
Laiki (*Cyprus*)	1.8	-
Kaupthing Bank (*Finland*)	-	200
Hypo Real State (*Germany*)	10	145
Piraeus Bank, Alpha Bank, Eurobank, National Bank of Greece (*Greece*)	18	-
Bank of Ireland (Ireland)	3.5	120
Caixa Geral de Depositos (*Portugal*)	1.65	-
Catalunya Caixa (*Spain*)	12.5	10.8
Norddeutsche Landesbank (*Germany*)	3.6	30.8
Cooperative Central Bank (*Cyprus*)	1.675	
Attica Bank (Greece)	-	0.38
Banca Popolare di Vicenza (*Italy*)	-	5.2
Veneto Banca (*Italy*)	-	4.9
Banca Popolare di Vicenza and Veneto Banca on sale to Intesa Sanpaolo (*Italy*)	4.785	12
Banca Monte dei Paschi (*Italy*)	1.9 (+ 5.4 precautionary)	24

§2.06 ASSET OR BUSINESS SALE

The previous chapters dealt with the possibility of nationalisation and liquidity measures to save failing banks. However, there are also other techniques that have been practised in the past.

[A] Facilitated Mergers

One example of a 'forced merger' was already given above and relates to an Austrian bank in the 1930s. It was the case of the merger between *Bodencreditanstalt* and *Creditanstalt* in 1928. In the further development of the business, the merger did not cure the problems but enlarged them. The merged entity was larger than all other Austrian banks together, and the problems that the heavily distressed *Bodencreditanstalt* brought along were far too large for *Creditanstalt* to bear. Hence, the merger really only delayed the problem and, by creating a large uncontrollable entity, it made the problem much more difficult to solve.

When there is a reference to a 'forced' merger, this does not always mean by way of a binding administrative act. Indeed, this could also take place in a much softer but nevertheless also quasi-binding way. One could better refer to this by means of an arranged or facilitated merger. Such types of mergers have also been quite frequently used in the 2008 financial crisis.

One example of such a facilitated merger is the one between Wells Fargo and Wachovia. Until the mid-2000s, Wachovia was among the top five North-American retail banks and seen as a vigorous market player. Circumstances rapidly became more serious, and the Federal Deposit Insurance Company informally started to coordinate the banks' next steps. Despite these losses, the solid market position of Wachovia made it a strong candidate for takeover bids. Wells Fargo got the deal. It was a traditional west coast bank that maintained relatively high lending standards and had minimal exposure to toxic assets. Wells Fargo could then complement its portfolio by aggregating Wachovia's south and south-eastern focus and expand businesses successfully.[247]

Bank mergers were very popular also in the Brazilian banking crisis and were used for the three largest failing banks (all among the top ten financial institutions in the country). As liquidity problems erupted in the local market, the Brazilian central bank sought assistance from national and foreign private banks by way of share deals. The country even enacted regulation allowing the central bank to order transfers of control of banks in distress, regardless of the decision of their own management.[248] In the midst of the turmoil, *Banco Econômico* was split into a poisonous entity that was liquidated and a healthy part, which was sold. The buyer received support from the government in the form of purchase of distressed assets in exchange for national treasury bonds worth about USD 7 billion.[249] Another similar example is the acquisition of *Banco Nacional* by *Unibanco* in 1995. To facilitate this acquisition, the Brazilian government bought problematic assets of *Banco Nacional*. As a final example in 1997, the central bank authorised the takeover of the sound segment of *Banco Bamerindus*. After that, HSBC-Bamerindus became the largest foreign control bank in Brazil and quickly implemented an austere management strategy, which brought long-term benefits to the restructured entity. This merger was partly financed with governmental resources under the Programme for Stabilisation and Strengthening of the National Financial System – PROER.[250] PROER authorised the merged entity to register the difference between the purchase price and the target's book value as a premium, which could later be deducted from the taxable income base. Also, they could register losses for assets whose value would be difficult to realise in order to further reduce taxable profits. These were key tax incentives granted by the Brazilian government in order to attract new investors to its newly structured financial market. A high concentration trend followed as a consequence of these (political) measures, but the country has not

247. On this case, *see Hirsch, Subramanian* and *Jo*. Sheila Bair, head of the FDIC during the financial crisis, said: 'We learned from the S&L crisis that putting two sick institutions together ends badly.' In: Tully, Shawn. CNN Money, 16 October 2012. At: https://fortune.com/2012/10/16/sheila-bair-im-sure-vikram-still-blames-me/.
248. *Salviano*, p. 76.
249. *Lundberg*, Saneamento, p. 10.
250. PROER – *Programa de Estímulo à Reestruturação e ao Fortalecimento do Sistema Financeiro Nacional*. *See* Banco Central do Brasil: https://www.bcb.gov.br/en/legacy?url=https:%2F%2Fwww.bcb.gov.br%2Fingles%2Fhimf1602.asp. *See Lundberg*, Rede.

seen such a severe banking crisis since.[251] The Brazilian central bank has created a strong network of monitoring and 'sanitation' network for local banks.[252]

Generally, when merging a distressed institution into a non-distressed institution, as the example from Austria in the past century shows, one has to be very careful not to enlarge or merely delay the problem. Certainly, a merger can bring and lift synergies, especially if the distressed bank has assets or contacts or networks that the bank offering the merger does not have. However, the distressed bank may also bring risks to the merged entity that the other bank is not aware of or cannot handle afterwards. Therefore, the scrutiny must be conducted cautiously on a case-by-case basis to make sure that the surviving entity will be strong enough to emerge from the financial crisis.

In the context of BRRD as well as in the German bank restructuring laws, there is also the possibility of a business sale to an investor, the investor being another bank. This only works if and insofar as the investor actually consents to a transfer. Moreover, the tools under BRRD allow for the possibility to reshape the balance sheet of the business that is being brought over into the merged bank cost-effectively. This is a comparable tool to the bridge bank. By orchestrating the business sale under BRRD, the resolution authority is able to leave certain liabilities behind so that only a healthier part, or only a more systemic part of the bank, is transferred to the investor. More details about this tool will be discussed below. An early example of such a comparable tool would be the acquisition of Washington Mutual. In September 2008, all of Washington Mutual's assets and most of its liabilities including covered bonds and other secured debt were transferred to an investor via an operative subsidiary.[253] Claims by equity, subordinated and senior unsecured debt holders stayed behind with the holding company. The latter filed for Chapter 11 bankruptcy on the following day and was delisted from the New York Stock Exchange. In the liquidation regime, the subordinated creditors only received a quota of their rights. Again, the Federal Deposit Insurance Corporation (FDIC) facilitated this transaction, even though it allegedly bore no residual costs.[254]

[B] Trust Structures ('Good Bank'–'Bad Bank')

Trust structures refer to the common theme that certain assets which are to be considered toxic assets are transferred from a bank to a vehicle, which is not under the obligation to have a banking licence and, hence, has lower capital requirements. This vehicle then holds the assets during a certain period with the purpose to sell them when

251. *Dewatripont*, Balancing their bank, p. 102, also mentions the fact that the Law on Fiscal Responsibility prohibited many forms of use of public funds for loans to banks and a stricter autonomy of the central bank as a positive regulatory change.
252. *Puga*, p. 418. *Siqueira* gives of the new structure; official data is to be found at Banco Central do Brasil: http://www.bcb.gov.br/htms/livrosfn.asp?idpai=ARTREGESP (26 December 2013).
253. *McCoy*, pp. 1352-1353.
254. *See* press release of the FDIC on the acquisition of the banking operations of Washington Mutual, dated 25 September 2008. Available at: https://www.fdic.gov/news/news/press/2008/pr08085.html.

the time is best and to realise the best possible value. These structures are well known in ordinary corporate restructurings, i.e. also in a non-banking environment.[255] This is because, sometimes, especially when assets are under stress, it is useful to transfer and to park them until markets have calmed down. However, with banks, a second component also comes along: a special purpose vehicle does not require a banking licence and, hence, assets transferred to that special purpose vehicle do not need the same amount of equity as the ordinary bank would need. Such transfers to special purpose vehicles also have a legal-technical aspect to it. Transfer of contracts usually requires the consent of the counterparties. To obtain the consent, it is often a difficult and lengthy process given the amount of contractual relations. Therefore, some jurisdictions have developed special laws according to which such transfers are implemented by hive down or spin-off rather than single transfer agreements. Hive downs or spin-offs do not require the consent of the contractual partner. However, if contracts are governed by foreign laws, it is sometimes uncertain as to whether under foreign laws such statutory spin-offs are recognised. Under those circumstances, consent to the transfer remains necessary and while that is pending, some form of 'synthetic' transfer can be applied according to which the formal ownership remains with the bank, while economic risks and benefits are transferred to the special purpose vehicle.

The combination of the following two aspects makes a trust structure desirable. First, there is an advantage of waiting until market uncertainties settle down combined with the fact that assets can be realised at a better value if they are not sold under pressure. Second, there is an easier equity-raising perspective of a special purpose vehicle in comparison with a regulated entity. Not surprisingly, there were examples of this in the 2008 crisis. In fact, the Fed applied a quite similar approach in relation to the Bear Stearns' risky assets. Given that the potential mortgage loans' losses could not be precisely determined at the time of the acquisition, the Fed assisted the buyer and purchased part of Bear Stearns' toxic assets via a special purpose vehicle, Maiden Lane LLC, in the amount of approximately USD 29 billion.[256]

Also, in Europe, such corporate reorganisations could be seen in a variety of cases. In Germany, they are found in connection with the *Abwicklungsanstalten* (wind-down corporations), which have exactly the same purpose as mentioned above. In Spain, an identical rationale prevailed with the SAREB vehicle. Often the 'bad bank' cannot be solved right at the moment of crisis, but it may be sold one day.

On the flip side, those structures can be quite expensive, because no further restructuring measures are actually taken. This means that often no balance sheet restructuring is conducted and there is no creditor that indeed bears losses. The special purpose vehicle must be funded in order to buy the assets from the original institution. Following that, the expectation is that these assets will be sold for a fair market value. The exact amount of those share market values is often difficult to determine

255. *See Undritz*, pp. 269-285.
256. Federal Reserve Board. Transaction Data: Bear Stearns, JPMorgan Chase, and Maiden Lane LLC, published on 2 August 2013. At: http://www.federalreserve.gov/newsevents/reform_bearstearns.htm. Also, *Webel*, p. 24.

beforehand. In many cases, it will be close to the book value of those assets transferred in order to avoid the transferring banks from slipping into a negative equity situation. As many of those schemes are still running, the experience will show which values can be realised over time with a prudent and forward-looking sales process without pressure to sell. This will also have an impact on the overall views regarding these systems.

§2.07 WHAT HAVE WE SEEN AFTER BRRD HAS COME INTO FORCE?

In 2015 the former bank Hypo Alpe Adria, then Heta, was placed under a moratorium.[257] The Austrian BRRD transposition law explicitly included bank wind-down vehicles, such as Heta, into its remit, with the purpose of eventually applying the bail-in tool to Heta's creditors. The debts of Heta, the former bank Hypo Alpe Adria, were guaranteed by the Austrian state of Carinthia, as Hypo Alpe Adria, a former Landesbank, was under the shield of the so-called Gewährträgerhaftung according to which the owners, the respective states, guaranteed their liabilities.[258] The Gewährträgerhaftung was according to the Commission Compromise dated 2006 which ended due to state aid reasons and existing guarantees phased out over time until 2018.[259] At the time Hypo Alpe Adria was becoming a severe restructuring case owing to a significant portion of toxic real estate assets in the south-eastern European countries, the guarantee by the state of Carinthia for the Heta liabilities were mostly still active, and hence, insolvency of Heta could have potentially triggered insolvency of the small state of Carinthia, with many ongoing discussions as to whether an Austrian state could be subject to insolvency proceedings.[260] The Moratorium under Austrian law which could have lasted for a period of up to one year leads to a stop of enforcement measures for the respective liabilities because it was not clear if the Moratorium was fully recognised EU wide as a measure under the bank winding-up directive.[261] The Moratorium further triggered political pressure on Austria on its refinancing costs and on its credibility to stand in for its liabilities. Finally, the Austrian government financed a settlement with the Heta Creditors.[262]

257. *See* Heta Asset Resolution. 28 July 2015. https://www.heta-asset-resolution.com/en/old_attachments/ad_hoc_haasang_28072015_final_engl.pdf.
258. Confidum Financial Management Consultants. Hypo Alpe Adria: Zukunftsszenarien und ihre möglichen Auswirkungen. February 2014. https://www.confidum.com/fileadmin/user_upload/pdf/download/Hypo_Alpe_Adria_Aussendung_12022014_EV.pdf.
259. *See* European Commission, Agreement on terms for the phasing-out of State guarantees for Austrian banks, 2 April 2003, https://ec.europa.eu/commission/presscorner/detail/en/IP_03_476.
260. Hans-Peter Siebenhaar. The lasting legacy of Austria's bad bank. Handelsblatt Today. 14 March 2016. https://www.handelsblatt.com/today/finance/failed-state-the-lasting-legacy-of-austrias-bad-bank/23536570.html?ticket=ST-3321637-py3fKrgZmVIOkvxSqKaP-ap4.
261. Directive 2001/24/EC of the European Parliament and of the Council of 4 April 2001 on the reorganisation and winding up of credit institutions.
262. Hans-Peter Siebenhaar. Austria cuts a deal with Heta creditors. Handelsblatt Today. 19 May 2016. https://www.handelsblatt.com/today/finance/debt-relief-austria-cuts-a-deal-with-heta-creditors/23538004.html.

In 2015 the Austrian cooperative Bank ÖVAG was further subject to a bad bank scheme with shareholders and government taking a share in the wind-down costs.[263]

In 2015 also the Greek banking sector started to undergo a severe crisis with a limitation of cash withdrawals over the summer to prevent a bank run. In the course of 2015, an AQR and a stress test were undertaken in respect of the four Greek banks supervised by the ECB.[264] Following the stress test in 2016, the four Greek banks were recapitalised with support of the HFSF and a burden sharing contribution by subordinated creditors under new legislation introduced by the Greek state. In particular, National Bank of Greece and Piraeus Bank received funds from the HFSF – in the form of subscription of ordinary shares and CoCo securities – amounting in total to EUR 2.71 billion and EUR 2.72 billion, respectively.[265] With regard to Alpha Bank and Eurobank, the HFSF acted as a backstop, meaning it provided 'a commitment to cover any capital needs not found from private investors or existing bondholders'.[266] This recapitalisation, which initially casts questions on such possibility under the regime of new BRRD and Single Resolution Mechanism Regulation (SRM-R), was the first application of the so-called precautionary recapitalisation which also played a role in connection with other banks in the Eurozone and which shall be described in principle in a separate chapter below. The rules under precautionary recapitalisation are currently under review and the Commission aims to amend and clarify these.[267]

In 2016 the Italian banking crisis emerged further. One institution, Banca Monte Paschi di Siena, was also recapitalised under the rules of the precautionary recapitalisation.[268] Two smaller banks, the so-called Venetian Banks, were placed under insolvency administration in 2017 following the SRB declaration that there is no public interest for resolution.[269] The insolvency proceedings were funded by the Italian government in a significant amount to avoid retail investors who had invested significantly in regulatory capital of the banks from falling short. Following this, a provision was introduced into BRRD to prevent the investment of retail in regulatory

263. Thomson Reuters. Austria to turn Volksbanken into 'bad bank'. 2 October 2014. https://uk.reuters.com/article/uk-austria-volksbanken-idUKKCN0HR1RI20141002.
264. ECB. Aggregate report on the Greek comprehensive assessment 2015. https://www.bankingsupervision.europa.eu/ecb/pub/pdf/aggregatereportonthecomprehensive assessmentexsum201510.en.pdf.
265. HFSF. Report of the HFSF for the period July – December 2015 at: http://www.hfsf.gr/files/announcement_20160406_en.pdf.
266. European Commission, Press release – State aid: Commission approves amended restructuring plans for Alpha Bank and Eurobank at: https://ec.europa.eu/commission/presscorner/detail/en/ip_15_6184.
267. European Commission, Report on the application and review of Directive 2014/59/EU (BRRD) and Regulation 806/2014 (SRM-R) at: https://ec.europa.eu/info/sites/info/files/business_economy_euro/banking_and_finance/documents/190430-report-bank-recovery-resolution_en.pdf.
268. European Commission's briefing on the precautionary recapitalisation of Monte dei Paschi di Siena on https://www.europarl.europa.eu/RegData/etudes/BRIE/2017/587392/IPOL_BRI(2017)587392_EN.pdf.
269. *See* SRB's press release dated 12 December 2017 on https://srb.europa.eu/en/node/341.

capital.[270] In 2016, German Maple Bank GmbH went into insolvency[271] due to alleged tax fraud claims. With its balance sheet of approx. EUR 3.7 billion it was the largest bank insolvency in Germany, since the bankruptcy of Lehman Bankhaus AG in 2008.

Also in 2017, the first and so far the only application of the resolution tools was in connection with Spanish Banco Popular which was sold by way of the sale of business tool in connection with the capital instrument write-down tool to an investor.[272] In some other cases in the Baltic countries, the public interest was denied and these banks went into ordinary liquidation.[273] In 2018, former German Landesbank HSH Nordbank was sold from public ownership to private investors.[274]

§2.08 PRECAUTIONARY RECAPITALISATION

In 2016 the systemic Greek banks were supported with capital by the HFSF.[275] In the same year, the Italian Bank Monte Dei Paschi di Siena (MPS) was supported with funds from the Italian Rescue fund 'Salva-risparmio'.[276] Given that: (i) BRRD aims to prevent the support of banks with public funds on the one hand and (ii) Article 32(4)(d) BRRD explicitly calls the 'extraordinary public financial support' a reason for a bank failing or likely to fail, the question arises, how such capital injections by the government were in compliance with the BRRD?

Article 32(4)(d) BRRD[277] has served and been developed as an exception from the application of the resolution tools. In that sense, public financial support in the form of an injection of own funds was possible to remedy a 'serious disruption' in the national economy and preserve financial stability, if granted:

- to solvent institutions;
- in compliance with the provisions of the Union state aid framework;
- the recapitalisation is precautionary, temporary and proportionate to remedy the consequences of disruption; and
- following to address a capital shortfall established in the national, Union or SSM-wide stress tests, AQRs or equivalent exercises conducted by the ECB, EBA or national authorities.

270. *See* Recital 15, Recital 16 and Article 44 of Directive (EU) 2019/879 of the European Parliament and of the Council of 20 May 2019.
271. www.bafin.de/massnahmen.
272. *See* SRB. Decision to take resolution action in respect of Banco Popular Español, S.A. (2017/C 222/05). Available at: https://eur-lex.europa.eu/legal-content/EN/TXT/?uri=uriserv%3AOJ.C_.2017.222.01.0003.01.ENG.
273. ABLV Bank, its subsidiary ABLV Bank Luxembourg S.A. and AS PNB Banka were determined to be 'failing or likely to fail' by the ECB, the SRB decided that resolution action is not necessary as it is not in the public interest for these banks. https://srb.europa.eu/en/content/ablv and https://srb.europa.eu/en/content/pnb.
274. www.ec.europa.eu/Presse with further details on the history and state aid aspects of this case.
275. HFSF. Report for the period January-June 2016. http://www.hfsf.gr/files/act_report_Jan_Jun_2016_en.pdf.
276. Alex Barker. Financial Times. EU agrees Monte dei Paschi rescue with Italian government. 1 June 2017. https://www.ft.com/content/eae10fa0-16bb-3af7-9a0d-4a362293d085.
277. Article 18(4) SRM-R.

Furthermore, public financial support may not be taken to offset losses that the institution has occurred or is likely to occur in the near future. In other words, support is granted by means of an injection of instruments 'at prices and on terms that do not confer an advantage upon the credit institution'.[278]

In respect of the Union state aid rules, these are described in the so-called Banking Communication (2013/C216/01). Key parameters for Directorate General for Competition in allowing such injections will be the: (i) capital raising measures by the bank under its own ability respectively private sector involvement[279] and (ii) a burden sharing by shareholders and subordinated creditors,[280] meaning a loss participation. In order to comply with the latter requirement in the case of Italy and Greece, special laws have been enacted that allowed the write-down of subordinated bonds outside the scope of BRRD.[281] During the COVID-19 crisis, the Commission clarified that they would consider the burden sharing as dispensable falling under Article 45 of the Banking Communication (2013/C216/01) if two conditions are met.[282] First, a credit institution would need extraordinary public financial support in the form of liquidity, recapitalisation or impaired asset measure due to this outbreak. Second, it is assessed that the conditions for precautionary recapitalisation are met and such measures address the problems linked to the outbreak.[283]

The crucial point for the use of the possibility of so-called precautionary recapitalisation is that such support may only be given to 'solvent' institutions.[284] Clearly, solvent institutions are not in a situation as described in Article 32(4)(a)–(c), i.e. failing or likely to fail (*see also* Chapter 5 section 5.10). On the other hand, the respective institutions are in need of additional capital; otherwise there would be no need for public financial support. An explanation for this friction could be given by the requirement that the capital injection needs to address a capital shortfall identified

278. Prof. Dr Christos V. Gortsos. A poisonous (?) mix: Bail-out of credit institutions combined with bail-in of their liabilities under BRRD – The use of 'government financial stabilisation tools' presented at the Workshop of the Financial and Monetary Law Working Group of the European University Institute (EUI. Florence. 12 October 2016) – section 4.2.1.2.1(iii). Available at: https://papers.ssrn.com/sol3/papers.cfm?abstract_id=2876508.
279. Section 3.1.1. EU/C 216/7.
280. Section 3.1.2 EU/C 216/7.
281. See Italian Law Decree No 237 of 23 December 2016. For Greece, see Law 4336/2015 (Government Gazette No 94/14.08.2015).
282. European Commission, Communication from the Commission on Temporary Framework for State aid measures to support the economy in the current COVID-19 outbreak, 8 May 2020, https://ec.europa.eu/competition/state_aid/what_is_new/sa_covid19_2nd_amendment_temporary_framework_en.pdf.
283. Point 17 of European Commission's COVID communication dated 8 May 2020. *See also* Chapter by Christos V. Gortsos. The application of the EU banking resolution framework amidst the pandemic crisis. In 'Pandemic Crisis and Financial Stability' European Banking Institute May 2020. Page 377.
284. European Commission, Precautionary recapitalisations under the Bank Recovery and Resolution Directive: conditionality and case practice, 5 July 2017, https://www.europarl.europa.eu/RegData/etudes/BRIE/2017/602084/IPOL_BRI%282017%29602084_EN.pdf. Page 2.

under a stress test or AQR.[285] However, the line to draw here may be rather thin. In the course of a planned reform of BRRD (third amendment to Directive 2014/59/EU), the European Commission is aiming to clarify the interpretation of solvency, its relation to 'failing or likely to fail' and the role of AQRs and stress tests.[286] A persuasive interpretation of solvency could be to link to the parameters of prudential regulation, i.e. to define solvent institutions as those which meet the Pillar 1 and Pillar 2 capital requirements currently and within the near future. In relation to stress tests and AQRs, only those shortfalls shall be covered which are identified in unlikely scenarios.

285. For capital injection estimated for Banca Monte dei Paschi di Siena (2017) and Banca Popolare di Vicenza and Veneto Banca, *see* European Commission. Precautionary recapitalisations under the Bank Recovery and Resolution Directive: conditionality and case practice. 5 July 2017.
286. *See* https://eba.europa.eu/risk-analysis-and-data/eu-wide-stress-testing.

CHAPTER 3

Recovery Planning

The concepts of recovery planning and resolution planning are relatively new pieces of regulatory architecture. They are the 'living wills' of financial institutions, which were developed in the aftermath of the 2008 financial crisis. Highly sophisticated institutions were at the forefront of this development. For instance, the Financial Services Authority developed recovery planning as well as resolution planning for the key institutions in the UK.[287] The European Commission introduced its draft of the proposed BRRD rules for recovery planning as well as for resolution planning.[288] In some countries, as, e.g., in Germany,[289] new laws for both had been introduced.

Given the differences in the planning designs already in place in the Member States, the EBA shall have crucial participation. It is expected to draft ITS and RTS to ensure comparability of plans among banks in different European jurisdictions.[290]

§3.01 BASIC DISTINCTION BETWEEN RECOVERY AND RESOLUTION PLANNING

While the resolution planning is conceptually quite clear, recovery planning is much more difficult to understand. On the other hand, the resolution plan is much more

287. *See Chan Ho*, p. 400 and *Moulton*, p. 17.
288. *See* Commission Delegated Regulation (EU) 2016/1075 of 23 March 2016. Also, *see* European Commission. Bank recovery and resolution. https://ec.europa.eu/info/business-economy-euro/banking-and-finance/financial-supervision-and-risk-management/managing-risks-banks-and-financial-institutions/bank-recovery-and-resolution_en#documents. In the US context, a similar course of action was enabled with the Dodd-Frank Act, which requires large banks to have plans for 'rapid and orderly resolution in the event of material financial distress or failure'. *Henkel*, p. 104. Also, *Feibelman*.
289. *See Schelo/Steck*.
290. *Schillig*, Bank Resolution Regimes in Europe I, p. 23. See also EBA Final draft RTS on the assessment of recovery plans under Article 6(8) of BRRD of 18 July 2014 and Commission Delegated Regulation (EU) 2016/1075 of 23 March 2016.

difficult to prepare and implement. Table 3.1 illustrates the key functions of each of them.[291]

The common characteristics are most obvious: both are *ex ante* crisis management measures and the main pillar for preparation and prevention.[292]

Table 3.1 Comparative Between Recovery and Resolution Planning

Aspect	*Recovery Plan*	*Resolution Plan*
Ultimate objective	To lower the probability of resolution of the bank	To lower the impact of the resolution on the society at large[293]
Short-run objectives	To assure business continuity in extreme disruption	To furnish the authorities with sufficient information for effective decision-making[294]
Basic pillars	Capital planning and liquidity planning	Systemic and societal protection
Good planning	Quick fixes (execution within a short time frame) and a wide range of options to choose from	Information on legal corporate structure of the group, map of main businesses, membership in payment and clearing infrastructures and deposit base[295]
Party responsible for drafting	The institution itself	The resolution authority together with the competent national authority[296]
Party responsible for implementation	The institution itself	Central bank, supervisor and head of government[297]
Instrumental role	A tool for sound risk management of an institution	A tool for defence of the financial system

Source: Compiled by author from various sources.

291. Based on the speech by Huertas, Thomas F. at the Financial Services Authority.
292. *Avgouleas*, Governance, p. 401.
293. *See* section 1.1.1 Role of the SRB in SRB Expectations for Banks March 2020.
294. See Principle 5.1 Management Information System (MIS) capabilities to provide information necessary for the preparation and update of resolution plans; Principle 5.2 MIS capabilities to produce necessary information for the execution of a fair, prudent and realistic valuation; and Principle 3 MIS capabilities to produce necessary information for the effective application of resolution actions in SRB's Expectations for Banks March 2020. Banks are expected to provide the SRB with all the information necessary for the preparation, update and implementation of resolution plans and, to this end, to cooperate as much as necessary with the SRB.
295. *See* Dimension 3 Liquidity and funding in resolution, and Dimension 4 Operational continuity in resolution and access to FMI services. Banks are expected to establish the necessary processes and arrangements to maximise the likelihood of maintaining access, ahead of, during and after resolution, to Financial Market Infrastructures (FMIs) and to payment, clearing, settlement and custody services provided by intermediaries.
296. *See* section 1.4.1 on Resolution planning in SRB's Expectations for Banks March 2020.
297. *See* section 1.4.3 Resolution weekend and implementation of resolution scheme in SRB's Expectations for Banks March 2020.

Under the final text of BRRD,[298] Member States shall ensure that each institution draws up and *maintains a recovery plan providing for measures to be taken by the institution to restore its financial position following a significant deterioration of its financial situation*. They shall not assume any access or receipt of extraordinary public financial support.

Hence, while resolution plans aim to prepare an institution structurally for a potential resolution, recovery plans are not meant to address a resolution but to implement and foresee measures, which the institution has to take in order to avoid coming to a resolution stage and to restore its financial stability beforehand. Hence, recovery plans are an instrument which are supposed to make an institution fit and proper to react to a future crisis with the knowledge of its weaknesses and risks so that it is able to react quickly in a predefined manner.

The key issue with recovery planning is that it is supposed to address a potential crisis rather than a real crisis. Hence, a hypothetical crisis scenario has to be developed which is then addressed in a hypothetical manner. Therefore, it is a double hypothetical event. One with respect to the potential crisis scenario and the other with respect to the potential reactions to such a scenario.

§3.02 WHICH POTENTIAL SCENARIOS SHOULD BE CREATED?

According to BRRD, EBA, in close corporation with the European Systemic Risk Board (ESRB), shall develop guidelines further specifying the range of scenarios to be used for the purpose of setting up recovery plans. According to the EBA,[299] system-wide events must be distinguished from idiosyncratic events. System-wide events mean events that have serious negative consequences toppling over the financial system or the real economy as a whole. Idiosyncratic events by contrast are events that unwind repercussions within a single institution or a single group. Under the proposed EBA standards, in their recovery plans, institutions will have to at least include one scenario for a system-wide event, one scenario for an idiosyncratic event, and one scenario with a combination of system-wide and idiosyncratic events which occur simultaneously or interactively. Similar concepts are to be found in the Financial Stability Board's (hereinafter 'FSB') key attributes.[300]

Under the EBA proposal, each scenario shall have a description and an analysis on how it evolves particularly on the capital of an institution and on the liquidity of an institution at buoyant markets times. Moreover, it shall have data on the business model, profitability, payment systems and reputation of the institution.[301]

298. Article 5(1) of BRRD.
299. Commission Delegated Regulation (EU) 2016/1075 of 23 March 2016.
300. The FSB is a forum where representatives of central banks and equivalent financial authorities, as well as international organisations like the International Monetary Fund and the Bank for International Settlements, meet to discuss international financial matters. *See* FSB. Recovery and Resolution Planning: Making the Key Attributes Requirements Operational. Consultative Document. November 2012.
301. EBA, Guidelines on the range of scenarios to be used in recovery plans, Title II para 10. *See also* Commission Delegated Regulation (EU) 2016/1075 of 23 March 2016.

[A] System-Wide Events

Taking the shortfall from public bonds as an example for a system-wide scenario, the realm of repercussions to be examined is wide. Here each bank would then have to analyse how this impacts the available capital and the available liquidity[302] in the business model, its profitability and whether it had an effect on payment settlement operations respectively on its reputation. An institution which has strongly invested in public bonds issued from countries in Southern Europe, for instance, would – in a case of shortfall of these – suffer losses which would have an effect on its capital. Especially if those bonds would be due within a short period of time, a shortfall would also have an effect on this available liquidity. The next step would be to assess whether it had an effect on its business model. The answers to these questions will depend on the amount of the investment in those bonds, the role this investment plays in the overall context of the bank's asset situation, and whether any shortfall and an effect on the available equity plays a role on the reputational side of the institution.

Once with the list of the potential adverse effects at hand, the bank then has to show how it would address those effects. For instance, on depletion of the equity, it would have to show how it could restore its equity position by means of the overall capital markets or by means of certain shareholder investments. If liquidity is the issue, the institution could potentially show that it could cure that problem by taking up interbank loans or shareholder loans or other loans from the available market. However, recovery plans shall not assume any access to extraordinary financial support.

Under the EBA standards, further examples of system-wide events are:

(i) the failure of significant counterparties affecting financial stability;
(ii) a decrease in liquidity available in the interbank lending market;
(iii) increased country risk and generalised capital outflow from a significant country of operation of the institution or the group;
(iv) adverse movements in the prices of assets in one or several markets; and
(v) a macroeconomic downturn.

The range of scenarios that the institution has to build shall include both slow-moving and fast-moving adverse events. A slow-moving event could be a macroeconomic downturn which usually has sent its signals sometime ahead. The failure of a significant counterparty could occur relatively instantaneously. Albeit it is known that depending on the factors that trigger these, it could be the other way around.

[B] Example for Idiosyncratic Events

While the failure of a significant counterparty or country risk as mentioned above rather serves as a system-wide event, an idiosyncratic event could, for instance, be a

302. *Leckow*, p. 318.

severe write-off in a certain product or asset class into which the institution has primarily invested.

Take for example the leveraged buyouts market and a bank that has invested into leveraged buyout loans to a large extent. If this type of market collapses or becomes subject to severe regulations, it is possible that a whole asset class suffers a severe loss. Same with respect to investment in subprime mortgage products, which have triggered the 2008 financial crisis. If those subprime loans had to be written down, the repercussions' purview on the valuation of the respective asset and on the institution's liquidity as payment on interest and principal on those subprime loans would not come through to the institution. In both scenarios, the institution would have to foresee and plan how to cope with depreciation and loss of equity.

The institution could, in its planning, also consider how it would reduce its exposure in this very market. Finally, the institution would have to consider divesting in the respective market or consider, if it comes to generating liquidity, selling off participation or other assets.

§3.03 THE STRUCTURE OF RECOVERY PLANS

The format and scope of the recovery plan will of course be proportionate to the systemic relevance of the institution and its interconnectedness.[303] BRRD authorises simplified obligations for institutions whose failure would have only a small impact in the wider economy.

BRRD sees relatively open how recovery plans are to be structured. Under other available laws, for instance under the laws in Germany, the recovery plan shall be divided into a descriptive part in which the structure, the bank, its activities, its balance sheet, its employees and its involvement in foreign countries are described.

In the next section, the potential crisis situations and scenarios are to be described under the rules as just set out. Also, crisis indicators are to be developed. This is the same under BRRD, where Article 9 prescribes that recovery plan indicators are to be developed. Those indicators may be of qualitative or quantitative nature and shall be capable of being monitored easily. Competent authorities shall ensure that institutions put in place appropriate arrangements for the regular monitoring of those indicators. Nevertheless, it is clarified in BRRD that those indicators are discretionary only; i.e., the institution at hand can either decide not to act even though one of the indicators is met or otherwise act even if no indicator is given.[304]

In further part of the recovery plan, the actual actions against those simulated crisis scenarios are set out in detail. This includes the conditions for those options, as well as any potential hurdles against implementing those options and how those hurdles are to be addressed. The latter point is of imminent importance. Say, for instance, that in order to cure a potential liquidity shortfall in any of its investments, an institution decides to sell off one of its foreign subsidiaries to generate cash. However,

303. Recital 16 of BRRD.
304. The EBA shall come up with a guiding minimum list of quantitative and qualitative indicators to be employed by banks in the recovery plan drafting.

if those foreign subsidiaries are subject to foreign regulatory impediments, it may well be that the sale of this subsidiary is not easily possible. Therefore, it has to be described as well how such regulatory impediments, if given as mentioned in this example, are to be solved. The same applies to institutions which are organised in a certain legal manner, for instance in a corporation manner rather than in the way of a public listed company. If its corporate institutional laws do only allow for a certain way of raising equity and not on the public stock markets, this has to be taken into consideration and addressed in a recovery plan, respectively.

Logically, the reliability and usefulness of a recovery plan depend on the reliability and 'truthfulness' of the potential crisis scenarios. Initially, the EBA has run stress tests, where 'only' systemic shocks on the financial markets were modelled.[305] If compared to such tests, crisis scenarios will come across as more three-dimensional and more individually designed to the respective institution. This is largely because the recovery planning is much more focused on the specific balance sheet and the specific risk of each institution and its very effects on the specific business model, profitability and reputation.

Annex A of BRRD sets out a helpful and detailed list of information to be included in recovery plans. Such a list includes:

(a) a summary of key elements of the plan, and the summary of the overall recovery capacity;[306]
(b) a summary of the material changes to the institution since the most recently filed recovery plan;
(c) a communication and disclosure plan outlining how the firm intends to manage any potentially negative market reactions;[307]
(d) a range of capital and liquidity actions required to maintain or restore the viability and financial position of the institution;
(e) an estimation of the time frame for executing each material aspect of the plan;
(f) a detailed description of any material impediment to the effective and timely execution of the plan, including consideration of the impact on the rest of the group, customers and counterparties;
(g) identification of critical functions;
(h) a detailed description of the processes for determining the value and marketability of the core business lines, operations and assets of the institution;

305. *Schelo/Steck*, p. 229. The new stress test conducted by the EBA in 2014 is more complex and included several components to assess credit risk, market risk, sovereign risk, securitisation risk, and cost of funding and interest income. *See* Results of 2014 EU-wide stress test published by the EBA, available at: http://www.eba.europa.eu/documents/10180/669262/2014+EU-wide+ST-aggregate+results.pdf.
306. Article 3(1) Commission Delegated Regulation 2016/1075. Also *see* Article 4 on Summary of the key elements of the recovery plan.
307. Article 3(4) Commission Delegated Regulation 2016/1075.

(i) a detailed description of how recovery planning is integrated into the corporate governance structure of the institution as well as the policies and procedures governing the approval of the recovery plan and identification of the persons in the organisation responsible for preparing and implementing the plan;[308]
(j) arrangements and measures to conserve or restore the institution's own funds;
(k) arrangements and measures to ensure that the institution has adequate access to contingency funding sources, including potential liquidity sources, an assessment of available collateral and an assessment of the possibility to transfer liquidity across group entities and business lines, to ensure that it can carry on its operations and meet its obligations as they fall due;
(l) arrangements and measures to reduce risk and leverage;
(m) arrangements and measures to restructure business lines;
(n) arrangements and measures necessary to maintain continuous access to financial market infrastructures (FMIs);
(o) arrangements and measures necessary to maintain the continuous functioning of the institution's operational processes, including infrastructure and IT services;
(p) preparatory arrangements to facilitate the sale of assets or business lines in a time frame appropriate for the restoration of financial soundness;
(q) other management actions or strategies to restore financial soundness and the anticipated financial effect of those actions or strategies;
(r) preparatory measures that the institution has taken or plans to take in order to facilitate the implementation of the recovery plan, including those necessary to enable the timely recapitalisation of the institution;[309]
(s) a framework of indicators which identifies the points at which appropriate actions referred to in the plan may be taken.

It is worth to be noted that the list of points to be included also includes remarks and information as to how arrangements and measures to restructure liabilities and business lines are to be made. The question is what is to be meant with 'restructure' in this context. Clearly, it is not a restructuring by way of resolution powers in the meaning of a write-off or write-down or conversion into equity as discussed further down. It is more of a restructuring by voluntary means, i.e. by negotiations with the respective stakeholders.

In this scenario, it is important to carefully plan which creditors should be addressed. Communication is of key importance too so that no information is being

308. Article 5 Governance Commission Delegated Regulation 2016/1075.
309. Article 3(5) Commission Delegated Regulation 2016/1075.

leaked to the market which could by any means lead to a damage to the bank's business and hence create a greater nuisance than benefit.[310]

§3.04 PROCEDURE

The procedure of creating and assessing the recovery plan is mostly in the hands of the respective Member States.[311] Surely it is the institution which draws up the recovery plan, in contrast to the resolution plan which is drawn up by the regulator or the resolution authority.

Recovery plans shall be updated on a yearly basis. Apart from that, competent national authorities - whichever they may be on the applicable national law - shall within six months from the submission of each plan, and after consulting other competent authorities in other Member States, review the plan, assess it, and check whether it meets the requirements under BRRD. These are:

(i) whether the implementation of the arrangements proposed in the plan is reasonably likely to maintain or restore the viability and financial position of the institution;
(ii) whether the plan and the specific options are reasonably likely to be implemented quickly and effectively in situations of financial stress and avoiding to the maximum extent possible any significant adverse effect on the financial system;
(iii) when assessing the appropriateness of the plans, the competent authority shall take into consideration the appropriateness of the institutions, capital and funding structure to the level of complexity of the organisational structure and the risk profile of the institution if the competent authority assesses that there are deficiencies in the recovery plan or material impediments, then it shall notify the institution or parent undertaking and require the institution to submit a revised plan demonstrating how those deficiencies are to be addressed;
(iv) if the institution fails to submit a revised plan or if the revised plan does in the view of the competent authority adequately remedy the deficiencies, then the competent authority may direct the institution to reduce the risk profile of the institution;
(v) to enable timely recapitalisation measures, review the institution's strategy and structure, make changes to the funding strategies so as to improve the resilience of the core business lines and critical functions;
(vi) to make changes to the governance structure of the institution.

This catalogue is similar, even though not identical, to the catalogue of measures that the resolution authority can take once it has found out and discovered that the

310. Recital 21b of BRRD stresses the sensitivity of the information included in recovery plans and, hence, stresses the vital importance of confidentiality obligations around it.
311. *Schillig* (2013), pp. 17 et seq.

institution is not resolvable and hence actions need to be taken to maintain, restore or for the first time assess resolvability.

Figure 3.1 shows the recovery planning process under BRRD.

Figure 3.1 Recovery Planning Process under BRRD

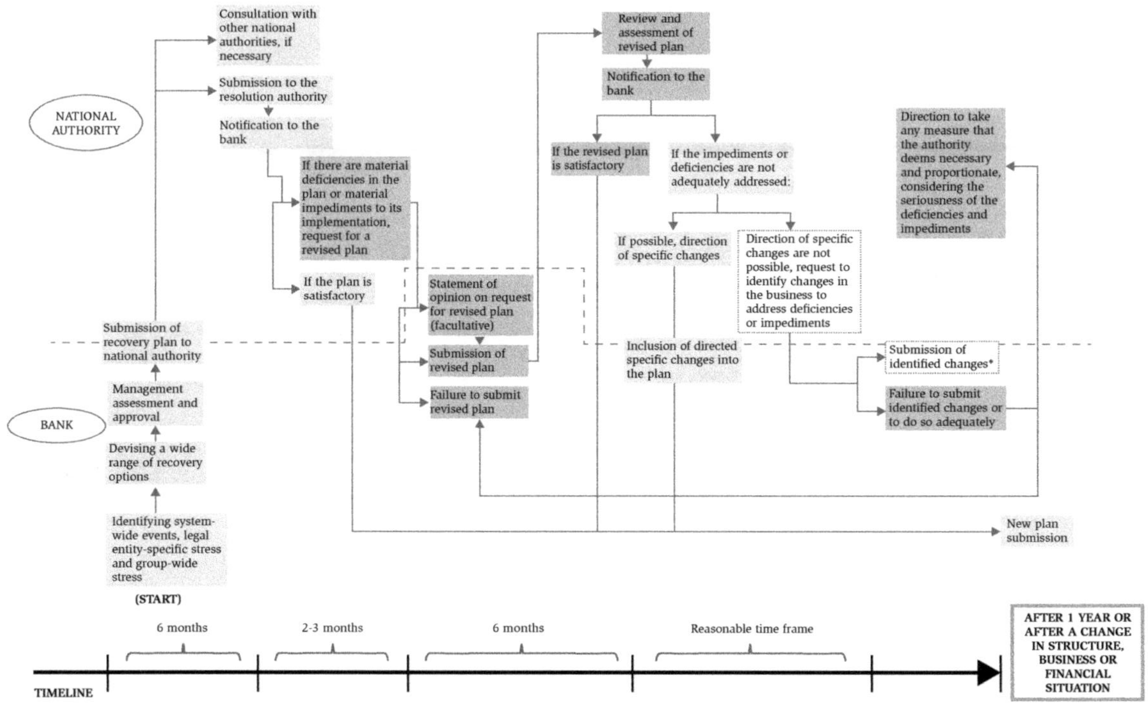

* BRRD does not specify what happens after the submission of the identified changes. However, one could expect that the process continues with the submission of a revised plan.
Source: Compiled by author from various sources.

§3.05 MARKET SPILLOVER EFFECTS OF THE RECOVERY PLANNING

Another important point is that recovery planning, in assuring sufficient robustness of the institution's capital and liquidity in extreme scenarios, has started to have an influence on the market *ex ante*.[312] Lastly, it is an instrument of market discipline enhancement.

As mentioned in the previous section, governments have been the largest provider of both liquidity and capital in the past crisis. This is obvious, for it is not very easy to find generous investors in a bearish market. Given that the reduction of financial burden is the ultimate goal of the new regulatory panorama, the case would not be different with recovery planning.[313] Hence, as institutions were pushed into a creative quest for alternative capital and liquidity sources, new instruments have started to emerge.[314]

This is the case, for instance, with contingent capital or enhanced capital notes, popularly called 'coco bonds'. These are high-coupon hybrid unsecured subordinated securities, which may turn into 'quality capital' – Additional Tier 1 or Tier 2, depending on the trigger level – upon the occurrence of certain events. The triggers may kick in depending on Basel ratios, share price, or rating of the issuing bank. In extreme threshold breaches, CoCos can also be set up to be completely written down – in a measure of full loss absorption. Constituting a strategy for raising capital standards in case of financial deterioration, CoCos are expected to become more and more usual in the years ahead. In theory, these notes have the aptitude of being more efficient than raising capital requirements from a risk management standpoint, as they require capital only when it is actually needed. Also, they discourage moral hazard, since investors are best compensated when healthy practices are undertaken.[315] The market is still seen as an infant, but some benchmark setters have issued contingent capital.[316]

Since governmental liquidity injections are now less than uncertain, contingent liquidity measures are also a core part of the planning. Satisfactory collateral reserves of unencumbered assets for securing future credit lines, committed contingent credit lines with private and reliable counterparts and readily saleable business units and affiliates are examples.

Finally, recovery planning also touches upon the avoidance of a cascade effect. In this context, a certain degree of flexibility in the contractual obligations of costumers is

312. Though not subject to a specific mandatory provision in BRRD, the recitals recognise the direct effects that recovery measures have on employees by stating that a mechanism of 'information and consultation' should be established with them.
313. Not surprisingly, Article 5(3) of BRRD expressly states that recovery plans should not assume any extraordinary public financial support.
314. Living wills are seen as a good alternative to combat excessive risk-taking by bank managers. *See Cecchetti*, p. 396.
315. *Kaal*, p. 296. *Petitjean*, p. 28.
316. *See Varriale* and several articles published in this respect in the International Financial Law Review.

also seen as a viable option. Hence, grace periods (as an alternative for direct default and acceleration) could be useful tools to adjust the balance sheet temporarily. They must be carefully planned and included in recovery plans for implementation upon the occurrence of fixed indicators.[317]

§3.06 GROUP RECOVERY PLANNING

BRRD prescribes for a relatively complex mechanism of group recovery planning, acknowledging that institutions are international institutions with a parent holding company and numerous subsidiaries and affiliated companies.[318]

Under BRRD, as each subsidiary may be subject to individual regulation, it is possible that for each subsidiary an individual recovery plan under the rules mentioned above is to be set up. Hence, the question is how those individual recovery plans are put together in the overall picture of the institution as a group. For this, BRRD prescribes and invents a mechanism for which those individual recovery plans are harmonised and fit together to form an overall group recovery plan. For this process, the parent's supervisor takes the lead; any discrepancies are to be mediated by EBA under a certain scenario.[319] Basically, every competent authority has the right to refer a matter of disagreement to the EBA. The other authorities are in agreement; they may reach a joint decision in relation to a group recovery plan regarding the entities in their jurisdiction. As per the part concerning the disputed entity, the decision on the plan shall be deferred until the EBA has reached its final decision.[320]

In order to mitigate the chances of disagreement between national authorities, certain key aspects should move towards deeper harmonisation in the next years, such as early intervention thresholds and powers, the ranking of creditors' positions, enforceability, and effects of netting arrangements as well as requirement relating to segregation of clients' assets and collateral.[321] Moreover, cross-border intragroup financial support will surely be an issue of tension. The issue will be dealt with in more detail in the next sections.[322] However, the *ex ante* obligation of a parent to provide financial means upon a call by a group entity in times of stress or unexpected loss may quickly increase the risk of loss to the support provider when the beneficiary subsequently fails.[323]

317. For the need of legal elasticity in the periphery of the financial system, *see Pistor*.
318. The Directive cross-references to definitions of parent companies in CRR and Directive 83/349.
319. The mechanism for settling disagreements between competent authorities in cross-border situations is in line with the one already defined in Regulation 1093/2010, which establishes the EBA.
320. Article 8(2)(c) of BRRD.
321. *See Hüpkes*, in *Lastra*, p. 124.
322. See Chapter 4.
323. Basel Committee on Banking Supervision, Report on intra group support measures, p. 3.

CHAPTER 4

Intragroup Financial Support and Early Intervention

§4.01 SCOPE AND IDEA

BRRD contains not only resolution powers but also measures that are aimed to prevent resolution. Among those measures are the early intervention powers,[324] consisting of power to remove management, to require the drafting of certain business plans, to take recovery plan measures. If the conditions for early intervention measures are met, intragroup financial support[325] agreement can be put into effect.[326]

The idea stems from the common problem within a group that faces a situation of distress. It is often legally and practically difficult to transfer liquidity from one part of the group to another part of the group. It is not unusual that some legal entities of a group in one Member State are comparably cash-rich, while other entities, or maybe even the top parent company, are in a compromised stadium.[327] Sometimes, there is a rapidly deteriorating financial condition, or a deteriorating liquidity situation,[328] as BRRD formulates. These are signals of relatively early distress compared to a stadium where the institution is already failing or likely to fail.

In such a situation, the management of the top company and also the management of the cash-rich entity may seek to help cure and support the situation. A way of doing so is a transfer of some of the cash in an intragroup loan.

324. *See* section 4.04.
325. *See* Report on intragroup support measures issued by the Bank for International Settlements in February 2012. http://www.bis.org/publ/joint28.pdf. The bail-in playbook guidance expects the banks to identify liabilities held by other group entities, as well as the intragroup liabilities guaranteed by the bank (see para 43).
326. Article 19 of BRRD.
327. Commission Delegated Regulation 2016/1075, in Article 33, lays out conditions for a reasonable prospect that the support provided significantly redresses the financial difficulties of the group entity receiving the financial support.
328. Article 27(1) of BRRD. *See also* Article 13 of SRM-R.

However, various Member States have quite strict capital and liquidity maintenance rules that prevent or limit the ability to make loans to other group companies. This is particularly true for upstream intragroup loans to entities which may be in a distressed situation. For instance, under German law, management may only grant loans to another group company if:

(a) there is a predominant likelihood that the loan will be repaid; and
(b) such withdraw of liquidity does not trigger the entity's own illiquidity.[329]

Sometimes, affiliated companies enter into so-called domination and profit-and-loss transfer agreements (*Beherrschungs – und Gewinnabführungsverträge*).[330] These agreements loosen the tight capital protection rules to a certain extent. Nonetheless, the two parameters above also apply to transfers under such agreements.

Similar rules are also found in other Member States.[331] First, company law may prohibit management from acting in the interest of the group, if this action might be detrimental to the managed company. Moreover, insolvency laws may also render invalid all intragroup transfers affected during the 'suspect' period prior to a failure.[332] The tax law rules regarding thin capitalisation and transfer pricing may also play a role. On top of that, national banking rules may give local supervisors the right to restrict any up-streaming of liquidity in order to protect local creditors and depositors.

BRRD acknowledges that it may be economically useful to transfer a cash overflow from one entity for the benefit of another.[333] Hence, it tries to give a little more flexibility to bank groups to manage their cash in an efficient manner during a distressed situation. However, this goal must be looked at very carefully, as European laws still function on entity-by-entity basis and not on a group basis. In a worst-case

329. Section 64 German Law for limited liability companies. '§ 64 Haftung für Zahlungen nach Zahlungsunfähigkeit oder Überschuldung. Die Geschäftsführer sind der Gesellschaft zum Ersatz von Zahlungen verpflichtet, die nach Eintritt der Zahlungsunfähigkeit der Gesellschaft oder nach Feststellung ihrer Überschuldung geleistet werden. Dies gilt nicht von Zahlungen, die auch nach diesem Zeitpunkt mit der Sorgfalt eines ordentlichen Geschäftsmanns vereinbar sind. Die gleiche Verpflichtung trifft die Geschäftsführer für Zahlungen an Gesellschafter, soweit diese zur Zahlungsunfähigkeit der Gesellschaft führen mussten, es sei denn, dies war auch bei Beachtung der in Satz 2 bezeichneten Sorgfalt nicht erkennbar. Auf den Ersatzanspruch finden die Bestimmungen in § 43 Abs. 3 und 4 entsprechende Anwendung.'

330. Banks are expected to identify, describe and document these arrangements in accordance with the bail-in playbook guidance (see para. 55).

331. The European Commission Internal Market and Services DG issued a feasibility report on 'asset transferability' within cross-border banking groups, dated 14 November 2008. The report lists the sanctions applicable to the companies, managers, and consequences of challengeable intragroup transfers under civil law, insolvency law, company law, banking law, criminal law, and others in each of the Member States. For example, in France, the transfer may be annulled for fraud, and the directors may be personally liable criminally and be compelled to bear the debts of the legal entity. *See* https://ec.europa.eu/info/sites/info/files/rep-14112008_en.pdf.

332. *See Hüpkes* (2009), pp. 377 et seq.

333. In the United States, the Code of Federal Regulations requires the banking holding company to ensure the soundness of the group: '§ 225.4 Corporate practices. (a) Bank holding company policy and operations. (1) A bank holding company shall serve as a source of financial and managerial strength to its subsidiary banks and shall not conduct its operations in an unsafe or unsound manner.'

scenario, a creditor will be a creditor of a legal entity in a certain Member State and not a creditor of a consolidated group. Streaming up cash and taking out cash from one entity for the benefit of another entity in a distressed situation can place depositors and other creditors at risk. From that perspective, transfers must be done in a way that it does not conflict with the rights of local parties. BRRD recognises this need and sets out the prerequisites and the process of such intragroup financial support quite carefully.

The conditions for group financial support are such that it may only be granted if:[334]

- there is a reasonable prospect that the support provided significantly redresses the financial difficulties of the group entity receiving the support;[335]
- the provision of financial support has the objective of preserving or restoring the financial stability of the group as a whole or any of the entities of the group and is in the interest of the group entity providing the support;
- there is the reasonable prospect, on the basis of information available of the management body of the group entity providing financial support that the consideration for the support will be paid and that the loan will be reimbursed by the group entity receiving the support;
- the provision of the financial support will not jeopardise the liquidity or solvency of the group entity providing the support.[336]

A key aspect of this prognosis element is the formula that there is 'a reasonable prospect on the basis of the information available to the management body' that the receiving entity will be able to reimburse the loan. This reasonable prospect is a lower degree of probability than the 'predominant likelihood' required under German and other laws. It indeed grants more flexibility to the management body.

§4.02 STRUCTURE OF THE AGREEMENT

For the management to be able to grant financial support, a previous group financial support agreement must be executed among various or all entities within the group.

This agreement shall set out the possibility of an intragroup liquidity transfer in a stadium where the receiving entities could be subject to early intervention measures.[337] This may happen due to a rapidly deteriorating financial condition, including: (a) a deteriorating liquidity situation and (b) an increasing level of leverage, NPLs, or concentration of exposures. These are to be assessed on the basis of a set of triggers,

334. Article 23(1)(a), (b), (d) and (e) of BRRD. *See* EBA. Final draft regulatory technical standards specifying the conditions for group financial support under Article 23 of Directive 2014/59/EU (EBA/RTS/2015/08) July 2015. Further, *see* Commission Delegated Regulation (EU) 2016/1075 of 23 March 2016.
335. Terms of such support are outlined in Article 34 Commission Delegated Regulation 2016/1075.
336. See Article 35 Commission Delegated Regulation 2016/1075.
337. Article 19 of BRRD.

which may include the institution's own fund requirements plus 1.5 percentage points.[338]

The intragroup financial support agreement shall set out the trigger point for the provision of support identical to the conditions for early interventions described above.[339] Furthermore, the agreement shall state the types of support that can be granted. The support may take the form of, i.e., loans, guarantees, or other securing measures by allowing assets to be transferred as a form of security.[340] Lastly, the intragroup financial support agreement must also set out the guidelines for the consideration that is to be made under it.[341]

There are several rules on consideration. The agreement shall not determine any consideration *ex ante*, but only guidelines for determination at the time of support provision. The consideration must be at arm's length, acknowledging that each party must be acting in its own best interest. In acting so, the parties may consider any direct or indirect benefit that may accrue as a result of the provision of financial support.[342] The principles for the calculation of the consideration do not need to consider any anticipated temporary impact on market prices arising from events external to the group.[343]

Once drafted according to the rules of BRRD, the agreement is reviewed by the competent authorities. These include the consolidating supervisor and the national authorities for each involved subsidiary.[344] The aim is to reach a joined decision among the competent authorities within four months. If that cannot be reached, the consolidating supervisor shall make its own decision on the case.[345] The EBA shall take the role of a mediator, in case one of the competent authorities refers the case to it.[346]

Finally, the group financial support agreement may only be signed if no party to it meets the conditions for early intervention.[347] The agreement must also be approved by the shareholders of all group entities that are a party to it.[348] Pursuant to Article 26 of BRRD, entities that are a party to a group financial support agreement shall make the general terms of such agreement public and annually update the information.

§4.03 PROCESS OF GRANTING FINANCIAL SUPPORT

Once the financial support agreement is approved and in place, financial support can then be granted if conditions for early intervention are met. The management body of the group entity providing financial support shall have the power to decide on the

338. Article 27(1) of BRRD. *See also* Article 13 of SRM-R.
339. The EBA shall issue guidelines to ensure consistent triggers in this context. Article 27(4) of BRRD.
340. Article 19(1) of BRRD.
341. Article 19(7) of BRRD.
342. Article 19(7)(b) of BRRD.
343. Article 19(7)(e) of BRRD.
344. Article 20 of BRRD.
345. Article 20(6) of BRRD.
346. Article 20(7) of BRRD.
347. Article 19(8) of BRRD.
348. Article 21 of BRRD.

granting of financial support.[349] The decision shall be reasoned and should state the objective of the support.

The management body shall notify the competent authorities of the intention to provide support.[350] Upon notification, the competent authorities may agree, totally or partially, or oppose to the management's initiative. If there are conflicting views among the consolidating supervisor, and/or the competent authorities, the matter may be referred to the EBA.[351]

§4.04 EARLY INTERVENTION

Early intervention is not a resolution measure but more of a preventive measure to avoid resolution. It is not the resolution authorities but competent authorities to order such measures. For instance, in the context of the ECB SSM, it is the ECB who is responsible for early intervention measures while the SRB is responsible for resolution measures. Measures can be:

- request update of the recovery plan;[352,353]
- request to draw up action or restructuring plans, including the calling of the shareholders' assembly;[354]
- require one or more members of the management board to be removed;[355]
- require changes to the institutions' business strategy or the institutions' legal and operational measures.[356]

In severe cases, competent authorities can request the removal of the senior management or management body in its entirety or with regard to individuals.[357]

In addition, the competent authorities can appoint a temporary administrator to the institution.[358] Its powers shall be specified by the respective competent authorities at the time of appointment. However, they can be far-reaching, including the possibility to manage or dispose of the assets of the institution or other powers as foreseen under national corporate law. The appointment shall generally not take longer than a year but can be prolonged in exceptional circumstances.[359]

Trigger points for early intervention are naturally different from trigger points for resolution. Article 27(1) of BRRD determines that:

> Where an institution infringes or, due, *inter alia*, to a rapidly deteriorating financial condition, including deteriorating liquidity situation, increasing level of

349. Article 24 of BRRD.
350. Article 25 of BRRD.
351. Article 25(4) of BRRD. *See also* Article 6(6) of SRM-R.
352. *See also* Article 13 of SRM-R.
353. Article 27(1)(a) of BRRD.
354. Article 27(1)(b), (c) and (e) of BRRD.
355. Article 27(1)(d) of BRRD.
356. Article 27(1)(f) and (g) of BRRD.
357. Article 28 of BRRD.
358. Article 29 of BRRD.
359. Article 29(7) of BRRD.

> leverage, non-performing loans or concentration of exposures, as assessed on the basis of a set of triggers, which may include the institution's own funds requirement plus 1,5 percentage points, is likely in the near future to infringe the requirements of Regulation (EU) No 575/2013, Directive 2013/36/EU, Title II of Directive 2014/65/EU or any of Articles 3 to 7, 14 to 17, and 24, 25 and 26 of Regulation (EU) No 600/2014, Member States shall ensure that competent authorities have at their disposal, without prejudice to the measures referred to in Article 104 of Directive 2013/36/EU where applicable, at least the following measures:
>
> (a) require the management body of the institution to implement one or more of the arrangements or measures set out in the recovery plan or in accordance with Article 5(2) of BRRD to update such a recovery plan when the circumstances that led to the early intervention are different from the assumptions set out in the initial recovery plan and implement one or more of the arrangements or measures set out in the updated plan within a specific time frame and in order to ensure that the conditions referred to in the introductory phrase no longer apply.

For exchange of senior management, the trigger points are tighter in a way that a 'significant deterioration in the financial situation or serious infringements of law' have to be given.

Generally, some of the early intervention measures will unavoidably become public. This will lead to a further decrease of creditworthiness or rating downgrade. Hence those measures may be the beginning of a 'self-fulfilling prophecy'. Therefore, they need to be handled carefully in order to avoid any further effect on the institution's viability.

CHAPTER 5
Bank Resolution

§5.01 INTRODUCTION

Bank resolution is actually a new term.[360] Traditionally, resolution meant that an entity is liquidated, and all creditors are repaid.[361] However, this is not always the meaning of resolution in the current context of bank resolution. As mentioned earlier in this book, resolution means either that a bank is liquidated or that it continues its business with contributions from shareholders and creditors. Often such contributions by creditors are referred to as 'haircut' because they do not entail new contributions per se but a cut of their credits against the institution. In this respect, as rights of creditors and shareholders can actually be impaired, it is comparable to an insolvency process where shareholders and creditors also do not often receive their full entitlement but only, if at all, a quota. That is why bank resolution is also referred to as a form of special insolvency law for banks.[362] On the other hand, a resolution can be something quite different from an insolvency process. When an entity is liquidated within an insolvency process, its creditors register their claims and its assets are sold. Instead, a bank resolution aims more at a partial continuation of the business with the support of

360. For instance, the report by the International Monetary Fund and the World Bank entitled *An Overview of the Legal, Institutional, and Regulatory Framework for Bank Insolvency* dated April 2009 refers to the measures with a view to securing the continuation of the bank's business as 'bank restructuring'.
361. *Bolzico* et al., define bank resolution as 'the set of procedures and measures taken by the authorities to solve the situation of an unviable bank' and explain the concept as a process that takes place after the bank crosses the 'point of no return', pp. 3 et seq.
362. Patrick S. Kenadjian (Ed.). Too Big to Fail – Do we need a special insolvency law for Banks? 2012 Institute for Law and Finance Series 9. https://www.degruyter.com/view/title/122850?tab_body=toc. *See also* International Monetary Fund. Chapter 25 Insolvency: Why a Special Regime for Banks?. Current Developments in Monetary and Financial Law. Vol. 3. 2005. https://www.elibrary.imf.org/view/IMF072/01499-9781589063341/01499-9781589063341/ch25.xml?language=en&redirect=true.

creditor contributions (or 'haircuts'). It may be combined with a normal insolvency process in some special cases, but not necessarily.

Sometimes, resolution tools can smooth the transition to insolvency. There are four common resolution tools: the bridge bank tool, the sale of business tool, the bail-in tool, and the asset transfer tool.[363] Each of these tools will relate to insolvency in a different manner.[364] The resolution proceedings may consist of a transitory phase which will involve bank insolvency in the future. For instance, in case of using a bridge bank tool, assets and liabilities are transferred to a bridge bank, while the remaining original bank entity could be placed - as a transition - under a moratorium and then after a certain period of time go into an ordinary insolvency process. Therefore, the study of resolution is closely linked to the quest of finding a system to let institutions go into a controlled insolvency process.

This book addresses resolution and recovery, including the applicable tools as set forth in the European context. Hence, it turns to the rules prescribed in BRRD and the SRM-R. A considerable part of the rules created under these set of rules is based on discussions with the FSB and the Group of Twenty (G20).[365] These discussions dealt with common principles and approaches to ensure harmonisation of bank recovery and resolution laws across jurisdictions. The European bank resolution system has become more transparent now and hence is more predictable that resolution tools have been introduced by BRRD and SRM-R.

The bridge bank tool involves the transfer of certain assets and liabilities to a new institution while leaving certain liabilities behind in a remaining institution.[366] The new bridge bank is up for continuation while only the remaining institution is liquidated within an insolvency process. This resolution tool aims at the continuation of the core parts of the bank's business.[367] These core parts survive under a different balance sheet because they leave certain liabilities behind at the remaining institution.

363. There has been a long political, legal and economic debate leading to the Directive final resolution structure. Many different views have been shared, especially in light of the costs of resolution to the society at large and the risk of moral hazard. For instance, in a Discussion Paper of the Deutsche Bundesbank, *Korte* argues that an automatic purchase and assumption or straightforward closure and liquidation of a bank in case of its failure to achieve a minimum capital ratio would be most efficient.

364. *Bolzico* et al. classify six bank resolution methods: bank closure and deposit payout, bridge bank, mergers and acquisitions, open bank assistance, purchase and assumption, and radical restructuring. They are to be applied depending on the most prominent need of the given situation, such as minimisation of contagion or no bailout for shareholders. Each of these methods is a combination of tools found in the Directive.

365. The G20 is a forum where representatives of the world's largest economies meet to cooperate and decide on international matters. It is composed by Argentina, Australia, Brazil, Canada, China, France, Germany, India, Indonesia, Italy, Japan, Republic of Korea, Mexico, Russia, Saudi Arabia, South Africa, Turkey, the United Kingdom, the United States, and the European Union. *See* https://www.g20.org.

366. A bridge bank may be simply defined as 'an entity that is established to temporarily take over and maintain certain assets, liabilities and operations of a failed firm as part of the resolution process'. *See* the Consultative Document of the FSB entitled Assessment Methodology for the Key Attributes of Effective Resolution Regimes for Financial Institutions of August 2013.

367. The rationale behind is that it is economically more efficient to keep the good business of the bank going and liquidate the bad parts only than liquidating the bank as a whole. Assets immediately suffer value depreciation once submitted to liquidation. *See Campbell*, 227.

On the one hand, it is a traditional resolution with respect to the remaining institution, because that entity is liquidated within an insolvency process. On the other hand, it is a continuation of core healthy businesses with respect to a bridge bank.

In contrast, the bail-in tool does not lead to an insolvency process of any part of the bank. It usually applies to cases where the bank can be rescued by an injection of equity. The bail-in basically works to convert certain types of debt into equity, making creditors convert into shareholders. Such conversion forces creditors to participate in the process to restructure and also to clean up the bank's balance sheet. In sum, this resolution tool focuses entirely on the continuation of the bank with an adjusted balance sheet.[368]

The sale of business tool and the asset separation tool compares to the bridge bank tool to a certain extent. This is due to the fact that they also involve a combination of continuation and insolvency.

When looking at the types of resolution tools, as set out, resolution can be defined as a special bank insolvency regime. All *pari passu* creditors share their losses according to the respective quota in the order set forth under the relevant insolvency laws. In an insolvency, shareholders usually do not receive payments on their equity. Similarly, in a bank resolution, creditors and shareholders share the burden of the restructuring.[369] However, ordinary insolvency regimes do not offer the tools and processes that are diverse and specific enough to fit a complex institution like a bank. The new bank resolution system precisely addresses this regulatory gap and provides a tailor-made approach.[370] It varies depending on the level of distress and the structure of the institution. In conclusion, the aim of many resolution tools is to lead a controlled restructuring process.

There are ongoing discussions about a further harmonisation of European bank insolvency regimes and the introduction of a new harmonised bank liquidation process.[371] The background of these attempts is that there seems to be a gap for midsized banks in respect of the sensible application of the resolution regime on the one hand and the normal insolvency proceedings on the other hand. Indeed, there are some banks which are 'too small' for resolution but 'too big' for national insolvency

---

368. Economists have conducted empirical research to assess what would have been the impact of a bail-in during the 2007 crisis. They have found that mostly equity and subordinated bond holders would have suffered losses, with little to no impact on sovereign institutions and depositors in Europe. *See Conlon* and *Cotter*.
369. Shareholders and other creditors have property rights over their credits against the bank. These rights are protected under the European Convention on Human Rights. Therefore, the resolution authority must follow a due process before acting in a way that adversely affects such property rights. *See Lastra*, pp. 114 et seq.
370. *Marinc* and *Vlahu* defend that given the bank-specific implications of a bank crisis, such as the risk of bank runs and the high associated social costs, bank insolvency must be subject to a differentiated proceeding. *See also Hüpkes*, 12 and *Sester*, 209.
371. European Commission. Study on the differences between bank insolvency laws and on their potential harmonization – Final report. November 2019. Available at: https://ec.europa.eu/info/sites/info/files/business_economy_euro/banking_and_finance/documents/191106-study-bank-insolvency_en.pdf.

processes.[372] Those banks are often dependent on deposits for their financing and have little access to capital markets that would allow them to create a sufficient amount of MREL. In addition, their business reach may only be regional and the critical functions limited, so there is no public interest in applying the resolution tools.[373] On the other hand, a normal insolvency process may not be adequate for those bank structures, not at least because it may trigger the call on the deposit protection schemes with significant amounts as already set out above.[374] Therefore some form of controlled insolvency or liquidation process that aims at selling the assets would be beneficial to close that gap. Due to tight prudential regulation, those bank assets often carry values that are sufficient to cover creditor claims, but not sufficient to cover shareholder values. A liquidation process, if initiated at the right time, could lead to the satisfaction of creditors' claims. However, the crucial element will be the deposits, their stabilisation, and, in turn, the deposit protection scheme funding as set out already.[375]

§5.02 GENERAL PRINCIPLES OF RESOLUTION

Although resolution is not insolvency, it is an insolvency-like process. Hence, the principles known from insolvency apply to resolution processes as well.

Resolution tools have the common characteristic of having an impact on the position of shareholders and creditors. They are alternatives to insolvency proceedings and lead to shareholders losing equity and creditors losing the value of their claims. Hence, insolvency proceedings and its principles may well serve as guidelines throughout these rules, however technical they may seem. The principles below demonstrate such guidelines.

§5.03 SHAREHOLDER SUBORDINATION AND CREDITORS' RANKING

The most important principle of insolvency processes is the ranking of creditors. This principle arises from the fact that the estate does not have sufficient funds to pay all creditors and to return the equity contributions to the shareholders. As a consequence, there must be a ranking about how the proceeds shall be distributed. In a banking context, this ranking is sometimes also referred to as 'waterfall'.

Normally, part of the funds is used to pay all costs relating to the insolvency proceedings first.[376] Then the following ranking is applied: in the reverse order of

372. European Commission. Study on the differences between bank insolvency laws and on their potential harmonization – Final report. November 2019. Page 44.
373. SRB has published a report on elements that constitute critical functions. Available at: https://srb.europa.eu/en/content/critical-functions.
374. See Section 1.04 [B] and Hupkes, Eva. Insolvency – why a special regime for banks?. 21 January 2003. International Monetary Fund. https://www.imf.org/external/np/leg/sem/2002/cdmfl/eng/hupkes.pdf. See also European Commission. Study on the differences between bank insolvency laws and on their potential harmonization – Final report. November 2019.
375. See Section 1.04 [B].
376. This applies to the large majority of jurisdictions globally. *See Fletcher*, 773 on the English law order of priority of distribution of assets.

preference, shareholders, subordinated creditors, unsecured creditors, and then secured creditors. Very often, the waterfall stops at the level of the unsecured creditors. They only receive a portion of their expected payments, while there is nothing left to distribute to subordinated creditors or shareholders.[377]

National laws substantially vary as to creating further subclasses within each of those main classes of creditors. This is one of the reasons why cross-border insolvency rules are so important.[378] For instance, claims by tax authorities or claims by employees may have a higher ranking within the group of unsecured creditors.[379,380] In a bank resolution, these principles apply analogously. Besides the attempts already mentioned to harmonise bank insolvency laws in Europe, there are also attempts to further harmonise the ranking of claims of creditors in a bank insolvency in order to reduce the risk of different treatments and unfair disadvantages as the ranking of creditors' claims can also have effects on the funding costs of a bank.[381] Despite certain differences, shareholder subordination is almost always legally prescribed.[382]

Article 34 of BRRD states that:[383]

(a) shareholders of the institution under resolution shall bear first losses;

---

377. *Hawkins* and *Turner* argue that shareholders should bear a higher burden to the extent their behaviour contributes to excessive risk-taking. In their opinion, not all shareholders can be held equally responsible as some minority shareholders are not as well informed about the banks' business.
378. The first significant step towards facilitation of cross-border insolvency of credit institutions within the European Union was Directive 2001/24. It is amended by the BRRD and shall remain in force according to Recital 119 of the BRRD, which states: 'Directive 2001/24/EC of 4 April 2001 on the reorganisation and winding-up of credit institutions provides for the mutual recognition and enforcement in all member states of decisions concerning the reorganisation or winding up of credit institutions having branches in member states other than those in which they have their head offices. That directive ensures that all assets and liabilities of the credit institution, regardless of in which country they are situated, are dealt with in a single process in the home member state and that creditors in the host States are treated in the same way as creditors in the home member state; in order to achieve an effective resolution, Directive 2001/24/EC should apply also in the event of use of the resolution tools both when these instruments are applied to credit institutions and when they are applied to other entities covered by the resolution regime.'
379. There is a recent trend and lobby for the recognition of environmental claims as an exception to the *pari passu* rule, giving it priority over other unsecured debt based on the communitarian gain principle. That might play an important role in future bank insolvencies in jurisdictions where there is increasing case law on lender liability for environmental damage. *See Symes*, pp. 197 et seq.
380. In addition to statutory subordination, credits may also be contractually subordinated. Particularly in the case of banks, subordinated debt is highly popular for capital requirements. Usually, it is contractually ranked behind senior debt but have priority of repayment over Tier 1 capital. *See* on contractual subordination *Benjamin*, 356.
381. European Commission. Study on the differences between bank insolvency laws and on their potential harmonization – Final report. November 2019. Page 32. *See also* J, Deslandes. M, Magnus. Further harmonizing EU insolvency law from a banking resolution perspective? April 2018. Economic Governance Support Unit. https://www.europarl.europa.eu/RegData/etudes/BRIE/2018/614514/IPOL_BRI(2018)614514_EN.pdf.
382. *See* Principle C.12 of the Revised World Bank Principles for Effective Insolvency and Creditor Rights Systems 2016.
383. *See* Article 15 of SRM-R.

(b) creditors of the institution under resolution bear losses after the shareholders in accordance with the order of priority of their claims under normal insolvency proceedings.

In the general framework of a bank's balance sheet, the cascade of liabilities (waterfall) is the following (in the order of loss bearing):

- First, Common Equity Tier 1.
- Second, Additional Tier 1 and Tier 2 instruments.
- Third, other subordinated creditors.
- Fourth, unsecured non-preferred claims.

§5.04 DETERMINATION OF LOSSES AND CUTS THEREOF: CAPITAL VERSUS LIQUIDITY EFFECT

The wording of the Directive includes 'losses' rather than positively specifying which 'proceeds' or 'moneys' shall be distributed to whom first. However, the key idea is exactly the same: creditors get paid before the shareholders receive their equity back. Why does the wording of the Directive refer to loss bearing instead of setting up a distribution order? The traditional distribution applies to proceeds generated when assets are liquidated, in cases of dissolution of an entity. However, by contrast, the Directive often aims at the continuance of institutions without liquidation. Therefore, it is correct to speak about loss bearing here.

Also, in other areas of banking, one will find loss absorption mechanisms. For instance, holders of subordinated debt notes often participate in annual losses in a way that the issuing bank's capital can be restored. However, those mechanisms are contractually agreed mechanism, while the loss sharing under Article 34 of BRRD is a statutory tool.[384] Also, the contractual loss sharing can be triggered earlier, i.e. when an institution is not yet at a stadium of resolution, i.e. failing or likely to fail. On the other hand, there is a nexus between those contractual loss-absorbing instruments and the application of the resolution tools. In order to restore the viability of the institution, the resolution authority will have to assess the amount of capital that has to be taken up. For that assessment also contractual loss absorption by way capital instruments will have to be taken into account. The authority must run such an assessment before initiating a resolution tool.

After the resolution authority ascertains the required amount of capital, it decides on how the institution shall obtain it. This capital should not be gained primarily in the capital markets through an increase of equity or other regulatory capital. In contrast, this capital is provided by reducing the liabilities of the institution.[385] This may happen

384. Article 15 of SRM-R.
385. Therefore, an obvious necessary precondition for the bail-in is that the failing bank has sufficient outstanding instruments to be converted or written down, as defended by *Huertas*, 171.

either by converting debt into equity in a bail-in tool scenario or by so-called partial transfers in a bridge bank tool scenario.

For instance, it is determined that an institution will need EUR 5 billion additional capital to achieve the required capital ratio of 8%. On the one hand, the use of the bail-in tool can generate the required capital by writing down liabilities. On the other hand, the bridge bank tool can do the same by leaving liabilities behind in the institution which then becomes insolvent, while other assets and liabilities are transferred to a bridge bank (partial transfer).

It should be mentioned that both the bail-in and the bridge bank not only can have a capital effect but can also have a liquidity effect. This liquidity effect may arise when a bail-in or a bridge bank tool is employed on subordinated or senior liability due to be paid by the institution. By converting this liability into equity or leaving it behind in the failing institution, the institution is then free from the payment of this liability. Even though this effect is not expressly mentioned in Article 34 of BRRD,[386] it is not to be forgotten in the reference of the word 'losses'[387] and can play an important role in the overall context. If liquidity can be generated by converting due liabilities into equity, less funds will be needed from a resolution financing arrangement.

§5.05 NO CREDITOR WORSE-OFF

Another very important principle of any resolution is that no creditor is worse off than it would be under normal insolvency proceedings.[388] This is described in Article 34(1)(g) of BRRD. It states that no creditor should incur greater losses than would have been incurred if the institution had been wound up under normal insolvency

386. Article 15 of SRM-R.

387. In most cases, the liquidity effect resulting from the resolution tool will not be enough and further liquidity funding will be required. In order to avoid this second-layer risk of taxpayer burden, the FSB recommends the creation of *ex ante* privately financed resolution funds in its Report entitled *Key Attributes of Effective Resolution Regimes for Financial Institutions* dated October 2011, section 6.1 (Funding of firms in resolution). *See also Institute of International Finance*, 38-41. Recital 55 of the BRRD clearly requires as follows: 'Save as expressly specified in this Directive, the resolution tools should be applied before any public sector injection of capital or equivalent extraordinary public financial support to an institution. This, however, should not impede the use of funds from the deposit guarantee schemes or resolution funds in order to absorb losses that would have otherwise been suffered by covered depositors or discretionarily excluded creditors. In that respect, the use of extraordinary public financial support, resolution funds or deposit guarantee schemes to assist in the resolution of failing institutions should comply with the relevant State aid provisions.'

388. In some jurisdictions, the sequence for write-down and conversion, established under the BRRD and SRM-R, may diverge from the ranking of priority claims under national insolvency law. It could lead to a potential breach of NCWO principle. The bail-in playbook guidance expects banks to reflect this divergence, particularly when the group is active in several jurisdictions (see para 43).

proceedings. A similar ruling is also found under existing national bank restructuring laws like in Germany.[389,390]

This principle is especially important in justification of applying resolution tools. The bail-in tool has been criticised for being unfair or unpredictable for creditors in case of a crisis. However, any creditor contracting with a bank or a non-bank entity always faces the possibility that the counterpart becomes insolvent. In the worst case, this tool simply realises the general insolvency risk for the bailed-in creditors. The safeguard is also expressed in Article 73 of BRRD:

> Member States shall ensure that, where one or more resolution tools have been applied and, in particular for the purposes of Article 75:
>
> (a) except where point (b) applies, where resolution authorities transfer only parts of the rights, assets and liabilities of the institution under resolution, the shareholders and those creditors whose claims have not been transferred, receive in satisfaction of their claims at least as much as what they would have received if the institution under resolution had been wound up under normal insolvency proceedings at the time when the decision referred to in Article 82 of BRRD was taken;
>
> (b) where resolution authorities apply the bail-in tool, the shareholders and creditors whose claims have been written down or converted to equity do not incur greater losses than they would have incurred if the institution under resolution had been wound up under normal insolvency proceedings immediately at the time when the decision referred to in Article 82 was taken.

The obedience of this principle is of uttermost importance for the correct utilisation of tools. For instance, take the case where a creditor is harmed and placed in a position worse than in normal insolvency proceedings as a consequence of a resolution strategy. Such creditor would be legally entitled to object to the various tools and, if successful in its objection, to receive payment of the difference.[391] Such compensation is limited to damages and no administrative act or transactions shall be affected. This limitation exists in order to not block the effectiveness of the resolution process. The assessment of how the position would be in a normal insolvency proceeding as compared to the position after a bail-in is subject to detailed valuation.[392]

389. 'The German rule works in the approval of the restructuring plan, in a way that even though the required majority of creditors of a given class have not approved the plan, it may be deemed approved if, among others, the creditors of such class are not worse off than they would be without the plan. Gesetz zur Reorganisation von Kreditinstituten, § 19(2) Annahme des Reorganisationsplans: Auch wenn die erforderlichen Mehrheiten in einer Gläubigergruppe nicht erreicht sind, gilt ihre Zustimmung als erteilt, wenn 1.die Gläubiger dieser Gruppe durch den Reorganisationsplan voraussichtlich nicht schlechter gestellt werden, als sie ohne einen Reorganisationsplan stünden. See Thole, 226. Similarly also the Swiss Banking Act. Bundesgesetz über die Banken und Sparkassen Article 31 Genehmigung des Sanierungsplans – Die FINMA genehmigt den Sanierungsplan, wenn er namentlich: [...] b. die Gläubiger voraussichtlich besser stellt als die sofortige Eröffnung des Bankenkonkurses.'

390. The NCWO principle also applies under English Law Banking Act of 2009. *See Marinc*, 193.

391. Under Swiss law, for instance, the creditor has a clear right to be compensated. This is also the case under Article 75 of BRRD and under Article 76(1)(e) of SRM-R.

392. Article 74 of BRRD establishes that an independent person shall evaluate whether shareholders and creditors would receive better treatment in normal insolvency proceedings and provides

With Delegated Regulation 2018/344,[393] the European Commission has set standards for this valuation of difference in treatment in resolution.[394] According to Delegated Regulation 2018/433, the valuer has to calculate the potential insolvency quota for unsecured creditors, subordinated creditors or shareholders, respectively. The cut-off date is the date of the resolution decision.[395] In its assessment, the valuer has to take into account applicable insolvency law and practice in the relevant jurisdictions, reasonably foreseeable administration, transaction and other costs and information on recent past insolvency cases of similar entities where relevant and available.[396] Thereafter, this basis should then be used for assessing the corresponding burden sharing to each creditor class.

§5.06 CREDITORS OF THE SAME CLASS ARE TREATED IN AN EQUITABLE MANNER

Under some insolvency regimes for ordinary corporates, reorganisation schemes, or insolvency plans are a common way to restructure entities. These schemes, such as the US's Chapter 11 Plan or the German Insolvency Plan, split the creditors into classes of similar interest and similar ranking. The general principle here is that creditors in the same class are treated in the same way.[397]

[A] Different Treatment of Creditors: Chapter 11 Lessons

Other jurisdictions may provide insights with respect to regimes for creditors' treatment. The Chapter 11 Plan[398] has been well tested and its practice has developed

the guidelines for this valuation exercise. Valuations are also set out in SRM-R, *see* Article 20 thereof. *See also* EBA's RTS on valuation for the purposes of resolution and on valuation to determine difference in treatment following resolution under Directive 2014/59/EU on recovery and resolution of credit institutions and investment firms – https://eba.europa.eu/sites/default/documents/files/documents/10180/1853532/88566587-ff6f-4116-a08e-282eb4ea2f78/Final%20draft%20RTSs%20on%20valuation%20in%20resolution%20(EBA-RTS-2017-05%20&%20EBA-RTS-2017-06).pdf. Also refer to Commission Delegated Regulation (EU) 2018/345 of 14 November 2017. Further *see* section 5.14 of this chapter on Valuation Principles.

393. Commission Delegated Regulation (EU) 2018/344 of 14 November 2017.
394. Such valuation is also referred to as 'Valuation 3' compared to 'Valuation 1' under Article 36(4)(a) BRRD and 'Valuation 2' under Article 36(4)(b)–(f) BRRD.
395. Article 1(3) Delegated Regulation 2018/344.
396. Article 4(3) Delegated Regulation 2018/344.
397. Article 34(1)(f) of BRRD. *See* Article 15(1)(f) of SRM-R. This principle is an example of the much discussed *pari passu* rule. In resolution scenarios, it does not apply across all creditors, but it is valid for creditors within a given class. *See Finch*, pp. 599 et seq.
398. Chapter 11 of the US Code section 1129 provides guidelines for an acceptable discrimination which is 'fair and equitable': '(b) (1) Notwithstanding s. 510 (a) of this title, if all of the applicable requirements of subsection (a) of this section other than para. (8) are met with respect to a plan, the court, on request of the proponent of the plan, shall confirm the plan notwithstanding the requirements of such paragraph if the plan does not discriminate unfairly, and is fair and equitable, with respect to each class of claims or interests that is impaired under, and has not accepted, the plan. (2) For the purpose of this subsection, the condition that a plan be fair and equitable with respect to a class includes the following requirements: (A) With respect to a class of secured claims, the plan provides – (i) (I) that the holders of such claims

standards. For instance, a certain group of senior creditors is offered a payment of 50% on their claims, while another group is only offered 40%. Such a different treatment would not be allowed under US's law unless exceptional circumstances are present. One case would be if this different treatment is duly and specifically justified. Another would be that the treatment being offered is indeed not exactly the same, but it is comparable in economic terms. In practice, this could translate into one group of senior creditors receiving a quota of 50%, and the other group receiving a quota of 25% plus a stake in the equity. If the economic result is proven to be the same, the apparently different ratio could be permitted. When compared, these two different treatments may indeed be economically comparable. Moreover, it may be equitable to treat those two classes differently. For example, one group of senior creditors may be institutional investors who would never take equity, while the other group would be opportunity fund creditors who are used to taking equity. This illustrates that sometimes it is necessary to treat creditors of the same ranking equitably, though in a different way.[399]

From an economic perspective, the bail-in tool, the bridge bank and the sale of business tool function to reduce the liabilities of the institution just like the Chapter 11 Plan. Hence, there are relevant lessons which are applicable from one model to the other. The question now is that under which situations is it possible to treat senior creditors differently in a bail-in scenario. One parameter could be to determine which group of creditors would economically be able to take a haircut and which would have difficulties to bear a haircut without follow-up insolvencies taking place on their

retain the liens securing such claims, whether the property subject to such liens is retained by the debtor or transferred to another entity, to the extent of the allowed amount of such claims; and (II) that each holder of a claim of such class receive on account of such claim deferred cash payments totaling at least the allowed amount of such claim, of a value, as of the effective date of the plan, of at least the value of such holder's interest in the estate's interest in such property; (ii) for the sale, subject to s. 363 (k) of this title, of any property that is subject to the liens securing such claims, free and clear of such liens, with such liens to attach to the proceeds of such sale, and the treatment of such liens on proceeds under clause (i) or (iii) of this subparagraph; or (iii) for the realization by such holders of the indubitable equivalent of such claims. (B) With respect to a class of unsecured claims – (i) the plan provides that each holder of a claim of such class receive or retain on account of such claim property of a value, as of the effective date of the plan, equal to the allowed amount of such claim; or (ii) the holder of any claim or interest that is junior to the claims of such class will not receive or retain under the plan on account of such junior claim or interest any property, except that in a case in which the debtor is an individual, the debtor may retain property included in the estate under s. 1115, subject to the requirements of subsection (a)(14) of this section. (C) With respect to a class of interests – (i) the plan provides that each holder of an interest of such class receive or retain on account of such interest property of a value, as of the effective date of the plan, equal to the greatest of the allowed amount of any fixed liquidation preference to which such holder is entitled, any fixed redemption price to which such holder is entitled, or the value of such interest; or (ii) the holder of any interest that is junior to the interests of such class will not receive or retain under the plan on account of such junior interest any property.'

399. There are arguments for substituting the *pari passu* rule with other criteria and to rank debts chronologically, ethically, on size or on policy grounds. However, most practitioners still see the rule as the best available method for ensuring fairness and efficiency of loss distribution. *See Finch*, 666-674. The UNCITRAL Legislative Guide on Insolvency Law admits equitable subordination by the court. This would be allowed, for instance, to prevent persons from using legal mechanisms to obtain advantages in priority and cause harm to other creditors.

end.[400] However, it is questionable whether this approach is correct. Stronger creditors would be disadvantaged, and weaker creditors are incentivised, regardless of the reason for their particular strength or weakness.

One must then analyse whether such a different treatment is legally possible at all. Under the former regime in Germany, which only comprised of the bridge bank tool, the authorities had free discretion to apply different haircuts within the same class of a creditor group.[401] When applying partial transfers, it may also decide that some creditors of a class stay behind in the failing institution, while other creditors of the same class are transferred to the going concern bridge bank. The important criterion for the decision was not equal treatment of classes but systemic relevance.

[B] Exceptions under BRRD

In the first step, BRRD and the SRM-R do not explicitly allow such a high degree of discretion. It says that except where otherwise provided in this Directive, creditors of the same class are treated in an equitable manner.[402]

As a second step, an expressly provisioned area of exception is laid out in the principles of the bail-in tool,[403] where it says that in exceptional circumstances where the bail-in tool is applied, the resolution authority may partially exclude certain liabilities from the application of the write-down or conversion where:

(a) it is not possible to bail in that liability within a reasonable time notwithstanding the good faith efforts of the resolution authority;
(b) the exclusion is strictly necessary and is proportionate to achieve the continuity of critical functions and core business lines in a manner that maintains the ability of the institution under resolution to continue key operations, services and transactions;
(c) the exclusion is strictly necessary and proportionate to avoid giving rise to widespread contagion, in particular as regards eligible deposits held by natural persons and micro-, small - and medium-sized enterprises, which would severely disrupt the functioning of financial markets, including of financial market infrastructures (FMIs), in a manner that could cause a serious disturbance to the economy of a Member State or of the Union; or
(d) the application of the bail-in tool to those liabilities would cause a destruction in value such that the losses borne by other creditors would be higher than if those liabilities were excluded from bail-in.

The Directive further states that:

400. *Avgouleas* highlights the systemic risk involved with such write-downs and how it may serve as a justification for a violation of the *pari passu* rule, p. 418.
401. Also under general English insolvency law are exceptions to the collectivity principle allowed in certain cases predefined in judicial and statutory rules. *See Fletcher*, 5.
402. Article 34(1)(f) BRRD.
403. Article 44 of BRRD. Article 27(3) of SRM-R.

> Where a resolution authority decides to exclude or partially exclude a bail-inable liability or class of bail-inable liabilities[404] under this paragraph, the level of write-down or conversion applied to other bail-inable liabilities may be increased to take account of such exclusions, provided that the level of write-down and conversion applied to other bail-inable liabilities complies with the principle in point (g) of Article 34(1) of BRRD.

What is expressed in these rather complicated terms is that it is possible to decide on different haircuts (or none at all) within one class of creditors. The resolution authority should also be able to exclude totally or partially liabilities where necessary to avoid the spreading of contagion and financial instability, i.e. where the creditors would end up in the brink of failure. Finally, some creditors may have to bear a deeper haircut so that the necessary thresholds for restoring the capital are reached. Whenever deeper haircuts are imposed, the affected creditors shall be protected under the no creditor worse-off (NCWO) principle.

This principle and its exclusions are one of the most sensitive rules in the application of the resolution tools. The more creditors of the same rank in insolvency are treated differently and 'privileged', the heavier burden others will have to bear. Consequently, the more potentially vulnerable will the resolution measure be. Therefore, treating creditors of the same class differently is something that should only be taken into account under very narrow and exceptional circumstances. The consequences are twofold. On the one side, the broader the pool of eligible creditors, the lower each haircut will be. On the other side, a fully comprehensive approach without any room for flexibility could lead to generalised higher costs of financing for the banking industry in a run for secured and insured debt.[405]

This concern is also one of the main drivers for the FSB criteria for TLAC (Total Loss Absorbing Capacity) under the TLAC term sheet.[406] Broadly speaking, the FSB proposed for respective institutions to draw upon subordinated liabilities for application of the bail-in tool, even though also senior liabilities are eligible for bail-in. This is driven by the concern that some senior liabilities are excluded from bail-in while others are not, and if those not excluded are taken up for burden sharing, the argument of different class treatment could be made and the tools can be challenged.[407] This principle of subordination (to a certain degree) of 'resolution capital'[408] was established under TLAC in 2015 and thereafter applied to G-SIIs has now been implemented into BRRD and the revised CRR under the reform of BRRD.[409]

404. As per Article 2(1)(71) BRRD, 'bail-inable liabilities' means the liabilities and capital instruments that do not qualify as Common Equity Tier 1, Additional Tier 1 or Tier 2 instruments of an institution or entity referred to in point (b), (c) or (d) of Article 1(1) BRRD and that are not excluded from the scope of the bail-in tool pursuant to Article 44(2) BRRD.
405. *See also* DG Internal Market and Services Working Document – Technical Details of a Possible EU Framework for Bank Recovery and Resolution dated January 2011, p. 87 (hereinafter 'the 2011 Commission Working Document').
406. *See* FSB TLAC Term Sheet of 9 November 2015 on https://www.fsb.org/wp-content/uploads/TLAC-Principles-and-Term-Sheet-for-publication-final.pdf. Adequacy of loss absorbing capacity of globally systemically important banks in resolution, 10 November 2014.
407. *See* section 5.16[G] for more details on the MREL, TLAC and GLAC.
408. Or 'MREL' under the terms of BRRD.
409. *See* Chapter 6 for a comprehensive overview of these changes.

Finally, it must also be mentioned that there is a considerable difference between treating creditors identically and treating creditors equitably. Equitable does not mean identical. As long as the treatments are economically comparable, they may seem equitable albeit not identical. The narrow exceptions cited above must be reviewed very carefully. Where the exceptions do not apply but nevertheless a different treatment would seem appropriate, other solutions must be developed. An alternative to meet the 'equitable test' could be to offer more equity to creditors with a deeper haircut than to those with a smaller haircut, albeit them being in the same class.[410]

§5.07 COVERED DEPOSITS ARE FULLY PROTECTED (RANKING UNDER ARTICLE 108 BRRD)

Another important principle of BRRD and of the SRM-R is the protection of covered deposits. According to the definition in BRRD,[411] covered deposits means covered deposits as defined in point (5) of Article 2(1) of Directive 2014/49/EU.[412] Under this Directive, covered deposits are deposits protected by a statutory DGS either set up by the relevant Member State or acknowledged by the protected Member State.[413,414] The general coverage level is up to EUR 100,000.[415] Therefore, the principle that covered deposits are fully protected is primarily safeguarded by the Directive on deposit guarantee schemes. At the same time, Article 44 explicitly excludes covered deposits from the bail-in tool. It gives rise to some general observations on the protection of deposits under BRRD.[416]

410. The 2011 Commission Working Document included a 'targeted approach' proposal, under which banks would be required to issue a fixed amount of 'bail-in able' debt to be automatically written down or converted into equity by force of a statutory trigger. Here, a second legal issue would arise. For this to be enforceable in the relevant jurisdictions, debt holders would have to contractually accept such potential bail-in *ex ante*. This proposal did not go through in BRRD's final text, *inter alia*, for technical complexity and limited market appetite issues. The 'comprehensive approach' policy was adopted. *See also* Commission Staff Working Document Impact Assessment Accompanying the Document Proposal for a Directive of the European Parliament and of the Council dated 2012, p. 234 (hereinafter 'the 2012 Commission Working Document').
411. Point (94) of Article 2(1).
412. Directive 2014/49/EU of the European Parliament and of the Council of 16 April 2014 on deposit guarantee schemes.
413. The more comprehensive protection of deposits in Europe had long been defended since the original Directive 94/19/EC on deposit guarantee schemes had many flaws, including Member States interpreting the definitions of deposits differently. *See Cariboni*, p. 83, and *Smits*.
414. Pursuant to Article 5 of Directive 2014/49/EU, deposits by credit institutions, investments firms, insurance and reinsurance undertakings, pension funds, public authorities and others are excluded from the definition of covered deposits.
415. The level of coverage is subject to much discussion and varies largely worldwide. If the level is too low, the deposit might be inefficient. If it is too high, it may lead to moral hazard by depositors and banks. In 2008, deposit guarantee schemes covered USD 37,000 in Portugal and USD 375,000 in Norway. *See Schich*, pp. 66 et seq.
416. Another issue involving the inclusion of deposit guarantees in the regulatory framework of financial markets is the necessity of strong governance rules to avoid reckless behaviour. *See* lessons from countries in North and Latin America in *Kane*.

Under Article 108 of BRRD,[417] a regime of ranking of deposits is introduced.[418] According to this provision:

> Member States shall ensure that in national law governing normal insolvency proceedings:
>
> (a) the following have the same priority ranking which is higher than the ranking provided for the claims of ordinary unsecured, non-preferred creditors:
>   (i) that part of eligible deposits from natural persons and micro-, small - and medium-sized enterprises which exceeds the coverage level provided for in Article 6 of Directive 2014/49/EU;
>   (ii) deposits that would be eligible deposits from natural persons, micro-, small - and medium-sized enterprises were they not made through branches located outside the Union of institutions established within the Union.
>
> (b) the following have the same priority ranking which is higher than the ranking provided for under point (a):
>   (i) covered deposits;
>   (ii) deposit guarantee schemes subrogating to the rights and obligations of covered depositors in insolvency.

As a consequence of this Article, national insolvency laws will have to reflect this ranking order. Table 5.1 shows an overview of the ranking of deposits in an insolvency scenario pursuant to Article 108 of BRRD.

Table 5.1 Treatment and Ranking of Deposits[419]

1	Covered deposits up to EUR 100,000	DGSs subrogating to the rights and obligations of covered depositors in insolvency
2	Deposits from natural persons and micro-, small - and medium-sized enterprises which exceed the EUR 100,000	Deposits that would be eligible deposits from natural persons, micro-, small- and medium-sized enterprises that were not made through branches located outside the union of institutions established within the Union
3	Ordinary unsecured, non-preferred creditors	

Source: Compiled by author from various sources.

417. *See* cross-reference in Article 17.1 of SRM-R.
418. Originally, the agreement was to leave deposits purely for the Member States to decide in their national insolvency laws, as in the proposal of December 2012 (COM/2012/0280 final - 2012/0150 (COD)). This amendment was then changed at a later stage of negotiations, as shown in Article 98a of the Council draft dated 28 June 2013 (Proposal for a DIRECTIVE OF THE EUROPEAN PARLIAMENT AND OF THE COUNCIL establishing a framework for the recovery and resolution of credit institutions and investment firms and amending Council Directives 77/91/EEC and 82/891/EC, Directives 2001/24/EC, 2002/47/EC, 2004/25/EC, 2005/56/EC, 2007/36/EC and 2011/35/EC and Regulation (EU) No 1093/2010 - General approach).
419. Article 108 BRRD.

This ranking may indeed have some very severe consequences. First, with respect to deposits coming from natural persons, micro-, small – and medium-sized companies which exceed EUR 100,000 will receive a priority in insolvency proceedings. In principle, these deposits do not qualify as covered deposits. Hence, they are not automatically excluded from bail-in by force of point (a) of Article 44(2) of BRRD. However, their subjection to a bail-in shall be restricted because of the NCWO principle. If these deposits are granted priority in insolvency, their hypothetical quota in an insolvency process will be higher, for they will be paid prior to any senior creditor. Under this new ranking, these depositors may theoretically receive a dividend of 100% in an insolvency scenario. Looking at the insolvency dividends paid by banks over the last years, such a dividend can be quite significant for a deposit creditor. This is even more significant when compared to unregulated industries, due to the various capital buffers applying to the banking industry.

A similar effect is observed with respect to the super priority of covered deposits and deposit of guarantee schemes. This is not because of their applicability in respect of bail-in. Covered deposits are not eligible anyhow, and DGSs have no claim against the institution prior to the protection trigger. However, according to Article 109 of BRRD,[420] the DGSs are obliged to contribute cash to the institution under resolution.[421] The amount shall be that of the covered deposits that would have been written down if a bail-in would be applicable. The maximum limit shall be the amount that the DGSs would have borne in an insolvency scenario, although the amount of payout in insolvency largely depends on the very circumstances of each case. This is a consistent approach, as covered deposits are excluded from bail-in. Hence, the deposit protection scheme generally is not called and does not incur any losses. Nevertheless, the framework requires the protection schemes to make a contribution to resolution. This contribution equals the amount of the hypothetical loss that the scheme would suffer, if covered deposits would be bailed in. Here the hierarchy set out in Article 108 of BRRD[422] becomes relevant again. According to it, the deposits under deposit protection schemes enjoy a priority even higher than that of deposits exceeding EUR 100,000. This means, in reality, the deposit protection scheme will probably not have to insert any cash contribution into the institution under resolution.

There have been further changes that have been introduced into Article 108 (2)–(7) BRRD under Directive 2017/2399 as of 21 July 2018.[423] Those changes are

420. *See* Article 79 of SRM-R.

421. This is a result of the intergovernmental agreement deciding that resolution measures should be financed by resolution funds and deposit guarantee schemes jointly. Needless to say that the way in which each of these actors contributes to the financing must be different. Deposit guarantee schemes and resolution funds are different in nature. The former aims to insure depositors, while the latter serves to cover costs of the resolution of failing institutions. The alleged rationale behind deposit guarantee schemes participating in the financing is that their contribution in a resolution measure would still be lower than the total payout to debtors in case of insolvency. *See* 2011 Commission Working Document, p. 85, and 2012 Commission Working Document, p. 45, 56-60.

422. *See* cross-reference in Article 17.1 of SRM-R.

423. Directive (EU) 2017/2399 of the European Parliament and of the Council of 12 December 2017 amending Directive 2014/59/EU as regards the ranking of unsecured debt instruments in insolvency hierarchy.

ultimately the result of the TLAC term sheet and the proposed subordination of the resolution capital (or MREL). Following that term sheet, the Member States developed different approaches to facilitate the subordination of bank liabilities. Some introduced a statutory subordination for bonds,[424] others introduced a more differentiated approach and allowed a subordination only by reference to an agreement.[425] The wording in Article 108(2) BRRD marks a compromise and introduces the new class of 'non preferred senior' which ranks below 'ordinary unsecured claims' (which would be characterised as 'preferred senior') and above own funds and other subordinated debt (*see* Article 108(3) BRRD). It can be taken from the minimum maturity of one year as foreseen under Article 108(2)(a) that this ranking is specifically linked to the MREL requirement and allows banks to choose as to whether they wish to refinance with senior non-preferred instruments (which would meet the subordination requirement under MREL or TLAC) but which bear a higher interest rate or with senior preferred bonds which may be less expensive (but on the other hand do not count for the subordination requirement should that be relevant to meet the respective MREL target).[426] Further paragraphs of Article 108 BRRD[427] focus on grandfathering rules for the years prior to 2018.

§5.08 MANAGEMENT BODY

Finally, Article 34(1) of BRRD[428] includes three principles that relate to the bank's management body:

> (c) management body and senior management of the institution under resolution are replaced, except in those cases when the retention of the management body and senior management, in whole or in part, as appropriate to the circumstances, is considered to be necessary for the achievement of the resolution objectives;
>
> (d) management body and senior management of the institution under resolution shall provide all necessary assistance for the achievement of the resolution objectives;
>
> (e) natural and legal persons are made liable, subject to member state law, under civil or criminal law for their responsibility for the failure of the institution.

Much attention has been paid to risk management after the crisis and how it relates to the general management body's functions.[429] The 2008 financial crisis revealed cases where the board of directors was not provided with timely financial

424. In Germany, under section 46(f) of the German Kreditwesengesetz (KWG; German Banking Act).
425. In France, the Sapin 2 law, enacted on 9 December 2016, modified the hierarchy of creditor claims in bank insolvency in line with BRRD. In particular, Article L.613-30-3-I-4 of the French Monetary and Financial Code created a senior non-preferred rank for liabilities that require contractual documentation to expressly refer to the ranking.
426. *See* Chapter 6 for an extensive description of the new MREL requirements.
427. Namely Article 108(4)–(7) BRRD.
428. Article 15 of SRM-R.
429. The Corporate Governance Lessons from the Financial Crisis. Grant Kirkpatrick. OECD http://www.oecd.org/finance/financial-markets/42229620.pdf.

information to act on prevailing and upcoming risks.[430] Hence, it is expected that corporate governance mechanisms shall address this issue and make sure that the flow of information to management happens more efficiently.[431] On the other hand, studies have also shown that management expertise had little influence on the vulnerability of the institution during the crisis. Rather, the studies found a positive correlation between financial distress, and institutional ownership and high independence of board members.[432] The conclusion is that empirical studies do not yet demonstrate how the management of the institution affects its likelihood to fail or not to fail. Nonetheless, BRRD provides resolution authorities with the powers to decide at their discretion if the management of a failing institution should be removed.[433]

For instance, recitals 40, 47, 69, and 84 of the Directive refer to removal or replacement of the management body and/or of senior management as part of the resolution process. Subject to an order by the competent authority, a temporary administrator may be ordered to substitute the previous management.[434] Management body and senior management are terms defined in the CRD. The management body includes the institution's bodies, which are appointed and empowered to set the strategy, objectives, and overall direction. It also oversees and monitors management decision-making and includes the persons who effectively direct the business of the institution.[435] The Directive also refers to the senior management, who are natural persons who exercise executive functions within an institution and who are responsible, and accountable to the management body, for the day-to-day management of the institution.[436]

Moreover, the Directive sets forth the obligation of the management to contribute to the execution of resolution actions and the liability if it is responsible for an institution's failure. However, the civil and criminal penalties shall be decided by each Member State in its national law. For example, Article 111(1)(d) states that Member States shall ensure that regulation addresses the management's omission to notify the competent authority that the institution is failing or likely to fail. As a consequence, the Directive recommends a temporary ban against the responsible manager to exercise professional functions in banks.[437]

430. Gone by the board? Why bank directors did not spot credit risks. Francesco Guerrera in New York and Peter Thal Larsen. Financial Times, 25 June 2008 http://www.ft.com/intl/cms/s/0/6e66fe18-42e8-11dd-81d0-0000779fd2ac.html#axzz3GhyS212G.
431. *See also* Expectations for Banks of the SRB dated March 2020, which puts emphasis on the role of governance in respect of resolvability, e.g. by appointing a member of the management body responsible for resolution planning and implementation of the resolvability work programme (pages 14 et seq.).
432. *See Erkens/Hung/Matos*.
433. Under Articles 27, 28 and 63 of BRRD, there is no obligation on the resolution authority to remove management. Rather, they have the power to do so at their disposal. *See* Article 13 of SRM-R. Under BRRD, European national authorities have been granted powers to conduct a resolution, similar to those that had already been given to the FDIC. *See Schelo* (2008).
434. Articles 29 of BRRD. *Wulfken*, p. 1055.
435. Article 3(1)(7) of Directive 2013/36/EU of 26 June 2013.
436. Article 3(1)(9) of Directive 2013/36/EU 26 June 2013.
437. Article 111(2)(c) of BRRD. Article 38 of SRM-R.

§5.09 TRIGGER POINTS FOR RESOLUTION

Since resolutions bear severe consequences for shareholders and creditors, there must be clear entry points that trigger a resolution tool.[438] The Bank Recovery sets a list of conditions for a resolution action in Article 32(1) of BRRD.[439] A resolution action[440] may be a decision to place an institution under resolution, the application of a resolution tool,[441] or the exercise of a resolution power.[442]

Trigger points will always be subject to some degree of flexibility on the part of the authorities which decide upon the commencement of resolution. Two different types of authorities are responsible for this decision in the European context. On the national level, the national authorities decide in the case of institutions located in countries outside the Eurozone and of institutions located in the Eurozone but which are not supervised by the ECB.[443] On the supranational level, the ECB decides after consulting with the SRB in the case of institutions under its supervision.[444]

§5.10 FAILING OR LIKELY TO FAIL

A key condition for resolution is that the institution is failing or likely to fail.[445] The threshold of likelihood to fail will be met if one of the circumstances below is present. Article 32(4) of BRRD spells out a list of such circumstances.[446]

[A] Withdrawal of Authorisation or of the Banking Licence

Point (a) of Article 32(4) of BRRD[447] refers to the maintenance of a banking licence:

438. Generally, in Europe, supervisors used to have wide discretion on determining when they should exercise intervention. The regulation also did not impose strict obligations on them to take action. The adopted approach was of 'constructive ambiguity', where supervisors 'reserved the right to intervene to preserve stability but give no explicit or implicit assurances to that end'. *Hüpkes*, pp. 16, 36-41. With time, clearer rules started to prove more efficient and avoid discrimination. Accordingly, recent regulation saw a shift to this direction.
439. Article 18 of SRM-R.
440. Article 2(40) of BRRD.
441. The sale of business tool, the bridge institution tool, the asset separation tool, and the bail-in tool, according to Article 37(3) of BRRD. Article 22(2)(c) of SRM-R.
442. The resolution powers are listed in Articles 63 and 72 of BRRD.
443. BRRD does not mandate the taking of action by the resolution authority. It simply states that action shall only be taken if the resolution authority is satisfied that all conditions are met, Article 32(1) of BRRD.
444. Recital 26 and Article 18(1) of SRM-R.
445. Article 32(1)(a) of BRRD. *See also* Article 18(1) of SRM-R. The wording is quite similar to the Banking Act 2009 of the United Kingdom, from which the Commission has obtained much inspiration. *See Randell.*
446. BRRD does not include hard capital triggers as discussed in the initial drafting stage. 2011 Commission Working Document, pp. 46-48 and 2012 Commission Working Document, pp. 38-40. As a consequence, the resolution authority has much more flexibility in the decision to intervene. The policy approach based on discretion requires transparency and clear accountability, which implies hard notification obligations for management. *See also Marinc*, p. 37.
447. Article 18(4) of SRM-R.

> the institution infringes or there are objective elements to support a determination that the institution will, in the near future, infringe the requirements for continuing authorisation in a way that would justify the withdrawal of the authorisation by the competent authority including but not limited to because the institution has incurred or is likely to incur losses that will deplete all or a significant amount of its own funds.

The legal wording requires that the breach be so grave as to justify the withdrawal of the authorisation by the competent authority. For instance, this could occur if the institution has incurred or is likely to incur losses that will deplete all or a significant amount of its required regulatory capital.

This prerequisite is closely linked to the regulatory requirement of holding a banking licence. Indirectly, the text remits to all potential factors that could lead to a withdrawing of the banking licence. This entry point serves as a general clause and provides flexibility for the resolution authority.[448]

There will also be failure or likelihood to fail if the assets of the institution are less than its liabilities. In insolvency terms, this is defined as over-indebtedness[449] or balance sheet insolvency.[450]

[B] Over-Indebtedness

Point (b) of Article 32(4) of BRRD[451] refers to over-indebtedness:

> the assets of the institution are or there are objective elements to support a determination that the assets of the institution will, in the near future, be less than its liabilities.

Over-indebtedness is given where the company's liabilities exceed its assets.[452]

Many evaluation questions arise when an authority assesses whether the liabilities exceed the assets. The most important of these questions is whether the assets of the institution are to be taken up with a going concern value or with a liquidation value. The going concern value is measured for an institution that is able to generate cash and whose business will continue to operate going forward. It takes past earnings, current trends, and prospects into account. The liquidation value is measured upon the assumption that all assets owned by the institution will be sold. It considers the

448. Commission Delegated Regulation (EU) 2018/345 of 14 November 2017 supplementing Directive 2014/59/EU of the European Parliament and of the Council with regard to regulatory technical standards specifying the criteria relating to the methodology for assessing the value of assets and liabilities of institutions or entities. It provides guidelines for valuation in connection with failing or likely to fail under Chapter II.
449. This term has a high importance in corporate insolvencies. In jurisdiction like Germany, extensive case law has been developed to define it.
450. *See* definitions in *Lastra*, pp. 29 et seq.
451. Article 18(4) of SRM-R.
452. *See* EBA Guidelines in failing or likely to fail (EBA/GL/2015/07), which speaks about the 'extreme case of inadequate capital position' to materialise if the institution has insufficient assets to cover its liabilities (page 14/para. 22). *See also* Chapter II of Commission Delegated Regulation (EU) 2018/345.

expected sales' proceeds and the costs of selling. The difference to the real end sale price is very often decisive.[453]

The determination of liquidation versus going concern values depends on the feasibility of going concern. Going concern is found if an institution is able to fulfil its liabilities for a certain period of time. In several corporate scenarios, this period of time can be one to two years (current and next business year). For a bank, however, this time frame may be too long, as the placing period for refinancing is often shorter due to the lower visibility of capital markets and the extreme amounts of liquidity needed for a bank. Therefore, the appropriate period could be less; in some cases, not longer than six months. Therefore, the assessment of over-indebtedness always carries an element of liquidity planning in it. However, if the liabilities exceed the assets even on a going concern basis, over-indebtedness is quasi certain. In this case, the institution would often also not be able to reach the capital ratio of 8% (and the authorisation withdrawal test would also be met). Nevertheless, it has to be noted that the over-indebtedness test takes into account all liabilities and all assets of the institution, therefore is closer to the 'leverage ratio' mentioned before, while the regulatory capital requirements also operate on a RWA approach, only taking certain assets into account for which a certain factor of equity needs to be taken up. Therefore, the approaches are not identical.

In some countries the over-indebtedness test is even modified further. In Germany, for instance, as part of the German Financial Markets Stability Act (*Finanzmarktstabilisierungsgesetz*),[454,455] to the extent that a positive going concern prognosis of the institution has been made, no further adjusted interim balance sheet (over-indebtedness status) is required. This change was made because of the rapid deterioration of values of assets versus the liabilities of institutions, while the cash flow and liquidity planning were still stable. In such circumstances, it was decided that liquidity would basically overrule balance sheet. Such a positive going concern prognosis can be made based on the company's business plan and financial planning. It is required that these documents could plausibly demonstrate that the solvency of the company will be maintained or restored during the forecast period. The forecast period should include the current and the next business year. If a positive going concern prognosis cannot be demonstrated, an adjusted interim balance sheet based on liquidation (break-up) values has to be prepared. In the latter case, the bank will most likely have to file for insolvency.[456] However, BRRD is silent on such an approach.

453. Bank crises often are associated with asset implosions, like a sudden drop in the price of securities of emerging markets or governmental bonds from developing countries. *Miller*, 735.

454. Gesetz zur Umsetzung eines Maßnahmenpakets zur Stabilisierung des Finanzmarktes dated 17 October 2008.

455. *Artikel 5 Änderung der Insolvenzordnung. § 19 Abs. 2 der Insolvenzordnung vom 5. Oktober 1994 (BGBl. I S. 2866), die zuletzt durch Artikel 9 des Gesetzes vom 12. Dezember 2007 (BGBl. I S. 2840) geändert worden ist, wird wie folgt gefasst: '(2) Überschuldung liegt vor, wenn das Vermögen des Schuldners die bestehenden Verbindlichkeiten nicht mehr deckt, es sei denn, die Fortführung des Unternehmens ist nach den Umständen überwiegend wahrscheinlich.'*

456. *Jaletzke/Veranneman, See* Gesetz zur Errichtung eines Finanzmarkt – und eines Wirtschaftsstabilisierungsfonds. Available at: http://www.gesetze-im-internet.de/fmstfg/, Article 5, paras 1-22.

Further special rules can apply to the formalities of setting up an over-indebtedness balance sheet. Usually, over-indebtedness is established by preparing an adjusted interim balance sheet to determine the over-indebtedness status.[457] This adjusted interim balance sheet deviates from Generally Accepted Accounting Principles (GAAP) balance sheet in some aspects. It aims at giving a more realistic picture of the debt to asset situation of the institution than a GAAP balance sheet would do. In that context, the valuation principles are set out in Commission Delegated Regulation (EU) 2018/345 in Chapter II. The valuations shall be based on, among others, fair and realistic assumptions and shall seek to ensure that losses under the appropriate scenario are fully recognised. Based on existing supervisory guidance or other generally recognised sources setting out criteria conducive to the fair and realistic measurement of different types of assets and liabilities, the valuer[458] may challenge the assumptions, data, methodologies and judgments on which the entity based its valuations for financial reporting obligations or for the calculation of regulatory capital and capital requirements and disregard them for the purposes of the valuation.[459] Further, the valuer shall determine the most appropriate valuation methodologies which may rely on the entity's internal models where the valuer deems it appropriate taking into account the nature of the entity's risk management framework and the quality of data and information available.[460]

Notably, not only over-indebtedness but according to Article 32(4) of BRRD[461] also impending over-indebtedness serves as a trigger point, if there are objective elements which support a determination that the assets of the institutions will be less than its liabilities in the near future. This means that currently the liabilities do not exceed the assets, but there are grounds to believe that this will happen in the future. It may be because, e.g., for a certain business unit losses are expected which will deplete the equity and, hence, will lead to an increasing amount of liabilities.[462] However, in a scenario where the occurrence of such liabilities is reasonably likely, an accrual will have to be built up in the over-indebtedness balance sheet such that from that perspective also actual rather than impending over-indebtedness would be given.

[C] Illiquidity

Point (c) of Article 32(4)[463] of BRRD refers to illiquidity:

> the institution is or there are objective elements to support a determination that the institution will, in the near future, be unable to pay its debts or other liabilities as they fall due.

---

457. Recital 14 Commission Delegated Regulation (EU) 2018/345.
458. Or the competent authorities, e.g. Art 36 (2) BRRD, as the case may be.
459. *See* Article 7 (1) of Commission Delegated Regulation (EU) 2018/345.
460. *See* Article 7 (2) of Commission Delegated Regulation (EU) 2018/345.
461. Article 18(4) of SRM-R.
462. *See* EBA Guidelines on failing or likely to fail, p. 13 which refers also to an asset quality review to assess those prognosis elements.
463. Article 18(1) of SRM-R.

In this case, the failure or likelihood to fail test is met on the basis of illiquidity. Illiquidity is usually defined as the inability of an institution to pay its debts as they fall due.[464]

Many corporate insolvency statutes and some national bank insolvency laws refer to this cash flow insolvency as illiquidity. The authority which assesses illiquidity should draw up a liquidity status to show the available funds compared to the liabilities on their respective due dates. The issues discussed below arise regularly when it comes to assessing illiquidity.

In some countries, the concept 'temporary illiquidity' exists, which is different from illiquidity. There is temporary illiquidity if a company is not instantaneously able to pay its due debts, but will be so within a short time period, e.g. if the company is able to generate the necessary cash within a few days.[465] Furthermore, there may also be temporary illiquidity if the liquidity gap is considerably small. Some jurisdictions apply a 10% threshold, in the meaning that if only less than 10% of liabilities are overdue, it is not considered as illiquidity.[466] These concepts of temporary illiquidity come from a corporate law background. They can only hardly be applied to a bank in distress. This is because capital markets and depositors assume constant liquidity – any late payment may be seen as a default and trigger rating downgrades with respective effects in the capital markets.

As set out, illiquidity is assessed on a cash flow plan, showing available assets and liabilities at their due dates. A further critical question for this calculation will always be how to account the deposits. This is because deposits differ from savings, which usually can only be terminated upon notice within a certain period of time. Unlike them, most of the bank's deposits are due daily and must be repaid immediately upon first demand. This stands for the expectation of the depositors that a bank is always liquid and always able to return depositors' funds. The problem however is that almost every bank in the world would be illiquid if the deposits would be accounted as immediately due. The calculation encompasses only those deposits which are actually being called upon, but not those that are at the bank and are not legally due and payable yet. If that is true, a further prognosis element will have to be taken into consideration: not only the deposits called at the date of the cash flow assessment but also how many deposits will likely be called in the near future. How this prognosis is made will depend on the overall experience of that very bank and on the speed of deposit withdrawals in the previous days and weeks. Comparing these results with other banks and their deposit withdrawal in that given banking sector seems appropriate. Usually, the bank can give a good estimate on how deposit withdrawal will develop over a certain period under certain assumptions. Usually, scenarios are being set up under which deposit withdrawals are estimated, measured, and counted against available assets and cash.

464. *See* EBA Guidelines on failing or likely to fail, p. 15, para. 23.
465. *Frege/Keller/Riedel*, paras 311-313. § 32. Unternehmenskrise und Insolvenz, para. 6.
466. *Frege/Keller/Riedel*, paras 308-310a. § 6 Die Insolvenzgründe als Verfahrensauslöser, para. 11.

To cover liquidity gaps, central banks may provide emergency liquidity lines for banks in financial distress.[467] In this context, the respective prerequisites for having access to and repaying such lines have to be reviewed in detail and taken into account in the assessment.[468] Usually the availability of bankable securities is key in order to access quick liquidity from central banks as lender of last resort.

Not only the liabilities but also the money available to cover those liabilities are of relevance. On the asset side, cash on account can be taken into equation as much as any assets that can be liquidated very quickly, like securities. Intuitively and in reality, assets that can only be liquidated within a longer period of time cannot be accounted for settling liabilities which are immediately due. Nonetheless, they may be relevant for long-term calculations or taken up as security for interbank or central bank lending.[469]

Different from illiquidity is the concept of impending illiquidity which is also referred to in Article 32(4) of BRRD.[470] It refers to situations where a bank is unable, or it appears likely that it will be unable, to pay its debts when they fall due in the future. One of the typical questions arising in this context is which time period is referred to with 'in the near future'. In Germany, in relation to corporates, the notion of future generally includes the current and next business year.[471] This complies with the length and standards of the going concern prognosis relevant for the corporate over-indebtedness test. However, as set out, in relation to banks, refinancing cycles and functioning of capital markets may require a shorter period, possibly of a year or even less. The second question often arising is of likelihood of such impending illiquidity: which degree of likelihood has to be given, in order to meet the test. Is it a degree of high likelihood or predominant likelihood or reasonable likelihood? BRRD gives no direct answer to these questions; however, again the consequences of the resolution tools and their effects have to be kept in mind.

Illiquidity in its most severe form, i.e. a bank not able to fulfil its liability when and if they are due, is often very clear, especially following a large deposit withdrawal. Any inability to counterbalance the withdrawal with collateral to secure liquidity from

467. *See* Chapter 2, section 2.05 above.
468. The liquidity amounts that must be kept by each bank are those determined under the rules of CRD IV, as discussed in Chapter 1, section 1.06 above. These rules also give guidelines on how the calculations shall be made.
469. In accordance with Article 415(3)(a), the EBA, in their Implementing Technical Standards amending ITS on additional liquidity monitoring metrics, has included Template C 66.00 (Maturity Ladder or Contractual Template) containing a liquidity progress report. This template aims to classify all future cash inflows and outflows in twenty-two maturity bands in accordance with their contractually agreed entry date. Liquid funds and lines are shown for individual maturity bands to cover liquidity shortage. This is the so-called Counter Balancing Capacity CBC. *See* template on https://eba.europa.eu/regulation-and-policy/liquidity-risk/implementing-technical-standards-its-amending-its-on-additional-liquidity-monitoring-metrics.
470. Article 18(4) of SRM-R.
471. *See* Uhlenbruck, Insolvenzordnung, 14 Auflage 2015, InsO § 18.

central banks can very quickly lead to a critical stadium of impending illiquidity and thereafter to illiquidity.[472][473]

[D] Public Financial Support

Point (d) of Article 32(4) of BRRD[474] refers to public financial support as a trigger point for resolution. A trigger for resolution is given, if:

> extraordinary public financial support is required except when, in order to remedy a serious disturbance in the economy of a Member State and preserve financial stability, the extraordinary public financial support takes any of the following forms:
>
> (i) a State guarantee to back liquidity facilities provided by central banks according to the central banks' conditions;
> (ii) a State guarantee of newly issued liabilities; or
> (iii) an injection of own funds or purchase of capital instruments at prices and on terms that do not confer an advantage upon the institution, where neither the circumstances referred to in point (a), (b) or (c) of this paragraph nor the circumstances referred to in Article 59(3) of BRRD are present at the time the public support is granted.

This trigger point may somewhat seem ambiguous. When banks need extraordinary public financial support, they are often already illiquid or over-indebted. The reasons for withdrawal of the authorisation might also already exist.[475] So in order to clearly distinguish the previous trigger points from this one, the Directive requires that the financial support be given to 'solvent'[476][477] institutions apparently setting aside illiquidity and over-indebtedness. Further, this is expressed in Article 32(4) (iii) of BRRD,[478] requiring that for the injection of own funds 'neither the circumstances referred to in point: (a) *i.e. failure of likelihood of failing*, (b) *i.e. over-indebtedness* or (c) *i.e. illiquidity*' be present. In addition, the financial support shall be conditioned upon final approval under the state aid rules. Hence, the Directive also makes sure that

472. *See* ECB on Banco Popular Español S.A. https://www.bankingsupervision.europa.eu/press/pr/date/2017/html/ssm.pr170607.en.html.
473. BCBS issued a Working Paper entitled Liquidity stress testing: a survey of theory, empirics and current industry and supervisory practices in October 2013 (available at: http://www.bis.org/publ/bcbs_wp24.htm). The paper states that both banks and external advisors have made relatively little progress on the methodologies for liquidity stress testing since the 2007 crisis. *See also* ECB. Sensitivity Analysis of Liquidity Risk - Stress Test 2019 Final Results. 7 October 2019. https://www.bankingsupervision.europa.eu/press/pr/date/2019/html/ssm.pr191007_annex~537c259b6d.en.pdf.
474. Article 18(4) of SRM-R.
475. In October 2010, the Commission issued a Communication about *An EU Framework for Crisis Management in the Financial Sector* (hereinafter 'the 2010 Commission Communication'). In this document, it admits the obvious degree of overlap between the triggers. The objective is to make sure that the resolution authority will have sufficient grounds to intervene as early as possible and by all means take action before a bank is balance sheet insolvent. *See* p. 7.
476. Article 32(4)(d), fourth paragraph.
477. *See also* above Chapter 2 on a description of the prerequisites for precautionary recapitalisation.
478. *See* Article 18(4) of SRM-R.

the public financial support trigger only applies to banks still holding an authorisation. This could possibly happen at a very early stage of distress.

For instance, this trigger point could kick in if a bank would be in early need of capital in order to meet capital requirements as set forth under national and regulatory law. This is in line with the legal wording of this trigger point which says that:

> Support measures [...] shall be limited to injections necessary to address capital shortfall established in the national, Union or SSM-wide stress tests, asset quality reviews or equivalent exercises conducted by the European Central Bank, EBA or national authorities, where applicable, confirmed by the competent authority.

The wording reflects the fact that the AQR or stress tests may reveal that capital basis will not be sufficient.[479] In this case the institution would not fulfil such tests[480] and the authorisation withdrawal could be triggered as well.

Points (i) and (ii) above regarding state guarantee to back liquidity facilities or of newly issued liabilities relate more closely to premature liquidity problems. Here again the border between a situation encompassed by these points and a situation of illiquidity or impending illiquidity is quite blurred. The proposal developed by the European Commission (*see* above Chapter 2) aims at defining institutions with a shortfall of capital in the future (under SSM stress tests or AQRs) still as solvent and draws a thin line between still solvent institutions which can be subject to precautionary recapitalisations and those which need public financial support beyond these proposed requirements.[481]

§5.11 NO REASONABLE PROSPECT OF MEASURES TO PREVENT FAILURE

Article 32(1)[482] of BRRD sets forth the following prerequisite for a resolution action:

> having regard to timing and other relevant circumstances, there is no reasonable prospect that any alternative private sector measures, including measures by an IPS, or supervisory action, including early intervention measures or the write-down or conversion of relevant capital instruments and eligible liabilities[483] in accordance with Article 59(2) taken in respect of the institution, would prevent the failure of the institution within a reasonable timeframe.

This condition serves to avoid intervention as a first resort. In other words, as long as permitted by time constraints, institutions shall seek other measures to prevent

479. *See* Chapter 1, section 1.06[E]. On the suitability of recapitalisation with public money, *see* *Gros*, The asset quality review (2013).
480. European banks are not only subject to the tests of the Single Supervisory Mechanism, but also of the EBA, and of the FSB. *Gros*, The asset quality review (2013).
481. European Commission. Precautionary recapitalisations under the Bank Recovery and Resolution Directive: conditionality and case practice. 5 July 2017. https://www.europarl.europa.eu/RegData/etudes/BRIE/2017/602084/IPOL_BRI%282017%29602084_EN.pdf.
482. *See* Article 18(1) of the SRM-R.
483. Article 2(1)(71a) 'Eligible liabilities' means bail-in-able liabilities that fulfil the conditions of Article 45b or point (a) of Article 45f(2) BRRD, and Tier 2 instruments that meet the conditions of point (b) of Article 72a(1) of CRR.

failure. Other measures may include private sector measures, such as a shareholder capital injection, or an institutional protection scheme (IPS). The measures may also include a supervisory action like management replacement or ordering changes in the business strategy of the institution.[484] Only if no alternative measure is reasonably expected to put a stop to the institution's failing, a resolution action shall be taken.

IPSs have been used in some countries like Spain and Germany. In Spain, savings banks created the *Sistema Institucional de Protección* in June 2010.[485] It is a contractual agreement between separate legal entities to ensure stability in their system. These banks have entered into mutual solvency and liquidity pacts, as well as certain profit pooling arrangements.[486] In Germany, the Cooperative Banking Network (*Genossenschaftliche FinanzGruppe Volksbanken Raiffeisenbanken*) created a scheme to protect clients of cooperated banks with respect to deposits above EUR 100,000 that are not covered under the European DGS.[487]

Such IPSs are allowed under Article 113(7) CRR subject to specific requirements. The competent national authorities may approve a 'contractual or statutory liability arrangement which protects those institutions and in particular ensures their liquidity and solvency to avoid bankruptcy where necessary', if, *inter alia*, the following conditions are met:

- the parties to the arrangement are either a bank, a financial holding company or a mixed financial holding company, financial institution, asset management company or ancillary services undertaking subject to appropriate prudential requirements;
- the parties to the arrangement are established in the same Member State;
- there is no current or foreseen material practical or legal impediment to the prompt transfer of own funds or repayment of liabilities among the parties to the arrangement;
- the arrangements ensure that the IPS is able to grant support necessary under its commitment from funds readily available to it;
- the IPS disposes of suitable and uniformly stipulated systems for the monitoring and classification of risk, which gives a complete overview of the risk situations of all the individual members and the IPS as a whole, with corresponding possibilities to take influence;
- the IPS conducts its own risk review which is communicated to the parties;

484. The early intervention measures are listed in Article 27 of BRRD. *See* Article 13 of the SRM-R.
485. *See* Bundesverband der Deutschen Volksbanken und Raiffeisenbanken. Study findings: The institutional protection scheme of the German Cooperative Banking Network is efficient and reliable - standardising deposit guarantee system in Europe is the wrong approach. 9 November 2010. https://www.bvr.de/p.nsf/B11B3AF5F355A69FC1257D2B0036E473/$FILE/PressRelease_GuaranteeSchemes.pdf.
486. *See* Javier Aríztegui. Savings bank restructuring and institutional protection schemes. Speech at the conference organised by Caja Granada. Granada. 17 December 2010. https://www.bis.org/review/r101222e.pdf.
487. *See* report by International Monetary Fund. Spain: The Reform of Spanish Savings Banks Technical Notes. June 2012. Country Report No 12/141. https://www.imf.org/external/pubs/ft/scr/2012/cr12141.pdf.

- the IPS draws up and publishes on an annual basis, a consolidated report comprising the balance sheet, the profit-and-loss account, the situation report and the risk report, concerning the IPS as a whole, or a report comprising the aggregated balance sheet, the aggregated profit-and-loss account, the situation report and the risk report, concerning the IPS as a whole;
- the parties are obliged to give advance notice of at least twenty-four months if they wish to end the IPS; and
- the scheme is based on a broad membership of credit institutions of a predominantly homogeneous business profile.

§5.12 PUBLIC INTEREST

In addition to the more quantitative criteria, the Directive also includes a typically qualitative requirement. Article 32(1)(c) of BRRD[488] states that a resolution action shall only be taken to the extent that it is necessary in the public interest.[489] Article 32 (5) BRRD offers some colour to this concept:

> a resolution action shall be treated as in the public interest if it is necessary for the achievement of and is proportionate to one or more of the resolution objectives referred to in Article 31 and winding up of the institution under normal insolvency proceedings would not meet those resolution objectives to the same extent.

Ultimately, this prerequisite serves to link any decision on resolution actions to the resolution objectives.[490] As mentioned, the tools entail significant interference with

488. *See* Article 18(1)(c) of the SRM-R.
489. Resolution authorities have to perform a public interest assessment in order to prepare resolution plans and when deciding whether to take a resolution action or not. The SRB has published its approach to such assessment in 2019 (https://srb.europa.eu/sites/srbsite/files/2019-06-28_draft_pia_paper_v12.pdf). It covers both public interest assessment at the time of resolution planning and when a bank is failing or likely to fail.
490. As per the SRB's approach, the public interest assessment is based on a comparison between credibility of winding up a bank under normal insolvency proceedings and resolution action. An option that puts one or more resolution objectives at risk shall not be considered credible. When assessing such credibility, SRB considers whether the bank performs any critical functions which would need to be preserved.

    The SRB will also assess if the bank failure will have significant adverse effects on the financial system of one or several Member States including financial markets' functioning and markets' confidence, FMIs, other financial institutions and the real economy. As the legal framework does not define the objective of avoiding 'significant adverse effects on financial stability', the SRB ultimately considers five risks. First, SRB considers the adverse impact on financial stability should the consequences of bank failure materialise at the level of one or more Member States. Second, it considers the consequences of financial distress that jeopardise the orderly functioning, efficiency and integrity of the internal market or the economy or the financial system of one or more Member States. Third, risk of direct contagion is accounted for. A direct contagion is a situation where the direct losses of counterparties of the institution in insolvency or resolution lead to the default or likely default of those counterparties or negatively affect their ability to perform their macroeconomic functions efficiently. Fourth, the risk of indirect contagion where the insolvency or resolution causes a negative reaction by market participants or other stakeholders that lead to severe disruption of the financial system are considered. Fifth, the effects of potential action on market discipline, i.e. the ability of

the property rights of creditors and shareholders. Hence, a proper balance must be found between this interference and the interests of the society at large. These resolution objectives are:[491]

(a) to ensure the continuity of critical functions;[492]
(b) to avoid a significant adverse effect on the financial system, in particular by preventing contagion, including to market infrastructures, and by maintaining market discipline;
(c) to protect public funds by minimising reliance on extraordinary public financial support;
(d) to protect depositors covered by Directive 2014/49/EU and investors covered by Directive 97/9/EC;
(e) to protect client funds and client assets.

The above are very similar to the objectives in the United Kingdom Banking Act of 2009, with one exception. The Act includes the objective to avoid interfering with property rights in contravention of the Charter of Fundamental Rights of the European Union. BRRD left this point out. This is because the non-violation obligation of the Charter is not an objective pursued in the use of resolution measures. In the European regulation, the non-violation obligation is a condition for the exercise of powers by the resolution authority.[493] Recital 50 of the Directive expressly refers to Article 52 of the Charter with respect to creditors and shareholder rights and requires authorities to take the principle of proportionality and the particularities of the legal form of an institution into account. The consequence is that there should be a proper balance between the protection of property rights and protection of public interests. In practice, both the Act and BRRD are supposed to achieve the same goal and respect the balance. Since the BRRD came into force, the resolution authorities have denied the public interest in various situations.[494]

The protection of the public interest also serves as a precondition to government stabilisation tools. These tools, like a temporary public ownership tool, may only be

---

informed stakeholders to identify risks in financial institutions and to act in a way that signals those risks to other stakeholders, are considered. In essence, these considerations are risks of potential spillovers to the real economy that indicate and measure the importance of a bank.

Following the determination from the above factors, if the objectives are not at a risk, SRB can conclude that winding up the bank under normal insolvency proceedings is normal or that, a resolution action is not in the public interest. If resolution objectives are deemed to be at a risk, SRB shall further assess the effectiveness of the resolution tools in mitigating the impact on financial stability.

491. Article 31(2) BRRD, Article 14(2) SRM-R.

492. Critical functions are defined as 'activities, services or operations the discontinuance of which is likely in one or more member states, to lead to the disruption of services that are essential to the real economy or to disrupt financial stability due to the size, market share, external and internal interconnectedness, complexity or cross-border activities of an institution or group, with particular regard to the substitutability of those activities, services or operations' (*see* Article 2(1)(35) BRRD).

493. *Randell*, p. 113.

494. Banco Popolare di Vincenca; Veneto Banca, ABLV, AS BNP Banca, *see* www.srb.europa.eu/ Resolution cases.

employed if the competent ministry or government and the competent resolution authority determine that the application of the resolution tools would not suffice to protect the public interest.[495]

§5.13 THE RESOLUTION TOOLS

There are four resolution tools: the bail-in tool, the bridge bank tool, the asset separation tool, and the sale of business tool.[496]

The bail-in tool is a tool to write down or to convert certain liabilities of the institution with the purpose of restoring its capital structure.[497] The bridge bank tool can have the same effect, but it offers broader and deeper restructuring powers to the competent resolution authority.[498] The sale of business tool enables the resolution authority to transfer assets, liabilities, and contracts directly to an investor rather than to a bridge bank.[499] The asset separation tool is not a stand-alone tool but always comes in combination with one of the other tools.[500] It serves the purpose of a supplement when it is necessary to combine a resolution technique with a bad bank scheme, by separating certain assets to preserve their value.

There is a further instrument which is not a resolution tool per se, but a financial reorganisation measure: the write-down and conversion of capital instruments under Article 59 of BRRD.[501,502] By contrast, this measure can be applied independently from

495. Article 56(4) of BRRD.
496. *Klimek* et al. have run empirical tests to compare the bail-in with the bailout and the purchase and assumption tools. The latter occurs when the failing bank is closed and its assets and liabilities are assumed by a healthy bank. Economists argue that the bail-in tool is the most effective in recession scenarios. Effectiveness in this study involves minimising financial contagion risk, liquidity provision to the real economy, reducing unemployment and leading to high economic output. The purchase and assumption is most effective in a business as usual scenario.
497. EBA has issued guidelines on treatment of liabilities and shareholders in bail-in – https://eba.europa.eu/regulation-and-policy/recovery-and-resolution/guidelines-on-the-treatment-of-shareholders-in-bail-in and https://eba.europa.eu/regulation-and-policy/recovery-and-resolution/guidelines-on-treatment-of-liabilities-in-bail-in.
498. *See* EBA's Regulatory Technical Standards and Guidelines on business reorganization plans under Directive 2014/59/EU https://eba.europa.eu/sites/default/documents/files/documents/10180/1312804/9ecf6b00-dbcf-493d-9ff4-016d7442e410/EBA-RTS-2015-12%20RTS%20and%20EBA-GL-2015-21%20GLs%20on%20Business%20Reorganisation%20Plans.pdf?retry=1. Also *see* Commission Delegated Regulation (EU) 2016/1400 of 10 May 2016.
499. EBA's guidelines on factual circumstances amounting to a material threat to financial stability and on the elements related to the effectiveness of the sale of business tool under Article 39(4) of Directive 2014/59/EU – https://eba.europa.eu/sites/default/documents/files/documents/10180/1080767/79c49d39-bd8e-44ae-9e23-d3cf04cc0609/EBA-GL-2015-04%20Guidelines%20on%20the%20sale%20of%20business%20tool.pdf.
500. *Chattopadhyay*, p. 412; Article 37(5) of BRRD. Article 22(4) of SRM-R. *See also* EBA's guidelines on the determination of when the liquidation of assets or liabilities under normal insolvency proceedings could have an adverse effect on one or more financial markets under Article 42(14) of Directive 2014/59/EU – https://eba.europa.eu/sites/default/documents/files/documents/10180/1080779/6441452a-d464-4618-9296-d71549a4f2c2/EBA-GL-2015-05%20Guidelines%20on%20the%20asset%20separation%20tool.pdf.
501. Article 21 of SRM-R.

resolution measures;[503] also, there is a group concept in that tool, while the resolution tools strictly apply to each legal entity.[504] In earlier versions of BRRD, trigger for the write-down tool was a point where the institution is otherwise no longer viable (while for the resolution tools it was the point of 'failing' or 'likely to fail'). However, the point of non-viability is now also defined as being a stadium of 'failing or likely to fail',[505] so that there is no difference in the entry point any more from that perspective. Conceptually, the write-down instrument has a lesser impact on the institution because it is not a resolution tool. Also, it only affects equity, Additional Tier 1, Tier 2 capital and MREL. The bail-in tool goes further to other subordinated debt and senior debt.

The Directive also sets forth government financial stabilisation tools.[506] These should only be used as a last resort, as the legal text expressly imposes.[507] Pursuant to Article 56(3) of BRRD, the competent ministry or the government must consult the resolution authority before taking such an action. For this consultation, they must previously assess and exploit the other resolution tools to the maximum extent practicable while maintaining financial stability. The Banking Union framework is structured so that governmental financial stabilisation tools are only used in exceptional cases.[508] Moreover, for these governmental stabilisation tools, shareholders' and creditors' participation is also a condition (as for the bail-in tool), Article 37(10) of BRRD. By this, it is clarified that these tools cannot be used to avoid BRRD clear rationale of loss participation.

Lastly, Member States may establish additional resolution tools in their national legislation. This is possible as long as these tools are compatible with the principles and objectives of BRRD and do not hinder cross-border group resolutions.[509]

§5.14 VALUATION PRINCIPLES

There are various circumstances during the phase of resolution where valuation plays a crucial role.[510] The valuation principles and guidelines have been further defined in Commission Delegated Regulation (EU) 2018/345.[511] The first valuation takes place

502. In the resolution of Banco Popular, the sale of business tool was combined with the capital instrument write-down tool. *See* www.srb.europa.eu/resolutiomn cases.
503. After the exercise of the power to write down or convert relevant capital instruments and eligible liabilities independently of resolution action, the valuation provided for in Article 74 BRRD shall be carried out, and Article 75 BRRD shall apply. See Article 59(1) BRRD.
504. *See* section 5.23 on group resolution.
505. Article 59(4)(a) of BRRD. Article 21(3) of SRM-R.
506. Articles 56 through 58 of BRRD.
507. *Chattopadhyay*, p. 409.
508. *See* section 5.10[D] on public financial support.
509. Article 37(9) of BRRD.
510. The resolution objectives of Article 31 of BRRD play a major role in the interpretation of all provisions in Title IV of the Directive. Also valuations shall be guided thereby. For instance, the principle in point (c) of Article 31(2) is crucial for the application of the asset separation tool. This principle says that public funds shall be protected. Hence, valuation must be precise as any overvaluation of an asset may indirectly constitute a prohibited state aid. *See Boudghene* et al., p. 21. *See* Article 14 of SRM-R.
511. Commission Delegated Regulation (EU) 2018/345 of 14 November 2017.

generally at the starting point of resolution when it comes to the assessment as to whether the institution is failing or likely to fail.[512] Second, it continues when it comes to the scope of the resolution measure and the potential losses that will need to be absorbed.[513,514] Finally, it serves for and the calculation of the hypothetical insolvency quota. This last point refers to the NCWO principle for which a separate evaluation is to be drawn up under BRRD and/or the SRM-R.[515]

Article 36 of BRRD determines that an independent person carries out a fair, prudent, and realistic valuation of the assets and liabilities of the relevant institution. The same is required under Article 17 of SRM-R. Independence[516] in this context means that this person must be independent from any relevant public authority and the relevant entity where all the following conditions are met:

(i) the valuer possesses the qualifications, experience, ability, knowledge and resources required and can carry out the valuation effectively without undue reliance on any relevant public authority or the relevant entity;
(ii) the valuer is legally separated from the relevant public authorities and the relevant entity; and
(iii) the valuer has no material common or conflicting interest.

Time is crucial in resolution scenarios. Resolution authorities will not have the time to wait for this independent assessment which may take several weeks or even months. Therefore, there must be a possibility for the resolution authorities themselves or for a mandated valuation expert to conduct a preliminary assessment to serve as a ground for urgent decisions.[517] The initial assessment may then usually be subject to the provision of a final independent valuation at a later stage. Then, where necessary, the values and assessments on which the resolution measures were based on shall be adapted.[518]

The course of the valuation generally will need to go into two directions. As both the Directive and the Regulation lay out, the first direction will be to assess the value of the assets and liabilities of the institution. Furthermore, the purpose of the valuation may also to assess whether or not the conditions for resolution are met. In this case, the second direction will be to assess whether the institution is failing or likely to fail. In

512. So-called Valuation 1, *see* Article 7 of Delegated Regulation 2018/345.
513. Recital 75 of BRRD: 'The minimum amount of contribution to loss absorption and recapitalisation of 8% of total liabilities including own funds or, where applicable, of 20% of risk-weighted assets should be calculated based on the valuation for the purposes of resolution in accordance with this Directive. Historical losses which have already been absorbed by shareholders through a reduction in own funds prior to such a valuation should not be included in those percentages.'
514. So-called Valuation 2, *see* Article 10 of Delegated Regulation 2018/345.
515. So-called Valuation 3, *see* Commission Delegated Regulation (EU) 2018/344 of 14 November 2017.
516. Article 38 of Commission Delegated Regulation (EU) 2016/1075 of 23 March 2016.
517. Article 36(2) of BRRD. Article 20(3) SRM-R.
518. It actually depends on the specific case and the applied resolution tools as to whether such an '*ex post* definitive valuation' is required. It is not required in case of the application of the sale of business tool, as the marketing process provides for another valuation base and the buyer will rely on the effectiveness of the transfer as it is.

fact, a liquidity assessment may also form part of the asset and liability value as it is relevant here as well, just not as evident as in the second direction.

[A] Purpose of Valuation

The purposes of the valuation are set out to be to:[519]

- support the determination of whether the resolution conditions or the conditions for the write-down or conversion of capital instruments are met;
- support the determination of the appropriate resolution action in respect of the failing institution;
- support the decision on the extent of cancellation or dilution of shares or other instruments of ownership, in case of write-down or conversion of capital instruments;
- support the decision on the extent of the write-down and conversion of eligible liabilities, in case of a bail-in tool;
- support the decision on which assets, contracts and liabilities are transferred and which stay behind in the remaining entity that is insolvent and which consideration is to be paid to the institution under resolution, in case of a bridge institution or asset separation tool;
- support the decision on which assets liabilities are to be transferred and to inform or support the authorities understanding of what constitute commercial terms for the purpose of application of the sale of business tool; and
- ensure that all losses on the assets of the institution are recognised at the moment the resolution tools are applied.

Moreover, the valuation shall be supplemented by:[520]

- an updated balance sheet and report of the financial position of the institution;
- an analysis and estimate of the accounting value of the assets; and
- a list of outstanding on-balance sheet and off-balance sheet liabilities with an indication of the respective credits and priority levels under the applicable insolvency law.

On the latter point, valuation shall indicate the subdivision of the creditors and classes in accordance with their priority levels under the applicable insolvency laws. Also, an estimate of the treatment that each class of shareholders and creditors would have been expected to receive if the institution or entity would be wound up under normal insolvency proceedings shall be made.

519. Article 36(4) of BRRD. Article 20(5) SRM-R.
520. Article 36(6) of BRRD. Article 20(7) of SRM-R. In accordance with the bail-in playbook guidance, banks are further expected to describe the capabilities and processes to produce financial information (according to Article 36(6) BRRD). Including estimations of own funds requirements, taking into account the available inputs and including provisional valuation results (see para 53).

This point relates to a legal assessment of the balance sheet. Shareholders and creditors will have to be divided and allocated to classes in accordance with priority levels under applicable insolvency law. Such division depends on the rankings of creditors in an insolvency procedure and will be governed by national laws applicable to the institution. Then, in a second step, a calculation has to be made regarding the potential quota which would have to be paid out in case of normal insolvency proceedings. At this stadium of evaluation, it is rather an 'estimate' than a precise calculation.

[B] Applicable Standards

Neither BRRD nor the SRM-R sets out the methodology to be used for assessing the value of assets and liabilities of the institution.[521] There are international accounting standards for assessment of corporation values, be it in distress or in a going concern scenario.[522] Also, there are standards for generally assessing and auditing assets and liabilities. Finally, there are standards for drawing up over-indebtedness balance sheets, which provide guidance for drawing up values in a liquidation scenario. Following recommendations by the EBA, as already mentioned, two technical regulations concerning the principles for valuation have been published.[523][524] Ultimately it will depend on the evaluation expert and the very circumstances, including which resolution tool is to be expected, what exact methodology is to be applied.[525] Whatever methodology is used, the valuation exercise will be extensive in such a complex institution like a large bank which often has a large number of subsidiaries.[526]

The valuation exercise will heavily depend on the structure of the bank's balance sheet and on whether a gone concern assumption of the bank has an effect on the valuation of its assets or liabilities. Some of the bank's assets may be relatively immune against a non-going concern of the bank. This will be the case where there is still a market for selling off such assets despite the liquidation of the selling institution. Other assets may depend on the institution's name and continuous network to be realised

521. In his speech of September 2012, Andrew Gracie, Director of the Special Resolution Unit of the Bank of England, defended indeed that no hard predetermination of methodology should be included in BRRD. However, he gives clear indications that write-down and conversion valuation should rather point to fair value. The valuation for comparison of resolution with insolvency should focus on liquidation value.
522. For example, the International Financial Reporting Standards developed by the International Accounting Standards Board. http://www.ifrs.org/Pages/default.aspx.
523. Delegated Regulation 2018/344 (on the no creditors worse-off principle) and Delegated Regulation 2018/345 on other types of valuation.
524. McGuire at the World Bank has drafted a set of Simple Tools to Assist in the Resolution of Troubled Banks. This document is aimed at resolution authorities and includes valuation methods regarding each item of a bank's balance sheet.
525. *See* recitals 6 and 7 of Delegated Regulation 2018/345.
526. Lehman Brothers had more than two hundred subsidiaries (excluding affiliates) in over twenty jurisdictions. *See* Michael J. Fleming and Asani Sarkar. The Failure Resolution of Lehman Brothers. 3 April 2014. Liberty Street Economics. https://libertystreeteconomics.newyorkfed.org/2014/04/the-failure-resolution-of-lehman-brothers-.html.

with its current value.[527] The same diversity is found in the liability side of the bank's balance sheet.[528] Some long-term contracts are not shown in the bank's balance sheet and may materialise in case of a non-going concern assumption. Lease contracts that may then have to be taken up with an accrual is one example. Another issue in a non-going concern assumption is that certain derivative contracts may have to be assumed to close out, so that a net amount of liabilities would have to be shown in the bank's balance sheet.

Generally, the following standards for valuation are to be kept:

- fair, realistic and prudent valuation of assets and liabilities;
- consideration of all costs of the resolution;
- no assumption of public financial support.

These standards can be loosened in case of a preliminary valuation. Such simplifications can be applied to the details of the supplementing information (e.g., updated balance sheet), as well as to the legal analysis of the respective creditor classes. Furthermore, cushions for additional loss estimates can be built in provisionally.[529]

[C] Derivatives

This latter point actually gives rise to some difficult questions. As mentioned earlier, derivatives deserve special consideration in a resolution context. There is always the risk that derivatives will automatically be terminated following a resolution measure. Thereby all liabilities under a standard framework agreement attached to such an agreement shall be netted against each other. The resolution authority has the power to suspend such closeout netting in connection with a resolution measure.[530] If bail-in is applied to derivative contracts, a manual closeout netting can be applied by the resolution authorities. However, such mechanism might not always work, as some of the derivative contracts may be governed by the law of a country outside of the EU. In that case, to some extent closeout netting will probably have to be taken into the equation. The appropriate methodology for assessing the respective liability or asset after the occurrence of closeout netting has been developed.[531]

An assessment of the conflict of laws situation beforehand is essential as well. In a bail-in scenario where the derivative contracts are to a large extent governed by the law of Member States, the stay of closeout netting will have to be recognised. In that

527. *See* Article 10 of Delegated Regulation 2018/345.
528. *See* Article 11 of Delegated Regulation 2018/345.
529. *See* Article 13 of Delegated Regulation 2018/345.
530. Article 71 of BRRD.
531. *See also* Article 49(4) of BRRD. EBA has published the Final Report on Draft Regulatory Technical Standards on the valuation of derivatives pursuant to Article 49(4) BRRD on https://eba.europa.eu/sites/default/documents/files/documents/10180/1312572/6d9950e7-47ce-49f8-aa35-0690b7740678/EBA-RTS-2015-11%20RTS%20on%20the%20valuation%20of%20derivatives.pdf. Further, *see* Commission Delegated Regulation (EU) 2016/1401 of 23 May 2016.

event, a liability will also not have to be taken up in the evaluation where the safeguard against termination applies. On the other hand, if there is a large derivative book governed by New York law, a stay of closeout netting might not be recognised.[532] Also, if the contractual trigger points under the master agreement of the ISDA give rise for a closeout in case of a bail-in, then it would be necessary to include a liability or provision for it in the valuation. In such a scenario, the amount of loss sharing among the creditor groups could be significantly higher than otherwise.[533]

[D] Depositors

In relation to the assessment of the liquidity position for the purpose of valuation, the depositors become key actors. This is not just with respect to assessing as to whether the institution is failing or likely to fail as a trigger point for resolution. Moreover, this is also to estimate the stability of the institution during and post resolution. The behaviour of depositors in a resolution scenario or in an impending resolution scenario will have a strong influence on the final figures. This is because, as mentioned, most of the deposits can be called on without notice on a daily basis. If it is anticipated that all depositors would call their deposits and demand repayment immediately, any institution would be immediately insolvent. Following a resolution, viability could never be restored. In most scenarios, the threat of such an institutional run would overstress the situation. Assessment can be based on comparable cases[534] or on the daily monitoring of depositors' behaviour at the respective institution. Some depositors may withdraw

---

532. So far, there have been solely non-binding memoranda of understanding among countries involved in the initiatives of the FSB. The Key Attributes is certainly among the most important ones. The International Swaps and Derivatives Association has also published Universal Resolution Stay Protocol in 2015 and Resolution Stay Jurisdictional Modular Protocol in 2016. *See* Consultative Document on Cross-border recognition of resolution action dated 29 September 2015 (https://www.fsb.org/wp-content/uploads/c_140929.pdf?page_moved=1) and the Overview of Responses to the Public Consultation by the FSB dated 3 November 2015 (https://www.fsb.org/wp-content/uploads/Cross-Border-Recognition-of-Resolution-Actions.pdf).
533. With respect to crisis prevention measures and crisis management measures defined in Article 2 paras (101) and (102) of BRRD, no default shall be triggered. Pursuant to Article 68(1) of the Directive, such measures shall not constitute insolvency for contractual purposes.
534. When it comes to comparable cases, the bank failures in 2007 and 2008, as well as that in Cyprus in 2013, may provide some guidance. It is possible to analyse if the underlying factors which led to such failures are present and so estimate depositors' behaviour. These would be excessive leverage of speculation funded by banks, lack of proper bank regulation, bad banking practices, corrupt banking, and lack of integrity of bank executives. Betz lists three main groups of reasons for the bank runs in 2007 and 2008, namely: (1) excessive leverage of speculation funded by banks: funding speculation by hedge funds in securitised derivatives from mortgage bonds; (2) lack of proper bank regulation: the repealing the Glass–Steagall separation of investment and commercial banking and allowing the lowering of lending standards; and (3) bad banking practices: banks lending 'short term' to hedge funds to buy 'long-term' mortgage bond, which also were fraudulently rated as to risk. In 2013, there were: (1) lack of proper bank regulation: no Euro-wide bank regulation for countries banking in the EU system; (2) bad banking practices: Cypriot banks buying too much Greek sovereign debt, so when the Greek government bonds declined, Cypriot banks collapsed; and (3) corrupt banking: the Cypriot financial system was set up to draw international deposits from questionable financial sources, such as tax evasion and money laundering. *Betz*, pp. 147-156.

their deposits following a bail-in. Others may trust the statutory provisions and DGSs under which deposits below EUR 100,000 will not be infringed. This is indeed a very critical point which affects not only valuation but also the overall viability planning of the institution.[535] In some cases during resolution, the withdrawal of deposits was limited for a certain period of time by way of a temporary moratorium. Such a moratorium has now also been implemented into BRRD (Article 33a BRRD). It is bound to strict conditions and can only last a for a very limited time period.[536] However, whether or not such moratorium would also work in a bail-in scenario with an institution fully continuing its operation will yet have to be tested.

[E] Hypothetical Insolvency Quota

This refers to one of the central points of BRRD and the SRM-R, namely the NCWO rule. In the context of valuation, the NCWO comes up in two instances. First, in the assessment of an estimate that creditors would have received otherwise. Second, in a separate valuation to be done under Article 74 of BRRD.[537] Here, the evaluation must be carried out by separate valuation exercise after the resolution action or actions have been effective. The same rationale is found in Articles 13(1) and 20(16) of SRM-R.

The second valuation [538]shall be distinct from the valuation that has been carried out at the beginning of the resolution exercise. A purpose of that valuation is to have an *ex post* view on the entity after resolution actions have been taken. It shall give the NCWO principle more weight and more credibility, as it is one of the key principles of the resolution laws.

Only if that principle is regarded, creditors cannot claim that they are being disadvantaged by the resolution actions. A creditor will always have to factor the risk that its contractual partner will fail, and it will only receive a quota from the insolvency proceedings. Such risk is inherent in any commercial dealings as long as the counterparty is subject to insolvency proceedings, which institutions generally are. Therefore, creditors can hardly argue that they have been disadvantaged or harmed by resolution actions, as long as this principle is obeyed. They could indeed say that other creditors have been privileged, but that is a different argument and topic.

For assessment of such a hypothetical insolvency quota, the critical question will then be which value could have been generated in insolvency for the assets in the estate. Usually, this value would not be higher than the value of those assets in a resolved institution after resolution actions have been taken. Therefore, the insolvency scenario usually is the floor for valuation. The quota assessed in such a scenario also sets the maximum amount of bail-in that eligible liabilities can bear.

Generally, the standards for the assessment under Article 74 of BRRD are the following:

535. *See* Chapter 3 on recovery planning.
536. Article 33a(4) BRRD: from the publication to midnight at the end of the business day following the publication.
537. So-called Valuation 3 in the overall context of valuations, see *supra* n. 515.
538. So-called Valuation 3 in the overall context of valuations, see *supra* n. 515.

- the valuation shall be carried out as soon as possible under the resolution actions have become effected;
- the valuations shall be based on fair and realistic assumptions and shall seek to ensure that losses under the appropriate scenario are fully recognised;[539]
- the valuer shall determine the most appropriate valuation methodologies which may rely on the entity's internal models where the valuer deems it appropriate taking into account the nature of the entity's risk management framework and the quality of data and information available;[540]
- the basis is the assumption of ordinary insolvency proceedings (instead of resolution action); and
- comparison of quota in such an insolvency scenario versus the treatment in resolution.

In case there is a difference in treatment in a way that the resolution leads to a worse scenario than in such hypothetical insolvency, the difference entitles to a compensation claim from the resolution financing arrangements.[541]

§5.15 ANCILLARY RESOLUTION POWERS

The aim of a resolution scenario is to continue with the bank business. After application of the bail-in tool, a business plan must be followed in order to make sure that the exercised restructuring continues to lead to a viable business.[542] Similarly, after the bridge bank tool, the assets and liabilities transferred to the bridge bank shall form an integral part of the viable institution going forward. In comparison, in a pure bankruptcy scenario, a continuation of the bank's business in almost every case is not an option. Rather, the focus is on pure liquidation. Assets are sold for the best possible price and quotas are distributed to creditors.

In view of this aim of continuation, it is key that the business activities are stable after the resolution tools have been applied.

However, this is not as easy because the most important capital of an institution may be its good name and reputation.[543] Financial markets do react in a very sensitive manner to bank crises and failures. In addition, they have developed sophisticated trigger points which kick in as soon as certain predefined crisis events occur.[544]

539. *See* Article 7(1) of Commission Delegated Regulation 2018/345.
540. *See* Article 7(2) of Commission Delegated Regulation 2018/345.
541. Article 75 of BRRD. Article 15(1)(g) of SRM-R.
542. Article 51 of BRRD. *See* Article 27(2) of SRM-R.
543. As highlighted by the European Commission, banks are special in comparison to other types of firms: 'Banks operate on the basis of public trust. If confidence in them is lost, depositors and other creditors may quickly withdraw their funds, which may lead to their failure. As well as depriving their customers of access to the socially valuable banking functions mentioned above, the failure of a large bank may undermine confidence in other banks, affect their finances and create instability across the financial system as a whole. Thus, through this contagion effect, the value and viability of other banks can be rapidly eroded and the entire financial system could be destabilised.' European Commission, MEMO/14/297, 15 April 2014.
544. This mechanism is solidly structured in worldwide-used standard agreements. For instance, under the 2002 International Swaps and Derivatives Association's Master Agreement, actions

Therefore, there are risk factors involved with a bank restructuring and the application of resolution tools. Among these, there are the following risks:

- Financial contracts are terminated and, following a closeout netting, a sum of liabilities is brought forward against the institution under or after resolution;
- Creditors enforce security and disturb or even destroy the going concern of the institution under or after resolution;
- Certain payment or delivery obligations unexpectedly become due; and
- Foreign law does not acknowledge the resolution measures.

[A] Contracts Terminate Automatically

The early termination of contracts most likely leads to acceleration of obligations. In the vast majority of cases, the counterparty will have the right to take steps towards the enforcement of its rights. These uncoordinated unilateral actions, if actually implemented by the contractual counterparties, may completely undermine the possibility of a successful resolution. For this reason, the widespread problem has been recognised by various laws. In US law, a twenty-four-hour moratorium with respect to termination rights under derivative contracts has been taken up.[545] Comparable solutions have been implemented into some continental European laws, as the German law.[546]

In BRRD, a broader approach was chosen.[547] It did not follow the rule of suspending contracts for a limited period of time. Rather, the Directive clearly defined

relating to a resolution scenario may be an issue, as well as the transfer of the agreement itself. In addition, even where the application of resolution tools per se does not constitute an event of default or a termination event, cross-default will be an issue. Almost any debt instrument documentation will include a cross-default at least in relation to other financial obligations.

545. Dodd-Frank Wall Street Reform and Consumer Protection Act. 'SEC. 210. POWERS AND DUTIES OF THE CORPORATION. (c) PROVISIONS RELATING TO CONTRACTS ENTERED INTO BEFORE APPOINTMENT OF RECEIVER. (10) NOTIFICATION OF TRANSFER. (B) Certain rights not enforceable. (i) Receivership A person who is a party to a qualified financial contract with a covered financial company may not exercise any right that such person has to terminate, liquidate, or net such contract under paragraph (8)(A) solely by reason of or incidental to the appointment under this section of the Corporation as receiver for the covered financial company (or the insolvency or financial condition of the covered financial company for which the Corporation has been appointed as receiver) – (I) until 5:00 p.m. (eastern time) on the business day following the date of the appointment; or (II) after the person has received notice that the contract has been transferred pursuant to paragraph (9)(A).'

546. German Bank Restructuring Act. Gesetz zur Reorganisation von Kreditinstituten. '§ 13 Beendigung von Schuldverhältnissen. Schuldverhältnisse mit dem Kreditinstitut können ab dem Tag der Anzeige nach § 7 Absatz 1 bis zum Ablauf des folgenden Geschäftstages im Sinne des § 1 Absatz 16b des Kreditwesengesetzes nicht beendet werden. Eine Kündigung gegenüber dem Kreditinstitut ist in diesem Zeitraum ausgeschlossen. Die Wirkung sonstiger in diesem Zeitraum eintretender Beendigungstatbestände ist bis zu seinem Ablauf aufgeschoben. Abweichende Vereinbarungen sind unwirksam. Dies gilt nicht für Gläubiger von Forderungen aus Schuldverhältnissen nach § 12 Absatz 2.' See also comments by Schelo (2010) on required powers for effective resolution.

547. The rule in BRRD is in line with para. 4.2 of the Key Attributes of Effective Resolution Regimes for Financial Institutions, published by the FSB.

that neither a crisis management measure nor a crisis prevention measure[548] shall constitute in an enforcement event[549] or insolvency proceedings[550] under the relevant contracts. Crisis management measures include any resolution action as well as the appointment of a special manager.[551] Crisis management measures include the write-down of capital instruments.[552] Hence, following the exercise of a resolution tool, no extraordinary termination, netting or set-off can be exercised. This will implicate changes to ISDA's and other master framework agreements for derivatives.[553] Also, other financial instruments under comparable contracts which follow a standard wording will be affected. Basically, these contracts will have to mirror the requirements set out under Article 68 of BRRD.

The Directive expressly sets the scope of this provision. First, the non-termination carve-out extends to subsidiaries of the entity which is the contractual partner itself. It covers situations where the parent or a holding company has issued a guarantee or where cross-default provisions have been included in the respective contracts.[554] Second, the carve-out only applies to termination rights based on a resolution action. Any other contractual or statutory termination right arising out of other circumstances remains unaffected. That is, if there is non-payment or non-compliance with any other terms outside of crisis management measures or crisis prevention measures, the counterparty may accelerate the contract.

Besides the automatic exception of termination rights based on the definition of enforcement or insolvency event, the Directive sets out a possibility to freeze termination rights. In practice, it is a power vested in the resolution authority to temporarily stay any early termination rights[555] of counterparties of any contracts of the bank under resolution. It is another example of a restriction of rights guaranteed under private law

548. '(101) "crisis prevention measure" means the exercise of powers to direct removal of deficiencies or impediments to recoverability under Article 6(6), the exercise of powers to address or remove impediments to resolvability under Article 17 or 18, the application of an early intervention measure under Article 27, the appointment of a temporary administrator under Article 29 or the exercise of the write-down or conversion powers under Article 59'. Article 2(1) of BRRD.
549. '(l) "enforcement event" means an event of default or any similar event as agreed between the parties on the occurrence of which, under the terms of a financial collateral arrangement or by operation of law, the collateral taker is entitled to realise or appropriate financial collateral or a close-out netting provision comes into effect'. Article 2(1) of Directive 2002/47/EC on financial collateral arrangements.
550. '(j) "insolvency proceedings" shall mean any collective measure provided for in the law of a member state, or a third country, either to wind up the participant or to reorganise it, where such measure involves the suspending of, or imposing limitations on, transfers or payments'. Article 2 of Directive 98/26/EC on settlement finality in payment and securities settlement systems.
551. '(102) "crisis management measure" means a resolution action or the appointment of a special manager under Article 35 or a person under Article 51(2) or under Article 72(1)'. Article 2(1) of BRRD.
552. Article 59 of BRRD. *See* Article 21 of SRM-R.
553. International Swaps and Derivatives Association. Position Paper on Challenges with Expanding BRRD Moratoria Powers. August 2017. https://www.isda.org/a/IkiDE/brrd-position-paper-final.pdf.
554. Article 68 of BRRD.
555. Article 71 of BRRD.

in order to achieve a public interest result in the Directive. Recital 94 of the Directive clarifies the specific objective in this case:

> Such a restriction would be necessary to allow authorities to obtain a true picture of the balance sheet of the failing institution, without the changes in value and scope that extensive exercise of termination rights would entail.

This more restricted approach is comparable to the aforementioned US law's twenty-four-hour moratorium. It applies to any type of termination right, such as a right to accelerate, closeout, set-off or net obligations. Hence, should early termination rights be exercisable regardless of Article 68 of BRRD, the resolution authority still may order to suspend their exercise. The period of validity of such suspension shall be from the publication of the resolution action order until midnight of the following day. The prerequisite is that payment and delivery obligations and the provision of collateral remain in place and continue to be performed. The resolution authority must always consider the impact of the stay in the stability of financial markets.[556]

[B] Creditors Enforce Their Security Interests

A further threat to the continued operation of the institution is the risk that creditors enforce their security. Security enforcement can be triggered under the relevant contractual or statutory terms when certain measures like resolution actions are adopted. The exact prerequisites for triggering security enforcement depend on each contractual or statutory rule. In order to mitigate such risk, BRRD grants resolution authority the power to temporarily restrict enforcement of security interest.[557] Like the stay of termination rights, this restriction shall be valid for a short period of time. Again, it lasts from the publication of the resolution action order until midnight of the following day.

With respect to group entities, the possibility to restrict enforcement is less wide than the one with respect to closeout netting and termination rights. This power only applies to the group entities that are actually under resolution.[558] The question arises in relation to security on a subsidiary level, where acceleration of the underlying contract on the failing institution is a prerequisite for the enforcement of the security. If termination is stayed for reason of resolution, then it does not constitute an enforcement event or insolvency proceedings and the enforcement of security could also be blocked. However, other views are possible and depend on the nature of the security and applicable laws.

556. Article 71(6) of BRRD.
557. Article 70 of BRRD.
558. Article 70(3) of BRRD.

[C] Payment Obligations Become Due

Further risk in the ongoing institution business is that certain payment obligations threaten the liquidity situation of the institution. This may particularly be relevant for those payment obligations which occur unexpectedly and are not included in a cash flow planning beforehand. In such case again, the resolution authorities have the possibility of a temporary suspension of obligations for a period consistent with the one mentioned above. This power applies not only to payment but also to delivery obligations irrespective of their nature and their legal basis.
There are three groups of exceptions. First, payment of eligible deposits cannot be suspended. Eligible deposits include all deposits other than deposits made by credit institutions, investments firms, insurance and reinsurance undertakings, pension funds, public authorities and others.[559] Second, payment and the delivery obligations relating to payment and securities settlement systems or operators of these systems, central counterparties and central banks shall not be stayed. This exception helps to ensure the orderly functioning of the financial markets.[560] Third, claims eligible for compensation under Directive 97/9/EC on investor-compensation schemes are claims arising out of an investment firm's inability to:

- repay money owed to or belonging to investors and held on their behalf in connection with investment business, or
- return to investors any instruments belonging to them and held, administered or managed on their behalf in connection with investment business, in accordance with the legal and contractual conditions applicable.[561]

[D] Foreign Law Contracts and Assets

While conceptually those rules are clear, a practical legal problem may occur. What happens if some of the contracts subject to a statutory or contractual termination right are governed by foreign law? Here, the harmonisation work is yet to be done.[562] This poses a large hurdle: the Bank of England governor coined the expression 'global banks are global in life, but national in death'[563] during the latest crisis. Countries outside the EU are under no obligation to recognise the provisions under BRRD, nor as transposed into national law. Hence, resolution authorities will face difficulties to legally prevent the termination rights of institutions with significant non-European operations.

559. Article 5 of Directive 2014/49/EU on deposit guarantee schemes.
560. Here the Directive also follows the Report and Recommendations of the Cross-Border Bank Resolution Group of the Bank for International Settlements dated December 2009: 'Clarity and predictability for the treatment of financial market contracts by preserving appropriate termination, netting, and collateral rights or, at the option of the resolution authority, providing for continuity through transfers to other market participants or a bridge financial institution.'
561. Article 2(2) of Directive 97/9/EC on investor-compensation schemes.
562. *See supra* n. 81.
563. Can banking regulation go global? Analysis by Steve Schifferes. Economics reporter, BBC News. Published on 18 March 2009. http://news.bbc.co.uk/2/mobile/business/7950758.st.

The road towards answering the question on recognition may pass by the nature of the relevant rules. They may have a material insolvency law nature or an administrative nature. It could be argued that these rules are based on administrative law and foreign jurisdiction may not recognise administrative orders. The enforcement would then face a deadlock. Another argument may be whether the *lex fori concursus*[564] and the principle of universality are acknowledged in the third country or not.[565] In light of these questions, resolution authorities and creditors might, depending on the jurisdictions involved, not have clear means to enforce their powers and rights.[566]

Hence, in cases where courts outside Member States have jurisdiction to decide, international agreements between the EU and these countries must be put in place. Ideally, these agreements would cover at least the 'most-wanted' bank subsidiaries and branches jurisdictions like Cayman Islands, Hong Kong, Singapore, Japan, Switzerland, and the US.[567] The FSB officially recommended this approach in 2011.[568]

The Directive creates a sophisticated conflict of laws design in this respect:

- First, it creates the procedure for European resolution authorities to cooperate with and recognise foreign resolutions. The resolution authorities shall effect such cooperation individually or via resolution colleges,[569] in case the third-country institution has subsidiaries and parent in more than one Member State.[570] European resolution authorities shall have a right to refuse to recognise or to enforce third-country resolution proceedings in special cases. For instance, in case the measure to be recognised or enforced would have adverse effects in a Member State.
- Second, it establishes a legal basis both for the EU and for Member States individually to negotiate bilateral agreements with third countries. Such

564. This is the law of the state in which the insolvency proceedings are commenced. *See* definition in Legislative Guide on Insolvency Law by United Nations Commission On International Trade Law http://www.uncitral.org/pdf/english/texts/insolven/05-80722_Ebook.pdf.
565. Within the European scope, these are recognised under Directive 2001/24/EC 4 April 2001 on the reorganisation and winding up of credit institutions. Recital 16 states: '(16) Equal treatment of creditors requires that the credit institution is wound up according to the principles of unity and universality, which require the administrative or judicial authorities of the home member state to have sole jurisdiction and their decisions to be recognised and to be capable of producing in all the other member states, without any formality, the effects ascribed to them by the law of the home member state, except where this Directive provides otherwise.'
566. Another undesired consequence is that creditors within the same class are treated differently depending on their jurisdiction. This would be against the Directive's resolution principle stated in Article 34(1)(f) of BRRD. *See also* Article 15(1)(f) of SRM-R.
567. According to the Discussion Note of the International Monetary Fund Staff: Subsidiaries or Branches: Does One Size Fit All? dated 7 March 2011, prepared by Jonathan Fiechter, İnci Ötker-Robe, Anna Ilyina, Michael Hsu, André Santos, and Jay Surti, p. 13.
568. Key Attribute 7.5 of the Key Attributes of Effective Resolution Regimes for Financial Institutions.
569. *See* EBA. Final draft regulatory technical standards on resolution colleges under Article 88(7) of Directive 2014/59/EU (EBA/RTS/2015/03) July 2015. Also *see* Commission Delegated Regulation (EU) 2016/1075 of 23 March 2016.
570. Articles 89 and 94 of BRRD. *See* Article 33 of SRM-R.

agreements may cover, *inter alia*, cooperation for information sharing, development of resolution plans, assessment of resolvability, application of intervention measures and of resolution tools.[571]

- Third, it offers an interim solution unless and until international agreements are signed. In this case, the EBA may enter into non-binding cooperation agreements with third-country authorities. The scope of these agreements may include the same areas of the described agreements in the previous paragraph.

Alternatively, the acknowledgement of foreign rules and orders must be taken up in the relevant contracts. Under Article 71a BRRD, a requirement is now introduced with respect to financial contracts governed by a third-country law to include recognition clauses covering the ancillary powers under Articles 68, 69, 70 and 81 BRRD, including the new moratorium powers under Article 33a BRRD. In addition, as mentioned already, Article 55 BRRD prescribes a procedure under which the recognition of the bail-in tool is required for third-country-governed liabilities. It allows for notifications in cases where it is not possible to include such recognition in the respective contracts (Article 55(2) BRRD). Following such notification, the resolution authority can either accept that status or insist on inclusion. In any event, absent the inclusion of such a contractual recognition clause, the respective liability shall not count towards the MREL target requirement.[572]

There is also a specific procedure with respect to assets, rights, liabilities, shares, or other instruments of ownership located or governed by the law of a third country. The resolution authority may ask the administrator or other person in charge to take all necessary steps so that the relevant resolution action becomes effective. However, if the resolution authority determines that such steps will not be successful, it may exclude the third-country elements from the given resolution action.[573]

[E] Power to Amend Terms of Contract

An unusual feature under BRRD shall be mentioned here. It is the power of the resolution authority set forth in point (f) of its Article 64(1). The authority may cancel or modify the terms of a contract of the institution under resolution or substitute a recipient[574] as a party to such a contract. The previously discussed powers relate to either termination rights or payment obligations, i.e. to typical main obligations under a contract. This power to amend terms of contract is much wider and seems to refer to any terms of a contract.

571. Article 93 of BRRD. More generally, Article 32 of SRM-R.

572. Article 55(2). Therefore, the notification only has the purpose to inform the resolution authority; however, it does not cure the issue in the sense that the respective liability is now included in the MREL quota.

573. Article 67 of BRRD.

574. As per Article 2(1) of BRRD, 'recipient' means the entity to which shares, other instruments of ownership, debt instruments, assets, rights or liabilities, or any combination of those items are transferred from an institution under resolution.

Given such a wide scope, it is crucial to understand the limits of such modifications. The two rather general limits are set out in that same Article. Namely, the resolution authority shall only exercise ancillary powers where it is appropriate to help: (a) to ensure the effectiveness of a resolution action or (b) to achieve resolution objectives. In addition, the 'NCWO principle' may also function as a qualitative limit to potential modifications. As a consequence thereof, resolution authorities should not be able to modify a term of a contract in a way that leaves the creditor in a worse position than in insolvency proceedings.

Another general power is the power to amend or alter the maturity of debt instruments or other eligible liabilities or the amount of interest payable under such instruments.[575] This is unusual for a resolution tool, for due dates of obligations normally cannot be changed in insolvency-like procedures. By this power, the resolution authorities can effectively oblige a counterparty to stay in contractual relations with an institution under resolution for longer than originally anticipated.

Resolution authorities also have the power to close out and terminate financial contracts or derivative contracts.[576] This power exists even if the respective contracts should not terminate due to the restrictions just described above. They may also affect a closeout netting for the purposes of writing down or converting liabilities relating to derivatives. Since the closeout netting is a condition for the bail-in of derivative contracts, the possibility to terminate discretionarily is a logical power vested in the resolution authority.

[F] Moratorium

Although not listed as a resolution power but under the chapter on objectives, conditions and general principles, the newly invented power to suspend certain obligations (Article 33a BRRD), the so-called moratorium, can also be classified as an auxiliary resolution power.[577] It was invented as it showed that there is no effective measure contained in BRRD or SRM-R against the dynamic and downwards spiral of a bank run. While various Member States already have such a moratorium power in their national law,[578] others had not.[579] Such an increase of deposit withdrawals can effectively limit the time available for executing proper resolution preparation, as the state of illiquidity can be reached quickly, followed by bank closures and possibly insolvency. Therefore, provided that the institution is deemed failing or likely to fail, the exercise to suspend payment obligations is justified where it is necessary to avoid the further deterioration of the financial conditions of the entity and to choose the appropriate resolution actions or to ensure the effective application of one or more of

575. Point (j) of Article 63(1) of BRRD.
576. Point (k) of Article 63(1) of BRRD.
577. Article 71 a BRRD includes its acknowledgement besides other auxiliary powers for third-country contracts.
578. For example, Germany in Article 46 German Bank Act.
579. For example, Spain did not have such a moratorium.

these tools.[580] It is also possible to extend that power to eligible deposits[581] if provided by the Member States and if resolution authorities ensure that depositors have access to an appropriate daily amount from those deposits.[582] In any event, the Moratorium may only last for a very limited period of time.[583]

§5.16 BAIL-IN

[A] Objective and Scope of the Bail-In Tool

In case the trigger points for resolution are given, resolution authorities shall have the power to exercise the bail-in tool.[584] Bail-in means the ability to recapitalise an institution and restore the conditions to maintain its banking licence[585] or alternatively to capitalise a bridge institution or bank business transferred to an investor as the case may be. To facilitate this, banks are required to develop their own bail-in playbook that addresses all internal and external actions to be taken for an effective bail-in.[586] This playbook shall be developed over time for each resolution group. For instance, where MPE approach is adopted, banks shall be expected to separate playbooks for all of the resolution groups. Pursuant to Article 43(2) of BRRD:[587]

> Member States shall ensure that resolution authorities may apply the bail-in tool to meet the resolution objectives specified in Article 31, in accordance with the resolution principles specified in Article 34 for any of the following purposes:
>
> (a) to recapitalize an institution or an entity referred to in point (b), (c) or (d) of Article 1(1) of this Directive that meets the conditions for resolution to the extent sufficient to restore its ability to comply with the conditions for authorisation (to the extent that those conditions apply to the entity) and to continue to carry out the activities for which it is authorized under Directive

580. Or to see whether the resolution action is in the public interest (Article 33a(1)(d)(i) and (ii)).
581. As defined under point (4) of Article 2(1) of Directive 2014/49/EU.
582. Article 33a(3) BRRD.
583. From the publication of the notice of suspension to midnight in the Member State of the resolution authority of the institution at the end of the business day following the day of the publication – which effectively lead to a moratorium from Friday 00:01 to Monday 23:59.
584. The bail-in tool has been very much welcomed as a way to avoid that taxpayers pay the bill of excessive risk-taking by bank managers. It solidifies the concept of burden sharing by shareholders. However, the initiative has also been accompanied by disagreement. *See De Grauwe* for strong criticisms to the bail-in approach employed in Cyprus and *MacNeil* for a general overview of the tool.
585. *Grünewald/Weber*, p. 556.
586. See SRB. Operational Guidance on Bail-in Playbooks. 2020 for SRB's expectations on the content of the playbook. At the minimum, the playbook is expected to cover: (a) an identification and description of relevant governance arrangements for the bail-in execution; (b) process and timelines for the identification of the perimeter of bail-in-able instruments and the generation of data points used as input for the resolution scheme, the national implementing act of the national resolution authority and the bail-in execution itself; (c) a detailed description of the procedural steps for the execution of the bail-in inside and outside the bank for each type of instrument covered by the playbook; and (d) a description of MISs that support the different processes (in line with principle 5.3 of SRB. Expectations for banks. March 2020).
587. Article 27(1) of SRM-R.

2013/36/EU or Directive 2014/65/EU, where the entity is authorized under those Directives, and to sustain sufficient market confidence in the institution or entity;

(b) to convert to equity or reduce the principal amount of claims or debt instruments that are transferred:
   (i) to a bridge institution with a view to providing capital for that bridge institution; or
   (ii) under the sale of business tool or the asset separation tool.

The extent to which the resolution authority may exercise the powers above depends on key circumstances:

(i) the assessment of the amount needed to restore viability and capital structure of the institution under resolution; and
(ii) the context in which the resolution tool is applied, i.e. if the tool is applied on a stand-alone basis[588] or in conjunction with other resolution tools.[589] For instance, if the bail-in is to be combined with the bridge bank tool, it may not be possible to convert claims into equity. The same would be with a sale of business tool. This is because new owners of the institution might be new investors or governmental authorities, which will not want minority shareholders involved. In this case, reduction of the principal amount rather than conversion into equity may be more appropriate, respectively the transferal of the shares post conversion.[590]

The bail-in tool is to be differentiated from the write-down of capital instruments tool.[591] The latter is not a pure resolution tool and has a more limited scope and only applies to capital instruments, which include Additional Tier 1, Tier 2 and MREL instruments.[592]

The bail-in tool aiming a recapitalisation will always be accompanied by a business reorganisation plan.[593] These plans must show how the business model of the institution will function and confirm that the institution will become viable after this resolution tool has been applied.[594] Article 43(3) of BRRD states that:

> Member States shall ensure that resolution authorities may apply the bail-in tool [...] only if there is a reasonable prospect that the application of that tool, together with other relevant measures including measures implemented in accordance with

588. So-called open bank bail-in.
589. In certain exceptional circumstances, the bail-in may also be applied in conjunction with state aid and the provisions in BRRD are consistent with the existing framework for such aid. *See Micossi* et al.
590. *See* SRB website on https://srb.europa.eu/en/content/resolution-cases for recent examples.
591. Article 59 of BRRD. Article 21 of SRM-R.
592. The write-down of capital instruments is discussed further below. *See* section 5.16[H].
593. Articles 43(3) and 51 of BRRD. Article 27(2) of SRM-R. The bail-in playbook guidance expects banks to lay out the arrangements in place to ensure sooth implementation of the bail-in tool and should therefore contain the arrangements that have to be taken to produce a business reorganisation plan. This should include a timeline, the responsible organisation unit(s) or committee(s), the tasks to be conducted and the flow of the information or outputs that are to be produced (see paras 35 and 38).
594. *Brandi/Gieseler*, p. 895.

> the business reorganisation plan [...] will, in addition to achieving relevant resolution objectives, restore the institution [...] in question to financial soundness and long-term viability.

[B] Liabilities Subject to Bail-In

Article 44 of BRRD[595] prescribes that all liabilities of the institution can be subject to bail-in, except for the ones listed below. The remaining liabilities are eligible liabilities, together with the Common Equity Tier 1, Additional Tier 1, and Tier 2:

- Deposits up to the coverage level in the Deposit Guarantee Schemes Directive, namely EUR 100,000.
- Secured liabilities and covered bonds.
- Liabilities relating to client money and client assets, including held on behalf of Undertakings for Collective Investment in Transferable Securities and Alternative Investment Funds, if protected by applicable insolvency law.
- Liabilities held by the institution as a trustee or another fiduciary position.
- Liabilities to other banks and investment firms with original maturity of less than seven days, excluding intercompany liabilities.
- Liabilities to systems operators with remaining maturity of less than seven days, excluding intercompany liabilities.
- Liabilities to employees, except for variable remunerations of material risk-takers.
- Liabilities to trade creditors, if they relate to activities that are essential to the daily functioning of the business, e.g. IT system services, utilities, rental, maintenance of premises.
- Tax and social security liabilities that are preferred under applicable law.
- Liabilities to DGSs; and
- Liabilities to institutions that are part of the same resolution group without being themselves resolution entities, except where those liabilities rank below ordinary unsecured liabilities under the relevant national law.

The exceptions above apply regardless of the liabilities' governing law.

With respect to secured liabilities and covered bonds, it is relevant to note that they are 'bail-in safe' only insofar as the value of the security covers the liability. Above the value of the security or above the value of the pool covering the bonds, bail-in is still possible. This opens the door for potential difficulties in security valuation if the authority pursues a bail-in on top of the value of the security or of the cover pool. While the valuation is easy for cash collateral, it is more difficult for other types of security. In some cases, it might be possible to separate covered secured liabilities from uncovered secured liabilities.[596]

595. Article 27 SRM-R.

596. This exception is especially important for German *Pfandbriefe*, whose related asset pools are carved out from insolvency by operation of national law. In relation to this type of covered

The BRRD defines secured liabilities as claims secured by a charge, pledge or lien, or collateral arrangements.[597] It includes liabilities arising from repurchase transactions and other title transfer collateral arrangements. This definition relates mostly to in rem security interests. As a consequence, it excludes guarantees although they may be considered a security interest under the law of some Member States. In the write-down of a guaranteed liability, the question may arise on whether the guarantee is released in written down proportion. The answer may depend on the wording of the respective guarantee and the national law governing the guarantee.[598]

[C] Exceptions: Do They Devaluate the Tool?

Whereas any other liabilities are consequently subject to bail-in, Article 44(3) of the BRRD lists further exclusions in 'exceptional circumstances' upon the decision of the resolution authority. These are supposed to be:

- it is not possible to bail in that liability within a reasonable time notwithstanding the good faith efforts of the resolution authority;
- the exclusion is strictly necessary and is proportionate to achieve the continuity of critical functions and core business lines in a manner that maintains the ability of the institution under resolution to continue key operations, services and transactions;
- the exclusion is strictly necessary and proportionate to avoid giving rise to widespread contagion, in particular as regards eligible deposits held by natural persons and micro-, small - and medium-sized enterprises, which would severely disrupt the functioning of financial markets, including FMI, in a manner that could cause a serious disturbance to the economy of a Member State or of the Union; or
- the application of the bail-in tool to those liabilities would cause destruction in value such that the losses borne by other creditors would be higher than if those liabilities were excluded from bail-in.

The exceptions mentioned above are worded in a far-reaching manner. Hence, they allow the resolution authority to assess which liabilities it considers to exclude at its discretion.[599]

---

bonds, it might be simpler to seek a full exemption regardless of the specific valuation being below estimated value of the secured assets.

597. According to estimates by the International Swaps and Derivatives Association, 90% of the derivative contracts in the market are collateralised and, hence, bail-in safe.

598. In the case of Hypo Alpe Adria Bank AG, the state guarantee relating to the bail-in debt was wiped out. The Austrian government enacted a law effecting a bail-in of EUR 890 million of subordinated debt. *See* report by the International Monetary Fund of September 2014 http://www.imf.org/external/np/sec/pr/2014/pr14423.htm#P18_327. Under the same law, shareholder loans with the Bayerische Landesbank were extinguished.

599. The guarantee that remains for creditors is that they will not receive less than they would in an insolvency scenario. *See Huertas*, p. 173.

If liabilities are excluded under Article 44(3) of BRRD and outstanding losses cannot be absorbed by the bailed-in creditors, then the resolution authority may decide to call upon financing arrangements.[600] In order to reduce the use of external funds in resolution, two thresholds were introduced. These minimum and maximum thresholds must be considered before the financing arrangements can be triggered.[601]

[D] The Eight-Percent Rule

Shareholders and other creditors subject to bail-in must contribute to loss absorption and recapitalisation in a minimum threshold. This means that an amount equal to at least 8 %[602] of the total liabilities including own funds must be converted or written down, as applicable.[603] The question arises whether this 8 % threshold measured at total liabilities including own funds would be sufficient for a first share of contribution to restore the viability of the failing institution.

First, the timing of assessment must be taken into account. The 8 % threshold[604] is calculated at a time when the resolution action is actually taken, rather than a time of the last orderly balance sheet. At that time, equity may be written down by losses or sometimes even be negative. Second, this once again highlights the importance of valuation in the context of resolution.[605] In the course of negotiations of that very paragraph, a review of recent bank recapitalisations in Europe has taken place. According to them, the bank restructuring scenarios would have been sufficiently restored by losses distributed to own funds and liabilities in the amount of 8 %.[606]

600. These include *ex ante* financing arrangements with contributions from credit institutions and certain investment firms pursuant to Article 103 of BRRD (Article 70 of SRM-R); *ex post* financing arrangements with contributions from credit institutions and certain investment firms pursuant to Article 104 of BRRD (Article 71 of SRM-R); and contract borrowings or other forms of support from credit institutions and certain investment firms, other financial institutions and other third parties pursuant to Article 105 of BRRD (Article 73 of SRM-R).
601. Article 44(5) of BRRD and Article 27(7) of SRM-R, which are in line with the Key Attribute 6.4 of the FSB's Key Attributes of Effective Resolution Regimes for Financial Institutions.
602. *See Wehling/Ockenga*.
603. Own funds include Common Equity Tier 1, Additional Tier 1 and Tier 2 capital.
604. The 8 % figure was agreed in June 2013. Germany and The Netherlands pushed for this agreement, while countries like France hoped to have more leeway for granting state aid. *See Spiegel*, Bail-Ins: EU Deal Protects Taxpayers in Bank Bailouts. Available at: http://www.spiegel.de/international/business/eu-deal-would-require-bail-ins-in-future-bank-rescue-plans-a-908175.html.
605. *See* EBA's Regulatory Technical Standards on criteria for determining the minimum requirement for own funds and eligible liabilities under Directive 2014/59/EU – https://eba.europa.eu/sites/default/documents/files/documents/10180/1132900/a0fc8387-e98e-4c3f-ae9d-11fb75511662/EBA-RTS-2015-05%20RTS%20on%20MREL%20Criteria.pdf?retry=1.
606. For instance, according to information published by the Bank of Cyprus, its bail-in entailed: (i) first, convertible bonds 2013/2018, capital securities and convertible capital securities, as well as convertible enhanced capital securities were converted into equity; (ii) second, a loss absorption haircut of EUR 2.4 billion was applied; and (iii) third, 47.5 % of unsecured deposits (those exceeding EUR 100,000) in the amount of EUR 3.8 billion were converted into shares. The contribution of capital instruments was indeed around 8 % of total liabilities (approximately EUR 31 billion).

Once the 8% threshold has been met, financing arrangements may be included in the resolution. Details of resolution financings[607] are described in section 5.22. Broadly these arrangements consist of so-called resolution funds. The resolution funds can either step in by way of acquiring equity or by any other means of debt instruments to cover losses.[608] However, the resolution funds may only contribute an amount that does not exceed 5% of the total liabilities including own funds. The 5% quota is measured again at the time of the resolution action.

In extraordinary circumstances, the resolution authority may seek further funding from alternative financing sources under Article 105 of BRRD[609] under two conditions: (a) it may only do so after the 8% limit described above has been reached; and (b) all unsecured, non-preferred liabilities other than eligible deposits must have been fully written down or converted into equity.

Alternatively, or in addition to alternative financing sources, the resolution authority may take additional contributions from financing arrangements (if the mentioned conditions under the previous paragraph are met). In many ways these are limited to *ex ante* raised payments by institutions. These arrangements must be in accordance with Article 100(6) and Article 103 of BRRD and must have not been used for prior capitalisation (i.e., monies left in the respective funds).[610,611]

[E] The Twenty-Percent Minimum

Instead of the 8% rule, a financing arrangement can be used if instead the recapitalisation by bail-in meets another ratio: namely, if shareholders and other creditors have contributed to loss absorption and recapitalisation at an amount of not less than 20% of the RWA.[612]

This may be more favourable to the institution and its creditors, depending on how the institution is financed and on the structure of the RWA. However, this exception is only available subject to specific requirements. The financing can only be drawn from *ex ante* contributions made to respective national resolution funds. The aggregate amount of those contributions must be at least 3% of the covered deposits of all of the credit institutions authorised in the relevant Member State. Also, the respective institution must have assets below EUR 900 billion on a consolidated basis.[613]

607. Article 101 of BRRD.
608. Article 44(4), points (a) and (b) of BRRD; Article 27(6) points (a) and (b) of SRM-R.
609. *See* Article 73 of SRM-R.
610. *See* Articles 68 et seq of SRM-R.
611. *See also* above Chapter 2 section 2.05 and Chapter 5 section 5.22[G] on the anticipated powers of the ESM to lend money to the SRF.
612. Article 44(8)(a) of BRRD.
613. Article 44(8) points (b) and (c) BRRD. However, SRM-R Article 27(11) purports that Article 44(8) of BRRD does not apply for purposes of SRM-R.

[F] A Practical Example

The principles laid out under BRRD and SRM are complex. It is difficult to see this system of bail-in work without a planning exercise. An *ex ante* resolution plan is simply essential given the complexity of banks' balance sheets. Otherwise, the speedy resolution implementation over a few weeks or even over a few days could be risky. For this reason, resolution planning is an instrument that is fundamental to all of the resolution tools. Not only the bail-in tool but also, for instance, the bridge bank tool is quite complex in its application to large systemic banks.[614]

Inevitably, the question as to how (if not by way of bail-in) the viability of the institution can be restored comes up in this context. Moreover, this brings in the interplay between the resolution fund and the bail-in. One expected reaction of the resolution authority would be to fill any gaps caused by excluded liabilities either:

- with further haircuts to other creditors; or
- with a participation of the resolution fund.

The first possibility may be limited given the principles that no creditor shall be worse off than in insolvency proceedings and that creditors of a same class shall be treated in an equitable manner. Therefore, the fund may step in and fill gaps by way of purchasing shares or other instruments to restore the net asset value and recapitalise the institution. Such fund is technically named financing arrangement and may derive contributions from different sources like credit institutions and investment firms.

The following example is just a rough sketch of how an 'open bank bail-in' would practically work. A large systemic bank is assessed to be failing or likely to fail in the meaning of BRRD or the SRM-R. If it is an institution supervised by ECB under the SSM, the SRM would apply to that institution.[615] Procedurally, the ECB will inform the SRB about the problems in that institution.[616] Ideally, this would take place before a point in time where the bank is already at the brink of resolution. The SRB together with ECB will then have to assess whether the bail-in tool would be the appropriate tool.[617]

The following actions would need to be taken:

- In a first step, a valuation exercise would have to be carried out.[618] The purpose would be to determine the amount of loss absorption and recapitalisation to restore the viability of the institution and capital adequacy in the meaning of the applicable regulation.
- In a second step, it would need to be assessed how much of own funds and eligible liabilities exist at all at this stage.[619] This would have to be measured against the figure revealed under the first step.

614. *See* Chapter 6 on resolution planning.
615. Hence, the SRM-R has a narrower geographical scope. *See* Articles 2 and 4 thereof.
616. Article 11 of SRM-R.
617. Article 18 of SRM-R.
618. Valuation 2 – *see* above Chapter 5 section 5.14.
619. This is not necessarily a valuation point but more a data and information point to be provided by the institution to the resolution authorities.

- The third step would be the decision on whether: (a) all of the eligible liabilities should be taken to loss absorption (i.e., bailed in) and recapitalisation or whether (b) certain amounts of liabilities should be excluded of the bail-in tool under the exceptions as set out in Article 44(3) of BRRD. For instance, such exclusions could be necessary to avoid widespread contagion, to achieve continuity of critical functions, or due to time factors.[620]
- Now assuming that certain liabilities are set aside from the bail-in and the existing eligible liabilities and own funds are fully bailed in but are not sufficient to restore viability and capital adequacy of the institution.
- The fourth step would be to consider the contribution from a financing arrangement. If it is a resolution governed by ECB and the SRB, the SRF will come to play and the respective intergovernmental agreement will be applicable.
- The fifth step would be to assess whether the 8 % test has been reached already prior to using the financing arrangement. As explained above, funds can only be drawn from that resolution fund, if the 8 % loss absorption and recapitalisation has been made by writing down own funds and converting eligible liabilities into equity.
- Once that has been assessed, the sixth step will be to assess whether the resolution fund contribution in its maximum amount of 5 % of own funds and all liabilities will be sufficient. If not, contributions beyond that will be necessary.
- In the seventh step, the resolution authority must decide on the procedure for contribution by the resolution fund. It may occur either by way of investing into equity, buying existing instruments or converting them into equity or by way of issuing a debt instrument. It will have to clear compliance with state aid rules. [621]
- In parallel, the resolution authority must establish how the loss allocation and recapitalisation to the various layers of the capital structure within the institution will be structured:
  - First, Common Equity Tier 1 will have to be written down.
  - Then, Additional Tier 1 and Tier 2 will be converted into Common Equity Tier 1. In that context, it will have to be assessed which amount of Common Equity Tier 1 equity will be given to those instruments given their relative juniority in the capital structure.
  - After that, subordinated instruments will be written down and converted into equity. Again, it will have to be assessed which amount of equity will be given to those subordinated instruments given their seniority in relation to Tier 2 instruments but juniority in relation to senior liabilities.
  - Finally, it will have to be assessed which eligible senior liabilities are to be converted into equity and whether they are fully written down or partially written down and which amount of equity they will get.

620. For an example of the bail-in effects on a fictional balance sheet, *see Gstädtner*, p. 187.
621. As fund aid counts like state aid, see Art 19 SRM-R.

All these measures must be performed under a valuation exercise following the principles laid out in BRRD und the SRM-R.[622] As mentioned, the ultimate bottom line is that no creditor is worse off than it would be in insolvency proceedings. Therefore, a hypothetical insolvency quota will have to be calculated prior to applying this long cascade. All creditors who rank prior to others in insolvency and who would presumably receive 100% dividends cannot be subject to bail-in.

Figure 5.1 roughly illustrates those steps.

622. Commission Delegated Regulation (EU) 2018/345 of 14 November 2017.

Figure 5.1 Balance Sheet Steps

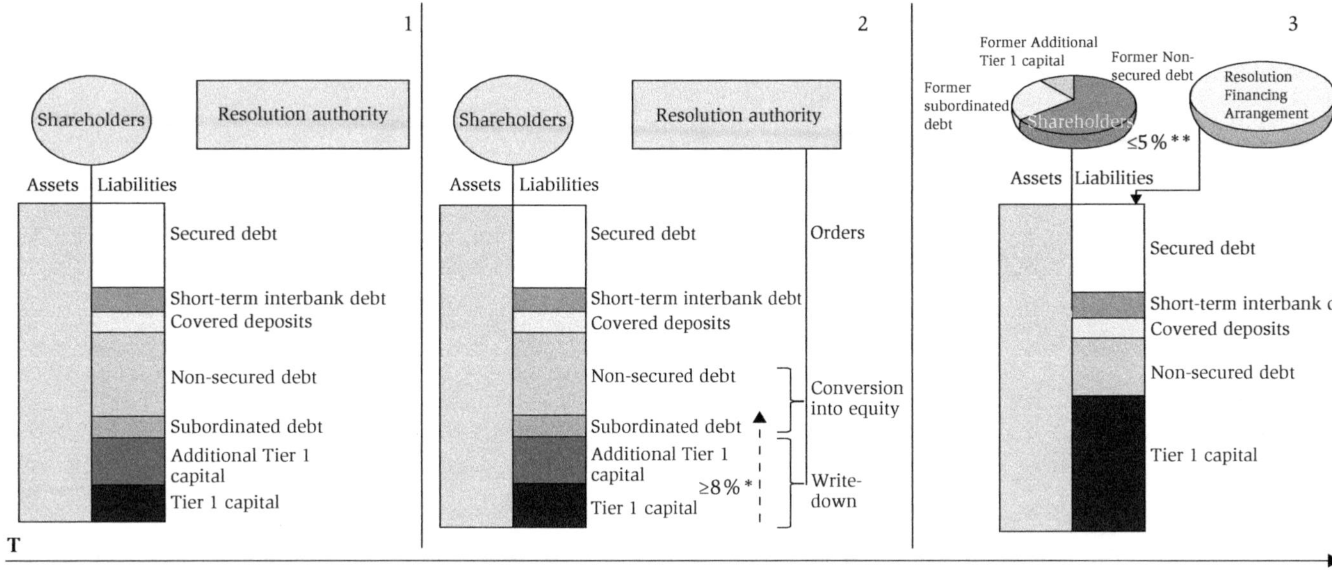

- (Impending) failure (i.e., (impending) illiquidity/(impending) over-indebtedness/(impending) withdrawal of authorisation)
- No reasonable prospect to prevent failure with alternative measures
- Resolution measures are necessary in the public interest

* If certain liabilities are excluded from bail-in, the relevant resolution authority can cover the capital shortfall through financing obtained by way of a Resolution Financing Arrangement. However, this requires that, prior to such financing, equity and debt in an amount equal to at least 8% of the institution's total liabilities including own funds have been written-down or converted into equity.

** Financing obtained through a Resolution Financing Arrangement will be limited to an amount equal to 5% of the institutuon's total liabilities.

Source: Compiled by author from various sources.

An important operational measure to accompany bail-in can be the appointment of an 'administrator'[623] for interim management. Inevitably it is necessary to set up a business reorganisation (or restructuring) plan with certain milestones.[624] It shall include at least the following elements:

(a) a detailed diagnosis of the factors and problems that caused the institution or entity referred to in point (b), (c) or (d) of Article 1(1) of BRRD to fail or to be likely to fail, and the circumstances that led to its difficulties;
(b) a description of the measures aiming to restore the long-term viability of the institution or entity referred to in point (b), (c) or (d) of Article 1(1) of BRRD that are to be adopted;
(c) a timetable for the implementation of those measures.

In addition, measures aiming to restore the long-term viability of an institution may include:[625]

(a) the reorganisation of the activities of the institution or entity referred to in point (b), (c) or (d) of Article 1(1) of BRRD;
(b) changes to the operational systems and infrastructure within the institution;
(c) the withdrawal from loss-making activities;
(d) the restructuring of existing activities that can be made competitive;
(e) the sale of assets or of business lines.

This serves to monitor the effectiveness of the resolution mid to long term and also to justify that the resolution action was actually able to restore the viability of the institution. It should be expected that the resolution authority has drawn up key elements of such plan beforehand in order to be able to estimate whether the resolution action is in fact foreseen to lead to a sustainable result.

§5.17 WRITE-DOWN OF CAPITAL INSTRUMENTS

The equity of banks consists of various layers of regulatory equity. The regulatory meaning of equity differs very much from the meaning of corporate law rules. Regulatory equity is core equity composed by Common Equity Tier 1, Additional Tier

623. Articles 51 and 72(1) of BRRD. *See* Article 27(2) of SRM-R.
624. Article 52 of BRRD. *See* Article 27(16) of SRM-R. The bail-in playbook guidance expects banks, in accordance with Article 52 BRRD, to address the processes needed for the production of business reorganisation plan, lay down the communication lines between authorities and the bank for comments on business reorganisation plan, describe the process supporting amendments to business reorganisation plan in line with the conclusions of the relevant authorities in a timely manner with the relevant control and approval steps, and identify internal units responsible for monitoring bank's progress towards targets foreseen in the business reorganisation plan (see para 38).
625. Article 52(6) of BRRD. *See* Article 27(16) of SRM-R.

1 capital, and Tier 2 capital. Only the core equity is 'real' equity in the meaning of statutory capital. Legally speaking, the other forms of regulatory equity (i.e., Additional Tier 1 and Tier 2) are debt positions which are very close to equity by virtue of contractual design. Issuing banks include deep subordination clauses, loss bearing mechanisms, or terms during which unilateral terminations by the instrument holders are excluded. These characteristics allow debts to count as part of core equity.

Looking at the bail-in tool, this applies throughout the whole capital layer starting with equity and ending with senior debt. However, a major principle of resolution and of any governmental action is that it shall be as minimally invasive as possible. Therefore, it seems logical to first conduct a write-down and conversion of Additional Tier 1 and Tier 2 capital before ordering a bail-in into subordinated or senior debt. In this spirit, BRRD and the SRM-R included powers for the resolution authority to write down capital instruments.[626] In the structure of BRRD, the write-down of capital instruments is not a resolution tool per se. Rather, it works as an ancillary tool or a tool that can be exercised independent of any resolution tool. The power to write down capital instruments has been extended to what is also called 'internal MREL' (IMREL). IMREL, which will be explained in more detail in Chapter 6, is a special form of intragroup capital instrument between a resolution entity (owner of the instrument) and its subsidiaries (issuing entity). IMREL is supposed to absorb losses within the resolution group by granting the resolution authority the possibility to write down that instrument - independently of a resolution action - similar to a capital instrument.[627] By doing this, the subsidiary of the resolution entity belonging to the resolution group is recapitalised, and the losses stemming from such recapitalisation are passed on to the resolution entity[628] which then in turn will need to absorb these by, e.g., applying the capital instruments write-down and (respectively) the bail-in tool.

[A] Prerequisites

In earlier versions of BRRD, the write-down power could also be exercised at a stage prior to the actual resolution tools. That stadium was defined as a stadium where the institution is or will no longer be viable. In the final draft, this was amended.

Under BRRD and the SRM-R, the main prerequisite for exercising this power is either:

- a determination has been made that conditions for resolution have been met before any resolution action is taken; or
- the appropriate authority determines that unless the power is exercised in relation to the relevant capital instruments, the institution will no longer be viable.

626. Article 59 of BRRD and Article 18 SRM-R.
627. Article 59(1a) BRRD, by referring to eligible liabilities that meet the conditions referred to in point (a) of Article 45f(2) BRRD.
628. By writing down the claims under the internal MREL.

Therefore, the non-viability test is still relevant. In the course of this paragraph of the Directive, no viability is defined as point in time where the institution is failing or likely to fail. Failure or likelihood to fail is again a condition for resolution under Article 32(4) of BRRD. This cross-reference implies that the write-down of capital instruments is actually only given when the institution is failing or likely to fail as set out in connection with the resolution tools.

As a consequence, the time at which the resolution authority can exercise the write-down is not earlier than the time of exercise for any other resolution tool. However, with regard to groups (*see* below and Article 59(6) of BRRD), trigger points are loosened to some extent. As the write-down of capital instruments is a less invasive measure, resolution authorities shall first consider this. Where the situation can be cured by writing down those instruments prior to exercising the resolution tools, the authority has discretion to assess this route. In exercising that discretion, the resolution authority will have to consider the relevant measure in detail. Therefore, it could potentially come to the conclusion that the write-down could be triggered practically a bit earlier than the bail-in tool and on a stand-alone basis.

Looking at the mechanics, the write-down of capital instruments is very similar to the bail-in tool. Here, debt instruments can either be written down or converted into equity. Equity in that sense means statutory equity, for those instruments are already own funds in the meaning of regulatory equity. Therefore, converting regulatory equity into equity means converting Additional Tier 1 and Tier 2 instruments into statutory equity. This is legally possible because those instruments are debt positions that can hence be converted into equity.

The question arises then in respect of the effect of such a write-down or conversion of capital instruments. Clearly, all those instruments will become equity after the conversion. The institution will then have a much stronger Common Equity Tier 1 ratio than before. In addition, the conversion can have the effect that any loss-absorbing capacity of those capital instruments will then be permanent.

Sometimes, loss absorption clauses in capital instruments can be drafted in a way that losses be absorbed as soon as accounted for and that gains in following year reduce the already absorbed losses. This can sometimes hinder third-party investors from making an investment in an institution, as those loss-absorbing instruments will always be senior to their pure equity. Hence, the write-down and conversion tool can be used to make an institution ready for a step-in by a third-party equity investor.[629]

Also, those capital instruments are not 'real' equity but hybrids or debts. They usually have a term until when a repayment of those instruments is due and along with periodic interest or coupon payments. These repetitive liquidity elements can also be an obstacle to the soundness of the institution. For instance, if a coupon payment obligation or if a repayment of capital instruments is due shortly, a conversion or a write-down of these instruments can also have an effect to stabilise the institution.

There is one distinction to the bail-in tool with respect to the approach in group resolution. While for bail-in and other resolution tools (as well as on MREL), BRRD

629. It is also possible in connection with the sale of business tool under Article 38 BRRD.

follows a clear entity-by-entity approach, this principle is loosened a bit regarding the write-down instrument. Article 59(4)(a) of BRRD rules not only that a trigger point is an institution or entity but also that 'the group is failing or likely to fail'.[630] This means that the write-down instrument can also be applied to an entity within the group, which per se is not failing, but the group as a whole would be. This can have positive effects on the capital ratio of the group on a consolidated basis. This is consistent with the approach of regulatory capital measurement which is also applied on a consolidated basis.[631]

§5.18 IMPLEMENTATION OF THE BAIL-IN TOOL

The idea of bail-in is relatively simple: in a situation of severe distress, equity holders and creditors have to bear the losses in order to recapitalise the institution.

Bearing losses, as mentioned earlier, means writing down or diluting equity to allow for new equity to come in, cancel debt, and convert debt into equity.

While these principles seem to be relatively straight forward, technical details can be complex.

The following points seem to be the most important:

- Ranking: What is the sequence of write-down or cancellation?
- In case of debt: Should debt be written down or always converted into equity?
- In case of conversion of debt into equity: What debt position is taken when it is converted into equity?
- What happens with equity or debt that is held by public bodies?

[A] Sequence

Prior to exercising a sequence of write-down or conversion, the resolution authorities must do some calculations. They need to assess how much Common Equity Tier 1 instruments and further regulatory capital must be reduced. They must assess the aggregate amount by which eligible liabilities must be written down or converted into shares and other types of capital instruments. These calculations must be carried out in a valuation pursuant to Article 36 of BRRD[632] and have two aims: to ensure that the net asset value of the institution under resolution is equal to zero and to restore the Common Equity Tier 1 capital ratio.[633,634]

630. Article 59(3)(c) of BRRD refers to the regulatory requirements ('own funds') on a consolidated basis. *See* Article 21(1)(c) of SRM-R.
631. *See* section 5.24 on group resolution for more details.
632. Article 20 of SRM-R.
633. Article 46 of BRRD.
634. *See also* EBA Guidelines on the treatment of shareholders in bail in or the write down and conversion of capital instrument, dates 5 April 2017.

Once each amount is assessed, the sequence follows the ranking of the relevant creditor's position in insolvency:[635]

- First, Common Equity Tier 1 items are fully reduced. This is consistent since such instruments have the weakest position in an insolvency scenario.
- Second, if Common Equity Tier 1 does not suffice, other capital instruments have to be fully reduced. This reduction starts with Additional Tier 1 instruments and continues with Tier 2 instruments.
- Third, if there is still the need to reduce debt, subordinated debt that is not Additional Tier 1 or Tier 2 capital is fully reduced.
- Fourth, if there is a need for further reduction, senior liabilities are reduced.

[B] Only Reduction or Also Conversion into Equity?

As mentioned above, Article 46 of BRRD requires that the authority assesses:

(i) the aggregate amount by which bail-in-able liabilities must be written down in order to ensure that the net asset value of the institution is equal to zero; and
(ii) where relevant, the amount by which bail-in-able liabilities must be converted into shares or other type of capital instruments in order to restore the Common Equity Tier 1 capital ratio.

In this context, one faces the question of whether a simple reduction of debt is possible without any conversion into equity. The careful answer to this question must go through a longer reasoning. Generally, according to the wording of Article 46 of BRRD, a division between write-down and conversion is technically possible. According to this wording, a write-down will be applied until the net asset value of the institution is equal to zero. Hence, a negative equity value of the institution is cured by writing down debt. As the sequence of write-down inevitably starts with the Common Equity Tier 1, it is not possible to reduce debt without reducing equity.[636] If the debt is subject to write-down, equity will necessarily have been reduced to zero already. This is the first conclusion.[637]

Theoretically, the exercise could stop at part of the equity and part of the debt. For instance, the market environment could change, and the institution could become attractive to investors following the haircut. The institution could then regain value and the old equity would participate in any upside. However, the hard-sequential rule

635. Article 48 of BRRD; *see also* Article 21(10) of SRM-R.
636. Or instead of reducing equity, transferring shares (equity) to creditors.
637. *See also* EBA Guidelines on the treatment of shareholders in bail in or the write down and conversion of capital instrument, dates 5 April 2017, para. 1.7 'if the net asset value ... is zero or negative, it will be necessary to write down, at least partially, creditors more senior in insolvency to shares or other instruments of ownership. Writing down creditors while shareholders retained some vale would be inconsistent both with the sequence of write-down in Article 48 and the respect for the creditor hierarchy in insolvency required by the resolution principles of Article 34'.

above hinders this scenario. This is adequate since shareholders' participation in an upside (which had basically been paid by creditors' loss contributions) would not be fair or equitable. The creditors that have been written down would not participate in such upside would be worse off. Therefore, the second conclusion follows. It seems only logical that a write-down of debt must always go along with a partial conversion of debt into equity or a transfer of existing shares to creditors.[638] Furthermore, any conversion implies an element of a write-down or of a waiver. This is because the conversion automatically leads to the debt position totally or partially disappearing and equity being created. Hence, these two instruments have to be seen as necessarily linked together.

In this context, the next question is why the BRRD separates conversion from write-down. The first reason may be of semantical nature. As mentioned, it is possible to transfer shares to creditors in combination with the write-down of liabilities or capital instruments as the case may be. In such circumstances, it may not be technically correct to use the expression 'conversion' as debt is not converted into equity, but rather existing equity is transferred. The second and possibly a more important reason is in order to have flexibility to adapt the process to different types of banks, creditors and national laws. In the case where the institution is state-owned, equity cannot possibly be given to the creditors. Also, in some circumstances, creditors may not be able to accept equity for regulatory reasons. In these cases, indeed only a write-down may be considered. In order to avoid a potential unjust upside, measures to counter-balance must be considered. For instance, a debt instrument that could economically represent such upside potential and payment would be triggered exactly like the upside (*Besserungsschein* or debtor warrant, participation note).[639]

With respect to the technical procedure of conversion, local law will guide the formalities.[640] Under German law, the creditor assigns its claims to the bank.[641] These claims disappear, as the creditor and debtor become the same entity. In that assignment, the claim is used as to pay up newly subscribed equity as equity in kind. The institution's statutory capital can then be increased by the value of that claim.

Clearly under ordinary corporate law rules a conversion of debt into equity follows many formalities, for instance, voting thresholds in general assemblies, invitation and publication requirements for general assemblies, binding public take-over offer requirements, valuation requirements, in case the capital is not increased by way of cash but rather by way of in rem consideration and formalities regarding the

638. *See* EBA Guidelines on the treatment of shareholders in bail in or the write down and conversion of capital instrument, dates 5 April 2017, para. 1.5.
639. Under IFRS, the original debt is novated into a new debt with a lower value, the fair value and the difference represents earnings for the institution. The probability of an upside will determine the fair value and the relevant earnings. *See Lüdenbach/Hoffmann*, p. 1721.
640. *See also* https://srb.europa.eu/en/content/resolution-cases for a recent example under Spanish law.
641. *Schelo* (2011), p. 188.

registration of these changes to public registers. It is here where the national transformation of BRRD will have to fill in technicalities and details. However, BRRD clearly states that any procedural impediments to bail-in shall be removed.[642,643]

[C] Which Conversion for Which Value?

An important question when it comes to debt-to-equity swap is the question of valuation of the equity rate.[644] As described above, the conversion works in a way that all or part of the claim is assigned to the company and a 'corresponding' equity value is created.[645] There are basically two possibilities to carry out that valuation: under the nominal value or under the actual value.

In some European jurisdictions, the nominal amount is relevant for assessing the amount of equity to be created. In Germany, on the other hand, only a fraction of the legal literature is in favour of assessing it at nominal value. Rather the real value, i.e. the actual value of the claim, is the relevant one. Then, of course, there are various possibilities to calculate the 'real' value in contrast to the nominal value. Real value can, for instance, be the value that the institution is able to pay to the creditor at that stage. If the claim has a nominal value of 100 and the institution would only be able to pay 70, taking into account its assets and overall liability position, the real value would be 70. Possibly, the real value could also be the market value, i.e. the value by which that claim can be sold to a third party.

Once the claim's value is determined, the corresponding equity amount shall be assessed. In the example above, the claim is worth 70 and statutory capital in the amount of 70 is created for it. Hence, the question arises, whether such valuation would not conflict with the NCWO principle. This is because the claim that was normally worth 100 with a real value of 70 could also have an expected value of 70 in insolvency. In this case, the creditor is given equity worth 70, for such claim. However, 70 of equity is a riskier position than a normal claim of 70.

Therefore, the assessment probably will have to be more distinguished. Assuming that a nominal amount of 100, a hypothetical insolvency quota of 60 and an actual value of 75 at the time of the resolution are used. In this scenario, an amount of 15 could be allocated to equity, while the 60 hypothetical insolvency quotas remain untouched. This example shows in many ways that the actual calculation of the conversion rate can be very complex.

In assessing which value is to be taken into consideration, i.e. nominal value or actual value, international standards and European law come into play. In 2009, as a consequence of the financial crisis, several entities started to renegotiate the repayment of debt instruments by equity issuances. The harmonisation of the reporting of such

642. Article 54 of BRRD.
643. Also important EU directives are amended to comply with this requirement: *see* Article 59(4) of BRRD and Article 21(3) of SRM-R.
644. *See* EBA Final Guidelines on the rate of conversion of debt into equity dated 5 April 2017.
645. Alternatively, shares can also be transferred to creditors in a respective amount subject to the conversion rate.

transactions became quite urgent since each debtor was applying a different approach and a different conversion. As a response, the International Financial Reporting Interpretations Committee ('IFRIC') issued a new interpretation, IFRIC 19, that was later endorsed by the EU.[646] This interpretation helped clarifying many open questions.

In sum, as per IFRIC 19, the financial statements should represent the *fair* value of the issued equity instruments. This fair value shall count as consideration paid against the converted and extinguished debt, either in total or in part. IFRIC 19 refers to the debtor's valuation only, but not to that of the creditor. Also, it does not apply to a situation where neither debtor nor creditor is a related party, nor where the debt was originally a convertible instrument. The applicability of this interpretation was not set aside in BRRD and may serve as a guideline for resolution authorities.

IFRIC 19 was applied in the bail-in of the Bank of Cyprus from March until July 2013.[647] After holders of shares and debt securities absorbed certain losses of this institution, deposits as well as remaining debt securities were converted into equity. In this case, it was not possible to reliably measure the fair value of the failing institution's equity because of several uncertainties. The trading of shares had been suspended before the conversion took place, there was not sufficient up-to-date financial information available, and the negotiations with the Troika were ongoing at the time of conversion. Hence, the Bank of Cyprus adopted the fair value of deposits and debt securities. For instance, each EUR 1.00 principal amount of subordinated debt and claims was converted into one Class D share at EUR 1.00 nominal amount.

The EBA Final Guidelines on the rate of conversion of debt into equity of 5 April 2017 has its focus on differential conversion rates applied to different classes of creditors and proposes guidelines under two overarching principles. The first principle is the 'NCWO' safeguard in combination with the protection of fundamental property rights. Hence, just as mentioned in the example of write-down and conversion above, the bottom limit for a conversion rate will always be the hypothetical quota that the creditor would be entitled to in an insolvency scenario. Second, the creditor hierarchy principles are laid out so that shareholders bear first losses and other creditors are ranked as if under normal insolvency proceedings. If these two principles are respected, the resolution authorities may apply differential conversion rates, but they are under no obligation to do so.[648] However, these guidelines provide no guidance on the actual valuation principles to be applied.[649]

[D] What Happens If Equity or Debt Is in Public Ownership?

Many states own banks or bank capital instruments, or sometimes grant loans or purchase subordinated debt and similar liabilities to capitalise institutions. Here, a

646. IFRIC's Interpretation 19 of 26 November 2009, and Regulation (EU) No 662/2010 amending Regulation (EC) No 1126/2008 in accordance with Regulation (EC) No 1606/2002.
647. Annual Financial Report 2013 https://www.bankofcyprus.com/globalassets/investor-relations/annual-reports/english/annual-financial-report-eng-not-signed.pdf.
648. Article 50(1) of the BRRD.
649. Neither do the EBA Final Guidelines on the treatment of shareholders in bail-in (dated 5 April 2017).

special problem may occur if such an institution later runs into a stage of potential failure.[650] In that situation, the resolution authority may have to consider writing down equity held by public bodies or converting debt held by public bodies into equity. The question is whether public ownership or public debt can be privileged to some extent.[651]

Starting with public debt, an exclusion of liabilities to the state could be justified under Article 44(3) of BRRD, by applying the exceptional circumstance rule. Here, it would be necessary that one of the justifications under this Article is present. Otherwise, the exclusion would not be legitimately justifiable. Basically, either: (a) the bail-in is not possible within the reasonable time frame; (b) the exclusion is strictly necessary and proportionate to achieve the continuity of critical functions and the core business lines of the institution; (c) the exclusion is strictly necessary in proportion to avoid widespread contagion; and/or (d) the exclusion is necessary because the bail-in tool would cause a significant destruction in value. The current wording does not imply that given the mere fact that debt is held by public bodies, an exclusion would be justified. In addition, if public debt is excluded, other creditors will have to bear the losses in a more extensive manner. In principle, public and private creditors should be treated equally if both have acquired debt or equity under the same conditions. This is because both have similar rights and responsibilities vis-à-vis the institution's financial distress. Therefore, the better arguments support an equal treatment of public and private creditors.

A second, and even more relevant question, is as to whether public equity can be excluded. Some European banks have been supported by government measures, and in the course of these measures, governments have become shareholders of institutions; under the new BRRD regime, further public support is in principle only possible if 8% loss contributions by shareholders and creditors have been made. However, such loss contribution will ultimately lead to the write-down of existing equity and therefore lead to a write-down of publicly owned ownership. This creates a clear conflict between various rationales of BRRD. On the one hand the rationale being that public support requires prior loss sharing – on the other hand the rationale that Tier 1 capital is reduced first. Possible solutions could be to:

- either grant an exception of the loss sharing rules for banks which are publicly owned; or
- write-down equity in publicly owned institutions, convert creditors into equity and then leave room for additional equity investments of the state – however, the equity will be shared between state and converted creditors; or
- not convert creditors into equity in such cases but to grant them other forms of participations or warrants and basically leave the existing public equity untouched.

650. It is valid to note here that certain state-related entities, such as bodies of state housing policy that are not mainly engaged in banking transactions are outside the scope of BRRD. For a complete list of excluded entities, *see* Article 2(5) of Directive 2013/36/EU.

651. In BRRD framework, this is more of a theoretical problem. National resolution authorities would hardly take the decision to wipe out their 'own' claims.

However, in BRRD, there is no explicit possibility to exclude equity or equity-like capital instruments from being written down, based on the public ownership. This is supported by Article 54 (3) BRRD which clearly states that any impediments to resolution shall be removed including those related to instruments of incorporation or statutes.[652] Therefore, better arguments support the position that BRRD does not distinguish here either and supports equal treatment of public and private shareholders in the light of achieving effectiveness of the bail-in tool.

§5.19 THE BRIDGE BANK TOOL

[A] Scope and Idea

The bridge bank tool is a more established resolution tool if compared to the bail-in tool.[653] In fact, it was operated in 2008 around the outskirts of the financial crisis. It was used and applied to a UK building society.[654] Later in 2012, the tool was applied to Greek banks[655] with respect to Dutch SNS Reaal.[656] The idea is that in a scenario where the institution is likely to fail, the resolution authority transfers certain assets, liabilities and contracts from the failing institution to a state-owned vehicle. This vehicle is usually called bridge bank because it serves as a preliminary harbour for those transferred parts of the business until an investor is found for the bank.[657] The bridge

652. Some Member States have included the possibility to change the type of the legal corporation, if current corporate status is an impediment, see § 149 German SAG (Rechtsformwechsel).

653. In the United States, the Competitive Equality Banking Act of 1987 authorised the Federal Deposit Insurance Corporation to establish bridge banks. It was later regulated in the United State Code of Laws: 12 US Code section 1821 '(n) Bridge depository institutions (1) Organization (A) Purpose: When 1 or more insured depository institutions are in default, or when the Corporation anticipates that 1 or more insured depository institutions may become in default, the Corporation may, in its discretion, organize, and the Office of the Comptroller of the Currency, with respect to 1 or more insured banks or 1 or more insured savings associations, shall charter, 1 or more national banks or Federal savings associations, as appropriate, with respect thereto with the powers and attributes of national banking associations or Federal savings associations, as applicable, subject to the provisions of this subsection, to be referred to as "bridge depository institutions"'. Since its creation, the bridge bank tool has been used many times in the North-American context. *See* Federal Deposit Insurance Corporation's historical study on bridge banks from 1987 until 1994. https://www.fdic.gov/bank/historical/managing/documents/history-consolidated.pdf. Also *see* list of failed banks by FDIC https://www.fdic.gov/bank/individual/failed/banklist.html.

654. The Dunfermline Building Society, in England. *See* Report by the Bank of England under section 80(1) of the Banking Act 2009 on the Dunfermline Building Society (DBS) Bridge Bank.https://www.bankofengland.co.uk/-/media/boe/files/news/2009/march/dunfermline-building-society.pdf?la = en&hash = E86698333E6647FCB08B6B373C6E3E6667B1EBBC.

655. These were Proton Bank and Hellenic Postbank. *See* press release by the European Commission dated 29 April 2014 entitled 'State aid: Commission approves restructuring aid for Greek bank'. http://europa.eu/rapid/press-release_IP-14-495_en.htm.

656. Communication by The Netherlands to the European Commission in the State Aid Case number SA.35382 (2013/N). http://ec.europa.eu/competition/state_aid/cases/247614/247614_1415897_100_2.pdf.

657. In some jurisdictions, e.g. in Germany, national law already included the possibility of transfers similar to that in the bridge bank tool. *See* Schelo (2010).

bank is totally or partially owned and administered by public authorities.[658] A phase of stabilisation starts after the transfer of assets and liabilities to the bridge institution. This phase includes a further phase of restructuring and is potentially followed by an M&A and exit process.[659]

By contrast, the outside investors may be ready to take the bank business in the form it would have been transferred to the bridge bank. Such a direct transfer to private investors is usually much more advantageous in economic terms. This scenario is referred to as sale of business tool[660] or a simple purchase and assumption transaction. However, experience shows that in a distressed situation of banks, investors are hesitant to take over the institution unless they are forced to do so. This is true even if the institution is reshaped only by partial transfers because the risk situation and the shape of the business are not always clear. In stress situations, authorities must act quickly because there is often a lack of time to conduct a proper due diligence. Hence, the bridge institution is to be seen as an interim solution for the bank business.

Article 40 of BRRD[661] determines that:

> In order to give effect to the bridge institution tool and having regard to the need to maintain critical functions in the bridge institution, member states shall ensure that resolution authorities have the power to transfer to a bridge institution:
>
> (a) shares or other instruments of ownership issued by one or more institutions under resolution
> (b) all or any assets, rights or liabilities of one or more institutions under resolution.

This means that by transfer order:

(i) the shares in the institution which is failing or likely to fail;
(ii) all assets, rights or liabilities of the institution which is failing or likely to fail; or
(iii) some assets, rights or liabilities of the institution which is failing or likely to fail

can be transferred to the bridge institution. In the first case (i), the bridge institution holds the shares in the failing bank, while the original shareholders are 'left behind'. In the second case (ii), the legal entity which is failing stays behind, while its assets, liabilities, and rights (i.e., its whole business) are transferred to the bridge bank. In the third case, not all liabilities, assets and rights are transferred, but only selected parts of it.

The focus of the transfer order will most likely lie on transferring assets, rights, or liabilities. In fewer cases, the authorities will consider whether they should transfer the shares of the failing institution or any other instruments of ownership of the failing

658. Articles 40(2)(a) and 41(1) of BRRD.
659. *Federal Deposit Insurance Corporation*, Purchase and Assumption Transactions, https://www.fdic.gov/bank/individual/failed/enloe-p-and-a.pdf.
660. *See* section 5.18.
661. Article 25 of SRM-R.

institution to a bridge bank. This is simply because the shares of the institution that is failing or likely to fail usually consist of little value to a bridge institution. Rather, if the waterfall of liabilities is applied as prescribed in BRRD, shareholders have to bear first losses followed by the further ranking of regulatory capital down to subordinated and senior liabilities. Consequently, shares in the institution are usually left where they are while the actual business (excluding a certain amount of liabilities and 'toxic' assets) is transferred.

There may be exceptional cases, in which the transfer of shares is appropriate. This could, for instance, happen in a situation where it is necessary to get the shareholder assembly under control to facilitate a transfer without any obstacles. In that context, it may be appropriate to transfer shares to another bridge institution.

It is clarified that any transfer may take place without obtaining the consent of the shareholders or any third party other than the bridge institution. The transfer may also occur without the need of previous compliance with any procedural requirements under company or securities law.[662]

[B] Partial Transfers

When transferring assets and liabilities to a bridge institution, the aim is to restructure it and make it sound for further investments. For this reason, in many circumstances, not the whole business, i.e. all assets and liabilities, will be transferred to the bridge institution. This is because in such case little or nothing would be gained in terms of balance sheet restructuring, as the institution is failing or likely to fail. The only effect this would have is effectively leaving the former shareholders behind with an empty shell company (or in case of transfer of shares without any corporate entitlement).

Therefore, in order to conduct a restructuring, usually certain liabilities are left behind in that failing institution. This is referred to as partial transfer; the institution left behind will then undergo an ordinary liquidation process, usually through some form of bankruptcy. The amount of those liabilities left behind corresponds to the amount that is necessary to restore the liability and the capital adequacy of the institution. In other words, the amount of liabilities left behind often equals to the amount that is necessary for a bail-in.

This demonstrates that, conceptually, the bail-in and the bridge bank tools have the same aim when it comes to restoring the balance sheet of the institution. With the bail-in tool, the balance sheet is reshaped without transferring assets or liabilities to a different legal entity. The legal entity per se is restructured. By contrast, in the bridge bank tool, the balance sheet is reshaped by transferring only certain assets and liabilities to a different legal entity. The methods are different, but – in case of a partial transfer – the economic result of both tools is identical (*see* Figure 5.2).

662. Article 40(1) of BRRD. *See* Article 25 of SRM-R.

Figure 5.2 Flowchart of the Bridge Bank Tool

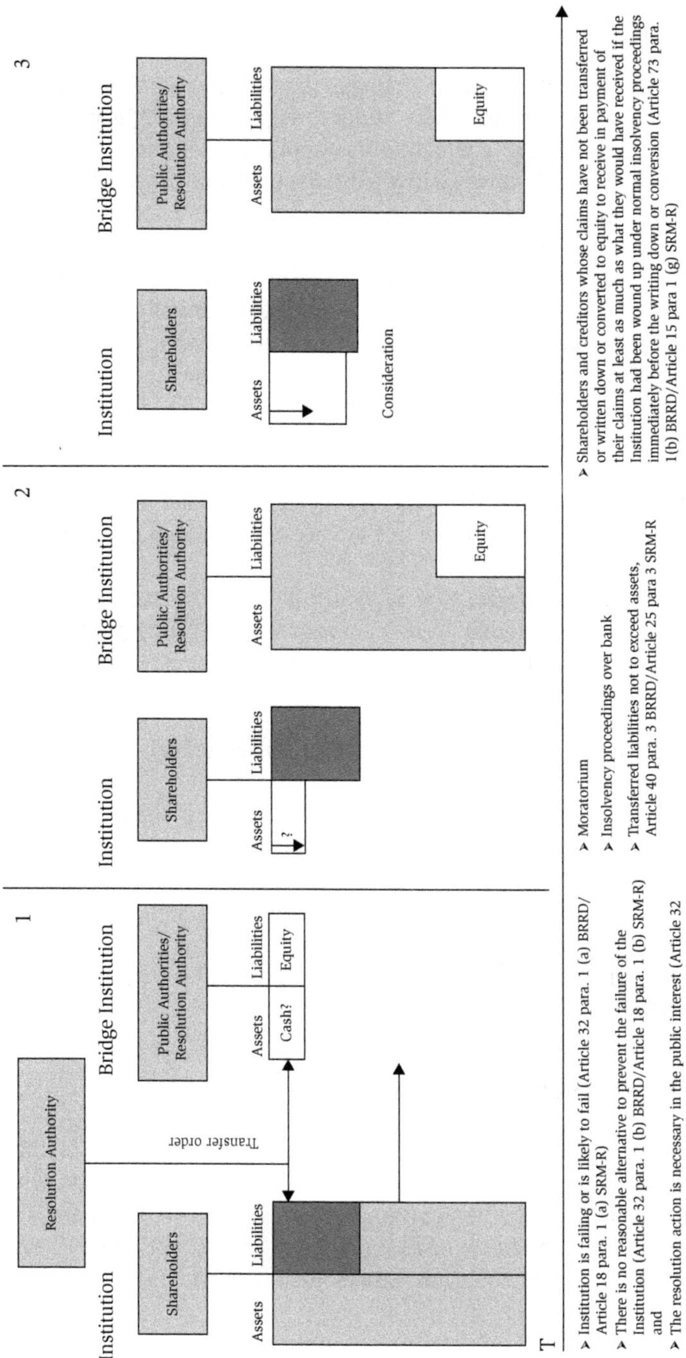

Source: Compiled by author from various sources.

In that context, the bridge bank tool certainly is technically a more complex tool. With the transfer of rights and obligations from one entity to another, several legal questions remain. Some of these questions are:

- if the transfer of rights and obligations will be acknowledged in different jurisdictions, especially where under foreign, non-European law.[663] However, this is a general theme which is also applicable to other resolution tools, like the bail-in tool. However, with the bridge bank tool assets and rights as well as certain liabilities have to be moved across. So, as there are more objects effected by the measure, the question of acknowledgement under foreign law may be more relevant. A solution could be to initially carve out foreign law assets, liabilities or rights and to transfer them manually (i.e., with the consent of the other side). There should often be an incentive to go across, as the bridge bank provides for greater certainty in going concern;
- if there will be uncertainty with respect to which classes of liabilities are transferred and which stay behind; also, this topic is similar to the one discussed with the bail-in tool. However, there may be more difficulties in actually identifying in the transfer order which exact liabilities are part of the transfer order and which are not. A very clear understanding of the creditors' identity is necessary;
- what type of compensation is being paid to the transferring entity? The question here is whether cash or shares are paid. BRRD is not specific here.[664] In many cases, shares in the bridge institution may be the right form of compensation.

These complex questions may be concrete disadvantages of the bridge bank tool in certain cases.

In contrast, the bridge bank has the advantage that it signals a new start to the market and potential investors and creditors. By transferring assets, liabilities, and contracts to a new legal entity, the signal is sent that the problematic liabilities are being carved out and left behind. Hence, the new entity is up for a fresh start and therefore more interesting to potential investors.

Ultimately, the decision about which resolution tool is the most appropriate has to be evaluated on a case-by-case basis.

[1] Safeguards in Partial Transfers

In case of a partial transfer, there are certain safeguards to be obeyed by the resolution authority. An especially important case is that of a partial transfer where not all liabilities are transferred. The first safeguard relates to the creditors and shareholders which stay behind in the failing institution. They should not receive less than they would have received in case of a normal insolvency of the institution. This complies

663. *See* discussion in *Huertas*, 2014, p. 15.
664. Article 40(4) of BRRD. *See* Article 25 of SRM-R.

with the NCWO principle.[665] Usually, the institution that stays behind will become part of a normal insolvency process and a liquidator will be appointed.[666]

Any assets or rights that have been transferred by the authorities cannot be set aside by the insolvency administrator of the failing institution.[667] Otherwise, the tool would not work. The same applies to shareholders and creditors in the institution which stayed behind. Article 40(11) of BRRD rules that they have no rights in respect of assets, rights, and liabilities transferred to the bridge institution.

A further safeguard is the protection of liabilities, which are subject to netting agreements or are subject to financial collateral.

Therefore, BRRD[668] prescribes that:

- when liabilities are transferred, any security that is attached to this liability is transferred at the same time;
- when liabilities that are tied into a certain netting agreement with counter-claims are transferred, then those netting rights may not be disturbed or changed to the negative by any transfer; and
- security arrangements, covered bonds, certain trading clearing, and settlement systems shall be protected.[669]

665. *See* section 5.05.
666. Article 37(6) of BRRD.
667. Article 37(7) of BRRD.
668. Article 77 of BRRD.
669. Article 78 of BRRD. Protection for security arrangements. '(1) Member States shall ensure that there is appropriate protection for liabilities secured under a security arrangement so as to prevent one of the following: (a) the transfer of assets against which the liability is secured unless that liability and benefit of the security are also transferred; (b) the transfer of a secured liability unless the benefit of the security are also transferred; (c) the transfer of the benefit of the security unless the secured liability is also transferred; or (d) the modification or termination of a security arrangement through the use of ancillary powers, if the effect of that modification or termination is that the liability ceases to be secured. 2. Notwithstanding paragraph 1, where necessary in order to ensure availability of the covered deposits the resolution authority may: (a) transfer covered deposits which are part of any of the arrangements mentioned in paragraph 1 without transferring other assets, rights or liabilities that are part of the same arrangement; and (b) transfer, modify or terminate those assets, rights or liabilities without transferring the covered deposits.' Article 79. Protection for structured finance arrangements and covered bonds. '1. Member states shall ensure that there is appropriate protection for structured finance arrangements including arrangements referred to in points (e) and (f) of Article 76(2) so as to prevent either of the following: (a) the transfer of some, but not all, of the assets, rights and liabilities which constitute or form part of a structured finance arrangement, including arrangements referred to in points (e) and (f) of Article 76(2), to which the institution under resolution is a party; (b) the termination or modification through the use of ancillary powers of the assets, rights and liabilities which constitute or form part of a structured finance arrangement, including arrangements referred to in points (e) and (f) of Article 76(2), to which the institution under resolution is a party. 2. Notwithstanding para. 1, where necessary in order to ensure availability of the covered deposits the resolution authority may: (a) transfer covered deposits which are part of any of the arrangements mentioned in para. 1 without transferring other assets, rights or liabilities that are part of the same arrangement, and (b) transfer, modify or terminate those assets, rights or liabilities without transferring the covered deposits.' Article 80. Partial transfers: protection of trading, clearing and settlement systems. '1. Member states shall ensure that the application of a resolution tool does not affect the operation of systems and rules of systems covered by Directive 98/26/EC, where the resolution authority: (a) transfers some but not all of the assets,

Ultimately these safeguards are also an outflow of the NCWO principle.
- In addition, there is a broad protection for structured finance arrangements so as to only transfer some but not all of the assets, rights and liabilities which constitute part of a structured finance arrangement. The term 'structured finance' arrangement is not defined; hence there may be some flexibility at this point.

Furthermore, there is no such catalogue on excluded liabilities in partial transfers as there exists for the bail-in tool.

A different question in case of a partial transfer is how the resolution authorities shall decide what is transferred and what stays behind and how the transfer order is technically drafted in order to address which liabilities are transferred and which liabilities are left behind. This is a question of resolution planning. Exact knowledge of the bank balance sheet and its creditor structure and identity is needed as well as knowledge about the asset and liability side. Especially if there are many foreign law (i.e., non-EU law) contracts and rights to be transferred whereas acknowledgement is uncertain, bail-in may be easier.

[C] Retransfer and Structural Issues

There is a possibility for the resolution authorities to transfer assets, rights, and liabilities more than once in order to make supplemental transfers.[670] Further, it may also retransfer assets, liabilities and rights (and indeed shares), back to the institution under resolution, if such retransfer possibility was explicitly stated in the transfer order or if the respective transfer object does not fit into the same class of objects transferred generally.[671]

Referring to the ownership structure of the bridge bank after transfer, this also depends on consideration granted to the institution under resolution (in case of asset, liabilities, and rights transfer). If a partial transfer is made and liabilities are left behind, some equity value is created with the bridge bank. In a bail-in scenario, such equity value is given to the bailed-in creditors. Consequently, in case of a partial transfer, such equity value should be allocated to the institution under resolution so that it becomes co-shareholder in the bridge bank and can then participate in an upside should the bridge bank be sold later on. However, BRRD is not explicitly clear on this (though it

---

rights or liabilities of an institution under resolution to another entity; or (b) uses powers under Article 64 to cancel or amend the terms of a contract to which the institution under resolution is a party or to substitute a recipient as a party. 2. In particular, a transfer, cancellation or amendment as referred to in para. 1 of this Article shall not revoke a transfer order in contravention of Article 5 of Directive 98/26/EC; and shall not modify or negate the enforceability of transfer orders and netting as required by Articles 3 and 5 of that Directive, the use of funds, securities or credit facilities as required by Article 4 thereof or protection of collateral security as required by Article 9 thereof.'

670. Article 40(5) of BRRD. *See* Article 25 of SRM-R, which makes cross-references to the provisions of BRRD.

671. Article 40(7) of BRRD.

allows partial private ownership), Article 40(2)(a) of BRRD. Certainly, technical questions will arise in respect of valuation and amount of equity to be allocated; but these questions are similar to the ones under the bail-in tool.

In the further course of running the bridge bank, Article 41 of BRRD contains specific conditions for operation, licensing and corporate governance requirements. Exit is supposed to happen two years after the last transfer.[672] It can be extended, however, for one or more additional year periods under the conditions set out in Article 41(6) of BRRD. Any proceeds from selling the bridge institution shall benefit the shareholders of the bridge institution.[673]

§5.20 SALE OF BUSINESS TOOL

[A] Scope and Idea

The sale of business tool is comparable to the bridge bank tool. In distinction to the bridge bank tool, the acquiring entity of the 'old banks' business is not the bridge bank but an external investor. In the past, external investors have taken over failed or nearly failing bank businesses by way of facilitation of the authorities.[674] Those mergers usually fail or are way too difficult if the entity to be acquired lacks viability in the long term and cannot be restructured by way of acquisition through a healthy institution. Hence, the idea of the sale of business tool is that the old institution is reshaped by partial transfers in a way that makes it attractive for an investor to acquire it.[675] This rationale is quite like one of the bridge bank tools. However, while the bridge bank tool is more of an interim solution which actually leaves the risk for the continuation of the bank with the government or state owning the bridge bank, the sale of business tool serves as a permanent solution. In fact, the first resolution case under the BRRD was resolved with the use of the sale of business tool.[676] Indeed placing the bank in difficulties in the hands of an experienced and solid market player can be a very powerful and effective tool. Its success will depend not only on the market the failing bank operates in but also on the amount of liabilities that resolution authorities can use for loss absorption in order to restructure the entity and make it a suitable target for M&A.[677] In that context, the MREL novelisation explained further down in Chapter 6 will play an important role. Generally speaking, the more reliable and credible eligible liabilities for bail-in are given in the very circumstances, there are more chances of success in an M&A process under the sale of business tool. It goes without saying that confidence in the failing institution can be reinstalled instantaneously under the new

672. Article 41 of BRRD.
673. Article 41(8) of BRRD.
674. *See* Chapter 2, section 2.06[A].
675. *Seelig* in *Hoelscher*, pp. 106-113.
676. The sale of Spanish Banco Popular, *see* https://srb.europa.eu/en/content/resolution-cases.
677. Basel Committee on Banking Supervision. Guidelines for identifying and dealing with weak banks. July 15. https://www.bis.org/bcbs/publ/d330.pdf. *See* section 6.2.3 Mergers and Acquisitions.

ownership of a reliable investor. By contrast, following an open bank bail-in, restoring confidence may need additional - possibly financial - efforts.[678]

The sale of business tool also provides for the possibility to transfer the institution as it stands. This would happen by way of a share transfer to an investor and may simply be to circumvent the necessary consent of the existing shareholders of the institution under resolution. However, in many cases, transferring the shares would not be attractive to an investor as the institution which is likely to fail has too many problems to be an attractive target.

Such 'more attractive target' could be delivered by transferring only certain assets and only certain liabilities to the investor (partial transfer). Ideally, these chosen assets and liabilities are those of systemic relevance and in the public interest to be transferred to an investor. The remaining assets and liabilities can be left with the existing institution under resolution to become the subject of an insolvency procedure. So far, the procedure does not differ much from that of the bridge bank tool.

Also, the safeguards and the possibility of partial transfers and retransfers are mostly identical to the bridge bank tool.

There is a difference with respect to retransfers. In the bridge bank tool, a retransfer requires an express authorisation in the original documentation[679] or that the classes of liabilities were not appropriately and equally transferred. In the sale of business tool, such retransfer is not foreseen by BRRD.

An alternative to restructure the balance sheet would be combining the sale of business tool with other tools, as the capital instrument write-down or the bail-in tool.[680] This may in most cases be less complicated than a partial transfer, as it would avoid the complex transferal of assets and liabilities on the one hand and the insolvency proceedings of the remaining bank on the other hand. Rather certain liabilities or capital instruments are reduced and converted into equity in the first step, and in second step, the shares are then transferred to the investor under the sale of business tool.

[B] Specific Requirements on the Sale of Business Tool

The main distinction to the bridge bank tool is that the acquirer is an external investor. In relation to this matter, there are some special formalities to be regarded.

One special feature is that the resolution authority is to effect the transfer on commercial terms and that a marketing of that bank business should take place.[681] It is possible to waive the marketing requirement, where there is a material threat to

678. The use of the SRF could be an option.
679. Article 40(7) of BRRD. Article 25 of SRM-R.
680. Article 37(4) BRRD. *See also* World Bank Group. Understanding Bank Recovery and Resolution in the EU: A Guidebook to the BRRD. April 2017. Chapter 16: The Sale of Business Tool. http://pubdocs.worldbank.org/en/609571482207234996/FinSAC-BRRD-Guidebook.pdf.
681. Article 38(2) and (3) and Article 39(2) of BRRD. *See* Article 24 of SRM-R.

financial stability, or if the compliance with this requirement would be likely to undermine the effectiveness of the tool.[682]

In distinction to the bridge bank tool, the purchase price in this case may, in fewer circumstances, be paid in shares. Rather, it is likely to be paid in cash, provided that there is a purchase price at all to be paid. Under certain circumstances, the appropriate purchase price may be EUR 1 or even be negative.[683]

Another distinction from the bridge bank tool is that the acquiring entity may need to obtain the permission from the competent authorities to take over the bank business. BRRD provides for a number of provisions in that respect. However, these provisions seem to focus on the case that shares of the institution under resolution are being transferred to the acquiring entity.

For this transfer, permission under European directives[684] is required vis-à-vis any holding company qualifications. However, in other cases, a transfer of shares may not be appropriate but rather a transfer of assets and liabilities to the acquiring entities may be more suitable. Also, in that case, permissions, business model or the regulatory capital ratio and related ratios may change or be impacted by the acquisition. BRRD does not contain specific provisions for the case of transfer of assets and liabilities. In that case, a tailor-made solution will have to be found.

In fact, also the provisions under BRRD with respect to obtaining permission focus on the suspension of voting rights in the relevant shares. This is also a requirement that is not necessary in case of an asset and liability transfer. For this alternative, the general clause in Article 38(7) of BRRD simply states that a purchaser shall have the appropriate authorisation to carry out the business it acquires when the transfer is made. The competent authority shall ensure that this application for authorisation shall be considered in conjunction with the transfer in a timely manner.

§5.21 ASSET SEPARATION TOOL

The chapters before have dealt with bail-in, bridge bank, and sale of business tool. There is one more tool, which serves as a hybrid between the other resolution tools and an ordinary bad bank scheme: the asset separation tool.[685] As a general point, the asset separation tool may not be used in isolation but only in conjunction with another resolution tool.[686]

By way of background, the technique of transferring assets of an institution into a special purpose vehicle was quite frequently used in restructurings for past years.

682. Article 39(3) of BRRD. *See* Article 24 of SRM-R. *See also* Title III of EBA Guidelines on the factual circumstances amounting to a material threat to financial stability and on the elements related to the effectiveness of the sale of business stool under Article 39(4) of BRRD.

683. The sale of business tool does not contain the requirement as in the bridge bank tool that 'the total value of liabilities transferred to the bridge institution does not exceed the total value of the rights and assets transferred from the institution under resolution or provided by other sources'. Article 40(3) of BRRD.

684. Directive 2013/36/EU of 26 June 2013 and Directive 2014/65/EU of 15 May 2014.

685. *Seelig* in *Hoelscher*, pp. 113-114.

686. Article 37(5) of BRRD; Article 22(4) of SRM-R.

This special purpose vehicle was called 'bad bank'. One of the purposes of this vehicle is to sell the assets which have suffered a loss of value over time in order to insulate and minimise the short-term losses. An asset which may now have a value of *x* may in two or three years have an increased value of *y*.

An interesting feature is that these special purpose vehicles were asset management companies that did not have a banking licence requirement. Consequently, they had lower capital requirements. Hence, such a structure was an effective and cheaper way of winding down banking activities. Examples are the German bad banks (*Abwicklungsanstalten*)[687] as well as the bad bank in connection with Hypo Alpe Adria[688] in Austria and SAREB,[689] the Spanish bad bank vehicle for the toxic assets of Spanish *cajas*. So far, these transfers have had the effect that any losses arising out of that transfer were directly or indirectly borne by the relevant governments. Creditors did not have to bear any losses.

Nowadays, there is a trend and need to transfer 'toxic assets' of banks to such vehicles to concentrate solely on the wind-down procedure in the most effective manner, without the banking licence and capital requirements attached to it.

This transfer element is reflected in the asset separation tool, as it is described that:

> member states shall ensure that resolution authorities have the power to transfer assets, rights or liabilities of an institution under resolution or bridge institution to one or more asset management vehicles. Such transfer may take place without obtaining the consent of the shareholders of the institution under resolution or any third party other than the bridge institution and without complying with any procedural requirements under company or securities law.[690]

When transferring those assets or contracts to the asset management vehicle:

> resolution authorities shall determine the consideration for which assets, rights and liabilities are transferred to the asset management vehicle in accordance with the principles established in Article 36 in an accordance with the Union State aid framework.[691]

This means that the transfer to the asset management vehicle will be basically effected at fair value.[692] Such transfer at fair value may be much lower than the value the actual assets or contracts may have in the accounts of the transferring institution. Any value being lower in the book value will trigger a loss which will deplete banks'

687. They were created under the *Gesetz zur Fortentwicklung der Finanzmarktstabilisierung* that entered into force on 23 July 2009.
688. *See* Josef Urschitz. Wir hatten noch ein paar Fragen. 12 February 2014. https://www.diepresse.com/1561946/wir-hatten-noch-ein-paar-fragen. The official page on *Bundesministerium für Finanzenon Hypo Alpe Adria* has been deleted. https://www.parlament.gv.at/PAKT/VHG/XXV/J/J_09441/index.shtml.
689. *Sociedad de Gestion de Activos Procedentes de la Restructuracion Bancaria*, created in November 2012. *See* https://www.sareb.es/en_US/about-us/who-we-are. Also *Bagus/Julian/Neira*, p. 95.
690. Article 42(1) of BRRD. *See* Article 26 of SRM-R.
691. Article 42(6) of BRRD. *See* Article 26(2)(b) of SRM-R.
692. Article 36(4)(e) of BRRD. *See* Article 20(5) of SRM-R.

equity, and which will have to be borne by either creditors or shareholders. The only exception is if there would be sufficient equity cushion in place. This is exactly the difference to the bad bank model seen in the past, where such loss effectively was covered by governmental institutions. In the asset separation tool, the other resolution tools come into place to avoid this.

The potential losses under the transfer to the asset management vehicle will have to be allocated either by a bail-in of creditors or by a partial transfer in connection with the bridge bank tool or sale of business tool. Given that it is anticipated that losses may be incurred in connection with the transfer, BRRD provides mechanisms for the allocation of such losses. In most cases, the allocation is to the creditors by one of the resolution tools. For this reason, the asset separation tool can only be used in conjunction with one of the resolution tools.

As an example, one larger institution may have a certain portfolio of NPLs. These loans are 'toxic' because their value is steadily decreasing. However, these loans may have some recovery potential later on. As the loans have to be depreciated in the accounts of the institution, this depreciation would deplete equity. The direct consequence would be a violation of regulatory equity requirements and the assessment of whether the institution is failing or likely to fail. In such a resolution scenario, there are various options:

- One option is that the resolution authority decides to conduct a bail-in on the institution. It could do so to cover the losses incurred by the depreciation of the portfolio. The loans would stay with the institution, and the focus of the bank's management would still be to find an appropriate approach for the portfolio. Management could either sell, write-off or otherwise potentially avoid further depreciation.
- Alternatively, the resolution authority could decide to establish a bridge bank and partial transfer scheme. It could either leave the NPLs behind in the old bank or transfer them to the bridge bank. In both cases, the authority would apply a haircut to creditors and leave certain liabilities behind.

In each of the two options above, there is a loss bearing by creditors. The second commonality is that the problematic assets continue to exist, in the bailed-in institution, or in a bridge bank, or in the institution under insolvency. The latter has the disadvantage that management capacities are still bound by these 'toxic' assets. Potentially equity cushions have to be built to make up for these assets' depreciation and to enable the bank's ongoing operations. Even the institution's name and reputation will be infected by those 'toxic' assets.

Therefore, an isolation of those assets as within a bad bank scheme can be very useful. The asset transfer tool does offer exactly such isolation, which can be combined with any of the other resolution tools. It leads to a ring-fencing of toxic assets into a separate legal entity held by the resolution authority or a public authority. In this case, partial ownership is sufficient; i.e., external investors may also be invited to invest in this vehicle.[693]

The consideration for the asset management vehicle does not necessarily have to be paid in cash but can also be paid by way of debt instruments.[694]

Furthermore, there are some additional conditions for the application of the asset separation tool. Those are:

(a) the situation of the particular market for those assets is of such a nature that the liquidation of those assets under normal insolvency proceedings could have an adverse effect on one or more financial markets;
(b) such a transfer is necessary to ensure the proper functioning of the institution under resolution or bridge institution; or
(c) such a transfer is necessary to maximise liquidation proceeds.

The wording implies that the requirement in paragraph (a) is always necessary and it must be combined either with the requirement in paragraph (b) or with the requirement in paragraph (c).

The asset separation tool may serve as an additional tool to facilitate the liquidation of a certain asset class in a more seamless and more effective way. It avoids that a depreciated asset class continues in the books of the old bank. Moreover, it is possible to offer those assets at an attractive price in the market if haircuts are applied. Potentially, the valuation and the debt instrument being issued to the selling entity could also be coupled with an upside kicker in case those toxic assets regain value.

Furthermore, it is possible to invite external investors into the funding of the asset management vehicle to potentially spread upsides and downsides among various creditors. These may include the creditors of the institution under resolution and the investors funding the asset management vehicle.

§5.22 RESOLUTION FINANCING

[A] Scope of Resolution Financing

At first sight, it seems necessary to explain why external financing is required in a scenario of resolution. That is because the balance sheet of the institution should be restructured in connection with a bail-in or partial transfers. The balance sheet should then be restructured for going concern, so that no external or support financing is necessary anymore. This is usually true for corporates, which are subject to less complex balance sheet requirements. As banks are special corporations, the following issues may arise in their resolution:

- By the time when the balance sheet is restructured, public discussion has probably adversely affected the overall confidence regarding the institution.

693. Article 42(2)(a) of BRRD. *See* cross-reference in Article 26 of SRM-R.
694. Article 42(7) of BRRD. *See* cross-reference in Article 26 of SRM-R.

Creditors, investors, and depositors may have suffered damage, even though the institution is restructured from a balance sheet standpoint. In this scenario, it is still possible that customers call their deposits, or certain creditors and investors do not have the confidence to provide capital or refinancing. In order to restore confidence, it may be essential to provide an additional source of financing for the institution under resolution.

- In the context of bail-in, certain bail-in-able liabilities might not have been bailed in but left out for the reasons foreseen under Article 44(3) of BRRD. In that case, the potential gap can be filled by a contribution through additional resolution financing arrangements.

The illustrative cases above show that an additional source of fresh liquidity must be made available. Under this rationale, one of the cornerstones of BRRD and SRM-R are provisions around resolution financing arrangements.

The purpose of the resolution financing arrangements is described as follows:[695]

(a) to guarantee the assets or the liabilities of the institution under resolution, its subsidiaries, a bridge institution or an asset management vehicle;
(b) to make loans to the institution under resolution, its subsidiaries, a bridge institution or an asset management vehicle;
(c) to purchase assets of the institution under resolution;
(d) to make contributions to a bridge institution and an asset management vehicle;
(e) to pay compensation to shareholders or creditors in accordance with Article 75;
(f) to make a contribution to the institution under resolution in lieu of the write-down or conversion of liabilities of certain creditors, when the bail-in tool is applied and the resolution authority decides to exclude certain creditors from the scope of bail-in in accordance with Article 44(3)–(8);
(g) to lend to other financing arrangements on a voluntary basis in accordance with Article 106;
(h) to take any combination of the actions referred to in points (a)–(g).

An identical scope is contained in the SRM-R with respect to the SRF.[696]

[B] National Financing Arrangements

The national financing arrangements are often also funding vehicles held by governments or governmental agencies in the Member States. Each Member State is required to set up such a fund under BRRD.[697,698]

695. Article 101 of BRRD.
696. Article 71 SRM-R.
697. Article 100 of BRRD; Article 68 of SRM-R.

National funds are responsible for collecting an annual contribution from all national banks. For those national funds located in the Eurozone, the collected funds are transferred to the Single Resolution Fund (SRF).[699] The contributions have two components. On the one hand, it shall consist of a fixed rate. The other component consists of a bank-related contribution mirroring risk exposure, strategy and size of the institution.[700]

In addition to the annual *ex ante* contributions, *ex post* contributions can also be drawn up in exceptional circumstances from the institutions. However, *ex post* contributions are limited to an amount of three times the annual contribution.[701]

Therefore, national funds set up in each Member State are responsible for collecting *ex ante* (regular) and *ex post* (extraordinary) contributions from the banking institutions in their territory. The total target to be filled by regular *ex ante* contributions is to be achieved by 2024. The envisaged amount is 1 % of all covered deposits.[702]

[C] External Financing

The national financing arrangements, the national funds or the SRF, as the case may be, can borrow money from third-party institutions. This may happen if:

> not sufficient to cover the losses, costs or other expenses incurred by the use of the financing arrangements, and the extraordinary ex-post contributions provided for in Article 104 are not sufficient or immediately accessible.[703]

Those external sources can also be the direct recapitalisation instrument by the ESM.[704] This may be used provided that the required funding complies with the rules and purposes of the ESM statutes.

[D] Deposit Guarantee Schemes

A further source for financing is found in the DGSs. In an insolvency situation, they are usually expected to step in and pay out to the covered amount of deposits. In contrast, in the context of a resolution, funds of DGSs may be spared. For instance, covered deposits are not eligible in a bail-in scenario. Also, in a bridge bank scenario, deposits

698. For instance, Germany has instituted a bank resolution fund at the beginning of 2011: Restructuring fund created under the Restructuring Act. *See* fundamental features of the Restructuring Act on https://www.bundesbank.de/resource/blob/707210/d60f5843069da07d666b02f2e8706c8f/mL/2011-06-fundamental-features-german-bank-restructuring-act-data.pdf.
699. See chapter [G] below.
700. Article 103(7) of BRRD; *see* Article 70(6) of SRM-R.
701. Article 104(1) of BRRD; Article 71(1) of SRM-R.
702. Covered deposits means the part of eligible deposits that does not exceed EUR 100,000. Article 2(1)(5) of Directive 2014/49/EU of the European Parliament and of the Council of 16 April 2014 on deposit guarantee schemes.
703. Article 105 BRRD. Similarly, Article 72 of the SRM-R.
704. *See* below Section Chapter 5 section 5.22[G] with respect to recent developments on the statues and powers of the ESM, respectively its ability to lend money to the SRF.

may be transferred in a partial transfer and not undergo an insolvency process. Therefore, when these resolution tools are applied, the DGSs are effectively saved.

However, such a saving is not an objective of the resolution process. Hence, BRRD and the SRM-R have a countermeasure. Both legal instruments foresee that the DGSs shall inject cash in the amount that would have been spent in case of an insolvency of the institution. This injection serves to assist in the financing of the resolution and is capped in an amount of 50% of the target level of the respective DGS.[705] This is another source of financing that is funded by contributions of the various private banks on a national level.[706]

[E] Borrowing Between Financing Arrangements

The final source of financing is the borrowing between national financing arrangements. It may be called upon, e.g., in case the amounts collected by the relevant national fund are not sufficient. Then, this national fund may request other funds to provide lending if:

(a) the amounts raised under Article 103 of BRRD are not sufficient to cover the losses, costs or other expenses incurred by the use of the financing arrangements;
(b) the extraordinary *ex post* contributions provided for in Article 104 of BRRD are not immediately accessible; and
(c) the alternative funding means provided for in Article 105 of BRRD are not immediately accessible on reasonable terms.[707]

[F] The Single Resolution Fund

The fundraising for the SRF is executed through the national financing arrangements. Even though the SRM is applicable in general to those banks which are subject to direct supervision by the ECB,[708] the *ex ante* contributions to the Single Resolution Fund are paid by all credit institutions in the Eurozone. Funds are nationally collected and are transferred to the SRF annually. The SRB holds the SRF.[709]

The purpose of the SRF is identical to the purposes of the national financing arrangements as described above. This Fund shall support the financing of the institution under resolution with the measures described in Article 71 of SRM-R. Also, the SRF has the same sources of further financing as the national financing arrangements, i.e. *ex ante* and *ex post* contributions. Both types of contributions are raised by

705. Article 109(5) of BRRD.
706. *See* Chapter 1, section 1.04[B].
707. Article 106 of BRRD.
708. And other cross-border groups, *see* Article 7(2)(b) SRM-R.
709. Article 64 of the SRM-R. *See also* SRB webpage https://srb.europa.eu/en/content/single-resolution-fund.

the national funds upon a decision by the SRB and transferred to the SRF. Similarly, alternative funding means and contributions by the DGSs can be used in the context of a resolution under the SRM.[710]

The SRF holds national compartments, where the national financing arrangements make transfers into. These compartments hold contributions for a period not longer than eight years. Starting from 2016, the compartments will be progressively merged. The use of the moneys collected in each of the compartments for financing of a cross-border resolution is explicitly stated and detailed in an intergovernmental agreement.[711]

The general approach is that the compartments are relatively strictly allocated to financing for situations in the respective Member State at first. Thereafter, they are slowly watered down and fully merged into one fund at the end of the transitional period.[712] As of 17 July 2019, SRB announced that the SRF received a cash injection of EUR 7.8 billion from 3,186 institutions for the year 2019. This brought the total amount in the SRF to just under EUR 33 billion. The target size of the SRF is intended to be at least 1 % of covered deposits by the end of 2023, which is expected to be about EUR 60 billion.[713]

Figure 5.3 sets out the mechanics of the interplay between various fundraising mechanisms.

710. Article 73 of the SRM-R.
711. Article 5 of the Intergovernmental Agreement dated 14 May 2014.
712. Article 69 of the SRM-R.
713. *See* SRB's press release titled SRF grows to €33 billion after latest round of transfers of 17 July 2019 on https://srb.europa.eu/en/node/804.

Figure 5.3 *European Resolution Financing Mechanisms*

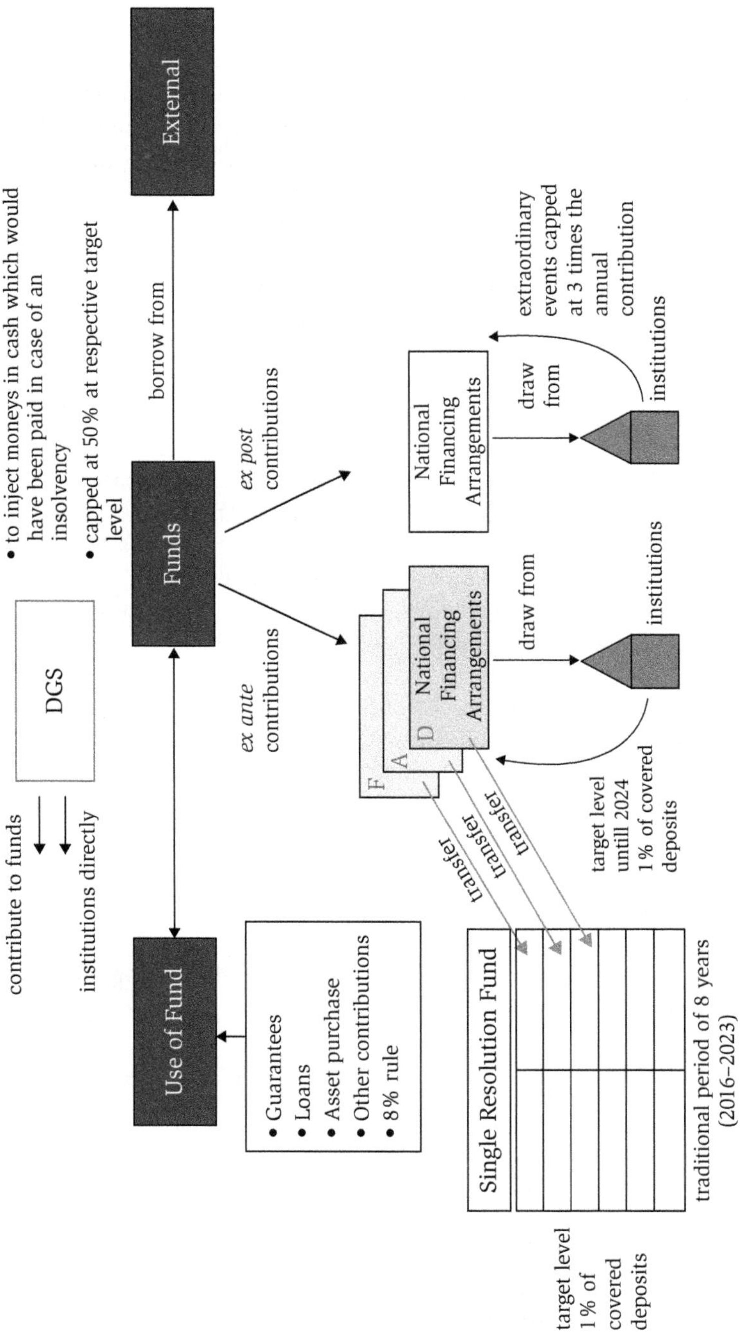

Source: Compiled by author from various sources.

§5.23 GROUP RESOLUTION

[A] General Background

Banks are rarely organised as a single entity corporation but in almost every case as a group of corporations. Large banking institutions very often have dozens, if not hundreds, of subsidiaries, spread all over the world. For instance, the Lehman group had over hundreds of affiliated companies, subsidiaries, and branches when Lehman became bankrupt.[714] Various insolvency processes started with office holders appointed by various national courts in different countries. One of the main elements of the various bankruptcy proceedings was to separate the assets of the various entities and allocate them properly to the respective states. Disconnecting and reallocating assets to single entities was a challenge as the firm was run on a group basis rather than on a single entity basis.[715]

The Lehman case is not an exception. Often the reality in going concern is that banks, cash flows, and assets are transferred centrally while legal entity responsibility remains locally. Therefore, the saying is true that groups live global but 'die' local.[716] Now, resolution generally is aiming for going concern rather than winding down and liquidating an entity. This is the case at least for the healthy and systemic part of the institution. Therefore, it is not as much about unwinding the group and isolating it on an entity-by-entity basis. Nonetheless, as resolution is a restructuring and an insolvency-related exercise, the single entity-by-entity approach plays an important role.

In light of that, the EU jurisdictions do not have a consolidated bankruptcy procedure. Under BRRD, resolution always takes place with respect to the affected legal entity. This matches the principle that creditors contract with a legal entity rather than with the whole group.[717]

From this reasoning, certain questions derive:

(i) In a group crisis, how should the trigger points for starting resolution be defined? Should they be defined on an entity or on a group basis?
(ii) If separate resolution authorities are competent for various entities, how should they interact? Also, how can the parent's resolution authority apply resolution measures against the will of the subsidiaries' resolution authorities?

714. First Joint Administrator's Progress Report regarding the Administration of Lehman Brothers International (Europe) by PriceWaterhouseCoopers on 14 April 2009, http://www.pwc.co.uk/en_uk/uk/assets/pdf/lbie-progress-report-140409.pdf.
715. Lehman Brothers International (Europe) has more than 4,000 counterparties all over the world.
716. 'Sir Mervyn King, the former governor of the Bank of England, famously commented that "global banks are international in life but national in death".' *See* http://www.economist.com/news/special-report/21587378-2008-global-financial-integration-has-gone-reverse-too-much-good-thing.
717. *Gleeson* in: *Dombret/Kenadjian*, p. 27.

(iii) How to establish exceptions to the general entity-by-entity rule in connection with the capital instruments, write-down provision?[718]

[B] Trigger Points in a Group Resolution

It may be the case that in a banking group the holding company is failing or likely to fail, while subsidiaries are still running on a relatively stable rhythm.

With respect to this constellation, BRRD is clear. Resolution measures shall apply only with respect to the very institution which is failing or likely to fail. It is not possible to apply them to the rest of the group if the other entities are still stable. This is reflected in Article 37(2) BRRD, which mentions the applicability of resolution tools only to an institution. Also, Article 32 mentions the conditions for resolution to be measured on an entity-by-entity basis:

> Member States shall ensure that resolution authorities shall take a resolution action in relation to an institution referred to in point (a) of Article 1(1) only if the resolution authority considers that all of the following conditions are met:
>
> (a) the determination that the institution is failing or is likely to fail has been made by the competent authority.

Therefore, a trigger point for a bail-in at an institution is assessed at the level of the very entity subject to the resolution. There is a loosening to this rule with respect to financial holding companies[719] and parent financial holding companies.[720] If two or more subsidiaries of a financial holding company or a parent financial holding company are failing, the resolution authority may have the power to act on the parent level.[721]

Furthermore, there is an additional exception to that rule with respect to the capital instruments and the write-down tool.[722]

---

718. Article 59 of BRRD and Article 21 of SRM-R.
719. 'Financial holding company means a financial institution, the subsidiaries of which are exclusively or mainly institutions or financial institutions, and which is not a mixed financial holding company; the subsidiaries of a financial institution are mainly institutions or financial institutions where at least one of them is an institution and where more than 50% of the financial institution's equity, consolidated assets, revenues, personnel or other indicator considered relevant by the competent authority are associated with subsidiaries that are institutions or financial institutions.' Article 4(1)(20) of CRR.
720. 'Parent financial holding company in a member state means a financial holding company which is not itself a subsidiary of an institution authorised in the same member state, or of a financial holding company or mixed financial holding company set up in the same member state.' Article 4(1)(30) of CRR.
721. Article 33(4) of BRRD.
722. *See* section 5.16[H].

[C] Single or Multiple Points of Entry

It is clear that in most cases the authority can only act with respect to one concerned legal entity and not generally within a group. However, there may be a situation where in fact a knock-on effect is taking place. Hence, if the top parent company is in difficulties, many of the subsidiaries may be as well, since they are all tied together.

In that circumstance, the resolution authority or authorities have the option to become active only at one point within the group or at several points within the group. This optionality is discussed under the word of single point of entry (SPE)[723] or multiple points of entry (MPE). Under Commission Delegated Regulation 2016/1075, SPE strategy is defined as a resolution strategy involving the application of resolution powers by a single resolution authority at the level of a single parent undertaking or of a single institution subject to consolidated supervision. MPE, on the other hand, is defined as a resolution strategy involving the application of resolution powers by two or more resolution authorities to regional or functional subgroups or entities of a group.[724]

BRRD generally focuses on an entity-by-entity basis and does not make any prescription for SPE or MPE.

Rather, it allows for both in the context of the MREL requirement:

> This Directive adopts a 'top down' approach to the determination of the minimum requirement for own funds and eligible liabilities (MREL) within a group. The approach further recognizes that resolution action is applied at the level of the individual legal person, and that it is imperative that loss-absorbing capacity is located in, or accessible to, the legal person within the group in which losses occur. To that end, resolution authorities should ensure that loss-absorbing capacity within a group is distributed across the group in accordance with the level of risk in its constituent legal persons. The minimum requirement necessary for each individual subsidiary should be separately assessed. Furthermore, resolution authorities should ensure that all capital and liabilities which are counted towards the consolidated minimum requirement are located in entities where losses are liable to occur, or are otherwise available to absorb losses.[725]

While the Directive is open on that point, institutions are working on suitable structures in their resolution plans. In the US, a structure with the SPE strategy at the holding level was introduced by FDIC in accordance with the authority granted by Title II of the Dodd-Frank Wall Street Reform and Consumer Protection Act (the 'Dodd-Frank Act').[726]

723. *See Maria J. Nieto,* Third-Country Relations in the Directive Establishing a Framework for the Recovery and Resolution of Credit Institutions, 2014. Banco de Espana, Documentos de Trabajo 1409 (2014) http://www.bde.es/f/webbde/SES/Secciones/Publicaciones/PublicacionesSeriadas/DocumentosTrabajo/14/Fich/dt1409e.pdf.

724. Commission Delegated Regulation (EU) 2016/1075- Article 2(5) for SPE and Article 2(6) for MPE.

725. Recital 80 of BRRD.

726. The Federal Deposit Insurance Corporation published the SPE strategy in December 2013. https://www.fdic.gov/news/board/2013/2013-12-10_notice_dis-b_fr.pdf.

By an SPE holding structure, the holding company pushes down the operational banking business into various subsidiaries. The holding structure itself neither has banking activities nor takes up deposits. Actually, it operates as a normal holding company, which issues bail-in-able liabilities on the capital markets, such as senior unsecured bonds or subordinated bonds. In a resolution scenario, such structure would enable the authorities to apply the bail-in at the holding level. This would restore the capital and equity of the holding level and leave the operational banking businesses intact. Various banks are currently assessing the SPE structure. They are also examining how this structure can be set up in a way that would work in a resolution scenario.[727]

One argument against such a structure is that a group's difficulties will often come from operating businesses. Hence, there must also be the possibility to apply resolution measures directly at such operating businesses.[728] However, looking from a mere capital structure perspective, operation at the holding company can be more efficient. The parent shall serve as the issuing company for bonds in the capital markets for only financing purposes. Once the parent restores the capital adequacy of the top company, it potentially also restores the financial soundness of the group. By introducing the concept of a resolution group and IMREL,[729] BRRD focuses on recapitalising the resolution group in case of a resolution by applying the resolution tools at the level of the resolution entity including the possibility to write down IMREL[730] at the level of the subsidiaries of the resolution entity. However, it is important to note that these provisions are for resolution planning purposes (and hence may be deviated from in an actual resolution scenario) and still leave options open for an MPE or SPE strategy.

[D] Authorities Responsible for Group Resolution Measures

As resolution is conducted on entity-by-entity basis, different resolution authorities may be competent for different legal entities.

In the reach of the SRM, the SRB will be the competent resolution authority. The covered institutions are those that form part of a group within and which are located in the Eurozone.[731] There should be no harmonisation difficulties under these circumstances, as the SRB decides on the resolution strategy. Thereafter, it instructs the national resolution authorities to execute the resolution decision. The whole idea and concept of setting up an SRM solely serves the purpose of avoiding a lengthy and

727. For instance, Bank of America has contemplated this structure in its resolution plan published on 1 July 2014. *See* Public Executive Summary for Bank of America Corporation Resolution Plan, Bank of America, N.A. Resolution Plan, and FIA Card Services, N.A. Resolution Plan. https://www.fdic.gov/regulations/reform/resplans/plans/boa-fia-idi-7114.pdf.
728. In order to deal with situations where a specific subsidiary is raising concern, entities should be 'sufficiently separable' so that they can be resolved separately in case this fallback approach is necessary. *See* p. 14 of Guidance on Developing Effective Resolution Strategies regarding Recovery and Resolution Planning for Systemically Important Financial, issued by the FSB on 16 July 2013. http://www.financialstabilityboard.org/publications/r_130716b.pdf.
729. *See* Articles 2(83b) and 45 f BRRD.
730. *See* above Chapter 5 section 5.17 and Chapter 6 below on internal MREL.
731. Article 2 of the SRM-R and Article 7(1) SRM-R.

complicated coordination among different competent authorities for institutions that are located within the Eurozone.

Outside the Eurozone, it may be possible that one resolution authority is competent for a subsidiary institution and another resolution authority is competent for the group's parent institution. An example could be the case of Poland or Hungary, which do not form part of the Eurozone. In this case, the resolution authorities competent for the parent may also seek to apply certain resolution measures with respect to one of the subsidiaries located abroad. This may well be a subsidiary in Warsaw, e.g.

As the entry triggers are assessed on an entity-by-entity basis, the competent authorities for applying resolution tools are assessed on an entity-by-entity basis. Hence, it is not possible for the parent resolution authority to order bail-in at a subsidiary outside its reach if a different resolution authority is competent. For instance, the German resolution authority would not be entitled to apply a bail-in to a subsidiary of the institution under resolution in Warsaw. In such a case, the various resolution authorities will have to coordinate among each other.

Articles 91 and 92 of BRRD lay out detailed procedural provisions for the coordination among resolution authorities. Group resolution authorities must form a resolution college.[732] They must agree on a resolution scheme which can be proposed by the top resolution authority within twenty-four hours.[733] Any of the relevant resolution authorities may disagree with the scheme or any of the proposed resolution measures by the parent resolution authority. In this case, the dissenting resolution authority can apply other resolution tools with respect to its own relevant institution. In order to do so, it has to set out detailed reasons for adopting a different approach in writing.[734]

When it comes to third-country involvement outside the EU, BRRD per se is not binding on them. The Directive envisages that individual agreements may be entered into with regards to the cooperation between the various resolution authorities.[735] Those agreements could also be of key importance, especially when the main financial hubs like New York, Tokyo, Hong Kong, or Singapore are involved. In respect of the UK, given the Brexit, it will have to be seen which arrangements between the UK and the EU are going to be entered into.

[E] Write-Down of Capital Instruments in a Group Context

In addition to the resolution tools in the narrow sense, there is also the possibility to write-down capital instruments and IMREL on a 'stand-alone' basis.[736] Those capital instruments are defined as Additional Tier 1 and Tier 2 capital instruments required for

732. *See* Article 88 of BRRD.
733. Article 91(4) of BRRD.
734. Article 91(8) of BRRD.
735. Article 93 of BRRD.
736. Article 59 of BRRD; Article 21 of SRM-R.

regulatory purposes to comply with the own fund requirements. Those capital instruments often come along as hybrid bond structures with loss bearing elements and a deep subordination that brings them very close to true equity. However, they can be issued less formally and spread broader on the capital markets. They are of interest for certain types of investors that may not be allowed to take real equity, such as insurance companies and pension funds. It is logical that those instruments need to be written down first and converted into real Tier 1 equity before subordinated and senior liabilities are bailed in.[737] For the purpose of own funds, regulatory requirements and capital ratios, a consolidated approach may be adopted. Thereunder, certain amounts of these capital instruments in a subsidiary count towards the consolidated own fund requirements. Hence, this consolidated approach is to some extent also carried on into the capital instruments write-down tool.

Article 59(4) BRRD sets out that not only the entity shall be deemed no longer viable but also the group shall be deemed no longer viable if the group is failing or likely to fail. Moreover, it sets out that:[738]

> For the purposes of point (a) of paragraph 4, a group shall be deemed to be failing or likely to fail where the group infringes or there are objective elements to support a determination that the group, in the near future, will infringe its consolidated prudential requirements in a way that would justify action by the competent authority including but not limited to because the group has incurred or is likely to incur losses that will deplete all or a significant amount of its own funds.

This wording means that the trigger point for starting the capital write-down tool does not cover the single entity, but the group as a whole. Furthermore, on group level, the trigger point is somehow loosened up if compared to the entity-by-entity approach, as there is reference to the infringement of the consolidated prudential requirements that would justify action by the competent authority. This appears less strict as the failing or likely to fail requirement under Article 32(4)(a) BRRD which refers - on an entity level - to the withdrawal of the authorisation.

Therefore, if a resolution authority decides to write down capital instruments, it can look at each entity under its scope of competence, and also look at the group as a whole. This is necessary to assess if the group will infringe its consolidated prudential requirements in the near future. The resolution authority could then start a capital instruments write-down with respect to a subsidiary which is not failing or likely to fail, provided that the group as a whole would on a consolidated basis breach its own fund requirements. Such an assessment would, under the remit of the SRM, be done according to the procedure laid out in Article 18 SRM-R, which means that in the first instance the ECB would be competent but also the SRB may make such an assessment after informing the ECB.[739]

Outside the remit of the SRM, the question is which authority is competent for making the determination under Article 59(3) BRRD. This issue is identical to the one

737. *See* section 5.16.
738. Article 59(6) of BRRD and Article 21(5) of SRM-R.
739. Article 18(1) SRM, if the ECB does not make such an assessment within three calendar days following a notification by the SRB.

above in relation to the resolution tools. The distinction is that it is possible to look at the group as a whole in respect of the write-down tool, but not for the regular resolution tools. Perhaps the group consolidated resolution authority could have been empowered to make that determination also with respect to a subsidiary institution located in a different Member State. However, the Directive takes the conservative approach of entity-to-entity level.[740] In case of a determination related to a group, both the consolidated supervisor and the supervisor at the level of the issuing entity will need to take a joint decision.[741]

740. Article 61 of BRRD.
741. Article 61(4) of BRRD.

CHAPTER 6

Resolution Planning and MREL

§6.01 SCOPE AND BACKGROUND

Logically resolution planning should come before actual resolution, hence should be included in a prior chapter. Why at the end of a book? The concept of resolution planning can only be understood after the complexity of the resolution has been explained. This is why it comes as final chapter and now is relatively self-explanatory. As the resolution tools like bridge bank or bail-in are highly complex, one of the key questions asked is whether they will actually work in practice. Often the argument is raised that the bail-in tool would not work, because there are either not enough bail-in-able liabilities or the liabilities would not be governed by relevant laws or simply because the interconnectedness of the banks' structure is too complex for a tool like this. Similar arguments are brought with respect to the bridge bank tool, especially in connection with partial transfers.

Therefore, in order to make these tools work, the concept of resolution planning comes into play. The rule is that each institution shall be resolvable either through ordinary insolvency proceedings or through the application of the resolution tools, however, without any extraordinary financial support.[742]

§6.02 MREL

'MREL is possibly the best-known condition to making banks resolvable.'[743] MREL stands for Minimum Requirement of Eligible Liabilities. That acronym has become well known since BRRD has come into force. It aims at ensuring that banks have sufficient

742. *See Schelo/Steck*, ZBB 2103, 227 seq. Article 10 of BRRD. *See also* Article 8(6)(a) of SRM-R.
743. Chair of the SRB, 22 July 2019.

bail-in-able liabilities ready for resolution. Sometimes MREL is also referred to as 'Resolution Capital'.[744]

A liability can only be counted for MREL if it has a remaining maturity of at least one year.[745] By contrast, liabilities with a maturity of less than seven days are excluded from a bail-in.[746] Therefore, there is an apparent discrepancy between eligible liabilities for bail-in catalogue and the MREL requirement. This is presumably so because an instrument with a maturity longer than seven days may be actually used for bail-in. On the other hand, it may be risky to account it as MREL. When it comes to a resolution planning scenario over the course of a year, such a liability may already have been repaid (or can be withdrawn in a crisis).[747] Since the MREL requirements are assessed on a yearly basis as included in the resolution plan, there must be an appropriate degree of caution.[748] A remaining year before maturity will be necessary for a liability to qualify for MREL calculation. For refinancing purposes, short-term liabilities less than seven days may be attractive for investors. However, this may be disadvantageous from the bank's perspective. Since those short-term liabilities are not 'bail-in-able', they would not count for the MREL requirement.

This also means that any deposits will not count against MREL as these – at least usually – have maturities with less than a year.[749] For the purposes of MREL, there may only be a few types of senior liabilities which can count against MREL. As deposits, secured liabilities, any short-term liabilities are excluded, basically senior bonds would count against MREL.[750]

The BRRD and SRM-R have been amended and the new versions are in force since 27 June 2019. The focus of the so-called banking package (i.e., BRRD, SRM-R and CRR collectively) lies on resolution planning. For these purposes, the banking package has extended the rules on MREL and implemented the TLAC standards into the EU legislation. Subordination requirement for MREL liabilities has been strengthened and streamlined.[751] Furthermore, a more effective process for removing the impediments to resolution has been introduced along with reporting and disclosure requirements for banks regarding their MREL quota.[752] While newly amended BRRD and SRM-R will become effective by the end of 2020, CRR has been effective as of 27 June 2019. As the TLAC standards have been implemented into CRR, this has the effect that for G-SIIs TLAC standards have to be fulfilled earlier than MREL standards for non-G-SIIs banks. This is also one of the reasons why the rule on eligible liabilities (section 6.02 [A]) has

744. EconoTimes. Moody's: European legislative developments and global resolution framework implementation impact creditor hierarchies, increase complexity. 5 May 2016. https://www.econotimes.com/Moodys-European-legislative-developments-and-global-resolution-framework-implementation-impact-creditor-hierarchies-increase-complexity-204766.
745. Article 72a(1)(b) CRR, Article 45b(9)(b) BRRD, Article 12c(9)(b) SRM-R.
746. Article 72a(2)(h) and (i) CRR.
747. SRB. MREL: Approach taken in 2016 and next steps. https://srb.europa.eu/sites/srbsite/files/srb_mrel_approach_2016_post_final.pdf, para. 11.
748. The plan shall also include a deadline for compliance with the defined MREL obligation. Article 8(9) of the SRM-R.
749. Article 72a(2)(a)–(d) CRR, Article 45b BRRD, Article 12c SRM-R.
750. Article 72a(2)(e) CRR, Article 45b BRRD, Article 12c SRM-R.
751. Article 72b CRR.
752. Article 45i BRRD, Articles 433 and 437 CRR.

been transferred from BRRD into CRR. Furthermore, BRRD provides for a more harmonised stay of enforcement powers (moratorium) and more extensive rules on the acknowledgement of third-country liabilities.[753] The focus of this chapter will be on the changes of MREL and resolution planning. While MREL is a key element of resolution planning, there is more to it.[754] Banks are, *inter alia*, expected to organise their governance and the collection of resolution-specific data.[755] In addition, banks are asked by means of 'bail-in playbooks' to rehearse and plan for a potential bail-in scenario.[756]

Since the first version of BRRD and SRM-R came into force in 2016, the meaning and role of MREL has expanded. For the purpose of resolution planning, MREL will play a key role. In a so-called open bank bail-in,[757] the more the losses can be absorbed and the better the bank can be recapitalised in principle, the higher the stability is. Even more in connection with the transfer tools, like the sale of business tool, the more reliable and predictable the availability of capital for loss absorption is, the easier it will be to find an investor to transfer the shares of the business.

In order to facilitate such transfer, it is important to have a predictable and reliable amount of bail-in-able capital available. But this principle is not new. The revision of the BRRD and SRM-R, however, has tried to provide uniformity to the quality and the amount of MREL for various types of institutions. According to Article 45b(1) BRRD,[758] eligible liabilities are now covered and dealt within CRR and hence have been transferred from the regime in previous BRRD to CRR.[759]

The parallel application and cross-references between BRRD (respectively SRM-R) and CRR make the understanding of these laws rather complex. In addition, the rules further differentiate between various types of banks in respect of MREL and

753. Article 55 BRRD. Also *see* above Chapter 5 section 5.15.
754. The SRB has recently started a process regarding expectations for banks which, in terms of resolution planning, goes far beyond MREL (*see* SRB. Expectations for Banks 2019. https://srb.europa.eu/sites/srbsite/files/srb_expectations_for_banks_2019.pdf and SRB. Expectations for Banks. March 2020. https://srb.europa.eu/sites/srbsite/files/efb_main_doc_final_web_0.pdf). It introduces bank governance specific requirements as well as specific actions to remove impediments to resolution like the transferability of contracts or introducing a bail-in playbook. The way forward for SRB for 2019-2020 has been to prepare the bail-in playbook. *See* the recently published Operational Guidance on Bail-In Playbooks available at: https://srb.europa.eu/sites/srbsite/files/srb_operational_guidance_on_bail-in_playbooks.pdf. *See also* SRB. Banking Industry Dialogue Meeting. 18 June 2019. https://srb.europa.eu/sites/srbsite/files/presentation_on_srb_resolution_planning.pdf slides 10-13.
755. *See* section 3 Governance, communication, disclosure obligations and business reorganisation plan of the SRB's Operational Guidance on Bail-In Playbooks.
756. *See* section 1,2 General Expectations for Playbooks in SRB's Operational Guidance on Bail-In Playbooks.
757. In an open bank bail-in, the bank remains a going concern and the bail-in process is triggered to effect bank recapitalisation to restore it to health – *see* Emilios Avgouleas and Charles Goodheart. Critical Reflections on Bank Bail-ins. March 2015. Journal of Financial Regulation Vol. 1 Issue 1. When applied to an operating subsidiary, this approach requires write-down and conversion of liabilities and instruments subject to bail-in into equity under a shorter time frame. *See* FSB. Principles on Bail in Execution. 21 June 2018. https://www.fsb.org/wp-content/uploads/P210618-1.pdf.
758. Article 12c(1) SRM-R.
759. The requirements for eligible liabilities have also been deleted from SRM-R.

between various types of parameters for measurement, i.e. an RWA approach (TREA), an approach based on the overall risk assets (Leverage Ratio Exposure Measure 'LREM') and an approach based on the total liabilities and own funds (TLOF) principle. Finally, although the new rules contain standardised minimum requirements of MREL, there are further provisions for flexible amounts and additional top-ups. Therefore, there are a lot of different elements that come into play which make the application of the amended rules difficult. However, the guiding principles have not changed.

[A] Eligible Liabilities for MREL

According to Article 45b(1) BRRD,[760] liabilities shall be included in the amount of own funds and eligible liabilities, if and where they satisfy the conditions of Article 72a and Article 72b CRR.[761] Liabilities that arise from debt instruments with embedded derivatives such as structured notes generally do not count towards MREL.[762] Furthermore, under some circumstances, according to Article 45b(3) in connection with Article 45f(2) BRRD, certain intragroup liabilities can count as MREL as laid down under the provisions of IMREL.[763]

In Article 72a CRR, eligible liabilities items shall consist of eligible liabilities instruments as defined in Article 72b CRR and Tier 2 instruments with a residual maturity of at least one year. The remaining provisions of Article 72a CRR work as an exclusion catalogue which was contained in Article 45(4) BRRD,[764] the prior version of BRRD. Now, this catalogue not only has been transferred and merged with the catalogue of excluded liabilities for bail-in but has also been further supplemented. It is to be noted that this catalogue still exists in the bail-in provisions in Article 44 of BRRD,[765] but logically would also not count as eligible liabilities for MREL.

The supplementation concerns some further wording around deposits, whereas now sight deposits, short-term deposits and deposits from small - and medium-sized companies above the EUR 100,000 deposit insurance threshold are also explicitly excluded from the MREL eligible liabilities catalogue.[766] Materially, this is not different from the prior version. The same result was effectively reached through the requirement that liabilities with a maturity of at least one year (which deposits usually would not have) will be counted as per previous Article 45(4)(d) of BRRD.[767] The maturity of at least one year has now been transferred into Article 72c CRR (amortisation of eligible liabilities instruments with some further provisions with respect to early redemption options prior to the original maturity date).

760. Article 12c(1) SRM-R.
761. This is albeit the exception of the subordination requirement mentioned in Article 72b(2)(d) and Article 72c CRR.
762. Article 12c(2) SRM-R, Article 45b(2) BRRD.
763. Article 12c(3) SRM-R in connection with Article 12g(2) SRM-R.
764. Article 12(16) SRM-R.
765. Article 27(3) SRM-R.
766. It complements Directive 2014/49/EU on deposit guarantee scheme for protection of deposits up to EUR 100,000.
767. Article 12(16)(d) SRM-R.

The main body of Article 72b CRR now defines the requirements for eligible liabilities instruments. Some of these requirements again stem from the original wording of Article 45(4) BRRD.[768] However, some of them are new and are flashed out in more detail. The key requirements are as follows:

- Liabilities are directly issued by an institution and are fully paid up. The acquisition of ownership is not funded directly or indirectly by the resolution entity. Liabilities are neither secured nor subject to a guarantee by the institution or its subsidiaries respectively a parent undertaking or an undertaking that has close links with these entities.
- Liabilities are not subject to set-off or netting arrangements that would undermine the capacity to absorb losses in resolution.
- Liabilities are not redeemable by the holders of the instruments prior to their maturity except in cases referred to in Article 70c(2) CRR.
- Provisions governing their liabilities do not give the holder the right to accelerate the future scheduled payment of interest or principle other than in the case of the insolvency or liquidation of the resolution entity.
- The level of interest or dividend payments due is not amended on the basis of their credit standing of the resolution entity.
- For instruments issued after 28 June 2021, the relevant contractual documentation and where applicable the prospectus related to the issuance explicitly refer to the possible exercise of the write-down and conversion powers in accordance with Article 48 BRRD.[769] This is to increase transparency for investors which might not be familiar with the statutory provisions.

The resolution authority may also accept contractual bail-in instruments for the MREL quota.[770] The conditions are that the instrument:

(a) contains a contractual term providing that, where a resolution authority decides to apply the bail-in tool to that institution, the instrument shall be written down or converted to the extent required before other eligible liabilities are written down or converted; and
(b) is subject to a binding subordination agreement, undertaking or provision under which, in the event of normal insolvency proceedings, it ranks below other eligible liabilities and cannot be repaid until other eligible liabilities outstanding at the time have been settled.

Contractual bail-in instruments may be relevant in case of foreign law liabilities, where it is uncertain that the bail-in tool may actually be recognised by that very

768. Article 12(16) SRM-R.
769. The bail-in playbook guidance expects banks to include a detailed description of all internal processes related to the decision of the resolution authority to reduce instruments and convert them into equity. This needs to be in line with the sequence of write-down and conversion envisaged in Article 4 48 BRRD (see par 49).
770. Article 12(12) of Regulation (EU) No 806/2014 of 15 July 2014.

jurisdiction. In order to create sufficient bail-in-able debt, such contractual bail-in clauses would need to be inserted.[771]

[1] Subordination

Of special importance within that paragraph is the subordination requirement which is listed in Article 72b(d) CRR as being a requirement for eligible liabilities instruments.

The question is how the rationale regarding subordination is justifiable. The FSB argues that bailing in senior debt could trigger uncertainties.[772] Those creditors bailed in could claim that they would receive a lower quota than in insolvency, as many senior creditors may be excluded from bail-in. However, that concern needs to be looked at closer. In an insolvency, senior bonds would under the insolvency ranking introduced by BRRD rank last under the senior claims, while other senior claims, like deposits from small - and medium-sized companies (above EUR 100,000) and covered deposits (until EUR 100,000) respectively deposit protection scheme recourse claims would rank ahead and would hence be paid before the senior bonds. Therefore, those creditors could not be taken up into the same class. It is rather the deposits above EUR 100,000 from large companies which would rank alongside the senior bonds. Now in an insolvency scenario, those senior creditors with prior ranking would be paid a quota first and only once they had received, a quota of 100%, senior bonds would receive a quota. Therefore, as long as in a hypothetical insolvency 'the value' breaks in classes prior to senior bonds, those creditors could not claim to be treated worse by a bail-in, as also in insolvency they had received a quota of 0%. In those circumstances, the resolution authority could exclude from bail-in further senior liabilities for systemic reasons[773] at the same rank without conflicts on the no creditors worse-off principle. It should be noted that in a hypothetical insolvency, liquidation values are commonly taken into account which usually lead to much lower values and lower quotas. This issue is addressed in section 11 of the FSB Draft Term Sheet:[774]

> 11. Priority. Eligible TLAC must absorb losses prior to liabilities excluded from TLAC in insolvency or in resolution and, in all cases, without giving rise to material risk of successful legal challenge or valid compensation claims; and authorities must ensure that this is transparent to creditors (see Section 20 for disclosure requirements). To ensure that eligible external TLAC absorbs losses prior to liabilities that are excluded from TLAC (see Section 10) and therefore to support the aim of ensuring that the G-SIB is credibly and feasibly resolvable, eligible instruments must be:
>   a. contractually subordinated to excluded liabilities on the balance sheet of the resolution entity ('contractual subordination'). They may, however, rank senior to capital instruments, including Tier 2 subordinated debt, in the insolvency creditor hierarchy if they meet all criteria;

771. CoCos may count as contractual bail-in instruments. *See* Chapter 3, section 3.05 above.
772. FSB. Principles on Bail in Execution. 21 June 2018. https://www.fsb.org/wp-content/uploads/P210618-1.pdf.
773. Article 44(2) and (3) of BRRD.
774. FSB. TLAC Term Sheet. 9 November 2015. https://www.fsb.org/wp-content/uploads/TLAC-Principles-and-Term-Sheet-for-publication-final.pdf.

b. junior in the statutory creditor hierarchy to excluded liabilities on the balance sheet of the resolution entity ('statutory subordination'); or
c. issued by a resolution entity which does not have any excluded liabilities (for example, a holding company) on its balance sheet that rank pari passu or junior to TLAC-eligible instruments on its balance sheet ('structural subordination').

Subordination of eligible external TLAC to excluded liabilities is not required if:

(i) the amount of excluded liabilities (Section 10) on the balance sheet of the resolution entity that rank pari passu or junior to the TLAC-eligible liabilities does not exceed 5% of the resolution entity's eligible external TLAC;
(ii) the resolution authority of the G-SIB has the authority to differentiate among pari passu creditors in resolution;
(iii) differentiation in resolution in favour of such excluded liabilities would not give risk to material risk of successful legal challenge or valid compensation claims; and
(iv) this does not have a material adverse impact on resolvability.

In all cases, the means of subordination of eligible external TLAC to excluded liabilities, the risk of successful legal challenge or valid compensation claims, and the transparency of the order in which creditors can expect to bear losses in the insolvency or in resolution, is subject to discussion in the CMG and review through the RAP. To assess the risk of legal challenge, authorities should consider, among other things,

(i) the amount of excluded liabilities, if any, that rank pari passu to TLAC in any given creditor class;
(ii) the applicable resolution law for the resolution entity; and
(iii) the agreed resolution strategy for the resolution entity.

The subordination requirement specified in this Section 11 does not apply in those jurisdictions in which all liabilities excluded from TLAC specified in Section 10 are statutorily excluded from the scope of the bail-in tool and therefore cannot legally be written down or converted to equity in a bail-in resolution. In this case, liabilities that rank alongside them and are included in scope of the bail-in tool and meet the eligibility criteria for TLAC would in fact be able to absorb losses in resolution and qualify for TLAC. If this option is used, authorities must ensure that this would not give rise to material risk of successful legal challenge or valid compensation claims, and that the terms of the TLAC-eligible liabilities specify that they are subject to bail-in.

In those jurisdictions where the resolution authority may, under exceptional circumstances specified in the applicable resolution law, exclude or partially exclude from bail-in all of the liabilities excluded from TLAC specified in Section 10, the relevant authorities may permit liabilities that would otherwise be eligible to count as external TLAC but which rank alongside those excluded liabilities in the insolvency creditor hierarchy to contribute a quantum equivalent of up to 2.5% RWA of the resolution entity's Minimum TLAC requirement when the TLAC RWA Minimum is 16%, and up to 3.5% RWA when the TLAC RWA Minimum is 18%. If this option is used, authorities must ensure that the capacity to exclude or partially exclude liabilities from bail-in would not give rise to material risk of successful legal challenge or valid compensation claims.

A resolution entity that uses one exemption under this Section cannot use any other exemption set out in this Section.

Figure 6.1 illustrates the issue.

Figure 6.1 No Creditors Worse-Off Rule in Connection with MREL/TLAC

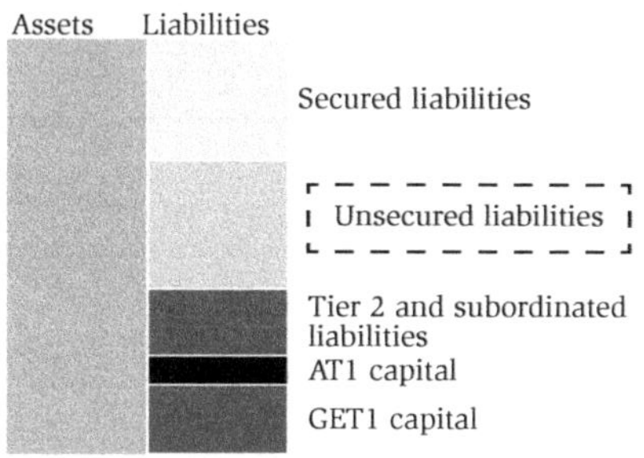

1. IR = Ranking order in insolvency (may differ in some countries).
2. If excluded liabilities.
3. Unless subordination requirement applies.
4. Capital instruments write-down tool.

Unsecured liabilities

IR[1]	Classification	Bail-In	MREL	TLAC
1.	Deposits ≤ EUR 100k	No	No	No
2.	Deposits > EUR 100k (SMCs)	Yes	No[2]	No
3.	Deposits > EUR 100k (large companies)	Yes	No[2]	No
3.	Bonds ('preferred senior')	Yes	(Yes)[3]	No
3.	Interbank credits (with a maturity of < seven days)	No	No[2]	No
3.	Liabilities from derivatives	Yes	No[2]	No
3.	Miscellaneous	Yes	Yes	No
4.	**Non-preferred senior (Art. 108 (2) BRRD)**	**Yes**	**Yes**	**Yes**
5.	Subordinated liabilities	Yes	Yes	Yes
6.	Tier 2	Yes[4]	Yes	Yes
7.	AT1 capital	Yes[4]	Yes	Yes
8.	CET 1 capital	Yes[4]	Yes	Yes

Source: Compiled by author from various sources.

However, that requirement is not applicable to all institutions but only to certain types of institutions. Like G-SIIs, it applies to banks with a balance sheet of more than EUR 100 billion and certain other types of banks which we will come to a bit further down. For this purpose, Article 45b(1)(b) BRRD[775] explicitly takes out point (d) of Article 72b(2) CRR. To institutions where subordination requirement applies, it can be met under the following circumstances:

- the contractual provisions governing the liabilities specify that in the event of normal insolvency proceedings, the claim on the principle amount of the instruments ranks below claims arising from any of the excluded liabilities referred to above; or
- the applicable law specifies that in the event of normal insolvency proceedings, the claim on the principle amount ranks below claims arising from any of the excluded liabilities; or
- the instruments are issued by a resolution entity which does not have on its balance sheet any excluded liabilities as referred to in Article 72a(2).

This subordination requirement is one of the actual core elements of the reform of BRRD and SRM-R, respectively.[776] While for the purposes of TLAC, the subordination requirement was included in the TLAC term sheet with an identical systematic subordination behind excluded liabilities, either contractually, structurally or statutory (*see* section 11 of the TLAC term sheet dated 9 November 2015),[777] the subordination requirement was not foreseen for MREL up until recently. This led to a disparity between G-SIIs, which effectively were bound by the TLAC standards and the requirements under BRRD/SRM-R. This gap has now been closed. This also explains the new methodology and mechanics of liabilities under Article 72a CRR, which effectively works in the same way as TLAC wording and mechanics.

However, there are still some gaps between the BRRD/SRM-R and CRR with regard to subordination requirements for different types of banks. Once the SRM-R and BRRD fully apply, the regime will be more complicated. Even though CRR includes subordination requirement in Article 72b(2)(d), BRRD switches off this criterion in non-G-SII context. For reference to such switch off, Article 45b(1)(b) BRRD refers to Article 72b CRR but except for (2)(d) such that there is no subordination requirement. To analyse the combined effect, mandatory subordination will apply to minimum MREL requirement of G-SII (with the limited exception stated in Article 72b(3)-(5))[778]

775. Article 12c(1)(b) SRM-R.
776. The concept of subordination can be viewed as an insurance provided by the holders of subordinated debt. *See* Jianping Zhou and others. From Bail-out to Bail-in: Mandatory Debt Restructuring of Systemic Financial Institutions. International Monetary Fund. Monetary and Capital Market Department and Legal Department. 24 April 2012. https://www.imf.org/external/pubs/ft/sdn/2012/sdn1203.pdf.
777. FSB. TLAC Term Sheet. 9 November 2015. https://www.fsb.org/wp-content/uploads/TLAC-Principles-and-Term-Sheet-for-publication-final.pdf.
778. The wording of these articles leaves the discretion in the hands of the resolution authority. Owing to this, there is 'uncertainty that bears on investors' capacity to predict their precise LGD [loss given default] ... To be sure, the regime aims at a high degree of transparency [Article 72b(5)]. Yet, this does not help much, where a re-evaluation of prior decisions affects existing

but will not apply in all other cases as per BRRD. Also, the mandatory subordination requirement does not necessarily apply to institution-specific MREL of G-SIIs, but this is subject to the minimum level of subordination requirement included in Article 45b(4) of BRRD.[779]

[a] G-SIIs

According to Article 92a CRR, G-SIIs have to maintain 18% of TREA and 6.75% of LREM. However, these limits are reduced for the certain period of time, i.e. from 27 June 2019 to 31 December 2021 as a result of 'grandfathering' rules under CRR wherein provisions were introduced to ensure that institutions have sufficient time to meet the requirements set out by the regulation. Article 494(1) CRR requires G-SIIs to maintain 16% TREA and 6% LREM from 27 June 2019 until 31 December 2021.[780]

As Article 92a CRR refers to the eligible liabilities' definition in Article 72a CRR, the subordination requirement is included. This applies as of CRR coming into force which is 27 June 2019. In addition, Article 45b(4) BRRD[781] introduces an 8% threshold of subordinated liabilities based on a TLOF parameter. This parameter has been introduced because, under BRRD rules, the resolution fund can only be accessed once an amount of 8% of TLOF has been taken up for loss absorption.[782] However, even though the BRRD/SRM-R become effective as of the end of 2020, the 8% threshold will apply as of 2024 (while the other thresholds TREA/LREM are effective earlier).[783]

The 8% TLOF threshold which is measured against the whole balance sheet can indeed lead to a high amount of subordinated MREL. For large G-SIIs with a balance sheet of more than a trillion EUR, the 8% amount can exceed EUR 80 billion. This can, depending on the applicable law and the priority provisions, lead to the requirement to issue significant amount of additional regulatory capital or subordinated MREL. For this reason, some countries, e.g. Germany, have included statutory provisions providing for a subordination of ordinary bonds in order to cope with the subordination requirement.[784] Other countries have opted for different solutions.[785] Under certain

investors' risk calculation'. *See* Tobias H. Tröger. Why MREL won't help much. 2017. Page 7. Available at: https://www.imfs-frankfurt.de/fileadmin/user_upload/IMFS_WP_117.pdf.

779. Article 12c(4) SRM-R.
780. *See also* SRB. Minimum Requirement for Own Funds and Eligible Liabilities (MREL). Addendum to the SRB 2018 MREL policy on new CRR requirements. 25 June 2019.
781. Article 12c(4) SRM-R.
782. This serves as an additional backstop 'thereby improving the ability of banks to be resolved and consequently the functional viability and thus the credibility of the resolution regime' – Deutsche Bundesbank. The European banking package – revised rules in EU banking regulation. June 2019. https://www.bundesbank.de/resource/blob/800764/d87f4df7102744e5b52f284fc03d186d/mL/2019-06-bankenpaket-data.pdf page 44. *See also* Section 5.16 [D].
783. Article 45m(1) BRRD, Article 12k(1) SRM-R.
784. Section 46(f) of the German Kreditwesengesetz (KWG; German Banking Act).
785. The European Commission has published a detailed study on the differences between bank insolvency laws of various countries and on their potential harmonisation. *See* European Commission, Study on the differences between bank insolvency laws and on their potential harmonization – Final report, November 2019. Available at: https://ec.europa.eu/info/sites/

circumstances, the resolution authority may permit a level lower than 8% TLOF but greater than amount resulting by application of a prudential formula.[786]

[b] Insolvency Hierarchy

In CRR, the ranking has been addressed by Article 72b(2)(d) which requires EU G-SII's eligible liabilities instruments to be wholly subordinated to excluded liabilities. It can be done by structural, and either contractual or statutory subordination. Here, 'excluded liabilities' include covered deposits, eligible deposits, deposits with maturity of less than one year, secured debt liabilities, derivatives, among others. The article goes further to ensure that no excluded liabilities rank *pari passu* or junior to eligible liabilities instruments, thereby ensuring subordination. In effect, such subordination is essentially creating a class of debt that ranks below excluded liabilities and other ordinary unsecured creditors.

The question that stems is how this subordination requirement complies with the ranking in insolvency hierarchy foreseen under Article 108 BRRD. Article 108 BRRD requires a new class of non-preferred senior debt to be introduced into the insolvency ranking. It provides that debt instruments that fulfil specific conditions will be ranked lower than ordinary unsecured claims but higher than capital instruments and subordinated liabilities that do not qualify as own funds instruments. The specific conditions for non-preferred senior debt are that they must be bonds or other transferrable debt instruments with a maturity of at least one year. These instruments must not be derivative or contain any derivative content. Also, the instruments need to be subordinated, and the subordination must be contractually agreed or published in the prospectus.[787]

The insolvency ranking in accordance with Article 108 BRRD in order of most protected to lowest subordinated will have covered deposits, eligible deposits and ordinary unsecured creditors, respectively. Then, it is the newly introduced category of non-preferred senior debt, followed by contractually subordinated instruments. Further down, the capital components are included in the specific order of Tier 2 instruments, Additional Tier 1 instruments and at the bottom, Common Equity Tier 1.[788]

To give the above meaning to Article 108 BRRD in context of 'non-preferred senior' instruments within the meaning of new creditor hierarchy would not be

---

info/files/business_economy_euro/banking_and_finance/documents/191106-study-bank-insolvency_en.pdf Annex 2 for a detailed analysis or page 30 for a brief overview of hierarchy of claims.

786. The formula is laid out in Article 45b(4) BRRD and Article 12c(4) SRM-R. The formula to be used is (1-(X1/X2)) X 8% TLOF where X1 = 3.5% of TREA; X2 = sum of 16% TREA if from 27 June 2019 to 31 December 2021 or 18% if on or after 1 January 2022 and amount of combined buffer requirement.
787. Article 108(2) BRRD.
788. *See also* page 71 of Deutsche Bundesbank. Bank recovery and resolution – the new TLAC and MREL minimum requirements. July 2016. https://www.bundesbank.de/resource/blob/654532/7046f093197a1e4ab2e1f2446aff8934/mL/2016-07-minimum-requirements-tlac-mrel-data.pdf.

possible without reading it simultaneously with Article 72 CRR. As discussed, Article 72 CRR fills in the legal blanks such as eligible liabilities.[789] Given that the articles need to be read together, they align with each other. However, it is to be noted that with certain exceptions stated in Article 72b(3)–(5), the regulation authority can permit minimum capital requirements to be satisfied without the liabilities being subordinated. Therefore, it is a rather fluid ranking as opposed to Article 108.

[c] Top-Tier Banks

For banks which are not G-SIIs but nevertheless exceed the EUR 100 billion balance sheet asset test are classified as Top-Tier Banks. As a result, Article 45b(4) BRRD[790] applies to these banks which imposes 8% TLOF test from 2024 onwards. In addition, Article 45c(5) BRRD[791] introduces alternative thresholds of 13.5% TREA and 5% LREM from 1 January 2022. Following the grandfathering rule mentioned above, the TREA and LREM requirements from 27 June 2019 to 31 December 2021 will be determined on an institution-specific basis. Again, both LREM and TREA have to be fulfilled and then compared to the 8% TLOF threshold. However, there is a cap of 27% of the TREA should the 8% TLOF be higher.[792]

[d] 'Fished Banks'

Article 45c(6) of BRRD[793] introduces a new category of banks which are commonly also called 'Fished Banks'. These are banks that are not G-SIIs or Top-Tier Banks with balance sheet of over EUR 100 billion but they are still likely to pose a systemic risk in

789. 'Inseparably linked to the eligibility criteria (Article 72b para. 2 of the [CRR]) is the harmonised amendment in Article 108 of [BRRD] to the ranking of unsecured debt instruments in the insolvency hierarchy in bank insolvencies.' *See* Comments on the Commission's proposal for amendments to the BRRD/CRR in conjunction with the MREL/TLAC-requirements 2017 – *see* Die Deutsche Kreditwirtschaft. Comments on the Commission's proposal for amendments to the BRRD/CRR in conjunction with the MREL/TLAC-requirements. 17 March 2017. Available at: https://bankenverband.de/media/files/20170317_DK-Papier_MRELVorgaben_in_CRRuBRRD_englisch.pdf. The proposal also advocates for a timely parallelism for the two articles in order to avoid the emergence of issuing gaps/delays in institutional issue activity and to ensure equal competitive conditions.
790. Article 12c(4) SRM-R.
791. Article 12d(4) SRM-R.
792. Article 45b(4) BRRD, Article 12c(4) SRM-R.
793. Article 12d(5) SRM-R. This could be viewed as a step towards the statement made in the BRRD proposal – 'Since the risk posed by any individual bank to financial stability cannot be fully ascertained in advance, these powers should be available to the relevant authorities in relation to any bank, regardless of its size or the scope of its activities.' *See* Proposal for a DIRECTIVE OF THE EUROPEAN PARLIAMENT AND OF THE COUNCIL establishing a framework for the recovery and resolution of credit institutions and investment firms and amending Council Directives 77/91/EEC and 82/891/EC, Directives 2001/24/EC, 2002/47/EC, 2004/25/EC, 2005/56/EC, 2007/36/EC and 2011/35/EC and Regulation (EU) No 1093/2010. COM/2012/0280 final – 2012/0150 (COD).

case of failure. Such determination is made by the national resolution authorities.[794] Following this determination, the same rules that apply to Top-Tier Banks shall also apply to Fished Banks. National resolution authorities, while deciding, take into account several factors. Those factors include prevalence of deposits and absence of debt in the funding model, the extent to which access to capital markets for eligible liabilities is limited, and the level of reliance of the resolution entity on Common Equity Tier 1 capital to meet the requirements on a consolidated basis at the level of the resolution group.

[e] Other Banks

Under Article 45b(5) BRRD,[795] the SRB can on its own initiative apply the subordination requirement up to the percentage amounts applicable for G-SIIs even if the national resolution authority did not request it, provided that:

- certain non-subordinated liabilities (as referred to in Article 45b(1) and (2))[796] have the same priority ranking in the national insolvency hierarchy as certain liabilities that are excluded from the application of the bail-in powers in accordance with Article 44(2) or Article 44(3) BRRD;[797] and
- there is an NCWO risk if claims are excluded from bail-in under Article 44(2) or Article 44(3) or if in order to reach the appropriate level of loss absorption, other liabilities of the same rank have to bear greater losses. This risk assessment is triggered if a level of more than 10% of that class is excluded from bail-in.[798]

794. Article 45c (6) BRRD; Article 12d (5) SRM-R, 'at the request of the national resolution authority of a resolution entity, the Board shall apply … '.
795. Article 12c(5) SRM-R.
796. Article 12c(1) and (2) SRM-R.
797. Article 27(3) or (5) SRM-R.
798. The valuation of banks assets differs from during different time period and such differences are critical when assessing conformity with NCWO principle. Two reasons have been outlined. 'First, in an insolvency, creditors' losses are judged ex-post once the firm has been liquidated or sold and the assets have been disposed of, whereas in a resolution, bank losses are determined either when the bank enters into resolution or shortly thereafter. Asset prices in resolution are normally marked against a depressed market, and both bank sales and asset sales are bound to attract a limited number of buyers, which compromises the concept of competitive market prices. The possibility of discrepancies in valuations upon entry into resolution is not possible.' *See* EBA. Handbook on Valuation for purposes of Resolution. 22 February 2019. Vanjhttps://eba.europa.eu/sites/default/documents/files/documents/10180/2613666/9f0772ea-a052-49e5-86ce-64c157adff10/Valuation%20Handbook.pdf. Page 15. The BRRD and EBA's technical standards recognise that the *ex post* valuation approach is important when determining whether shareholders and creditors do not receive worse treatment under resolution than they would have expected in a counterfactual liquidation under normal insolvency proceedings. *See* page 6 of EBA. Regulatory Technical Standards on valuation for the purposes of resolution and on valuation to determine difference in treatment following resolution under Directive 2014/59/EU on recovery and resolution of credit institutions and investment firms. 23 May 2017. https://eba.europa.eu/sites/default/documents/files/documents/10180/1853532/88566587-ff6f-4116-a08e-282eb4ea2f78/Final%20draft%20RTSs%20on%20valuation%20in%20resolution%20%28EBA-RTS-2017-05%20%26%20EBA-RTS-2017-06%29.pdf. Further, *see* Commission Delegated Regulation (EU) 2018/345 of 14

[f] Increase of Subordinated MREL Amount

Under certain circumstances, according to Article 45b(7) BRRD,[799] the resolution authority can increase the amount of subordinated MREL for G-SIIs or Top-Tier or Fished Banks to the greater amount of 8% of the total liabilities including own funds or a certain prudential formula[800] taking into account combined buffer requirements referred to in Article 92a CRR. However, this increase is limited to a threshold of 30% of the total number of all G-SIIs or Top-Tier or Fished Banks. More importantly, the SRB shall take into consideration certain conditions when deciding. First, substantive impediments to resolvability have been identified in the preceding resolvability assessment. Post identification of such impediments to resolvability, either no immediate action has been taken or identified substantive impediments cannot be addressed. And, if increasing the subordinated MREL amount will partially or fully compensate for the negative impact of the substantive impediments to resolvability, then the first condition is deemed satisfied. Second, the resolution authority will also determine whether the feasibility and credibility of the resolution entity's preferred resolution strategy is limited considering the entity's size, interconnectedness, nature, scope, risk, complexity of its activities, legal status and its shareholding structure. The third consideration is based on the level of risk. If the resolution entity is among the top 20% of institutions for which the resolution authority determines the MREL requirements, it could be subject to increased MREL requirements.[801]

[B] No Set-Off

Further important novelty is the no set-off requirement included in Article 72b CRR.[802] This effectively stems from the situation that certain creditors of the bank may at the

November 2017. Also, *see* Ed. Douglas W. Arner et al., Systemic Risk in the Financial Sector – 10 years after the great crash. 2019. CIGI Press. Further, SRB, in the Banking Industry Dialogue Meeting held 16 December 2019, discussed its intention to apply a value-based assessment of NCWO risk in the 2020 planning cycles where the approach would seek to quantify NCWO risk by comparing the value of instruments held by senior creditors of a given bank in resolution with their value in insolvency using a dedicated quantitative tool. The bank-specific input values would be derived from the liability structure of the bank. The quantitative tool may serve to assess NCWO risk as a precondition for any case-by-case adjustments of subordination targets and allowances for Pillar 1 banks. For non-pillar 1 Banks, the tool may be used to set bank-specific subordination requirements. *See* further on SRB. Banking Industry Dialogue Meeting. The Banking Package and the next SRB MREL policy. 16 December 2019. https://srb.europa.eu/sites/srbsite/files/industry_dialogue_16_december_2019_-_srb_-_the_banking_package_and_the_next_srb_mrel_policy_1.pdf.

799. Article 12c(7) SRM-R.
800. The prudential formula is Ax2 + Bx2 + C, wherein A = amount resulting from the requirement referred in Article 92(1)(c) CRR; B = amount resulting from the requirement referred in Article 104a of Directive 2013/36; and C = amount resulting from the combined buffer requirement. *See also* Article 12c(7) SRM-R.
801. Article 45b(8) BRRD, Article 12c(8) SRM-R.
802. No set-off clause is considered as a surprise clause in accordance with section 309(3) of the Bürgerliches Gesetzbuch ('BGB'; German Civil Code). Surprise clauses are clauses that are so unusual in a contract that their recipient cannot be expected to anticipate them (section 305c

same time be customers. This quite often is the case for depositors who at the same time have taken out a loan from the bank. However, deposits are not eligible to MREL in any event; therefore, the requirement mainly applies to other forms of creditors, i.e. owners of bonds or regulatory capital which at the same time have taken out a loan from the bank. This can effectively jeopardise a bail-in, as a set-off would likely lead to an NCWO claim effective in an insolvency. On the other hand, it would be not only important but also a challenge for banks to filter the respective information related to those creditors and instruments and apply and bail in through to their MREL assessment. This may at the same time also be problematic for resolution authorities in the resolution scenario where the relevant data may not be available at short notice. Needless to say, the data requirement also forms a central cornerstone in respect of the resolution planning as recently confirmed by the SRB in the expectations for banks statement.[803]

[C] Amount of MREL

There is a distinction between the amount of MREL and the amount of subordinated MREL generally. Not all MREL has to be subordinated. Therefore, Article 45b(1)(b) BRRD[804] carves out the subordination requirement under CRR, namely Article 72b(2)(d). Except for the G-SIIs, Top-Tier Banks and Fished Banks, the subordination requirement is bank-specific and is set individually. Generally, it can be said that subordinated MREL facilitates the application of the resolution tools. It avoids or reduces the risk of a bail-in of senior class liabilities which may have an impact on the NCWO principle and also on the market confidence.[805]

Also, in the prior version of BRRD, there were provisions about the amount of MREL contained in Article 45.[806] These provisions have mainly been moved to Article

BGB). A no set-off clause is regarded as a surprise clause because in civil law jurisdictions, set-off provisions are implied; i.e., they do not require the existence of an express agreement for the set-off to take place. It operates automatically when all the legally required conditions are met. Having a no set-off clause is therefore unusual and could be invalid. However, since courts will take the practices and customs that apply in business dealings into reasonable account, German courts will have to consider the requirements under the banking package, and subsequently, it will be regarded as a custom in the agreements that banks have for instruments counting towards MREL. Also, it could potentially be a conflict of law between the national law and EU legislation, in which case, the courts must give precedence to EU legislation. In this light, it can be validly included.

803. *See* SRB's Expectations for Banks March 2020. https://srb.europa.eu/sites/srbsite/files/efb_main_doc_final_web_0.pdf.
804. Article 12c(1)(b) SRM-R.
805. '[MREL] could be seen as a reserve parachute, which could efficiently mitigate any spread of the panic and thus prevent any contagion effect on other market participants or financial sectors in other European countries' – page 24 of Martina Miskova. Lucia Országhovál. Národná banka Slovenska. MREL: Gone Concern Loss Absorption Capacity. 2015. Available at: https://www.nbs.sk/_img/Documents/_PUBLIK_NBS_FSR/Biatec/Rok2015/03-2015/06_biatec_3-15_miskova-orszaghova.pdf.
806. Article 12(7)-(15) SRM-R.

45c BRRD[807] and have been further enhanced. Specific MREL minimum quantities are only given for G-SIIs, Top-Tier and Fished Banks.

For G-SIIs, the respective minimum quantities are contained in Article 92a and 92b of CRR. They are measured on a risk-based ratio of 16% of TREA[808] and a non-risk-based ratio of 6%[809] expressed as a percentage of the total exposure measure over the asset side of the balance sheet in accordance with grandfathering rule under Article 494(1) CRR.[810] Concerning Top-Tier Banks, Article 45c(5) BRRD[811] contains the rule that the MREL amount shall be 13.5% of TREA and 5% of LREM from 1 January 2022 and until 31 December 2021, such will be determined on an institution-specific basis. For Fished Banks, under Article 45c(6), the same requirements as for Top-Tier Banks apply.

Despite the differences, the general principle has not changed. MREL should always be sufficient to contain an element of loss absorption and an element of recapitalisation.[812]

[1] The Loss Absorption Amount

According to Article 45c(2) BRRD,[813] the amount of MREL shall consist of a loss absorption amount (LAA) and a recapitalisation amount (RCA). This principle of LAA and RCA is not new and was introduced by Articles 1 and 2 of the Delegated Regulation 2016/1450 ('Delegated Regulation').[814] The Delegated Regulation supplements the BRRD with regard to RTS specifying the criteria relating to the methodology for setting the MREL. It applies alongside the banking package; however, parts of it have been merged into BRRD and SRM-R. The LAA and RCA requirements were previously contained in Articles 1 and 2 but now have been transferred to Article 45c of BRRD and Article 12d of SRM-R. In specific, Article 45c(3) BRRD which, in turn, refers to Article 92 of CRR sets forth the requirements as such.

Subsequently, this means that MREL generally requires an amount equal to 8% total capital ratio plus buffers for firm-specific risks and 3% leverage ratio both at consolidated level.[815] This amount stands for the LAA because the own fund requirements – as generally is equity – stands for loss absorption. Practically, the losses are

807. Article 12d SRM-R.
808. Calculated in accordance with Article 92(3) and (4) CRR.
809. Calculated in accordance with Article 429(4) CRR.
810. From 2022, the TREA and LREM ratios will be 18% and 6.75%, respectively.
811. Article 12d(4) SRM-R.
812. 'MREL provides a reassurance that the loss absorption and loss recapitalisation amount, in case of failure, will be sufficient to gain market confidence and prevent a bank run.' James McAndrews et al., What Makes Large Banks Failures So Messy and What to Do about It? 2014. FRBNY Econ Pol Rev 229. 236-240.
813. Article 12d(2) SRM-R.
814. Commission Delegated Regulation (EU) 2016/1450 of 23 May 2016 supplementing Directive 2014/59/EU of the European Parliament and of the Council with regard to regulatory technical standards specifying the criteria relating to the methodology for setting the minimum requirement for own funds and eligible liabilities.
815. Article 45c(3)(a)(i) and (b)(i) BRRD, Article 12d(3)(a)(i) and (b)(i) SRM-R. It is to be noted that the prudential leverage ratio requirement applies from 28 June 2021 and is to be taken into

absorbed by writing down these own funds,[816] by way of bail-in, capital instrument write-down tool or transfer tools in a resolution.

[2] *The Recapitalisation Amount*

In addition, the RCA is there to recapitalise the institution in a resolution. The RCA amounts to again 8% total capital ratio plus buffers for firm-specific risks and 3% leverage ratio both at consolidated level.[817] Practically, this means that after applying the respective resolution tools, the institution needs to be well capitalised again and market confidence needs to be restored. Effectively this would happen by bailing in own funds and liabilities and converting them into equity that is sufficiently high for the institution to be sustainable in its field. Correspondingly, there is a possibility for the resolution authority to adapt the RCA by an appropriate amount to ensure that, following resolution, the entity is able to sustain sufficient market confidence for an appropriate period which shall not exceed one year.[818]

[3] *Adjustments to LAA/RCA*

[a] *Strategic Considerations*

While there are certain minimum amounts for MREL as shown above for certain types of banks, there are possibilities for banks to either avoid an additional increase of

account when calibrating targets based on the non-risk-based formula in decisions issued in the 2020 planning cycle, including the intermediate target to be met by 1 January 2022. *See* SRB. Minimum Requirements for own funds and eligible liabilities (MREL). SRB Policy under the Banking Package. 20 May 2020. https://srb.europa.eu/sites/srbsite/files/srb_mrel_policy_2020.pdf.

816. 'Although this appears to be a somewhat academic point, it actually has great significance. The write-down power is explicitly designed to fall outside the constraints which normally apply to resolution actions – by Article 59(1) [BRRD] it should be exercised independently of resolution action and is only required to be exercised within a resolution when the criteria for the commencement of resolution have been determined to have been met. Thus, write down took is explicitly a pre-resolution as well as a resolution tool. This means that its exercise is not constrained by the general principles governing resolution, and it is therefore not subject either to the equal treatment of creditors obligations [Article 34(f) BRRD] or to the NCWO principle [Article 34 (g) BRRD], and any creditor who suffers loss as a result of the exercise of the power will receive no compensation apart from the issue of equity [Article 60(3) BRRD]. It therefore makes a significant difference to MREL holders whether the resolution tool applied is the write down tool or the bail-in tool.' – Simon Gleeson. The Single Resolution Mechanism and the EU crisis management tools. 2016 in The European Banking Union and the Role of Law. 2019. Edited by Gianni Lo Schiavo (page 225).
817. Article 45c(3)(a)(ii) and (b)(ii) BRRD, Article 12d(3)(a)(ii) and (b)(ii) SRM-R.
818. Article 45c(3) BRRD, Article 12d(3) SRM-R. 'The analysis was performed on a sample of 91 systemically important banks in the EU and the US, covering the period from 2006 to 2015. We found that a higher amount of recapitalisation increased bank profitability with a lag of one year' – Page 319 of Matej Tomec and Timotej Jagric. Does the Amount and Time of Recapitalization Affect the Profitability of Commercial Banks? 2017. Czech Journal of Economics and Finance (67, number 4). https://journal.fsv.cuni.cz/storage/1390_318-341_jagric_final_issue_4_2017.pdf.

subordinated MREL or to benefit from a discount. Given the high costs that can be carried along with additional subordinated MREL, it should be a strategic priority for banks to search for structures or possibilities to fit such discounts or at least avoid increases. Some of those discounts or increases have been mentioned already, like the increase of subordinated MREL under Article 45b(7) and (8) BRRD or the reduction under Article 45b(4) BRRD and Article 72b(3) CRR. Another option is set out in Article 45c(2) BRRD[819] according to which no RCA is necessary if the resolution plan provides that the entity shall be wound up under normal insolvency proceedings (*see also* section 6.02 [C][3][a][i] and [ii]).

Further possibilities include the reduction of RWAs in the balance sheet under divestment plans, respectively a reduction of the balance sheet (and RWAs) following the application of the resolution tools.[820] A further important reduction of the RCA can follow from the anticipated application of transfer strategies in a resolution scenario, as the idea behind such strategy is that the acquirer of assets or shares following a transfer will help set up market confidence so that the amount for recapitalisation will be lower. While there will generally be no adjustments to the LAA, some of the points just mentioned to reduce the RCA will be discussed in more detail.

[i] Transfer Strategies

There is a possibility to be granted a discount or reduction on the RCA in case of transfer strategies. It is not directly mentioned in BRRD (or SRM-R) but stems from the wording in Article 45c(2)(b) BRRD[821] and its underlying rationale. In case of a transfer of shares in an institution under resolution by way of applying the sale of business tool to an acquirer, the acquirer will help to stabilise the business of the entity under resolution following the transfer. Part of that stabilisation will come by the transfer itself, i.e. by bringing the institution under resolution to a safe harbour of – assumingly – a sound and stable bank. However, the acquiring bank will need to demonstrate to the markets that it is able to digest and integrate the acquisition. For this purpose, additional capitalisation measures may need to be taken by the acquiring bank. The amounts that are necessary depend on the very circumstances, but especially on the market position of the acquiring bank, i.e. its capital position and the marked confidence it enjoys.[822] Therefore, if a transfer strategy in the form of transferring the

819. Article 12d(2) SRM-R.
820. SRB has discretion to allow such adjustments on a bank-by-bank basis with due justification. *See* page 11 of SRB. Minimum Requirement for Own Funds and Eligible Liabilities (MREL) 2018 SRB Policy for the second wave of resolution plans. 16 January 2019. https://srb.europa.eu/sites/srbsite/files/public_mrel_policy_2018_-_second_wave_of_plans.pdf.
821. Article 12d(2)(b) SRM-R.
822. 'Certain potential purchasers may be more likely to ensure financial stability, in particular due to factors such as their financial or market position, their structure and business model, which may facilitate the business integration and the legal and organisational feasibility or may have positive effects on the time required for the implementation of the resolution action and the expectation that critical functions can be continued. Resolution authorities should take into account the needs and expectations of counterparties, infrastructure providers, depositors and liquidity providers and those of the wider market.' – Title III (5)(b) in EBA. Guidelines on

'bank' to an investor is a credible option under the resolution planning scenario, it is logical to reduce the RCA, since part of the recapitalisation is done by the acquirer. The same logic would apply to structural variances of this theme, say if not shares but rather assets and liabilities are transferred under the sale of business tool, possibly also if a transfer is performed under the asset separation tool.[823] In all of these potential circumstances, it has to be assessed what happens to the remaining entity in case the whole bank has not been transferred. If it is wound down under insolvency proceedings, no RCA for the remaining entity will be needed.[824] In order to plan for that scenario in a resolution planning exercise, some factors will need to be adhered. One, it seems clear that a strategy comprising the transfer of shares to an investor is likely the most stable way of resolving a bank, as the acquirer, under the assumptions set out, is immediately able to provide confidence and help stop the deposit run and liquidity drain, in case it has already occurred and can be a likely trigger for the failing or likely to fail analysis.

However, in order to take it up in a resolution plan, such a transfer strategy will have to have a strong likelihood to be implemented. This again depends on marketability of the target (i.e., the bank under (hypothetical) resolution and the group of potential investors). The marketability of the target in turn may depend on various elements, the business model of the target, its products, clients and market share, and also its structure in terms of separability (if the whole bank is not transferred).[825] A key factor will also be the LAA available, i.e. whether the bank can be transferred with a restructured balance sheet, i.e. losses which have been assessed on the basis of Valuation 2[826] can be absorbed sufficiently and without legal risk. For this purpose, the amount of MREL, especially subordinated MREL ready for loss absorption, will be an important factor. Generally speaking, the clearer the market footprint of the target bank is and the easier liabilities on the balance sheet can be erased for loss absorption, the more persuasive the transfer option is in a resolution planning scenario.

---

factual circumstances amounting to a material threat to financial stability and on the elements related to the effectiveness of the sale of business tool under Article 39(4) of Directive 2014/59/EU. https://eba.europa.eu/sites/default/documents/files/documents/10180/1080767/79c49d39-bd8e-44ae-9e23-d3cf04cc0609/EBA-GL-2015-04%20Guidelines%20on%20the%20sale%20of%20business%20tool.pdf.

823. *See* EBA. Guidelines on the determination of when the liquidation of assets or liabilities under normal insolvency proceedings could have an adverse effect on one or more financial markets under Article 42(14) of Directive 2014/59/EU. https://eba.europa.eu/sites/default/documents/files/documents/10180/1080779/6441452a-d464-4618-9296-d71549a4f2c2/EBA-GL-2015-05%20Guidelines%20on%20the%20asset%20separation%20tool.pdf.

824. *See* SRB. Resolution Q&A. https://srb.europa.eu/en/content/resolution-qa.

825. 'Potential conflicts between the marketing requirements and the resolution objective can, for example, arise where there is the risk that full compliance may cause additional uncertainty and a loss of market confidence or where certain potential purchasers may be more likely to ensure financial stability than others, and in general with respect to the legal and organisational feasibility, the practicability and the timely implementation of the sale.' – EBA. Guidelines on factual circumstances amounting to a material threat to financial stability and on the elements related to the effectiveness of the sale of business tool under Article 39(4) of Directive 2014/59/EU. 2015. Also *see* Title II Circumstances amounting to a material threat to financial stability.

826. *See* SRB. Framework for Valuation February 2019. https://srb.europa.eu/sites/srbsite/files/framework_for_valuation_feb_2019_web_0.pdf. Also *see* Chapter 5 section 5.14 above.

The banks aiming to rely on such strategies will have to prove the reliability of this path. Besides the structural elements and the existence of subordinated loss-absorbing MREL, a diligent screening of potential buyers will have to be undertaken and assessed.[827] This exercise will have to remain theoretical, as on the one hand, the resolution scenario itself is theoretical, and even if it occurs, it is uncertain whether the respective investor will actually buy the target bank. On the other hand, the more reliable and credible this scenario is, naturally the more persuasive it will be towards the resolution authorities. Now, there are steps that can be taken to make this scenario more persuasive even though it is not possible to run a real M&A process. Such factors could be some form of opinion by recognised M&A advisors. They could also be preparatory works, like installing a virtual data room with all necessary information at hand for such a sale or linking this process to the recovery plan.[828] The recovery plan could then describe how in crisis per-resolution an M&A process including data room is organised. If this fails, then interested parties are known and vice versa they know of the target bank. A sale by way of application of the sale of business tool then may become more credible.

Should the resolution authority accept in general the feasibility of this transfer option, the next question is, how large the discount will be. As mentioned, BRRD splits the MREL amount into an LAA and an RCA.[829] However, the minimum amounts as per Article 45c BRRD (in particular, Article 45c(5) and (6) BRRD)[830] do not distinguish between loss absorption and recapitalisation but provide for a minimum absolute amount. It is therefore not fully clear, if a reduction in light of the transfer strategy will be deducted from the 8% TLOF or whether the reduction will be applied in respect of additional MREL charges, e.g. those under Article 45b(7)/(8) BRRD[831] or Article 45d BRRD[832] or Article 45c(3) BRRD.[833][834] In any event, sharpening of this strategy will be

827. *See* Title III (5)(b) in EBA. Guidelines on factual circumstances amounting to a material threat to financial stability and on the elements related to the effectiveness of the sale of business tool under Article 39(4) of Directive 2014/59/EU. https://eba.europa.eu/sites/default/documents/files/documents/10180/1080767/79c49d39-bd8e-44ae-9e23-d3cf04cc0609/EBA-GL-2015-04%20Guidelines%20on%20the%20sale%20of%20business%20tool.pdf.

828. 'The process of merging or acquiring two banking organizations is extremely complex; it requires a great deal of time and effort from both buyer and seller. The business, legal, operational, organizational, accounting, and tax issues all must be addressed if the merger or acquisition is to be successful.' *See* Chapter 14 Bank Merger and Acquisition Process in Zabihollah Rezaee. Financial Services Firms: Governance, Regulations, Valuations, Mergers, and Acquisitions. 2011. Wiley. 3rd Edition.

829. Article 45c(2) BRRD, Article 12d(2) SRM-R.

830. Article 12d(4) and (5) SRM-R.

831. Article 12c(7)/(8) SRM-R.

832. Article 12e SRM-R.

833. Article 12d(3) SRM-R.

834. In its recent communication, the SRB has considered the maximum amount to be deducted under this strategy as 25% reduction of the RCA measured according to TRA or LREM. *See* para. 37 SRB Policy under the Banking Package. 20 May 2020. https://srb.europa.eu/sites/srbsite/files/srb_mrel_policy_2020.pdf – 'SRB intends to tailor the adjustment factor to bank-specific characteristics within a 10% corridor range, with an upper limit of 25% and a lower limit of 15% for the 2020 planning cycle. A flat scaling factor of 20% was applied in the 2017 to 2019 resolution planning cycles. The adjustment factor as of 2020 will be determined on case-by-case basis, based on criteria that capture the marketability and capital needs of the resolved

beneficial, as it avoids impediments to resolution with the risk of Pilar 2 MREL charges under Article 45b(8) BRRD.[835]

[ii] Liquidation Strategies

Liquidation strategies can according to Article 45c(2) BRRD[836] lead to a full reduction in respect of the existence of the RCA, if the resolution plan provides that the entity is wound up under normal insolvency proceedings. In such a scenario, it is logical that solely loss absorption factors are taken up because in an insolvency, there is no need for a recapitalisation since the institution will be wound up and liquidated. The question that therefore arises is that for which banks do such insolvency or liquidation strategies seem feasible.

Under Article 32(5) BRRD[837] in conjunction with Article 31 BRRD,[838] a resolution action is not in the public interest if, *inter alia*, winding the institution up under normal insolvency proceedings would meet the resolution objectives to the same extent (as any of the resolution actions). Also, the credibility of any foreseen resolution action shall be taken into account.[839] This means that insolvency proceedings would need to meet the resolution objectives, which are: (i) ensure the continuity of critical functions; (ii) avoid significant adverse effects on financial stability, in particular by preventing contagion, including to market infrastructure, and by maintaining market discipline; (iii) protect public funds by minimising reliance on extraordinary public financial support; (iv) protect depositors covered by the Deposit Guarantee Schemes Directive and investors covered by the investor-compensation schemes Directive; and (v) protect client funds and client assets.[840] While each of the assessments will be difficult to predict, it can be said that the following parameters could practically be decisive for this assessment: (i) size of the banks, meaning that insolvency procedures would generally only be feasible for small or midsized banks with balance sheets (significantly) smaller than EUR 100 billion;[841] (ii) reach of the bank – if a bank has either a limited local appearance or limited market share, it is likely that its discontinuance is

entity.' This seems to signal that the 8% threshold will (except for the exceptions already mentioned) not be subject to deductions. However, this may not be entirely logical as the 8% TLOF does stand not only for loss absorption but also for recapitalisation (*see* Article 44(5)(a) BRRD).

835. Article 12c(8) SRM-R.
836. Article 12d(2) SRM-R.
837. Article 18(5) SRM-R.
838. Article 14 SRM-R.
839. Article 23(1) Commission Delegated Regulation (EU) 2016/1075 of 23 March 2016.
840. The SRB has published a report to describe the approach taken when performing the public interest assessment. https://srb.europa.eu/sites/srbsite/files/2019-06-28_draft_pia_paper_v12.pdf.
841. Even though size is a parameter, in the 2012 proposal for BRRD, the intention was to resolve every bank regardless of the size – 'Since the risk posed by any individual bank to financial stability cannot be fully ascertained in advance, these powers should be available to the relevant authorities in relation to any bank, regardless of its size or the scope of its activities.' *See* Proposal for a Directive of the European Parliament and of the Council establishing a framework for the recovery and resolution of credit institutions and investment firms and amending Council Directives 77/91/EEC and 82/891/EC, Directives 2001/24/EC, 2002/47/EC,

of less significance and hence poses less risk to financial stability;[842] (iii) interconnectedness – if a bank is less interconnected with other financial institutions its failure is less likely to lead to financial contagion;[843] (iv) deposit base – if a bank has predominant deposits up to the amount of EUR 100,000 so as to ensure protection under the DGS and there is no risk that the DGS will be able to cover; and (v) no critical mass in terms of providing lending, deposit taking or payment services so that critical functions are not at risk.[844] Looking at those parameters, this route will probably only be open to regional or local banks, with a limited market activity which can be taken up by other market participants in case of failure. In addition, its activity and access to the capital markets is likely limited. These characteristics could also fit to solve a dilemma: the concept of MREL might be difficult to be fulfilled by banks which have limited access to the capital markets. This is because MREL requires a certain type of instruments to be issued not necessarily but likely through capital markets. Hence, banks with a deposit-based funding scheme will often have difficulties to cope with MREL requirements, especially if they are focused locally or regionally. For those banks, effective resolution may not be available since 'material' for bail-in or loss absorption is rare and is limited to own funds section. Hence, winding banks up under normal insolvency proceedings may be a consequential alternative and default option.[845] However, if that is the conclusion, then those banks will need to potentially modify their structures in order to clearly fit with the no public interest test. The reward would be a waiver of the RCA and hence significant reduction of MREL. For the investors and creditors of the banks, such message (if given or concluded) may of course trigger actions in a way that protection is sought, e.g. limit deposits to an amount of EUR 100,000, or for larger deposits create a set-off situation against a loan or seek other forms of security.

2004/25/EC, 2005/56/EC, 2007/36/EC and 2011/35/EC and Regulation (EU) No 1093/2010. COM/2012/0280 final – 2012/0150 (COD).

842. One of the factors in the public interest assessment for ABLV Group (ABLV Bank AS in Latvia and ABLV Bank S.A. in Luxembourg) was that the failure of the bank was not likely to result in significant adverse effects on financial stability in Latvia or in other Member States.

843. Application of this parameter was seen in Banca Popolare di Vicenza S.p.A and Veneto Banca S.p.A where SRB concluded that the resolution action was not necessary in the public interest as the institutions had low financial and operational interconnectedness with other financial institutions as they were of minor importance in the Italian funding market.

844. The term 'critical functions' is defined by Article 2(35) BRRD as activities, services or operations, the discontinuance of which is likely in one or more Member States, to lead to the disruption of services that are essential to the real economy or to disrupt financial stability due to size, market share, external and internal interconnectedness, complexity or cross-border activities of an institution or group, with particular regard to the substitutability of those activities, services and operations. The SRB has further adopted the five relevant economic functions that constitute critical functions as identified by the FSB. These are: (i) deposits; (ii) lending; (iii) payment, cash, settlement, clearing, custody; (iv) capital markets; and (v) wholesale funding. Details can be found on https://srb.europa.eu/en/content/critical-functions.

845. 'The problem with this is twofold. On one hand, the difference in [normal] insolvency frameworks implies that failing banks would face different insolvency proceedings in different countries. [Secondly], the fact that insolvency is regulated under national law also makes it easier for governments to amend the ordinary insolvency framework. This could give rise to peculiar situations whereby senior creditors [are far] better in insolvency than they would in resolution.' – Page 11 of Silvia Merler. Bank liquidation in the European Union: clarification needed. January 2017. https://bruegel.org/wp-content/uploads/2018/01/PC-01_2018.pdf.

However, that does not differ from the situations ordinary corporates and their creditors are in. Finally, in those circumstances, a solution with respect to the DGS will need to be found. These schemes will have to step in an insolvency and fund significant amounts of deposits. Those funds will, in large cases, be paid in by national bank *ex post*, which could in turn create funding problems for these banks and lead to contagion.[846] However, it has to be noted that covered deposits have priority status in insolvency proceedings[847] and with the DGS systems stepping in as well leads to a very high chance of full recovery for these systems in insolvency, given the capital ratios of a failing bank. Therefore, it should be assessed whether in such scenario the DGS insurance can possibly be prefunded (e.g., by the SRF or ESM) or whether the reimbursement claim in insolvency can be taken up as collateral for the ECB funding line.[848]

[D] Relevant Calculation Parameters

According to Article 45 BRRD,[849] MREL requirements are calculated according to either the TREA of the relevant entity calculated in accordance with Article 92(3) of CRR or the total exposure measure of the relevant entity calculated in accordance with Article 429 and 429a of CRR.

The first calculation method under Article 45(2) BRRD[850] is referring to TREA which in turn refers to an RWA approach. For this calculation, only certain amount of assets which are seen riskier in terms of losing value are taken into account.[851] In comparison to the TREA, the total exposure measure referred to in Article 45(2)(b)[852] (which is referenced in Article 429 and Article 429(a) of CRR) is measured on a broader asset spectrum, i.e. not only on assets which are considered to lose value but also generally on all assets as set out in the relevant provisions under CRR. Consequently,

846. 'DGSs should assess the adequacy of extraordinary ex-post contributions and alternative funding means to meet the shortfall within the repayment deadline. In this regard, reliance on ex-post funding should take into account the constraints laid down in Article 10(8) [BRRD], including whether some institutions' payments may be deferred in whole or in part on the grounds that the payments would jeopardise their liquidity or solvency position.'– *see* page 23 of EBA's Guidelines on stress tests of deposit guarantee schemes under Directive 2014/49/EU of 24 May 2016. https://eba.europa.eu/sites/default/documents/files/documents/10180/1472555/dea33e8f-d902-433a-ab85-7b95c0b4d6b3/EBA-GL-2016-04%20(Final%20report%20on%20GL%20on%20DGS%20stress%20tests).pdf.
847. Article 108 BRRD.
848. *See* Chapter 1 section 1.04 [B].
849. Article 12a SRM-R.
850. Article 12a(2) SRM-R.
851. Different classes of assets held by banks are subject to different risk weights. First, the assets are grouped into classes based on the level of risk and potential of loss. For instance, unsecured loans will be assigned in a higher risk weight class as compared to cash or treasury bills. The higher the risk is, the higher the capital adequacy ratio and capital requirements. So, under this approach, risk-weighted assets are used as a measure of a bank's assets (mostly loans since they are categorised as having higher level of risks) adjusted for their perceived risks. Further risk-based calculations can be found on Bank for International Settlements. RCB20 – Calculation of minimum risk-based capital requirements. 15 December 2019. https://www.bis.org/basel_framework/chapter/RBC/20.htm?inforce=20191215.
852. Article 12a(2)(b) SRM-R.

the TREA number is smaller than the total exposure measure, also referred to as LREM which produces a higher number. In terms of calculating the overall amounts of MREL (notwithstanding the amounts to be subordinated), both parameters are relevant. For instance, for Top-Tier Banks, the amount of MREL shall be at least equal to 13.5% when calculated in accordance with TREA and 5% when calculated in accordance with LREM. Therefore, for Top-Tier Banks, both parameters need to be fulfilled with the respective amounts. For smaller banks, i.e. those with asset volumes smaller than EUR 100 billion, the respective MREL amounts will be set on an individual, case-by-case assessment following the parameters set out in Article 45c(1), (2), (3) BRRD.[853]

Besides the two calculation parameters, LREM and TREA, a third parameter is introduced. This third parameter is the parameter measured according to TLOF. So other than the first two parameters which basically look at the asset component of the relevant balance sheet, this parameter looks at the liability and equity/own funds side of the balance sheet. It originally stems from the 8% rule in connection with the bail-in and the use of the resolution fund.[854] According to Article 45b(4) BRRD,[855] G-SIIs and resolution entities with a balance sheet size over EUR 100 billion and Fished Banks shall ensure that a part of the requirement referred to in Article 45e BRRD[856] equal to 8% of TLOF shall be fulfilled by own funds and subordinated eligible instruments.[857] There are some exceptions to that rule. For instance, the resolution authority may permit at a level lower than 8% of TLOF but greater than the amount resulting from the application of a prudential formula outlined above to be used instead. However, this is possible provided that all the conditions set out in Article 72b(3) CRR are met. Another exception is that for banks with a balance sheet volume larger than EUR 100 billion (but not G-SIIs), where the application of the 8% TLOF rule leads to a requirement of greater than 27% TREA, the SRB may impose 27% limit under certain circumstances.

A more general question arises as to why all these different calculation methods are set out in BRRD/SRM-R. Partly this may stem from the TLAC term sheet, which took a risk-rated and leverage approach, i.e. TREA and LREM respectively for G-SIIs in 2015. The TLOF approach, however, was unique to BRRD, and in order to preserve consistency with the 8% rule, it probably had to be maintained in the regulation. This means that various parameters need to be run to assess the amount and subordination requirement according to asset-based denominators and TLOF denominators.

[E] Group Resolution and Resolution Entities

As before, BRRD and SRM-R do not prescribe whether within a banking group the resolution authorities go for an SPE or MPE strategy. SPE strategy is defined as a resolution strategy involving the application of resolution powers by a single resolution

853. Article 12d(1), (2), (3) SRM-R.
854. Article 27(7) SRM-R.
855. Article 12c(4) SRM-R.
856. Article 12f SRM-R.
857. Article 2(1)(71b) BRRD, 'subordinated eligible instruments' means instruments that meet all of the conditions referred to in Article 72a CRR other than paragraphs (3) to (5) of Article 72b CRR.

authority at the level of a single parent undertaking or of a single institution subject to consolidated supervision.[858] MPE, on the other hand, is defined as a resolution strategy involving the application of resolution powers by two or more resolution authorities to regional or functional subgroups or entities of a group.[859]

The SRM-R introduces the concept of resolution entity. It is defined as a legal person established in a participating Member State and is identified by the SRB as an entity in respect of which the resolution plan provides for a resolution action.[860] A resolution group means a resolution entity together with one or more subsidiaries that are themselves not resolution entities (or subsidiaries of other resolution entities).[861] Therefore, it is possible that within a banking group there are only one or several resolution entities. It is also possible that within a banking group there is one resolution group or several resolution groups. The MREL requirement as described above always needs to be fulfilled on a consolidated basis within the relevant resolution group (Article 45e(1) BRRD).[862]

When looking at banking groups, there are some subsidiaries which are institutions and some subsidiaries which are non-institutions (i.e., are neither a credit institution nor an investment firm covered by consolidated supervision). Subsidiaries in the meaning of SRM-R/BRRD would not necessarily mean direct subsidiaries but could also mean indirect subsidiaries as long as there is a predominant influence.[863] Therefore, when we speak about resolution groups, they can consist of both direct and indirect credit institutions but not non-institutions. This is because the resolution tools are only available with respect to institutions but not with respect to non-credit institutions. Following that, resolution will take place at the level of resolution entity which is bound to be an institution (i.e., credit institution or financial holding companies).

The MREL requirement for a resolution entity is calculated on a consolidated basis at the level of the resolution group in accordance with Article 45e(1) BRRD.[864] Whereas, institutions that are subsidiaries of a resolution entity who are not themselves resolution entities are required to comply with the MREL requirements on an individual basis.[865] The rationale behind consolidated MREL is the accumulation of

858. Article 2(5) Commission Delegated Regulation (EU) 2016/1075.
859. Article 2(6) Commission Delegated Regulation (EU) 2016/1075. The FSB in Recovery and Resolution Planning for Systemically Important Financial Institutions: Guidance on Developing Effective Resolution Strategies 2013 has outlined some questions to consider when deciding between SPE and MPE as a preferred resolution strategy. https://www.fsb.org/wp-content/uploads/r_130716b.pdf page 16 and 19. *See* Chapter 5 section 5.23[C].
860. Article 3(24a) SRM-R.
861. Article 3(24b) SRM-R.
862. Article 12f(1) SRM-R.
863. Article 4(114) CRR.
864. Article 12f(1) SRM-R. 'MREL is meant to create extra loss-absorbing capacity, i.e. to shift losses to external shareholders and bondholders. This seems to imply that MREL should be applied at the consolidated level, where there are external share and bond holders, rather than at the individual internal level.' - Bennet Berger, Pia Hüttl, Silvia Merler. Total Assets versus risk weighted assets: Does it matter for MREL? 2016. Bruegel Policy Contribution. No 2016/12. Bruegel, Brussels.https://www.econstor.eu/bitstream/10419/165979/1/87733787X.pdf. It also offers further comparison with TLAC approach.
865. Article 45f(1) BRRD, Article 12g SRM-R.

losses at the level of resolution entity. In a resolution group, the losses from the subsidiaries are upstreamed and accumulate at the level of the resolution entity/parent level.[866] Given that, the resolution entity requires more MREL for resolution purposes, and therefore, MREL is calculated on consolidated basis at the level of the resolution group to account for the losses and to enable effective application of resolution strategy.

In terms of resolution strategy for banking groups, this can, as set out above, vary between SPE or MPE[867] and the various resolution tools. However, in terms of setting the scene in relation to MREL and its quality, it seems clear that the bail-in tool will play a very important role as a resolution tool. This can be either solely or possibly more likely in connection with the sale of business tool to an investor. Generally, as mentioned above, the more clearly bail-in-able material is available at the level of the resolution entity and the resolution group, the more attractive and easier it is to transfer the shares to an investor after write-down of the respective eligible liabilities.

For those groups which are organised by means of a holding structure[868] having the operative bank subsidiaries underneath but carrying most of the MREL in the holding group, the logical resolution strategy could be to write down the liabilities at the holding level and the respective intercompany liabilities to the bank subsidiaries (*see* above section 5.23 [E]).

[F] Internal MREL

Article 45f BRRD[869] prescribes that institutions that are subsidiaries of a resolution entity but are not themselves resolution entities shall comply with the requirement by way of so-called IMREL. In other words, these subsidiaries need to comply with MREL on an individual basis. This individual basis requirement applies to 'resolution group'. A resolution group means a resolution entity, together with its subsidiaries that are not resolution entities themselves; or subsidiaries of other resolution entities; or entities

866. *See* para. 11 of SRB Policy under the Banking Package. 20 May 2020. https://srb.europa.eu/sites/srbsite/files/srb_mrel_policy_2020.pdf.
867. '[MPE, as a resolution strategy,] requires high-level coordination works on behalf of respective EU Member States' resolution organs, because their actions must be cohesive and supportive of one another, if intervention is applied simultaneously towards several subsidiaries of the same group.' – page 162 of Jakub Kerlin. The Role of Deposit Guarantee Schemes as a Financial Safety Net in the European Union. 2017. Palgrave Macmillan. 1st edition. In Table 5.4 on Page 163, the book also further offers a comparative approach on SPE and MPE resolutions. Also *see* Charles Randell 'Group Resolution under EU Resolution Directive' in The Bank Recovery and Resolution Directive: Europe's Solution for 'Too Big To Fail?' 2017 edited by Andreas Dombret and Patrick S. Kenadjian. Applying bail-in to multiple group entities is highly complex and risks fragmenting the ownership of the group.
868. 'Generalization about "bank groups" are impossible because each large bank group is to some extent unique, and even simple generalisations about "the holding company" or "the group" are liable to counterexamples.' Therefore, it is important to examine various holding structures. Big Bank, Bank/non-bank, Global multi-bank and the financial conglomerate models have been discussed *by* Simon Gleeson in Legal aspect of bank bail-ins. January 2021. LSE Financial Markets Group Paper Series. http://www.lse.ac.uk/fmg/assets/documents/papers/special-papers/SP205.pdf.
869. Article 12g SRM-R.

established in third countries that are not included in the resolution group under the resolution plan, and their subsidiaries.[870] Following that, the individual MREL requirement applies only to subsidiaries that are part of the same resolution group, and not all subsidiaries of a resolution entity.

As per Article 45f BRRD and the requirement for IMREL, the regulation foresees that these liabilities shall be broadly subordinated instruments bought by the resolution entity or other entities in the same resolution group.[871] Alternatively, IMREL can also be produced by way of own funds under Article 45f(2)(b) BRRD.[872] The liabilities that have been prescribed here as subordinated instruments in a broad sense have to comply with further requirements set out in Article 45f(2)(a)(i–viii).[873] Basically, this means that the liability from the parent to a subsidiary or an affiliated entity under control of the parent also needs to fulfil certain eligibility criteria under Article 72a CRR.

As an alternative to these subordinated instruments or own funds, the resolution authority may permit the requirement of IMREL to be met in full part with a guarantee provided by the resolution entity according to Article 45f(5).[874] The requirements for this guarantee are set out in a way that provides for at least an amount that is equivalent to the amount for IMREL. The guarantee is triggered when the subsidiary is unable to pay its debts or liabilities as they fall due or when the entity has been determined to be failing or likely to fail in accordance with Article 59(4) BRRD.[875] The guarantee is collateralised through the financial collateral arrangement and thereby fulfils further requirement as set out under Article 45f(5)(d–g) BRRD.[876]

[G] Non-institution Subsidiaries

A banking group can have various subsidiaries that include both institutions and non-institutions. However, when looking at resolution groups, the question that arises is whether the non-institution subsidiaries form part of it and are subject to MREL requirements. In accordance with BRRD and SRM-R, an institution is defined as a credit institution or an investment firm covered by the consolidated supervision of the parent undertaking carried out by the ECB.[877] Further, a subsidiary is defined as a credit institution that is permanently affiliated to a central body, the central body itself, and their respective subsidiaries.[878] The resolution authority also has discretion to decide which institutional subsidiaries in the resolution group are required to comply with MREL requirements depending on the features of the solidarity mechanisms for bank cooperative groups and preferred resolution strategy.[879] Given the definitions do not

870. Article 2(42) BRRD, Article 3(24b) SRM-R.
871. Article 45f(2)(a) BRRD, Article 12g(2)(a) SRM-R.
872. Article 12g(2)(b) SRM-R.
873. Article 12g(2)(a)(i-viii) SRM-R.
874. Article 12g(3) SRM-R.
875. Article 21(3) SRM-R.
876. Article 12g(3)(f–i) SRM-R.
877. Article 2(23) BRRD, Article 3(13) SRM-R.
878. Article 2(5) BRRD, Article 3(21) SRM-R.
879. Article 45e(3) BRRD, Article 12f(3) SRM-R.

take into account non-institutional holdings in the banking group, it can be inferred that they are excluded from the resolution group and hence are not required to comply with MREL.[880]

The concern that arises subsequently is that certain types of non-institutional holdings might pose risk to the resolution group. Or, they may even be used to perform critical functions without being subject to regulatory requirements.[881]

[H] Subsidiaries of Non-EU Institutions

MREL calculations require a distinction to be made in respect of where the respective institutions are located. They can be located within the Eurozone. They can also be located within the EU. Finally, they can also be located in a third country, i.e. non-EU states. While the rules are throughout applicable for institutions within the EU, the only distinction is as to whether SRM-R is directly applicable (for participating Member States/Eurozone countries) or via BRRD or via national laws for non-participating Member States.

For subsidiaries of banking groups which are mainly domiciled outside of the EU, i.e. have the parent country in a non-EU country, special rules apply. Article 45d BRRD[882] defines requirements for material subsidiaries of non-EU G-SIIs with respect to amount and quality of MREL that can be set. Given that, such subsidiaries that are material subsidiaries of non-EU G-SIIs, even though they are not resolution entities, are required to satisfy the MREL requirements equal to 90% of the requirements for MREL required by institutions that are G-SIIs in the EU.[883]

In order to comply with MREL, Additional Tier 1/Additional Tier 2/eligible liabilities instruments will only count where these are held by third-country parent and are issued directly/indirectly through other entities in the same group given that those entities are established in the same third country as the parent or in an EU Member State.[884] Eligible liabilities instruments must also be subordinated and subject to write-down or conversion powers.[885] Further, the MREL is calculated on a consolidated basis to allow for an upstream of losses to the third-country parent in case of resolution.

880. Although institutions in the European Union complying with MREL are not required to also comply with TLAC requirements, Guiding Principles on the Internal Total Loss-Absorbing Capacity of G-SIBs by the FSB outline various scenarios where non-institutional holdings can be subject to MREL requirements. *See* Guiding Principal 4 by FSB. Guiding Principles on the Internal Total Loss-absorbing Capacity of G-SIBs ('Internal TLAC'). 6 July 2017. https://www.fsb.org/wp-content/uploads/P060717-1.pdf.
881. *See also* the recent Wirecard AG issue. Financial Times. Wirecard: the downfall of Germany's fintech star. 26 June 2020. https://www.ft.com/content/8569779b-64e5-4008-a634-0a97a7cf9eb5 and Financial Times. Wirecard collapses into insolvency. 25 June 2020. https://www.ft.com/content/ac949729-6167-4b6c-ac3f-f0aa71aca193.
882. Article 12e SRM-R.
883. Article 92b (1) CRR, Article 45d(2)(a) BRRD, Article 12e(2)(a) SRM-R.
884. Article 92b (2) CRR.
885. Article 92b (3)(b) CRR.

Following that, additional requirements for MREL may be determined by the resolution authorities to further ensure a reliable resolution at a national level.[886]

[I] Reporting and Disclosure Requirements

As the banking package has implemented the TLAC into EU standards while also amending the MREL, the requirements for TLAC and MREL must be met at all times. In order for markets and authorities to ensure compliance with the requirements, reporting and disclosure requirements have been imposed. The reporting and disclosure requirements for institutions subject to TLAC and MREL are set out separately. TLAC applies to resolution entities that are G-SIIs or part of G-SIIs and institutions that are material subsidiaries of non-EU G-SIIs but are not resolution entities themselves. Whereas, MREL applies to a broader population of institutions that include G-SIIs and non-SIIs. As both TLAC and MREL apply to G-SIIs, MREL is actually composed of TLAC requirement, and if needed, an institution-specific MREL is added on based on a case-to-case basis. The institutions that are subject to be wound up under normal insolvency proceedings are exempted from complying reporting and disclosure requirements.

[1] Reporting

For reporting requirements for TLAC, Article 430(1)(b) CRR does not go beyond simply requiring institutions to report to their competent authorities on requirements for TLAC and internal TLAC itself. Also, no minimum requirements or limits with regard to frequency of reporting are set out in Article 430 CRR.

However, for MREL and IMREL, the reporting requirements are contained in Article 45i(1) BRRD.[887] Institutions have to report to their competent and resolution authorities stating the amount of own funds and eligible liabilities counting towards MREL and IMREL on a semi-annual basis. The amount of 'other bail-in-able liabilities' are to be reported on an annual basis. With respect to both reports, institutions must also include composition, maturity profile, ranking in insolvency and whether they are governed by third-country law. If they are governed by third-country law, report must mention the third-country law and whether the instruments contain bail-in recognition clause. However, in accordance with Article 45i(2) BRRD, the competent authority or resolution authority has the option to request more frequent reporting. Further, Article 45i(5) BRRD also mandates the EBA to set the frequency of reporting with regard to the minimum standard already set.

886. Article 45d (3) and (5) BRRD; Article 12e (3) and (4) SRM-R.
887. Article 12(2) SRM-R.

[2] Disclosure

Disclosure requirements go beyond reporting requirements and are more elaborate. They require the information to not only be reported to the authorities but also to be made publicly available.[888] For TLAC disclosure requirements, Article 437a of CRR requires institutions to disclose information regarding the composition of their own funds and eligible liabilities along with their maturities and main features along with order of ranking of eligible liabilities in the creditor hierarchy. Also, the total amount of each issuance of eligible liabilities instruments, that is subordinated and senior, and the total amount of excluded liabilities shall need to be disclosed too. The frequency of disclosures of TLAC for large institutions is set to semi-annually by Article 433a CRR. However, the key matrices, such as own funds and eligible liabilities ratios along with their components, numerator and denominator, and the break down at the level of each resolution group needs to be disclosed quarterly. In accordance with Article 433 CRR, semi-annual and quarterly disclosures shall be published on the same date as the date on which the institutions publish their financial reports for the corresponding period where applicable or as soon as possible thereafter.

The disclosure requirements for MREL are laid out in Article 45i(3) BRRD and require institutions to disclose the amount of own funds and eligible liabilities, their composition including maturity profile and ranking in insolvency proceedings, and the applicable MREL requirement for the institution, i.e. whether MREL is calculated on a consolidated or individual basis. This information must be made publicly available at least on an annual basis. Annual disclosures shall be published on the same date as the date on which institutions publish their financial statements or as soon as possible thereafter.

On 3 August 2020, EBA published draft ITS on disclosure and reporting of MREL and TLAC.[889] Template for both reporting and disclosure has been enshrined in a single set of ITS document. The provisions of MREL disclosures will apply from the date of expiration of transition periods pursuant to Article 45m BRRD, i.e. from 1 January 2024 or if the resolution authority sets a compliance date later than that, it will apply from that deadline.

The first reporting date in accordance with the ITS is estimated to be 30 June 2021 for both TLAC and MREL giving institutions about one year from the deemed date of application. For reporting requirements, EBA will also publish data-point model, XBRL taxonomy and validation rules based on the final draft of ITS in the third quarter of 2020.

888. The playbook guidance expects banks to assess and reflect on disclosure obligations under Market Abuse Regulation (Regulation (EU) no 596/2014), Prospectus Regulation (Regulation (EU) no 2017/1129) and national transposition of the Transparency Directive (Directive 2004/109/EC) which might arise prior to and during the bail-in period (see para 31).

889. EBA. Draft Implementing Technical Standards on disclosure and reporting of MREL and TLAC. 3 August 2020. https://eba.europa.eu/sites/default/documents/files/document_library/Publications/Consultations/2020/CP%20on%20ITS%20on%20disclosure%20and%20reporting%20of%20MREL%20and%20TLAC/898092/Final%20report%20on%20draft%20ITS%20on%20disclosure%20and%20reporting%20on%20MREL%20and%20TLAC.pdf.

§6.03 CONTENTS OF RESOLUTION PLAN

In order to assess resolvability, the resolution authorities are obliged to set up a resolution plan for each institution and groups. For groups, the group-level resolution authorities are competent together with the resolution authorities of the subsidiaries.[890]

The resolution plan shall include:[891]

(a) a summary of the key elements of the plan;[892]
(b) a summary of the material changes to the institution that have occurred after the latest resolution information was filed;[893]
(c) a demonstration of how critical functions and core business lines could be legally and economically separated, to the extent necessary, from other functions so as to ensure continuity upon the failure of the institution;[894]
(d) an estimation of the time frame for executing each material aspect of the plan;[895]
(e) a detailed description of the assessment of resolvability carried out in accordance with paragraph 2 of this Article and with Article 15;[896]
(f) a description of any measures required pursuant to Article 17 to address or remove impediments to resolvability identified as a result of the assessment carried out in accordance with Article 15;[897]
(g) a description of the processes for determining the value and marketability of the critical functions, core business lines and assets of the institution;

890. Article 12 of BRRD and Commission Delegated Regulation (EU) 2016/1075 of 23 March 2016. *See also* Article 8(10) of SRM-R.
891. Article 10(7) of BRRD, Articles 8 et seq of SRM-R. *See also* Chapter 3 section 3.03.
892. As per SRB's recommendation for the bail-in playbook (section 3.1.1 para 21), the framework should include preparatory phase, resolution weekend and the implementation phase along with a closing phase.
893. *See* SRB's Expectations for Banks March 2020 Principle 1.2 Governance for Resolution Activities – 'Banks are expected to inform resolution authorities without undue delay on material changes planned to inform resolution authorities without undue delay on material changes planned to elements such as the business model, the structure, the operational set-up (e.g. changes to the IT infrastructure) and the governance having an impact on resolution planning activities or the implementation of the preferred resolution strategy and resolvability.' Further, the bank 'bail-in playbook' in accordance with SRB guidance needs to be updated at least annually in accordance with feedback from internal resolution team, guidance from resolution authorities, material changes within the bank, requirements of external stakeholders for external execution, trading venues and legal changes (see para 15).
894. *Ibid. See* 2.4.3 Principle 4.1 Operational continuity in resolution, Principle 4.4 Identifying, Mapping and Assessing dependencies on FMI service providers. *See also* page 40 for separability and restructuring. In the playbook, the bank is also expected to describe how it plans to ensure that an entity in its group remains operational in resolution, i.e. enhancing resilience of this entity (see para 25).
895. The bail-in playbook guidance places utmost importance on time. The playbook is expected to estimate and provide a timeline for the completion of all necessary tasks and map staff to processes if additional resources are needed to prevent bottlenecks or operational constraint, or if synergies could be created by merging procedures (see para 23).
896. *Ibid., see* role of SRB to proactively ensure that banks are resolvable.
897. *Ibid., see* page 7 for proposal of measures to address or remove impediments.

(h) a detailed description of the arrangements for ensuring that the information required pursuant to Article 11 is up-to-date and at the disposal of the resolution authorities at all times;[898]
(i) an explanation by the resolution authority as to how the resolution options could be financed without the assumption of any of the following: (i) any extraordinary public financial support besides the use of the financing arrangements established in accordance with Article 100; (ii) any central bank ELA; or (iii) any central bank liquidity assistance provided under non-standard collateralisation, tenor and interest rate terms;[899]
(j) a detailed description of the different resolution strategies that could be applied according to the different possible scenarios and the applicable timescales;
(k) a description of critical interdependencies;[900]
(l) a description of options for preserving access to payments and clearing services and other infrastructures and an assessment of the portability of client positions;[901]
(m) an analysis of the impact of the plan on the employees of the institution, including an assessment of any associated costs, and a description of envisaged procedures to consult staff during the resolution process, taking into account national systems for dialogue with social partners where applicable;[902]
(n) a plan for communicating with the media and the public;[903]
(o) the requirements referred to in Article 45e and Article 45f and a deadline to reach that level in accordance with Article 45m;
(p) where a resolution authority applies Article 45b(4), (5) or (7), a timeline for compliance by the resolution entity in accordance with Article 45m;
(q) a description of essential operations and systems for maintaining the continuous functioning of the institution's operational processes;[904]
(r) where applicable, any opinion expressed by the institution in relation to the resolution plan.

898. *Ibid.*, 'SRB will closely cooperate with competent authorities, taking into account information that is already available as well as assessments performed under supervisory tasks (e.g. on-site inspections).'
899. *Ibid.*, *see* 2.3 Liquidity and funding in resolution and Principle 3.1 Estimation of liquidity and funding needs in resolution.
900. *Ibid*- Principle 7.1 Structure, complexity and interdependencies.
901. *Ibid*- Principle 4.6 FMI contingency plan and measures to ensure continuity in access to FMI services.
902. *Ibid*- Principle 6.1 Communication Plan.
903. *Ibid*- Principle 6.2 Communication Governance. The playbook guidance goes further than this and expects banks to describe for each step which information needs to be communicated to which external stakeholder (relevant market authorities, trading venues, agents and CSDs). In terms of timelines, banks are expected to determine which information can be communicated to whom and at what point in time owing to legal requirements and restrictions, market reactions and potential threats to financial stability or successful resolution (see para 28-29).
904. *Ibid.*, section 2.4 Operational continuity in resolution and access to FMI services page 25.

The group resolution plan shall include the following:[905]

(a) set out the resolution actions that are to be taken for resolution entities in the scenarios referred to in Article 10(3), and the implications of those resolution actions in respect of other group entities, referred to in points (b), (c) and (d) of Article 1(1), the parent undertaking and subsidiary;

(aa) where a group comprises more than one resolution group, set out the resolution actions that are to be taken for the resolution entities of each resolution group and the implications of those actions on both of the following:

  (i) other group entities that belong to the same resolution group;

  (ii) other resolution groups.

(b) examine the extent to which the resolution tools could be applied and the resolution powers exercised, with respect to resolution entities established in the Union in a coordinated manner, including measures to facilitate the purchase by a third party of the group as a whole, of separate business lines or activities that are provided by a number of group entities, or of particular group entities or resolution groups, and identify any potential impediments to a coordinated resolution;

(c) where a group includes entities incorporated in third countries, identify appropriate arrangements for cooperation and coordination with the relevant authorities of those third countries and the implications for resolution within the Union;

(d) identify measures, including the legal and economic separation of particular functions or business lines, that are necessary to facilitate group resolution when the conditions for resolution are met;

(e) set out any additional actions, not referred to in this Directive, which relevant resolution authorities intend to take in relation to the entities within each resolution group;

(f) identify how the group resolution actions could be financed and, where the financing arrangement would be required, set out principles for sharing responsibility for that financing between sources of funding in different Member States. The plan shall not assume any of the following: (i) any extraordinary public financial support besides the use of the financing arrangements established in accordance with Article 100; (ii) any central bank ELA; or (iii) any central bank liquidity assistance provided under non-standard collateralisation, tenor and interest rate terms.

Those principles shall be set out on the basis of equitable and balanced criteria and shall take into account in particular Article 107(5) of BRRD and the impact on financial stability in all Member States concerned.

905. Article 12(3) of BRRD, Article 8(11) of SRM-R. *See also* Chapter 6 section 6.02[5] on group resolution.

There is a process for both resolution and group resolution plans laid out in Article 10 and Article 13 of BRRD, respectively.[906]

§6.04 IMPEDIMENTS FOR RESOLVABILITY

Key for the process is the possibility of the resolution authorities to remove impediments to resolution which have come up in the course of the planning process. To facilitate the process, the Member States shall ensure that pursuant to an assessment of resolvability of an entity, if a resolution authority determines that there are substantive impediments to resolvability, a notice of such findings is given in writing to the entity concerned, the competent authority and to resolution authorities of jurisdictions in which significant branches of the entity are located.[907] Following this notification, the requirement for resolution authorities to draw up resolution plans and reach a joint decision on group resolution shall be suspended. Such suspension lasts until resolution authority accepts measures to remove impediments to resolvability.[908]

The entity concerned shall propose to the resolution authority within two weeks of notice possible measures and the timelines for their implementation where the substantive impediment to resolvability is due to the following situations: (a) the entity meets the combined buffer requirement when considered in addition to Article 141(a)(1)(a), (b) and (c) of Directive 2013/36/EU but does not meet the combined buffer requirements when considered in addition to the MREL requirement (Article 45c and 45d of BRRD); or (b) the entity does not meet the requirements in Article 92a CRR (requirements for own funds and eligible liabilities for G-SIIs) and Article 494 CRR (transitional provisions concerning the requirement for own funds and eligible liabilities). Otherwise, the entity shall, within four months of the date of receipt of notice, propose to the resolution authority possible measures to address or remove the substantive impediments identified in the notification.[909] The resolution authority shall then assess if the proposed measures effectively address or remove the impediments in question with the consultation of the competent authority.

Where the resolution authority determines that the measures are ineffective, it shall either directly or indirectly, through the competent authority, require the entity to take alternative measures and notify the entity in writing of such measures. The entity shall then propose a plan to comply with the alternative measures within one month. When identifying alternative measures, the resolution authority shall demonstrate how the measures proposed by the entity were insufficient and how the alternative measures are proportionate in removing impediments.[910] The resolution authority

906. *See* corresponding processes in Part II (Specific Provisions), Title I (Functions Within The SRM And Procedural Rules), Chapter 1 (Resolution planning) of SRM-R.
907. Article 17(1) of BRRD, Article 10(7) and (8) SRM-R.
908. Article 17(2) of BRRD.
909. Article 17(3) of BRRD, Article 10(9) SRM-R. The bail-in playbook guidance expects banks to provide further details on the impact, if any, of a bail-in on the by-laws/articles of association and to clearly state if there are obstacles to the application of the bail-in related to the legal form of the bank (see para 53).
910. Article 17(4) of BRRD, Article 10(10) SRM-R.

shall also consider the potential effect of these measures not only on the particular entity but also on the internal market for financial services and on the financial stability of other Member States and in the Union as a whole.[911]

In the context of alternative measures, resolution authorities can:[912]

(a) require the entity to revise any intragroup financing agreement or review the absence thereof, or draw up service agreements, whether intragroup or with third parties, to cover the provision of critical functions;
(b) require the entity to limit its maximum individual and aggregate exposures;
(c) impose specific or regular additional information requirements relevant for resolution purposes;
(d) require the entity to divest specific assets;
(e) require the entity to limit or cease specific existing or proposed activities;
(f) restrict or prevent the development of new or existing business lines or sale of new or existing products;
(g) require changes to legal or operational structures of the entity or any group entity, either directly or indirectly under its control, so as to reduce complexity in order to ensure that critical functions may be legally and operationally separated from other functions through the application of the resolution tools;
(h) require an entity or a parent undertaking to set up a parent financial holding company in a Member State or a Union parent financial holding company; (ha) require an institution or an entity referred to in point (b), (c) or (d) of Article 1(1) of this Directive to submit a plan to restore compliance with the requirements of Article 45e or 45f of this Directive, expressed as a percentage of the TREA calculated in accordance with Article 92(3) of Regulation (EU) No 575/2013 and, where applicable, with the combined buffer requirement and with the requirements referred to in Article 45e or 45f of this Directive expressed as a percentage of the total exposure measure referred to in Article 429 and 429a of Regulation (EU) No 575/2013;
(i) require an institution or entity referred to in point (b), (c) or (d) of Article 1(1) to issue eligible liabilities to meet the requirements of Article 45e and Article 45f;
(j) require an institution or entity referred to in point (b), (c) or (d) of Article 1(1), to take other steps to meet the MREL under Article 45e and Article 45f, including in particular to attempt to renegotiate any eligible liabilities, Additional Tier 1 instrument or Tier 2 instrument it has issued, with a view to ensuring that any decision of the resolution authority to write down or convert that liability or instrument would be effected under the law of the jurisdiction governing that liability or instrument; (a) for the purpose of ensuring ongoing compliance with Article 45e or Article 45f, require an institution or entity referred to in point (b), (c) or (d) of Article 1(1), to change the maturity profile of: (i) own fund instruments, after having obtained the agreement of the

911. Article 17(7) of BRRD.
912. Article 17(5) of BRRD, Article 10(11) of SRM-R.

complex authority, and (ii) eligible liabilities referred to in Article 45b and in point (a) of Article 45f(2); and

(k) where an entity is the subsidiary of a mixed-activity holding company, requiring that the mixed-activity holding company set up a separate financial holding company to control the institution, if necessary in order to facilitate the resolution of the entity and to avoid the application of the resolution tools and the exercise of the powers referred to in Title IV having an adverse effect on the non-financial part of the group.

Hence the powers are far-reaching, and correspondingly resolution planning can have a severe impact in the structure and business model of an institution. In fact, the MREL and TLAC requirements as discussed above form part of that planning to require institutions to hold or obtain respective liabilities for bail-in. The requirement to set up holding structures to allow SPE bail-in concepts is a first sign of structural changes triggered by the aim of resolvability.

Another far-reaching power that the resolution authority has is to prohibit certain distributions where the entity meets the combined buffer requirement when considered in addition to Article 141(a)(1)(a), (b) and (c) of Directive 2013/36/EU but does not meet the combined buffer requirements when considered in addition to the MREL requirement (Article 45c and 45d of BRRD), and could be a reason for impediment to resolvability. The resolution authority of that entity shall have the power to prohibit that entity from distributing more than the Maximum Distributable Amount relating to MREL ('M-MDA').[913]

The M-MDA is calculated by first adding the sum of:

(a) any interim profits not included in Common Equity Tier 1 capital pursuant to Article 26(2) CRR, net of any distribution of profits or any payment resulting from the actions including (i) making a distribution in connection with Common Tier Equity 1 capital; (ii) creating an obligation to pay variable remuneration or discretionary pension benefits, or to pay variable remuneration if the obligation to pay was created at a time when the entity failed to meet the combined buffer requirement; or (iii) making payments on Additional Tier 1 instruments;

plus

(b) any year-end profits not included in Common Equity Tier 1 capital pursuant to Article 26(2) CRR, net of any distribution of profits or any payment resulting from the actions referred to in point (a) above;

minus

(c) amounts which would be payable by tax if the items specified in points (a) and (b) of this paragraph were to be retained.[914]

The sum is them multiplied by the following factors:[915]

(a) where the Common Equity Tier 1 capital maintained by the entity which is not used to meet any of the requirements set out in Article 92a of CRR and in Articles

913. Article 16a(1) of BRRD, Article 10a(1) SRM-R.
914. Article 16a(5) of BRRD, Article 10a(5) SRM-R.
915. Article 16a(4) of BRRD, Article 10a(4) SRM-R.

45c and 45d of BRRD, expressed as a percentage of TREA calculated in accordance with Article 92(3) of CRR, is within the first (that is, the lowest) quartile of the combined buffer requirement, the factor shall be 0;

(b) where the Common Equity Tier 1 capital maintained by the entity which is not used to meet any of the requirements set out in Article 92a of CRR and in Articles 45c and 45d of BRRD, expressed as a percentage of TREA calculated in accordance with Article 92(3) of CRR, is within the second quartile of the combined buffer requirement, the factor shall be 0.2;

(c) where the Common Equity Tier 1 capital maintained by the entity which is not used to meet the requirements set out in Article 92a of CRR and in Articles 45c and 45d of BRRD, expressed as a percentage of TREA calculated in accordance with Article 92(3) of CRR, is within the third quartile of the combined buffer requirement, the factor shall be 0.4;

(d) where the Common Equity Tier 1 capital maintained by the entity which is not used to meet the requirements set out in Article 92a of CRR and in Articles 45c and 45d of BRRD, expressed as a percentage of TREA calculated in accordance with Article 92(3) of CRR, is within the fourth (that is, the highest) quartile of the combined buffer requirement, the factor shall be 0.6;

wherein the lower bound and upper bound of each quartile of combined buffer requirement shall be calculated as:

$$\text{Lower bound} = \frac{\textit{Combined buffer requirement}}{4} \; x \; (Qn-1)$$

$$\text{Upper bound} = \frac{\textit{Combined buffer requirement}}{4} \; x. \; Qn$$

where 'Qn' = the ordinary number of the quartile concerned.[916]

The factors influencing resolution authority's decision to use the power include:[917] (a) reason, duration and magnitude of failure and its impact on resolvability; (b) development of entity's financial situation and likelihood of fulfilling it in the foreseeable future; (c) prospect that the entity will be able to ensure compliance with MREL requirements within a reasonable time frame; (d) where the entity is unable to replace liabilities that no longer meet the eligibility or maturity criteria laid down in Article 72b and 72c of CRR, or in Article 45b or Article 45f(2) of BRRD, if that inability is idiosyncratic or is due to market-wide disturbance; and (e) whether the exercise of the power is the most adequate and proportionate means of addressing the situation of the entity, taking into account its potential impact on both the financing conditions and resolvability of the entity concerned. The assessment of these factors shall be revisited at least every month for as long as the entity continues to be compliant with Article 141a (1)(a), (b) and (c) of Directive 2013/36/EU but non-compliant with Article 45c and 45d of BRRD. Should such situation last for more than nine months after the entity has been notified of it, the resolution authority shall exercise the power to prohibit distributions.[918]

916. Article 16a(6) of BRRD, Article 10a(6) SRM-R.
917. Article 16a(2) of BRRD, Article 10a(2) SRM-R.
918. Article 16a(3) of BRRD, Article 10a(3) SRM-R.

CHAPTER 7

Epilogue by Dr Mariana Wiederkehr:[919] Comparative Bank Recovery and Resolution – The Swiss Legal Framework

§7.01 BANKING REGULATION IN SWITZERLAND

Switzerland was one of the first jurisdictions in the world to adopt regulations relating to the restructuring of banks, in response to the key attributes set out by the FSB.[920] The Swiss Banking Act[921] was reformed with effect as of September 2011. Soon after, the Swiss Financial Market Supervisory Authority (FINMA) enacted the new Banking Insolvency Ordinance (BIO-FINMA)[922] with original effect as of November 2012. Several amendments have been made to Swiss banking regulations since then. However, these two instruments provide a coherent set of rules to be applied in the case an institution suffers some sort of financial distress.[923]

919. Dr Mariana Wiederkehr is a lecturer at the University of St. Gallen in Switzerland. She undertook a Bachelor's in Legal Studies at the Pontificia Universidade Catolica do Parana in Brazil, followed by an LLM in International Economic Law at the Martin-Luther-University in Germany and a doctoral programme at the University of St. Gallen in Switzerland.

920. *See* report of the FSB dated 12 November 2014, entitled *Towards full implementation of the FSB Key Attributes of Effective Resolution Regimes for Financial Institutions*. Available at: http://www.financialstabilityboard.org/wp-content/uploads/Resolution-Progress-Report-to-G20.pdf.

921. Bundesgesetz über die Banken und Sparkassen (Bankengesetz, BankG consolidated as of 1 January 2019). Unofficial translation by KPMG available at: https://assets.kpmg/content/dam/kpmg/ch/pdf/ch-banking-act-en.pdf.

922. Verordnung der Eidgenössischen Finanzmarktaufsicht über die Insolvenz von Banken und Effektenhändlern (Bankeninsolvenzverordnung-FINMA, BIV-FINMA, consolidated as of 1 April 2017). Translation for information purposes only published by the Swiss Federal Council, available at: https://www.admin.ch/opc/en/classified-compilation/20112977/index.html. *See* discussion in Nobel, p. 454.

923. *Schiltknecht*, New FINMA Banking Insolvency Ordinance, p. 2.

The BIO-FINMA innovates mostly in terms of restructuring[924] of institutions and adopts the essential terms of the former Bank Bankruptcy Ordinance[925] in respect of bank insolvency and liquidation without any relevant changes. The Bank Bankruptcy Ordinance ceased to have an effect upon the entry into force of BIO-FINMA.[926]

The final BIO-FINMA was enacted a few months after the European Commission published the first draft of the BRRD.[927] Therefore, one cannot imply that either set of regulation has influenced the other. Rather, it is safer to say that both were influenced by the recommendations of the FSB, as discussed multilaterally within the G-20.[928]

Another relevant piece of legislation in the context of bank restructuring is the Swiss Banking Ordinance.[929] This Ordinance contains rules relating to depositor protection schemes and to systemically important institutions.

§7.02 SCOPE OF APPLICATION OF BIO-FINMA

[A] Covered Institutions

The institutions covered by BIO-FINMA[930] are banks under the Banking Act, securities firms under the Financial Institutions Act,[931] and central mortgage bond institutions under the Mortgage Bond Act.[932]

Under Article 1(1) of the Banking Act, the term banks shall include banks - being the sole proprietorship, general partnerships or limited partnerships - private banks, and savings banks.[933] Scholars criticise the lack of a precise legal definition of a 'bank' under Swiss regulation and refer to the practice of the Swiss National Bank to describe

924. The term used in BIO-FINMA for recovery and resolution is 'restructuring'. For the purpose of consistency with the examined Swiss regulation, this chapter uses the term 'restructuring' to refer to the set of measures described thereunder. Another difference is that while the BRRD applied the term 'institutions', BIO-FINMA chose to use the term 'banks' instead.
925. Verordnung der Eidgenössischen Finanzmarktaufsicht über den Konkurs von Banken und Effektenhändlern (Bankenkonkursverordnung-FINMA, BKV-FINMA) dated 30 June 2005, available at: http://www.admin.ch/opc/de/classified-compilation/20051042/index.html.
926. Article 60(1) of BIO-FINMA.
927. First draft reference and date. At the time of enactment of BIO-FINMA, FINMA confirmed that it was compatible with the European Commission's draft BRRD. *Schiltknecht*, New FINMA Banking Insolvency Ordinance, p. 3.
928. Bankeninsolvenzverordnung-FINMA - Erläuterungsbericht, published by the Swiss Financial Market Supervisory Authority on 16 January 2012, available at: https://www.finma.ch/en/news/2012/10/mm-inkraftsetzung-bankeninsolvenzverordnung-finma-20121022/.
929. Verordnung über die Banken und Sparkassen (Bankenverordnung, BankV1) dated 17 May 1972 (consolidated as of 1 January 2020), available in German at: https://www.admin.ch/opc/de/classified-compilation/20131795/202001010000/952.02.pdf.
930. Article 2 BIO-FINMA.
931. Federal Act on Financial Institutions (Financial Institutions Act, FinIA, consolidated as of 18 February 2020), available at: https://www.admin.ch/opc/en/classified-compilation/20152662/index.html.
932. Pfandbriefgesetz (PfG, consolidated as of 1 January 2015). Available in German at https://www.admin.ch/opc/de/classified-compilation/19300030/index.html.
933. Original text in German: '*Diesem Gesetz unterstehen die Banken, Privatbankiers (Einzelfirmen2, Kollektiv - und Kommanditgesellschaften) und Sparkassen, nachstehend Banken genannt.*'

the local banking system.[934] Basically, this authority categorises the banks as cantonal banks; big banks; regional banks and savings banks; Raiffeisen banks; stock exchange banks; other banking institutions; foreign-controlled banks; branches of foreign banks; and private bankers.[935] All of these may in principle be subject to BIO-FINMA restructuring proceedings.

As defined in Article 41 of the Financial Institutions Act:

> A securities firm is an entity that, on a commercial basis:
>
> a. trades in securities in its own name for the account of clients;
> b. trades in securities for its own account on a short-term basis, operates primarily on the financial market and: 1. could thereby jeopardise the proper functioning of the financial market, or 2. is a member of a trading venue; or
> c. trades in securities for its own account on a short-term basis and publicly quotes prices for individual securities upon request or on an ongoing basis (market maker).

As per Article 1 of the Mortgage Bond Act, central mortgage bond institutions have the purpose of making available long-term mortgage loans to real estate owners at the cheapest and constant interest rates.[936]

The personal scope of BIO-FINMA is quite similar to that of the BRRD, with the exception that the latter only applies to investment firms which required an initial capital of EUR 730,000.[937] In practice, however, the scope may be almost the same, as security firms authorised in Switzerland are required to have a minimum capital of CHF 1,500,000.[938]

Some special rules apply in the case of systemically important institutions, as defined in Articles 7 and 8 of the Banking Act. Basically, these are institutions whose failure would cause considerable damage to the Swiss economy and the Swiss financial system. For this reason, new rules were created to ensure the continuation of these institutions' economically critical functions and to avoid the use of state aid. Functions shall be deemed critical if they are indispensable and cannot be substituted at short notice, such as payment transactions, deposit and lending. Currently, Credit Suisse, UBS, Zürcher Kantonalbank, Raiffeisen Group and Post Finance are deemed to be systemically important.[939]

---

934. *Kunz*, p. 99.
935. Swiss National Bank, Banks in Switzerland 2019, p. 9, available at: https://www.snb.ch/en/mmr/reference/banks_2019/source/banks_2019.en.pdf.
936. Original text in German: '*Die Pfandbriefzentralen haben den Zweck, dem Grundeigentümer langfristige Grundpfanddarlehen zu möglichst gleichbleibendem und billigem Zinsfusse zu vermitteln.*'
937. Articles 1 and 2(1)(3) of the BRRD.
938. Article 69(1) of the Financial Institutions Ordinance (Finanzinstitutsverordnung, FINIV, consolidated as of 1 January 2020) available at: https://www.admin.ch/opc/en/classified-compilation/20192376/index.html.
939. As determined by Swiss National Bank - Determination of systemically important banks, available at: https://www.snb.ch/de/iabout/finstab/finstab_pub/id/finstab_pub_banksector. Bertschinger, p. 548.

[B] Covered Assets

The rules on the scope in terms of assets are set out in Article 3 of BIO-FINMA. In accordance with the principle of universality, the applicability of this Ordinance extends over all assets held by the covered institution in Switzerland and abroad. National and foreign creditors of the institution, as well as creditors of the institution's foreign branches, shall be given equal privileges.

§7.03 GENERAL OVERVIEW OF RESTRUCTURING PROCEEDINGS

[A] Principles

The principle of NCWO[940] assumes great relevance in BIO-FINMA, as a condition for restructuring. Hence, a restructuring may only take place if thereafter creditors are likely to be in a better position than they would be in an insolvency scenario.[941] A second important principle is the shareholder subordination and the creditors' ranking. The applicable waterfall of payment of claims shall start, first, with all costs relating to the restructuring proceedings which have been approved by the restructuring agent.[942] Thereafter, the specific rules on bail-in and loss bearing will apply as discussed below.

[B] Confidentiality

Just as in Article 84 of the BRRD, confidentiality is also a procedural obligation under BIO-FINMA. In the latter, parties with a sufficiently credible claim have the right to request an inspection of the restructuring proceeding documents. The restructuring agent shall decide on whether to grant it or not, provided that the relevant person will use the information for the protection of its immediate financial interests only.[943]

On the other hand, transparency in the resolution proceedings is a key objective of BIO-FINMA, provided that it is balanced with flexibility of FINMA to make ad hoc decisions on a case-by-case basis.[944] For instance, relevant decisions on restructuring proceedings shall be made public immediately.[945]

940. *See* Chapter 5, section 5.05. Also *Andreotti*, p. 465.
941. Article 40(1)(a) of BIO-FINMA.
942. Article 43 of BIO-FINMA.
943. Article 3 of BIO-FINMA. A breach of this commitment shall entail criminal penalties to the inspecting person.
944. Bankeninsolvenzverordnung-FINMA – Erläuterungsbericht, published by the Swiss Financial Market Supervisory Authority on 16 January 2012, available at: https://www.finma.ch/en/news/2012/10/mm-inkraftsetzung-bankeninsolvenzverordnung-finma-20121022/.
945. Article 41(4) of BIO-FINMA.

[C] Trigger Points for Restructuring

The course of action leading to a restructuring is set out in Article 25 of the Banking Act. Thereunder, an institution may be at a threat of insolvency, by over-indebtedness, serious liquidity problems, or no longer being able to fulfil its capital requirements. The Banking Act does not define these terms; hence other legislative instruments, such as the Swiss Civil Code[946] and the Swiss Debt Enforcement and Bankruptcy Law,[947] are used to supplement them.[948] In general terms, the concepts are applied as follows:

- Over-indebtedness corresponds to the situation in which the total liabilities exceed the total assets of the institutions, and the institution is no longer able to fulfil its payment obligations.
- Serious liquidity problems relate to illiquidity or inability to pay, meaning that the institution may not be able to settle its debts even though it is not over-indebted. Usually, it is required that this situation is expected to last for a longer period of time and is not merely temporary;[949] and
- The non-fulfilment with the capital requirements is more objective as it refers to the parameters set in the Capital Requirements Ordinance. This trigger can only be pulled after the expiry of a term set out by FINMA. It presents a higher supervision aspect, as capital requirements compliance is a prerequisite for the banking licence.[950]
- If there are justified concerns in relation to one of the circumstances above, FINMA shall have three options: (i) to adopt protective measures, (ii) to start restructuring proceedings, or (iii) to move to liquidation of the institution.
- Protective measures assume a similar effect as the early intervention measures of the BRRD.[951] They may be adopted individually or together with restructuring or liquidation proceedings. Article 26 of the Banking Act contains a non-exhaustive list of protective measures:[952]
  - To issue instructions to the governing bodies of the bank.
  - To appoint an investigator.
  - To remove representation powers of the bank's governing bodies or withdraw their mandate.

946. Federal Act on the Amendment of the Swiss Civil Code (Part Five: The Code of Obligations) dated 30 March 1911 (consolidated as of 1 January 2020), available at: https://www.admin.ch/opc/en/classified-compilation/19110009/202004010000/220.pdf.
947. *Bundesgesetz über Schuldbetreibung und Konkurs*, consolidated as of 1 January 2020, available at: https://www.admin.ch/opc/de/classified-compilation/18890002/202001010000/281.1.pdf.
948. *Kähr* (2013), p. 479. *See also Kähr* (2014).
949. *Kähr* (2013), p. 480.
950. *Kähr* (2013), p. 481. The capital requirements are described mainly in a FINMA ordinance, as supplemented by a series of FINMA circulars (*Rundschreiben*). *See* Capital Requirements Ordinance – Verordnung über die Eigenmittel und Risikoverteilung für Banken und Effektenhändler (Eigenmittelverordnung, ERV), consolidated as of 28 March 2020, available at: https://www.admin.ch/opc/de/official-compilation/2020/1105.pdf.
951. *See* Chapter 4, section 4.04.
952. *See Pulver*, pp. 94 et seq.

- To withdraw the mandate of the audit firm appointed under corporate law or banking regulation.
- To restrict the bank's business operations.
- To prohibit the bank to make payments, to accept payments, or to carry out securities transactions.
- To close the bank; and
- To declare a moratorium or to postpone maturity dates, except for secured receivables of central mortgage bond institutions.[953]

If FINMA is convinced of a prospect of restructuring, the respective proceeding will start. In principle, FINMA will need sufficient evidence of two prerequisites to justify the decision not to liquidate:

(a) 'the creditors are likely to be placed at a better position in restructuring than in bankruptcy; and
(b) the restructuring plan is feasible in terms of time and scope'.[954]

If these conditions are given, FINMA will rule on the commencement of restructuring proceedings and appoint a restructuring agent.[955] This appointment shall specifically determine which powers are delegated to the restructuring agent, as well as how reporting, control, and costs are to be administered.

§7.04 RESTRUCTURING PLAN

[A] *Ex ante* Planning

With respect to planning, BIO-FINMA differs slightly from the BRRD. The latter indeed imposes an obligation on all covered institutions and the resolution authority to draft living wills. While institutions shall draw up a recovery plan for restoration of the financial position, resolution authorities draw up a resolution plan in respect of resolution actions to be adopted in distress scenarios.

A similar provision exists for systemically important institutions in the Swiss regulation. The Banking Ordinance requires these institutions to deliver to FINMA an emergency plan (*Notfallplan*), a recovery plan (*Stabilisierungsplan*), and a resolution plan (*Abwicklungsplan*).[956] Once a year, at the end of the second calendar quarter, the institutions shall deliver and update the emergency plan, the recovery plan, and the information necessary for drafting the resolution plan. While the institution is entitled to draw up the emergency plan and the recovery plan, FINMA produces the resolution plan based on information provided by the institution.

953. Article 26 of the Banking Act.
954. Article 40 of BIO-FINMA.
955. Articles 41 and 42 of BIO-FINMA. FINMA may also decide to carry out the restructuring actions itself.
956. Article 9(2)(d) of the Banking Act; Articles 60-66 of the Banking Ordinance. *See Bösch.*

The emergency plan specifies measures aiming at the continuation of the systemically relevant functions, to be adopted in case of a risk of insolvency. It shall take into account the issues of time, legal obstacles, technical infrastructure, cross-guarantees within a financial conglomerate, maintenance, and restoration of capital requirements.[957] The recovery plan shall establish the measures to ensure that the systemically relevant bank can stabilise after a crisis in a sustainable manner and without state support. In the resolution plan, FINMA describes how it shall conduct the resolution or liquidation of the institution. It shall foresee detailed steps to ring-fence the risky areas from the rest of the institution from an economic and a legal perspective.[958]

[1] Capital Requirements

In Switzerland as elsewhere, the regulation of living wills is very much connected with capital requirements.[959] BIO-FINMA does not set forth a resolution fund, as established under the European Banking Union. Hence, the financing of the resolution will be partly anticipated in the capital structure of the institution, and partly financed (preferably, from market participants) in accordance with the restructuring plan. As part of a good management strategy, the institution shall hold sufficient own funds to ensure that such plans are viable.[960] Swiss capital requirements - so-called Swiss Finish - are Basel III compliant.[961] A general set of ratios applies across all financial institutions, while increased targets are established for systemically important institutions.

The Capital Adequacy Ordinance establishes the ratios applying in relation to financial institutions' RWA.[962]

FINMA carries out stress tests of relevant banks but does not publish the results in detail. Under the revised circular of FINMA governing liquidity risk management requirements,[963] banks and financial conglomerates shall also conduct their own tests with respect to severe liquidity stress scenarios.[964] The IMF has issued a report in June 2019 confirming that the Swiss financial sector remains resilient but encouraged close risk monitoring.[965]

957. Article 61 of the Banking Ordinance.
958. Article 66 of the Banking Ordinance.
959. *Von der Krone/Monferrini*, p. 506.
960. *Ibid.*
961. *Bösch*, p. 267.
962. Verordnung über die Eigenmittel und Risikoverteilung für Banken und Effektenhändler (Eigenmittelverordnung, ERV, consolidated as of 28 March 2020), available in German at: https://www.admin.ch/opc/de/official-compilation/2020/1105.pdf.
963. Rundschreiben 2015/2 – Liquiditätsrisiken, consolidated as of 7 December 2017, available in German at: https://www.finma.ch/de/~/media/finma/dokumente/rundschreiben-archiv/2015/rs-15-02/rs-15-02-02-20171207.pdf?la=de.
964. Neue Zürcher Zeitung, Kein Stress für Schweizer Banken, dated 27 October 2014, http://www.nzz.ch/wirtschaft/kein-stress-fuer-schweizer-banken-1.18412651.
965. International Monetary Fund, Country Report No 19/189 Switzerland: Financial Sector Assessment Program; Technical Note-Stress Testing the Banking Sector dated June 2019, available at: https://www.imf.org/~/media/Files/Publications/CR/2019/1CHEEA2019009.ashx.

[B] *Ex post* Planning

For all non-systemically important institutions, the restructuring plan shall only be drawn up *ex post*, for concrete implementation. Thereunder, the restructuring plan can only be prepared if it is likely that the institution is able to recover or can continue to provide banking services.[966] If there is no prospect of restructuring the institution, FINMA will revoke its banking licence and consequently place it under liquidation.[967]

The function of a restructuring plan is quite similar to that of *ex ante* plans, though. Just as recovery and resolution plans, it aims at setting forth measures for dealing with a failing institution. The restructuring plan shall ensure that its implementation will lead to the institution fulfilling the requirements to maintain a banking licence and complying with the applicable regulations.[968] To achieve this purpose, the plan may mandate a transfer of assets and liabilities solution and/or, as a last resort, a bail-in of liabilities.

The restructuring agent shall draw up the restructuring plan, which is then approved by FINMA.[969] The general assembly of shareholders of the institution does not need to approve the plan.[970] Nonetheless, there are objective criteria that guide the approval of the restructuring plan and serve as prerequisites for an approval to be legitimate. The plan must:

(a) be based upon a prudent valuation of the bank's assets;
(b) place the creditors in all probability in a more favourable position than they would be in the case of a liquidation of the bank;
(c) take into consideration the precedence of the interests of the creditors over those of the shareholders;
(d) consider the legal and economic connection between assets, liabilities and contractual relationships.[971]

As in the BRRD, the Swiss regulation also requires an independent valuation of assets, liabilities and contractual relationships (item (a) above). The valuation must be carried out efficiently and in a reasonably short period of time, in order not to delay the finalisation of the restructuring plan. Finally, FINMA shall decide on the appropriate compensation after considering the results of the valuation.

The plan shall include the capital structure and the business model to be implemented by the bank upon restructuring and include detailed information on the following matters:[972]

- future compliance with the licensing requirements;

966. Article 28(1) of the Banking Act.
967. Article 33 of the Banking Act.
968. Article 29 of the Banking Act.
969. Article 44 of BIO-FINMA.
970. The institution itself has a right to challenge legal aspects of the plan based on Articles 285-292 of the Swiss Debt Enforcement and Bankruptcy Law.
971. Article 31 of the Banking Act.
972. Article 44 of BIO-FINMA.

- the bank's assets and liabilities;
- the bank's future organisation and management and, if the bank is part of a banking group or a banking conglomerate, the future organisation of the group or conglomerate;
- whether and how the restructuring plan affects the rights of the bank's creditors as well as the owners;
- whether the bank's right to contest the restructuring plan and assert civil responsibility claims under Article 32 of the Banking Act are excluded;
- which current members of the bank's governing bodies are to retain responsibility for its management, and why this is in the interests of the bank, its creditors and its owners;
- the severance settlements for departing members of governing bodies;
- those transactions which require an entry in the Commercial Register or in the Land Register; and
- the provisions in sections 3 (Corporate Actions) and 4 (Continuation of Certain Banking Services) of this chapter which are to be applied to a specific restructuring case.

Once FINMA approves the restructuring plan, its decision shall be published so that creditors and shareholders may inspect it.[973] The approval decision shall have all necessary constitutive effects, including those relating to the transfer of property or other in rem rights.[974] For instance, the registration of a change of creditor in a mortgage deed with the relevant real estate registry shall have a declaratory effect only, since the approved plan has immediate *erga omnes* effect.[975]

The FINMA-approved plan may be set aside if a majority of creditors reject it.[976] They may do so within a timeline set out by FINMA, which cannot be shorter than ten business days.[977] The request for rejection must be duly justified, and BIO-FINMA already excludes the mere transfer of liabilities and contractual relationships and the change of debtor as possible rejection grounds.[978]

The consequence of such a rejection is then that the bank shall be liquidated. This possibility of creditors' rejection only applies to banks that are not considered systemically important institutions. For these institutions, higher risks are at stake for the financial system as a whole and, hence, FINMA has the final decision power to try and ensure the continuation of critical services. The dissenting creditors of systemically important institutions shall have, however, a right to compensation for damages.[979]

973. Article 45(2) of BIO-FINMA.
974. Article 45(3) of BIO-FINMA.
975. Entwurf Bankeninsolvenzverordnung-FINMA – Kernpunkte, published by the Swiss Financial Market Supervisory Authority on 16 January 2012, available at: https://www.finma.ch/de/~/media/finma/importiertedokumente/regulierung/anhoerungen/17-biv-finma/kp-biv-finma.pdf?la=de.
976. Article 45 of BIO-FINMA and Article 31a of the Banking Act in connection with Article 8 of BIO-FINMA.
977. Article 46(1) of BIO-FINMA.
978. Article 46(2) of BIO-FINMA.
979. Article 24(4) of the Banking Act.

§7.05 RESTRUCTURING TOOLS

[A] The Transfer Tool

[1] General Overview

The BIO-FINMA also allows for the continuation of certain critical banking services by the transfer of the relevant assets and liabilities, as well as contractual relationships to another entity.[980] The transferee may be either a bridge bank or another entity approved by FINMA.[981] This tool is in fact much similar to the bridge bank tool provided for in the BRRD.[982]

Article 51 of BIO-FINMA specifies clearly the content of the restructuring plan that orders a transfer to ensure that it envisages the necessary structure for a transfer to take place: the transfer plan shall:

(a) name the legal entity or entities to which such banking services and assets are to be transferred;
(b) describe the assets, liabilities and contractual relationships to be transferred and the compensation to be provided for them;
(c) describe the banking services that are to be continued and transferred;
(d) list the corporate actions undertaken and, where banking services are to be transferred to a bridge bank, describe how assets and liabilities will be shared between the bank and the bridge bank;
(e) stipulate an obligation on the bank's part to take any action necessary to ensure that all of the assets and objects to be transferred, including in particular those located abroad or subject to foreign law, can be transferred to the other legal entity;
(f) explain whether compensation is to be paid, how such compensation is to be calculated and whether a maximum compensation amount is to be imposed;
(g) explain whether systems and applications will be used jointly by the bank and the other legal entity and, if banking services are to be continued by a bridge bank, how the latter will be guaranteed access to payment transaction and financial market infrastructure and how it will be able to use this;
(h) describe how to preserve the legal and economic connections between assets, liabilities and contractual relationships, thereby ensuring that only the following can be transferred: (1) all claims and liabilities on the bank's part vis-à-vis a counterparty or several counterparties that can be offset, in particular those that are subject to a netting agreement; (2) secured claims and liabilities together with their collateral; and (3) structured financing

980. Section 4 of BIO-FINMA.
981. The bridge bank may function for a period of two years, with a possible extension. Article 52(2) of BIO-FINMA.
982. *See* Chapter 5, section 5.19.

arrangements or comparable capital market agreements to which the bank is a party, together with all rights and obligations pertaining to them.[983]

[2] Stay of Early Termination Rights

If certain financial contracts, mainly derivative contracts, are transferred, FINMA has the authority to order a stay of termination rights.[984] This stay may last for forty-eight hours with a view of guaranteeing the continuity of critical functions, as well as the protection of the domestic and international financial systems. Should there be reasons other than the transfer or protective measure that would entitle the institution's counterparty to terminate the contract, the stay shall not apply to that contract.

Article 56 of BIO-FINMA includes a definition of the financial contract whose early termination rights may be stayed:

(a) the following contracts relating to securities and book-entry securities: contracts for buying, selling, repurchasing, and lending securities and book-entry securities and trading with options on securities and book-entry securities irrespective of whether it is done individually, in groups or as indices;
(b) the following contracts relating to commodities: contracts for buying and selling commodities with future delivery and for options trading on commodities or commodity deliveries;
(c) the following contracts relating to futures and forwards: contracts for buying, selling or transferring goods, services, rights or interest yields at a certain price set in advance and at a future date;
(d) the following contracts relating to swaps: contracts for foreign exchange, currency, precious metals, credit as well as securities and book-entry securities, commodities and their indices; and
(e) all other contracts with an effect equivalent to those specified under points (a)-(d).

[B] Bail-In

[1] Objective and Scope

The corporate actions set forth in BIO-FINMA entail the conversion of debt into equity and the write-down of claims. As a general rule, all liabilities are convertible except for those expressly excluded.[985] This is basically the Swiss version of the bail-in tool. As in the BRRD, excluded liabilities shall be those of employees, client deposits up to CHF

983. *See also* Article 55 of BIO-FINMA in this respect.
984. Article 30a of the Banking Act.
985. Article 49 of BIO-FINMA.

100,000 covered by the depositor guarantee scheme, secured liabilities, as well as off-settable liabilities.[986]

BIO-FINMA does not set forth a MREL, as does the BRRD. Nonetheless, Swiss regulation requires the systemically important institutions maintain a considerable amount of contingent capital, such as CoCo bonds. These may be either automatically convertible bonds or write-down bonds, in each case subject to the occurrence of a trigger event.[987] The conditions leading to a conversion or write-down trigger shall be those of threat of insolvency or the point of no viability.[988] In order to be considered for the purpose of capital requirements calculation, such CoCo bonds must be approved by FINMA.[989]

[2] Implementation

Under the BIO-FINMA bail-in tool,[990] shareholders and debt holders bear the costs of the restructuring, whereby debt holders shall have an economic advantage over shareholders. In practice, this means that, first, all equity capital and hybrid debt instruments such as CoCo bonds must be written down.[991] For this reason, it is said that the bail-in is a subsidiary measure, which takes place after the contractual trigger of conversion under the CoCo bonds has been pulled. Only after all legal write-downs and contractual debt-to-equity conversion have occurred may a conversion of other 'traditional' debt liabilities into equity take place under the restructuring plan.[992] The conversion shall be so that the institution holds sufficient capital to continue its business activities after the restructuring.[993]

In sum, Article 48(1) of BIO-FINMA mandates the sequence of bail-in as follows:

(1) the share capital must be completely written down;
(2) all CoCo capital must be converted;
(3) other debt claims may be converted into equity in the following order:
  (i) subordinated claims without capital adequacy eligibility;
  (ii) other claims not excluded from the conversion, with the exception of deposits; and
  (iii) deposits, in so far as they are not privileged.

The above shows that there is not a very tight rank among the claims subject to bail-in, so that FINMA has a certain degree of flexibility to distribute losses across different classes of junior and senior creditors. The only exception is the ranking of

986. *Ibid.*
987. *Schiltknecht/McHale*, p. 511.
988. *Grünewald/Weber*, p. 559.
989. Article 127(2) of the Capital Requirements Ordinance.
990. The Swiss Code of Obligations applies *mutatis mutandis* to the corporate actions set forth in section 3 of BIO-FINMA. Article 47(1)(b) of BIO-FINMA.
991. *Grünewald/Weber*, p. 555.
992. Article 31(1)(c) of the Banking Act and Articles 48 and 49 of BIO-FINMA.
993. Article 48(1)(a) of BIO-FINMA.

depositors as a last resort in the order of conversion. The conversion of liabilities may be total or partial. It may also be combined with or substituted by a reduction of the debt claims, depending on what is set out in the restructuring plan at the discretion of FINMA.[994]

§7.06 DEPOSIT GUARANTEE SCHEMES

The Banking Act determines that deposits up to CHF 100,000 per creditor are insured in the event of a crisis.[995] The so-called privileged deposits are:[996]

- client claims arising from banking or securities dealing operations that are booked or should be booked to the balance sheet as liabilities to clients (savings and investments), other amounts due to customers, or medium-term notes;
- Medium-term notes deposited at the bank in the depositor's name.

Bearer claims, medium-term notes that are not held at the bank, as well as contractual and non-contractual compensation claims such as compensation claims for custody assets no longer at the bank's disposal are excluded from the scope of the insurance.[997]

Switzerland has a deposit insurance fund in place, to cover privileged deposits up to the amount of six billion Swiss francs. The insurance fund shall only be called upon if the institution's liquid assets are not sufficient to make the payments at the time of a crisis. The restructuring agent shall make the payments to depositors without any netting within a period of twenty business days after a protective measure has been ordered by FINMA.[998]

Institutions are not required to make *ex ante* contributions to the deposit insurance fund.[999] Rather, they must hold domestic claims and assets (including illiquid) summing up at least 125% of their privileged assets.[1000] In case the deposit insurance fund needs to step in and make payments to depositors, the fund shall subrogate in the depositors' rights against the bank in the amount of the disbursements made.[1001] Hence, in this case, institutions make *ex post* reimbursement contributions.

994. Article 50 of BIO-FINMA.
995. Article 37a(1) of the Banking Act.
996. Article 25 of BIO-FINMA in conjunction with Article 37a of the Banking Act.
997. In the first draft of BIO-FINMA, bank accounts where the holder's identity cannot be easily revealed such as those under pseudonyms and numbered accounts were privileged under the deposit protection scheme. This was, however, deleted due to market pressure. *Rayroux/Conti*, p. 3.
998. Article 37i of the Banking Act.
999. *See* discussion and critique in *Reiser*.
1000. Article 37a of the Banking Act.
1001. Article 37j of the Banking Act.

§7.07 CROSS-BORDER RESTRUCTURING

This final section probably best reveals the relevance of a chapter on the Swiss regulation. Indeed, Swiss systemically relevant institutions are not only locally relevant conglomerates but also relevant on a European and global level.[1002] Also, European institutions have significant businesses as well as group entities established in Swiss territory. National authorities often have conflicting interests because of the asymmetric positions of the supervised entities.[1003] If the balance sheet of a group would be looked at nationally, probably subsidiaries in some countries would be cash-positive, while subsidiaries in other countries would have a cash-negative position. Nonetheless, the effectiveness of a group's restructuring depends on the coordination of the multiple competent authorities. Hence, there is a need for regulation of the relationship between cross-border authorities and the cross-border effects of legal measures.

BIO-FINMA does not have an express methodology for group resolutions, but the banking regulation includes instruments that enable cooperation. The Swiss Banking Act sets forth that the restructuring agent shall coordinate with foreign authorities and governing bodies with respect to restructuring measures.[1004] For this purpose, FINMA has the authority to recognise the measures of foreign authorities, as long as they do not adversely affect the interests of creditors:[1005] FINMA may even conduct such recognition regardless of reciprocity and ex officio, i.e. without a specific request by the interested party.[1006] With respect to Swiss financial groups, FINMA has adopted the SPE approach, because the orderly restructuring of a too-big-to-fail bank should be designed at its consolidated balance sheet.[1007] In order to effectively be able to carry out this centralised type of restructuring, it will certainly need to count on the cooperation of authorities in Europe and in the US. These jurisdictions have also similar rules on cooperation, but it is still not clear how they will be implemented in practice.

1002. *Schiltknecht*, p. 463.
1003. *Wünsch*, p. 534.
1004. Article 9 of BIO-FINMA.
1005. Article 37f and 37g of the Banking Act; Article 10 of BIO-FINMA.
1006. *Schwob/Müller*.
1007. *Grünewald*, p. 276.

Appendix Secondary Legislation and Technical Standards Still to Come

Certain issues were too specific and technical to be established in BRRD. For this reason, it is expected that the Commission, together with the EBA, adopts RTS[1008] and ITS[1009] over the next months. The EBA shall also issue guidelines and recommendations on certain issues.[1010] This Appendix lists the upcoming regulatory acts that are expected to follow BRRD.

1008. Article 290 of the Treaty on the Functioning of the European Union: (1) A legislative act may delegate to the Commission the power to adopt non-legislative acts of general application to supplement or amend certain non-essential elements of the legislative act. The objectives, content, scope and duration of the delegation of power shall be explicitly defined in the legislative acts. The essential elements of an area shall be reserved for the legislative act and accordingly shall not be the subject of a delegation of power. (2) Legislative acts shall explicitly lay down the conditions to which the delegation is subject; these conditions may be as follows: (a) the European Parliament or the Council may decide to revoke the delegation; (b) the delegated act may enter into force only if no objection has been expressed by the European Parliament or the Council within a period set by the legislative act. For the purposes of (a) and (b), the European Parliament shall act by a majority of its component members, and the Council by a qualified majority. (3) The adjective 'delegated' shall be inserted in the title of delegated acts.

1009. Article 291 of the Treaty on the Functioning of the European Union: (1) Member States shall adopt all measures of national law necessary to implement legally binding Union acts. (2) Where uniform conditions for implementing legally binding Union acts are needed, those acts shall confer implementing powers on the Commission, or, in duly justified specific cases and in the cases provided for in Articles 24 and 26 of the Treaty on European Union, on the Council. (3) For the purposes of para. 2, the European Parliament and the Council, acting by means of regulations in accordance with the ordinary legislative procedure, shall lay down in advance the rules and general principles concerning mechanisms for control by Member States of the Commission's exercise of implementing powers. (4) The word 'implementing' shall be inserted in the title of implementing acts.

1010. Article 16(1) of Regulation (EU) No 1093/2010 of the European Parliament and of the Council of 24 November 2010 establishing a European Supervisory Authority (EBA): the authority shall, with a view to establishing consistent, efficient and effective supervisory practices within the ESFS, and to ensuring the common, uniform and consistent application of Union law, issue guidelines and recommendations addressed to competent authorities or financial institutions.

The Commission must notify these adopted regulatory acts to the European Parliament and to the Council. The European Parliament or the Council may each express its objection within three months of notification, with a possibility of extension for three additional months. If there is no objection, the act shall enter into force.[1011]

The EBA has created a permanent internal committee for the purpose of preparing decisions relating to draft RTS and draft ITS.[1012] This committee is structurally independent from the other functions performed by the EBA. National resolution authorities shall be part of such committee.[1013]

Also, in the SRM-R, the Commission is empowered to adopt delegated acts for matters relating to the regulation.[1014]

1011. Article 115 of BRRD.
1012. Articles 10 through 15 of Regulation (EU) No 1093/2010 of the European Parliament and of the Council of 24 November 2010 establishing a European Supervisory Authority (EBA). *See also* EBA's decision of 22 January 2020 concerning establishment of the Standing Committee on Resolution (ResCo) on https://eba.europa.eu/sites/default/documents/files/document_library/About%20Us/Legal%20Framework/Updated%20Files%2026022019/854483/2020%2001%2022%20BoS%20ESAs%20Review%20-%20ResCo%20RoP.pdf.
1013. Article 127 of BRRD, Article 4 para. 11 of EBA's decision concerning establishment of ResCo.
1014. Article 93 of the SRM-R.

Reference	*Scope*	*Type of Act*	*Authority*	*Status*	*Deadline*
Article 2(2) of BRRD	To specify the criteria for the determination of the activities, services and operations as regards the definition of 'critical functions' in point (35) of Article 2(1) of BRRD[1015]	Delegated act	Commission	Commission Delegated Regulation (EU) 2016/778 of 2 February 2016 Technical advice on delegated acts EBA/Op/2015/05 published on 6 March 2015	Indeterminate
Article 2(2) of BRRD	To specify the criteria for the determination of the business lines and associated services as regards the definition of 'core business lines' in point (35) of Article 2(1) of BRRD[1016]	Delegated act	Commission	Commission Delegated Regulation (EU) 2016/778 of 2 February 2016 Technical advice on delegated acts EBA/Op/2015/05 published on 6 March 2015	Indeterminate

1015. 'Critical functions' means activities, services or operations the discontinuance of which is likely in one or more Member States, to lead to the disruption of services that are essential to the real economy or to disrupt financial stability due to the size, market share, external and internal interconnectedness, complexity or cross-border activities of an institution or group, with particular regard to the substitutability of those activities, services or operations.
1016. 'Core business lines' means business lines and associated services which represent material sources of revenue, profit or franchise value for an institution or for a group of which an institution forms part.

Reference	*Scope*	*Type of Act*	*Authority*	*Status*	*Deadline*
Article 4(5) and (6) of BRRD	To specify the criteria relating to recovery and resolution plans, for assessing the impact of an institution's failure on financial markets, on other institutions and on funding conditions	Guidelines followed by RTS	EBA to draft; Commission to adopt	Guidelines EBA/GL/2015/16 adopted and submitted to the Commission on 7 July 2015 RTS EBA/RTS/2017/11 adopted and submitted to the Commission on 19 December 2017 Commission Delegated Regulation (EU) 2019/348 of 25 October 2018	Guidelines 3 July 2015; RTS 3 July 2017
Article 4(11) of BRRD	To specify uniform formats, templates and definitions for the identification and transmission of information by competent authorities and resolution authorities to EBA for the purposes of Article 4(7) BRRD	ITS	EBA to draft; Commission to adopt	Final ITS EBA/ITS/2015/05 adopted and submitted to the Commission on 7 July 2015 Commission Implementing Regulation (EU) 2016/962 of 16 June 2016	3 July 2015
Article 5(7) of BRRD	To specify further the range of scenarios of severe macroeconomic and financial stress to be used in recovery plans	Guidelines	EBA to issue, in close cooperation with the ESRB	Guidelines EBA/GL/2014/06 published on 18 July 2014	3 July 2015

Reference	*Scope*	*Type of Act*	*Authority*	*Status*	*Deadline*
Article 5(10) of BRRD	To further specify the information to be contained in the recovery plan	RTS	EBA to draft; Commission to adopt	EBA final draft EBA/RTS/2014/11 adopted and submitted to the Commission on 18 July 2014 Commission Delegated Regulation (EU) 2016/1075 of 23 March 2016	3 July 2015
Article 6(8) of BRRD	To specify the minimum criteria that the competent authority is to assess recovery plans pursuant to Article 6(2) of BRRD and group recovery plans pursuant to Article 8(1) of BRRD	RTS	EBA to draft; Commission to adopt	EBA final draft EBA/RTS/2014/12 adopted and submitted to the Commission on 18 July 2014 Commission Delegated Regulation (EU) 2016/1075 of 23 March 2016.	3 July 2015
Article 9(2) of BRRD	To specify the minimum list of qualitative and quantitative indicators for recovery plans	Guidelines	EBA to issue	Guidelines EBA/GL/2015/02 adopted and submitted to the Commission on 6 May 2015	3 July 2015

Reference	*Scope*	*Type of Act*	*Authority*	*Status*	*Deadline*
Article 10(9) of BRRD	To further specify the contents of the resolution plan	RTS	EBA, after consulting the ESRB, to draft; Commission to adopt	EBA final draft EBA/RTS/2014/15 adopted and submitted to the Commission on 19 December 2014 Commission Delegated Regulation (EU) 2016/1075 of 23 March 2016	3 July 2015
Article 11(3) of BRRD	To specify procedures and a minimum set of standard forms and templates for the provision of information to resolution authorities from institutions and competent authorities	ITS	EBA to draft; Commission to adopt	Final ITS EBA/ITS/2015/06 adopted and submitted to the Commission on 7 July 2015 Final ITS EBA/ITS/2018/02 adopted and submitted to the Commission on 17 April 2018 Commission Implementing Regulation (EU) 2016/1066 of 17 June 2016 Commission Implementing Regulation (EU) 2018/1624 of 23 October 2018	3 July 2015

Reference	*Scope*	*Type of Act*	*Authority*	*Status*	*Deadline*
Article 12(6) of BRRD	To specify the contents of group resolution plans, by taking into account the diversity of business models of groups in the internal market	RTS	EBA, after consulting the ESRB, to draft; Commission to adopt	EBA final draft EBA/RTS/2014/15 adopted and submitted to the Commission on 19 December 2014 Commission Delegated Regulation (EU) 2016/1075 of 23 March 2016	3 July 2015
Article 15(4) of BRRD	To specify the matters and criteria for the assessment of the resolvability of institutions or groups provided for in Article 15(2) of BRRD and in Article 16 of BRRD	RTS	EBA, after consulting the ESRB, to draft; Commission to adopt	EBA final draft EBA/RTS/2014/15 adopted and submitted to the Commission on 19 December 2014 Commission Delegated Regulation (EU) 2016/1075 of 23 March 2016	3 July 2015
Article 17(8) of BRRD	To specify the further details on measures to reduce or remove impediments to resolvability	Guidelines	EBA to issue	Guidelines EBA/GL/2014/11 published on 19 December 2014	3 July 2015

Reference	*Scope*	*Type of Act*	*Authority*	*Status*	*Deadline*
Article 23(2) of BRRD	To specify the conditions for group financial support	RTS	EBA to draft; Commission to adopt	Final RTS EBA/RTS/2015/08 adopted and submitted to the Commission on 9 July 2015 Commission Delegated Regulation (EU) 2016/1075 of 23 March 2016 Commission Implementing Regulation (EU) 2016/911 of 9 June 2016	3 July 2015
Article 23(3) of BRRD	To specify the conditions for group financial support	Guidelines	EBA to issue	Guidelines EBA/GL/2015/17 published on 9 July 2015	3 January 2016
Article 26(2) of BRRD	To specify the form and content of the description of the general terms of a group financial support agreement	ITS	EBA to draft; Commission to adopt	Final draft EBA/ITS/2015/07 adopted and submitted to the Commission on 9 July 2015 Commission Delegated Regulation (EU) 2016/1075 of 23 March 2016 Commission Implementing Regulation (EU) 2016/911 of 9 June 2016	3 July 2015

Reference	*Scope*	*Type of Act*	*Authority*	*Status*	*Deadline*
Article 27(5) of BRRD	To specify a minimum set of triggers for the use of early intervention measures	Guidelines	EBA to issue	Guidelines EBA/GL/2015/03 published on 8 May 2015	3 July 2015
Article 27(5) of BRRD	To specify a minimum set of triggers for the use of early intervention measures	RTS	EBA may draft; Commission to adopt	Discussion Paper EBA/DP/2020/02 published on 26 June 2020. Comments to be provided by 25 September 2020	Not applicable (optional)
Article 32(4) of BRRD	To clarify the type of tests, reviews or exercises which may lead to public support measures such as injection of own funds or purchase of capital instruments	Guidelines	EBA to issue	Guidelines EBA/GL/2014/09 published on 22 September 2014	3 January 2015
Article 32(6) of BRRD	To propose interpretation of the different circumstances when an institution shall be considered to be failing or likely to fail	Guidelines	EBA to issue	Guidelines EBA/GL/2015/07 published on 26 May 2015	3 July 2015

Reference	*Scope*	*Type of Act*	*Authority*	*Status*	*Deadline*
Article 36(14) of BRRD	To specify the circumstances in which a person is an independent valuer from both the resolution authority and the institution for the purposes of valuation under Article 36(1) of BRRD or Article 74 of BRRD	RTS	EBA to draft; Commission to adopt	Final RTS EBA/RTS/2015/07 adopted and submitted to the Commission on 6 July 2015 Commission Delegated Regulation (EU) 2016/1075 of 23 March 2016	3 July 2015
Article 36(15) of BRRD	To specify the following criteria for the purposes of valuation under Article 36(1) of BRRD or Article 74 of BRRD: (a) the methodology for assessing the value of the assets and liabilities of the institution; (b) the separation of the valuations under Articles 36 and 74; (c) the methodology for calculating and including a buffer for additional losses in the provisional valuation	RTS	EBA may draft; Commission to adopt	Final RTS EBA/RTS/2017/05 adopted and submitted to the Commission on 23 May 2017 Commission Delegated Regulation (EU) 2018/345 of 14 November 2017	Not applicable (optional)

Reference	*Scope*	*Type of Act*	*Authority*	*Status*	*Deadline*
Article 39(4) of BRRD	To specify factual circumstances amounting to a material threat and the elements relating to the effectiveness of the sale of business tool	Guidelines	EBA to issue	Guidelines EBA/GL/2015/04 published on 20 May 2015	3 July 2015
Article 42(14) of BRRD	To promote the convergence of supervisory and resolution practices regarding the determination when the liquidation of the assets or liabilities under normal insolvency proceeding could have an adverse effect on one or more financial markets	Guidelines	EBA to issue	Guidelines EBA/GL/2015/05 published on 20 May 2015	3 July 2015
Article 44(11) of BRRD	To specify further the circumstances when exclusion is necessary to achieve the objectives in the context of exclusion of liabilities from the bail-in tool	Delegated act	Commission to adopt	Commission Delegated Regulation (EU) 2016/860 of 4 February 2016	Indeterminate

Reference	*Scope*	*Type of Act*	*Authority*	*Status*	*Deadline*
Article 45c(4) of BRRD	To specify the methodology to be used by resolution authorities to estimate the requirement referred to in Article 104a of Directive 2013/36/EU and the combined buffer requirement for resolution entities at the resolution group consolidated level where the resolution group is not subject to those requirements under that Directive	RTS	EBA to draft; Commission to adopt	Consultation Paper EBA/CP/2020/16 published on 24 July 2020. Comments to be provided by 24 October 2020.	December 2020[1017]

1017. The original deadline was 28 December 2019; however, EBA expects some delays and therefore has published a new deadline. *See* EBA. Risk Reduction Package Roadmaps. November 2019. https://eba.europa.eu/sites/default/documents/files/document_library/EBA%20Risk%20Reduction%20Package%20Roadmaps.docx.pdf.

Reference	*Scope*	*Type of Act*	*Authority*	*Status*	*Deadline*
Article 45f(6) of BRRD	To specify methods to avoid instruments recognised for the purposes of this Article indirectly subscribed, in part or in full, by the resolution entity hamper the smooth implementation of the resolution strategy	RTS	EBA to draft; Commission to adopt	Consultation Paper EBA/CP/2020/18 published on 22 July 2020. Comments to be provided by 23 October 2020.	December 2020[1018]
Article 45i(5) of BRRD	To specify uniform reporting templates, instructions and methodology on how to use the templates, frequency and dates of reporting, definitions and IT solutions for the supervisory reporting.	ITS	EBA to draft; Commission to adopt	Final RTS EBA/ITS/2020/06 adopted and submitted to the Commission on 03 August 2020.	28 June 2020

1018. *Ibid.*

Reference	*Scope*	*Type of Act*	*Authority*	*Status*	*Deadline*
Article 45i(6) of BRRD	To specify uniform disclosure formats, frequency and associated instructions in accordance with which disclosures shall be made	ITS	EBA to draft; Commission to adopt	Final draft ITS EBA/ITS/2020/06 published on 3 August 2020.	28 June 2020
Article 45j(2) of BRRD	To specify uniform reporting templates, instructions and methodology on how to use those templates, frequency and dates of reporting, definitions and IT solutions for the identification and transmission of information by resolution authorities, in coordination with competent authorities, to EBA	ITS	EBA to draft; Commission to adopt	Consultation Paper EBA/CP/2020/17 published on 24 July 2020. Comments to be provided by 24 October 2020.	December 2020[1019]

1019. The original deadline was 28 June 2020 but has been revised by EBA. *See* EBA. Letter to Commission. June 2020. https://eba.europa.eu/sites/default/documents/files/document_library/About%20Us/Missions%20and%20tasks/Correspondence%20with%20EU%20institutions/2020/885560/2020%2006%2012%20Letter%20to%20Mr%20Berrigan%20re%20Request%20for%20new%20deadlines%20under%20the%20RRM_rev.pdf.

Reference	*Scope*	*Type of Act*	*Authority*	*Status*	*Deadline*
Article 47(6) of BRRD	To describe the circumstances in which each of the bail-in or write-down or conversion of capital instruments would be appropriate	Guidelines	EBA to issue	Guidelines EBA/GL/2017/04 published on 5 April 2017	3 July 2016
Article 48(6) of BRRD	To provide guidelines on any interpretation relating to the interrelationship between the provisions of this Directive and those of Regulation (EU) No 575/2013 and Directive 2013/36/EU	Guidelines	EBA to issue	Guidelines EBA/GL/2017/02 published on 5 April 2017	3 January 2016
Article 49(5) of BRRD	To specify methodologies and the principles on the valuation of liabilities arising from derivatives, including for closeout set out in the netting agreement	RTS	EBA, after consulting the ESMA, to draft; Commission to adopt	Final RTS EBA/RTS/2015/11 adopted and submitted to the Commission on 17 December 2015 Commission Delegated Regulation (EU) 2016/1401 of 23 May 2016	3 January 2016
Article 50(4) of BRRD	To provide guidelines on the setting of conversion rates	Guidelines	EBA to issue	Guidelines EBA/GL/2017/03 published on 5 April 2017	3 January 2016

Reference	*Scope*	*Type of Act*	*Authority*	*Status*	*Deadline*
Article 52(12) of BRRD	To specify further: (a) the minimum elements that should be included in a business reorganisation plan; and (b) the minimum contents of the reports by the management	RTS	EBA to draft; Commission to adopt	Final RTS EBA/RTS/2015/12 adopted and submitted to the Commission on 17 December 2015 Commission Delegated Regulation (EU) 2016/1400 of 10 May 2016	3 January 2016
Article 52(13) of BRRD	To specify further the minimum criteria that a business reorganisation plan is to fulfil for approval by the resolution authority	Guidelines	EBA to issue	Guidelines EBA/GL/2015/21 adopted and submitted to the Commission on 17 December 2015 Commission Delegated Regulation (EU) 2016/1400 of 10 May 2016	3 January 2016
Article 52(14) of BRRD	To specify further the minimum criteria that a business reorganisation plan is to fulfil for approval by the resolution authority	RTS	EBA may draft; Commission to adopt	Final RTS EBA/RTS/2015/12 adopted and submitted to the Commission on 17 December 2015 Commission Delegated Regulation (EU) 2016/1400 of 10 May 2016	Not applicable (optional)

Reference	*Scope*	*Type of Act*	*Authority*	*Status*	*Deadline*
Article 55(5) of BRRD	To further determine the list of liabilities to which the exclusion in Article 55(1) of BRRD on the contractual recognition of bail-in applies, taking into account banks' different business models	RTS	EBA to draft; Commission to adopt	Final RTS EBA/RTS/2015/06 adopted and submitted to the Commission on 3 July 2015 Commission Delegated Regulation (EU) 2016/1075 of 23 March 2016	3 July 2015

Reference	*Scope*	*Type of Act*	*Authority*	*Status*	*Deadline*
Article 55(6) of BRRD	To specify: (a) the conditions under which it would be legally or otherwise impracticable for an institution or entity to include the contractual term in certain categories of liabilities; (b) the conditions for the resolution authority to require the inclusion of the contractual term; (c) the reasonable time frame for the resolution authority to require the inclusion of a contractual term	RTS	EBA to draft; Commission to adopt	Consultation Paper EBA/CP/2020/15 published on 24 July 2020. Comments to be provided by 24 October 2020.	December 2020[1020]
Article 55(8) of BRRD	To specify uniform formats and templates for the notification to resolution authorities	ITS	EBA to draft; Commission to adopt	Consultation Paper EBA/CP/2020/15 published on 24 July 2020. Comments to be provided by 24 October 2020.	December 2020[1021]

1020. Deadline of 28 June 2020 delayed to December 2020 in EBA's letter to Commission dated 12 June 2020. https://eba.europa.eu/sites/default/documents/files/document_library/About%20Us/Missions%20and%20tasks/Correspondence%20with%20EU%20institutions/2020/885560/2020%2006%2012%20Letter%20to%20Mr%20Berrigan%20re%20Request%20for%20new%20deadlines%20under%20the%20RRM_rev.pdf.

Reference	*Scope*	*Type of Act*	*Authority*	*Status*	*Deadline*
Article 65(5) of BRRD	To specify the minimum list of services or facilities that are necessary to enable a recipient to effectively operate a business transferred to it	Guidelines	EBA to issue	Guidelines EBA/GL/2015/06 published on 20 May 2015	3 July 2015
Article 71(8) of BRRD	To specify the following elements for detailed records of financial contracts: (a) a minimum set of the information on financial contracts that should be contained in the detailed records; and (b) the circumstances in which the requirement should be imposed	RTS	EBA to draft; Commission to adopt	Final RTS EBA/RTS/2015/13 adopted and submitted to the Commission on 17 December 2015 Commission Delegated Regulation (EU) 2016/1712 of June 2016	3 July 2015

1021. *Ibid.*

Reference	*Scope*	*Type of Act*	*Authority*	*Status*	*Deadline*
Article 71a(5) of BRRD	To further determine the contents of the term required, taking into account institutions' and entities' different business models	RTS	EBA to draft; Commission to adopt	Consultation Paper EBA/CP/2020/04 published on 15 May 2020. Comments to be provided by 15 September 2020.	December 2020[1022]
Article 74(4) of BRRD	To specify the methodology for carrying out the valuation, in particular the methodology for assessing the treatment that shareholders and creditors would have received if the institution under resolution had entered insolvency proceedings at the time when the decision relating to a resolution action was taken	RTS	EBA may draft; Commission to adopt	Final RTS EBA/RTS/2017/05 adopted and submitted to the Commission on 23 May 2017 Commission Delegated Regulation 2018/344 of 14 November 2017	Not applicable (optional)

1022. *Ibid.*

Reference	*Scope*	*Type of Act*	*Authority*	*Status*	*Deadline*
Article 76(4) of BRRD	To further specify the classes of arrangement that fall within the scope of security arrangements, title transfer financial collateral arrangements, set-off arrangements, netting arrangements, covered bonds, structured finance arrangements	Delegated act	Commission to adopt	Commission Delegated Regulation 2017/867 of 7 February 2017 Technical advice EBA/Op/2015/15 published on 14 August 2015	Indeterminate
Article 82(3) of BRRD	To specify the procedures and contents relating to the following requirements: (a) the notifications referred to in Article 81 of BRRD from the management body of an institution, competent authorities, and resolution authorities; (b) the notice of suspension referred to in Article 83 from resolution authorities	RTS	EBA to draft; Commission to adopt	Final RTS EBA/RTS/2015/04 adopted and submitted to the Commission on 3 July 2015 Commission Delegated Regulation 2016/1075 of 23 March 2016	3 July 2015

Reference	*Scope*	*Type of Act*	*Authority*	*Status*	*Deadline*
Article 84(7) of BRRD	To specify how information should be provided in summary or collective form with respect to confidentiality matters	Guidelines	EBA to issue	Guidelines EBA/GL/2016/03 published on 19 April 2016	3 July 2015
Article 88(7) of BRRD	To specify the operational functioning of the resolution colleges for the performance of tasks relating to group resolution, taking into account international standards	RTS	EBA to draft; Commission to adopt	Final RTS EBA/RTS/2015/03 adopted and submitted to the Commission on 3 July 2015 Commission Delegated Regulation (EU) 2016/1075 of 23 March 2016	3 July 2015
Article 102(4) of BRRD	To determine the appropriate reference point for setting the target level for resolution financing arrangements, and in particular whether total liabilities constitute a more appropriate basis than covered deposits	Recommendations	EBA to submit	Report EBA/OP/2016/18 published on 28 October 2016	Report submission by 31 October 2016

Reference	*Scope*	*Type of Act*	*Authority*	*Status*	*Deadline*
Article 102(5) of BRRD	To determine the target level for resolution financing arrangements	Legislative proposal	Commission to submit legislative proposal to the European Parliament and to the Council	To come	Legislative proposal submission by 31 December 2016
Article 103(7) of BRRD	To specify the notion of adjusting contributions in proportion to the risk profile of institutions	Delegated acts	Commission to adopt	Commission Delegated Regulation (EU) 2015/63 of 21 October 2014 Commission Delegated Regulation (EU) 2016/1434 of 14 December 2015	Indeterminate
Article 103(8) of BRRD	To specify: (a) the registration, accounting, reporting obligations and other obligations intended to ensure that the contributions are in fact paid; (b) the measures to ensure proper verification of whether the contributions have been paid correctly	Delegated acts	Commission to adopt	Commission Delegated Regulation (EU) 2015/63 of 21 October 2014 Commission Delegated Regulation (EU) 2016/1434 of 14 December 2015	Indeterminate

Reference	*Scope*	*Type of Act*	*Authority*	*Status*	*Deadline*
Article 104(4) of BRRD	To specify the circumstances and conditions under which the payment of contributions by an institution may be deferred	Delegated acts	Commission to adopt	Commission Delegated Regulation (EU) 2016/778 of 2 February 2016 Technical advice EBA/Op/2015/06 published on 6 March 2015	Indeterminate
Article 19(8) of SRM-R	To create detailed rules of procedure concerning: (a) the calculation of the interest rate to be applied in the event of a recovery decision; (b) the guarantees of the right to good administration and the right of access to documents	Delegated acts	Commission to adopt	To come	Indeterminate

Reference	*Scope*	*Type of Act*	*Authority*	*Status*	*Deadline*
Article 65(5) of SRM-R	To create rules on contributions in order to: (a) determine the type of contributions and the matters for which contributions are due, the manner in which the amount of the contributions is calculated, and the way in which they are to be paid; (b) specify registration, accounting, reporting and other rules necessary to ensure that the contributions are paid fully and in a timely manner; and (c) determine the annual contributions necessary to cover the administrative expenditure of the SRB before it becomes fully operational	Delegated acts	Commission to adopt	Commission Delegated Regulation (EU) 2017/2361 of 14 September 2017 Commission Delegated Regulation (EU) 1310/2014 of 8 October 2014	Indeterminate

Reference	*Scope*	*Type of Act*	*Authority*	*Status*	*Deadline*
Article 69(5) of SRM-R	To specify: (a) criteria for the spreading out in time of the contributions to the fund; (b) criteria for determining the number of years by which the initial period of contribution can be extended; (c) criteria for establishing the annual contributions	Delegated acts	Commission to adopt	Commission Delegated Regulation (EU) 2017/747 of 17 December 2015	Indeterminate
Article 71(5) of SRM-R	To specify the circumstances and conditions under which the payment of *ex post* contributions by an entity may be partially or entirely deferred	Delegated acts	Commission to adopt	Commission Delegated Regulation (EU) 2017/747 of 17 December 2015	Indeterminate
Article 75(4) of SRM-R	To create the detailed rules for the administration of the fund and general principles and criteria for its investment strategy	Delegated acts	Commission to adopt	Commission Delegated Regulation (EU) 2016/451 of 16 December 2015	Indeterminate

Bibliography

Maria J. Nieto. Third-Country Relations in the Directive Establishing a Framework for the Recovery and Resolution of Credit Institutions. 2014. Working Papers 1409, Banca de España.

Uhlenbruck, Insolvenzordnung, 14 Auflage 2015.

ECB. Banco Popular Español S.A. https://www.bankingsupervision.europa.eu/press/pr/date/2017/html/ssm.pr170607.en.html.

SRB. Operational Guidance on Bail-in Playbooks. Available on https://srb.europa.eu/sites/srbsite/files/srb_operational_guidance_on_bail-in_playbooks.pdf.

EBA. Draft Implementing Technical Standards on disclosure and reporting of MREL and TLAC. 3 August 2020. https://eba.europa.eu/sites/default/documents/files/document_library/Publications/Consultations/2020/CP%20on%20ITS%20on%20disclosure%20and%20reporting%20of%20MREL%20and%20TLAC/898092/Final%20report%20on%20draft%20ITS%20on%20disclosure%20and%20reporting%20on%20MREL%20and%20TLAC.pdf.

Italian Law Decree No. 237 of 23 December 2016.

Greek Law 4336/2015 (Government Gazette No 94/14.08.2015).

Accenture. Basel III Handbook – https://fitc-ng.com/vlearning/fvltest/BCAM%20Demo/story_content/external_files/Accenture-Basel-III-Handbook1.pdf.

Act to Accelerate Financial Market Stabilisation (Finanzmarktstabilisierungsbeschleunigungsgesetz) 17 October 2008.

Ahrend, R. and A. Goujard. International Capital Mobility and Financial Fragility – Part 1. Drivers of Systemic Banking Crises: The Role of Bank-Balance-Sheet Contagion and Financial Account Structure. OECD Economics Department Working Papers, No. 902, OECD Publishing. 2012.

Aktiengesetz. Available at https://www.gesetze-im-internet.de/aktg/.

Alex Barker. Financial Times. EU agrees Monte dei Paschi rescue with Italian government. 1 June 2017. https://www.ft.com/content/eae10fa0-16bb-3af7-9a0d-4a362293d085.

Alfon, Isaac / Isabel Argimon / Patricia Bascuñana-Ambrós. The Determinants of Capital Held by UK Banks and Building Societies and the Role of Individual

Capital Requirements. In Edward Elgar Publishing, Inc., Research Handbook on International Financial Regulation. Cheltenham, UK. 2012.

Allen N. Berger (Editor), Phillip Molyneux (Editor), John O. S. Wilson (Editor). The Oxford Handbook of Banking (Oxford Handbooks) Hardcover - 7 November 2019.

Allen, Franklin /Douglas Gale. Comparing Financial Systems. MIT Press 2000.

Allen, Roy E. Financial Crises and Recession in the Global Economy. Edward Elgar Publishing; 3 edition (28 February 2010).

Alston, Lee J. and Grove, Wayne A. and Wheelock, David C. Why Do Banks Fail? Evidence from the 1920s (1994). Explorations in Economic History, Vol. 31, No. 409-431, 1994. Available at SSRN: http://ssrn.com/abstract=2271698.

Altvater, Christian, Dr. and von Schweinitz, Dr., Oliver. Trennbankensystem: Grundsatzfragen und alternative Regulierungsansätze. Wertpapiermitteilungen, Zeitschrift für Wirtschafts - und Bankenrecht, Nr. 14, 6. April 2013, Seiten 625-633.

Andenas, Mads / Iris H. - Y. Chiu. Financial stability and legal integration in financial regulation. European Law Review: 2013.

Andreotti, Fabio Andrea. Wirtschaftsrecht: 'Die heilige Kuh soll geschlachtet werden' - zum bankenrechtlichen bail-in von Kundeneinlagen - Analyse des neuen Paradigmas im Bankensanierungsrecht. In: Fahrländer, Lukas; Heizmann, Reto A. Europäisierung der schweizerischen Rechtsordnung. Dike Verlag AG, 2013.

Avdjiev, Stefan / Kartasheva, Anastasia / Bogdanova, Bilyana. CoCos: a primer. BIS Quarterly Review, September 2013.

Avgouleas, Emilios Charles Goodhart, Dirk Schoenmaker. Bank Resolution Plans as a catalyst for global financial reform. Journal of Financial Stability 9 (2013) 210–218.

Avgouleas, Emilios. Governance of Global Financial Markets: The Law, the Economics, the Politics. Cambridge University Press (26 April 2012).

Ayadi, Ryan. Lastra, Rosa. Proposals for reforming deposit guarantee schemes in Europe. Journal of Banking Regulation, 210-222 (2010). http://www.palgrave-journals.com/jbr/journal/v11/n3/pdf/jbr20109a.pdf.

Ayadi, Rym. Lierman, Frank; Balling, Morten. Crisis Management at Cross-Roads: Challenges facing cross-border financial institutions at the EU level. SUERF - The European Money and Finance Forum. Vienna 2010. SUERF Study 2010/1.

Baily, Martin Neil / Douglas J. Elliott. The Causes of the Financial Crisis and the Impact of Raising Capital Requirements. In The International Financial Crisis: Have the Rules of Finance Changed? Asli Demirguc-Kunt (Author, Editor), Douglas D. Evanoff (Editor), George G. Kaufman - World Scientific Studies in International Economics (Book 14).

Banco Central do Brasil. O Banco Central e as novas técnicas de saneamento do Sistema Financeiro Nacional após a estabilização monetária. 26 December 2013 http://www.bcb.gov.br/htms/livrosfn.asp?idpai=ARTREGESP.

Banco Central do Brasil. PROER - Programa de Estímulo à Reestruturação e ao Fortalecimento do Sistema Financeiro Nacional. 26 December 2013 https://www

.bcb.gov.br/en/legacy?url=https:%2F%2Fwww.bcb.gov.br%2Fingles%2Fhimf1602.asp.

Banco de Espana. Directive Establishing a Framework for the Recovery and Resolution of Credit Institutions. Documentos de Trabajo 1409 (2014).

Bank for International Settlements. Basel II: International Convergence of Capital Measurement and Capital Standards: A Revised Framework – Comprehensive Version. Available at https://www.bis.org/publ/bcbs128.htm.

Bank for International Settlements. Basel III: A global regulatory framework for more resilient banks and banking systems. Basel Committee on Banking Supervision December 2010 (rev June 2011).

Bank for International Settlements. Consultative Document: Report and Recommendations of the Cross-border Bank Resolution Group. Basel Committee on Banking Supervision December 2009.

Bank for International Settlements. G10. https://www.bis.org/list/g10publications/index.htm.

Bank for International Settlements. Global systemically important banks: updated assessment methodology and the higher loss absorbency requirement. Basel Committee on Banking Supervision July 2013.

Bank for International Settlements. History of the Basel Committee. https://www.bis.org/bcbs/history.htm.

Bank for International Settlements. Liquidity stress testing: a survey of theory, empirics and current industry and supervisory practices. 23 October 2013. https://www.bis.org/publ/bcbs_wp24.htm.

Bank for International Settlements. Quarterly Review. Basel Committee on Banking Supervision December 2013.

Bank for International Settlements. RCB20 – Calculation of minimum risk-based capital requirements. 15 December 2019. https://www.bis.org/basel_framework/chapter/RBC/20.htm?inforce=20191215.

Bank for International Settlements. Report and recommendations of the Cross-border Bank Resolution Group. 18 March 2010. https://www.bis.org/publ/bcbs169.htm.

Bank for International Settlements. Report on intra-group support measures. 15 February 2012. https://www.bis.org/publ/joint28.htm.

Bank for International Settlements. Risk-based capital requirements and Boundary between the banking book and the trading book. Dated 15 December 2019. Effective as of 15 December 2019. https://www.bis.org/basel_framework/chapter/RBC/25.htm?inforce=20191215.

Bank for International Settlements. The Basel Framework. https://www.bis.org/basel_framework/.

Bank for International Settlements. The Joint Forum. Basel Committee on Banking Supervision February 2012.

Bank of Cyprus Group. Annual Financial Report 2013. https://www.bankofcyprus.com/globalassets/investor-relations/annual-reports/english/annual-financial-report-eng-not-signed.pdf.

Bank of England. 'A practical process for implementing a bail-in resolution power'. 'Speech given by Andrew Gracie, Director, Special Resolution Unit, Bank of England At the British Bankers' Association, London. 17 September 2012'.

Bank of England. Consultation on credit adjustment spread methodologies for fallback in cash products referencing GBP LIBOR. December 2019. https://www.bankofengland.co.uk/-/media/boe/files/markets/benchmarks/consultation%20on%20credit%20adjustment%20spread%20methodologies%20for%20fallbacks%20in%20cash%20products%20referencing%20gb.

Bank of England. Discussion Paper on Supporting risk-free rate transition through the provision of compounded SONIA. February 2020. https://www.bankofengland.co.uk/-/media/boe/files/paper/2020/supporting-rfr-transition-by-providing-compounded-sonia.pdf?la = en&hash = 2ED72FBB529C17999D3F948A55BD7C6D5F839E62.

Bank of England. Dunfermline Building Society. 30 March 2009. https://www.bankofengland.co.uk/-/media/boe/files/news/2009/march/dunfermline-building-society.pdf?la = en&hash = E86698333E6647FCB08B6B373C6E3E6667B1EBBC.

Bank of England. SONIA interest rate benchmark. 26 February 2020. https://www.bankofengland.co.uk/markets/sonia-benchmark.

Bank of England. The Bank's risk management approach to collateral referencing LIBOR for use in the Sterling Monetary Framework – Market Notice. 26 February 2020. https://www.bankofengland.co.uk/markets/market-notices/2020/risk-management-approach-to-collateral-referencing-libor-26-february-2020.

Bank of Japan. Provision of Subordinated Loans to Banks. 17 March 2009. https://www.boj.or.jp/en/announcements/release_2009/fsky0903a.htm/.

Barofsky, Neil. Bailout: An Inside Account of How Washington Abandoned Main Street While Rescuing Wall Street. Simon and Schuster, 24 July 2012 – Political Science – 288 pages.

Basel Committee on Banking Supervision, Core Principles for Effective Deposit Insurance Systems: A proposed methodology for compliance assessment, dated December 2010, p. 15. Available at: http://www.bis.org/publ/bcbs192.pdf.

Basel Committee on Banking Supervision, Recognising the cost of credit protection purchased, dated March 2013. Available at: http://www.bis.org/publ/bcbs245.htm.

Basel Committee on Banking Supervision. Basel III: international regulatory framework for banks. https://www.bis.org/bcbs/basel3.htm?m = 3%7C14%7C572.

Basel Committee on Banking Supervision. Consultative Document. Basel III: The Net Stable Funding Ratio. http://www.bis.org/publ/bcbs271.pdf.

Basel Committee on Banking Supervision. Guidelines for identifying and dealing with weak banks. July 15. https://www.bis.org/bcbs/publ/d330.pdf.

Basel Committee on Banking Supervision. Liquidity Coverage Ratio 15 December 2019. https://www.bis.org/basel_framework/chapter/LCR/40.htm?tldate = 20201231&inforce = 20191215&export = pdf.

BBC News. Can banking regulation go global? Published: 2009/03/18 22:29:06 GMT.

BBC. Spanish savings banks agree merger as debt crisis bites. 29 May 2012. http://www.bbc.co.uk/news/business-18246886.

Benjamin, Joanna. Financial Law. Oxford: Oxford University Press, 2007.

Bennet Berger, Pia Hüttl, Silvia Merler. Total Assets versus risk weighted assets: Does it matter for MREL? 2016. Bruegel Policy Contribution. No. 2016/12. Bruegel, Brussels. https://www.econstor.eu/bitstream/10419/165979/1/87733787X.pdf.

Bernhard Bomke. Bausparkassen: Diese Anbieter überzeugten im Test. 13.09.2019. https://www.fundresearch.de/Bauen/bausparkassen-diese-anbieter-ueberzeugten-im-test.php.

Bertschinger, Urs. Das Finanzmarktaufsichtsrecht Mitte 2013 bis Mitte 2014. Schweizerische Zeitschrift für Wirtschafts - und Finanzmarktrecht, 2014, p. 545.

Betz, Frederik. Why Bank Panics Matter - Cross-Disciplinary Economic Theory. Springer International Publishing Switzerland 2014.

BIO-FINMA

Blair / Walker. Financial Services Law. OUP Oxford; 2 edition (19 March 2009).

Bolzico, Javier. Yira Mascaró. Paola Granata. Practical Guidelines for Effective Bank Resolution. The World Bank - Latin America and the Caribbean Region Poverty Reduction and Economic Management Department November 2007 Policy Research Working Paper 4389.

Bösch, René. Grossbankenregulierung: Status - Quo Vadis? / I.-III. EIZ - Europa Institut Zürich Volume 144, Kapitalmarkttransaktionen VIII, Schulthess Juristische Medien AG, 2014.

Bösch, René. Grossbankenregulierung: Status - Quo Vadis? / IV.-VII. EIZ - Europa Institut Zürich Volume 144, Kapitalmarkttransaktionen VIII, Schulthess Juristische Medien AG, 2014.

Boudghene, Yassine and Maes, Stan and Scheicher, Martin. Asset Relief Measures in the EU: Overview and Issues. (14 September 2010). Available at SSRN: http://ssrn.com/abstract=1677310 or http://dx.doi.org/10.2139/ssrn.1677310.

Brandi, Tim Oliver and Gieseler, Konrad. Banking Resolution und Bail-in - gesetzliche, europäische Vorgaben. Kreditwesen 18/2013, Nr. 894, Seite 16-18.

Breilmann, Anja and Fuchs, Karl. Bankenregulierung, Insolvenzrecht, Kapitalanlagegesetzbuch, Honorarberatung - Bericht über den Bankrechtstag am 28. Juni 2013 in Berlin. Wertpapiermitteilungen, Zeitschrift für Wirtschafts - und Bankenrecht, Nr. 31, 3. August 2013, Seiten 1437-1445.

Broome, Lissa / Chris Brummer, Michael Helfer, Robert Hockett, Cyrus Amir-Mokri, and Nick O'neill. Domestic Bank Regulation in a Global Environment - A Comparative Dialogue. North Carolina Banking Institute Journal Volume 17 - Citation: 17 N.C. Banking Inst. (2013), Page 1.

Building Societies Association. Fact Sheet - Mergers and conversions. 01 October 2018.

Bundesgesetz über die Banken und Sparkassen (Bankengesetz, BankG) as of 1 January 2019. Unofficial translation by KPMG available at: https://assets.kpmg/content/dam/kpmg/ch/pdf/ch-banking-act-en.pdf.

Bundesgesetz über die Banken und Sparkassen. 22 March 2013. https://www.admin.ch/opc/de/federal-gazette/2013/2485.pdf.

Bundesgesetz über die Banken und Sparkassen. 8 November 1934 (Stand am 1 Juni. 2004). https://www.admin.ch/opc/de/classified-compilation/19340083/200501010000/952.0.pdf.

Bundesgesetz über Schuldbetreibung und Konkurs dated 11 April 1889 (consolidated as of 1 January 2020), available at: https://www.admin.ch/opc/de/classified-compilation/18890002/202001010000/281.1.pdf.

Bundesverband der Deutschen Volksbanken und Raiffeisenbanken. Study findings: The institutional protection scheme of the German Cooperative Banking Network is efficient and reliable – standardising deposit guarantee system in Europe is the wrong approach. 9 November 2010. https://www.bvr.de/p.nsf/B11B3AF5F355A69FC1257D2B0036E473/$FILE/PressRelease_GuaranteeSchemes.pdf.

Calomiris, Charles W. The great depression and other 'contagious' events. Nber Working Paper Series Bank Failures In Theory And History: Working Paper 13597 National Bureau Of Economic Research Cambridge, MA November 2007.

Campbell, Andrew. Bank Insolvency and the Problem of Non-Performing Loans. In: Omar, P. (ed.) International Insolvency Law, Ashgate. 2008.

Cariboni, Jessica. The promptness of European Deposit Protection Schemes to face banking failures. Journal of Banking Regulation. 191-209 (2010). http://www.palgrave-journals.com/jbr/journal/v11/n3/pdf/jbr201013a.pdf.

Cariboni. Deposit protection in the EU: State of play and future prospects. Journal of Banking Regulation Vol. 9, 2 82-101 2008.

Carnell, Richard Scott / Jonathan R. Macey / Geoffrey P. Miller. The Law of Banking and Financial Institutions. Aspen Publishers; 5 edition (16 August 2013).

Cecchetti Stephen and Kermit Schoenholtz. Money, Banking and Financial Markets. 5th edition. 2017.

Cecchetti, Stephen Giovanni; Schoenholtz, Kermit L. Money, banking, and financial markets. 'Ausgabe: 4th Edition; Erschienen: New York: McGraw-Hill Education, 2014; Erscheint ca. Februar 2014'.

Central Bank of Cyprus. Rescue Programme for Laiki Bank. 30 March 2013. https://www.centralbank.cy/en/announcements/30-03-2013.

Chan Ho, Look. Bank Insolvency Law in the United Kingdom. In: Lastra, Rosa. Cross-Border Bank Insolvency. Oxford: Oxford University Press, 2002 MLE: PE 600: 03.

Chapter 11 of the US Code

Chapter 14 Bank Merger and Acquisition Process in Zabihollah Rezaee. Financial Services Firms: Governance, Regulations, Valuations, Mergers, and Acquisitions. 2011. Wiley. 3rd Edition.

Charles Randell 'Group Resolution under EU Resolution Directive' in The Bank Recovery and Resolution Directive: Europe's Solution for 'Too Big To Fail?' 2017 edited by Andreas Dombret and Patrick S. Kenadjian. Applying bail-in to multiple group entities is highly complex and risks fragmenting the ownership of the group.

Chattopadhyay, Robi. Der Vorschlag für eine Richtlinie zur Sanierung und Abwicklung von Kreditinstituten. WM Heft 9/2013, S. 405-415.

Christos V. Gortsos. The application of the EU banking resolution framework amidst the pandemic crisis. In 'Pandemic Crisis and Financial Stability' European Banking Institute May 2020.

CoCos and Bail-Ins Bank Recovery and Resolution Directive: Europe's Solution for Too Big to Fail?, Institute for Law and Finance Series Vol. 13, De Gruyter, 2013 (Ed. by Patrick S. Kenadjian).

Commission Delegated Regulation (EU) 2015/61 of 10 October 2014 to supplement Regulation (EU) No 575/2013 of the European Parliament and the Council with regard to liquidity coverage requirement for Credit Institutions.

Commission Delegated Regulation (EU) 2015/63 of 21 October 2014 supplementing Directive 2014/59/EU of the European Parliament and of the Council with regard to ex ante contributions to resolution financing arrangements.

Commission Delegated Regulation (EU) 2016/1075 of 23 March 2016 supplementing Directive 2014/59/EU of the European Parliament and of the Council with regard to regulatory technical standards specifying the content of recovery plans, resolution plans and group resolution plans, the minimum criteria that the competent authority is to assess as regards recovery plans and group recovery plans, the conditions for group financial support, the requirements for independent valuers, the contractual recognition of write-down and conversion powers, the procedures and contents of notification requirements and of notice of suspension and the operational functioning of the resolution colleges.

Commission Delegated Regulation (EU) 2016/1400 of 10 May 2016 supplementing Directive 2014/59/EU of the European Parliament and of the Council with regard to regulatory technical standards specifying the minimum elements of a business reorganisation plan and the minimum contents of the reports on the progress in the implementation of the plan.

Commission Delegated Regulation (EU) 2016/1401 of 23 May 2016 supplementing Directive 2014/59/EU of the European Parliament and of the Council establishing a framework for the recovery and resolution of credit institutions and investment firms with regard to regulatory technical standards for methodologies and principles on the valuation of liabilities arising from derivatives.

Commission Delegated Regulation (EU) 2016/1434 of 14 December 2015 correcting Delegated Regulation (EU) 2015/63 supplementing Directive 2014/59/EU of the European Parliament and of the Council with regard to ex ante contributions to resolution financing arrangements.

Commission Delegated Regulation (EU) 2016/1450 of 23 May 2016 supplementing Directive 2014/59/EU of the European Parliament and of the Council with regard to regulatory technical standards specifying the criteria relating to the methodology for setting the minimum requirement for own funds and eligible liabilities.

Commission Delegated Regulation (EU) 2016/1712 of 7 June 2016 supplementing Directive 2014/59/EU of the European Parliament and of the Council establishing a framework for the recovery and resolution of credit institutions and investment firms with regard to regulatory technical standards specifying a minimum set of the information on financial contracts that should be contained in the detailed records and the circumstances in which the requirement should be imposed.

Commission Delegated Regulation (EU) 2016/451 of 16 December 2015 laying down general principles and criteria for the investment strategy and rules for the administration of the Single Resolution Fund.

Commission Delegated Regulation (EU) 2016/778 of 2 February 2016 supplementing Directive 2014/59/EU of the European Parliament and of the Council with regard to the circumstances and conditions under which the payment of extraordinary ex post contributions may be partially or entirely deferred, and on the criteria for the determination of the activities, services and operations with regard to critical functions, and for the determination of the business lines and associated services with regard to core business lines.

Commission Delegated Regulation (EU) 2016/860 of 4 February 2016 specifying further the circumstances where exclusion from the application of write-down or conversion powers is necessary under Article 44(3) of Directive 2014/59/EU of the European Parliament and of the Council establishing a framework for the recovery and resolution of credit institutions and investment firms.

Commission Delegated Regulation (EU) 2017/2361 of 14 September 2017 on the final system of contributions to the administrative expenditures of the Single Resolution Board.

Commission Delegated Regulation (EU) 2017/747 of 17 December 2015 supplementing Regulation (EU) No 806/2014 of the European Parliament and the Council with regard to the criteria relating to the calculation of ex ante contributions, and on the circumstances and conditions under which the payment of extraordinary ex post contributions may be partially or entirely deferred.

Commission Delegated Regulation (EU) 2017/867 of 7 February 2017 on classes of arrangements to be protected in a partial property transfer under Article 76 of Directive 2014/59/EU of the European Parliament and of the Council.

Commission Delegated Regulation (EU) 2018/344 of 14 November 2017 supplementing Directive 2014/59/EU of the European Parliament and of the Council with regard to regulatory technical standards specifying the criteria relating to the methodologies for valuation of difference in treatment in resolution.

Commission Delegated Regulation (EU) 2018/345 of 14 November 2017 supplementing Directive 2014/59/EU of the European Parliament and of the Council with regard to regulatory technical standards specifying the criteria relating to the methodology for assessing the value of assets and liabilities of institutions or entities.

Commission Delegated Regulation (EU) 2019/348 of 25 October 2018 supplementing Directive 2014/59/EU of the European Parliament and of the Council with regard to regulatory technical standards specifying the criteria for assessing the impact of an institution's failure on financial markets, on other institutions and on funding conditions.

Commission Delegated Regulation (EU) No 1310/2014 of 8 October 2014 on the provisional system of instalments on contributions to cover the administrative expenditures of the Single Resolution Board during the provisional period.

Commission Implementing Regulation (EU) 2016/1066 of 17 June 2016 laying down implementing technical standards with regard to procedures, standard forms and templates for the provision of information for the purpose of resolution plans for credit institutions and investment firms pursuant to Directive 2014/59/EU of the European Parliament and of the Council.

Commission Implementing Regulation (EU) 2016/911 of 9 June 2016 laying down implementing technical standards with regard to the form and the content of the description of group financial support agreements in accordance with Directive 2014/59/EU of the European Parliament and of the Council establishing a framework for the recovery and resolution of credit institutions and investment firms.

Commission Implementing Regulation (EU) 2016/962 of 16 June 2016 laying down implementing technical standards with regard to the uniform formats, templates and definitions for the identification and transmission of information by competent authorities and resolution authorities to the European Banking Authority according to Directive 2014/59/EU of the European Parliament and of the Council.

Commission Implementing Regulation (EU) 2018/1624 of 23 October 2018 laying down implementing technical standards with regard to procedures and standard forms and templates for the provision of information for the purposes of resolution plans for credit institutions and investment firms pursuant to Directive 2014/59/EU of the European Parliament and of the Council, and repealing Commission Implementing Regulation (EU) 2016/1066.

Commission Implementing Regulation (EU) 2018/308 of 1 March 2018 laying down implementing technical standards for Directive 2014/59/EU of the European Parliament and of the Council with regard to formats, templates and definitions for the identification and transmission of information by resolution authorities for the purposes of informing the European Banking Authority of the minimum requirement for own funds and eligible liabilities.

Commission of the European Communities. White Paper on the Integration of EU Mortgage Credit Markets. Brussels 18.12.2007. Available at – https://ec.europa.eu/transparency/regdoc/rep/1/2007/EN/1-2007-807-EN-F1-1.Pdf.

Commission Regulation (EU) No 662/2010 of 23 July 2010 amending Regulation (EC) No 1126/2008 adopting certain international accounting standards in accordance with Regulation (EC) No 1606/2002 of the European Parliament and of the Council as regards International Financial Reporting Interpretations Committee's (IFRIC) Interpretation 19 and International Financial Reporting Standard (IFRS).

Competitive Equality Banking Act of 1987 (US)

Confidum Financial Management Consultants. Hypo Alpe Adria: Zukunftsszenarien und ihre möglichen Auswirkungen. February 2014. https://www.confidum.com/fileadmin/user_upload/pdf/download/Hypo_Alpe_Adria_Aussendung_12022014_EV.pdf.

Corazza, Gentil. Crise e reestruturação bancária no Brasil. Porto Alegre: UFRS, 2000 (Texto para Discussão, 8).

Council of The European Union. Agreement on the transfer and mutualisation of contributions to the Single Resolution fund. 14 May 2014.

Cranston, Ross. Principles of banking law. Oxford: Oxford University Press, 2002 MLE: PE 600: 03.

Credit Agricole. Business Lies and Brands. https://www.credit-agricole.com/en/business-lines-and-brands/all-brands/credit-agricole.

Credit Agricole. Financial Publications 2020. https://www.credit-agricole.com/en/finance/finance/financial-publications.

Crisis and change in the Japanese financial system. Ed. by Takeo Hoshi ... [et al.] Boston: Kluwer Academic, 2000. Cargill.

Cysne, Rubens Penha; Costa, Sergio Gustavo da Silveira. Reflexos do Plano Real sobre o Sistema Bancário Brasileiro. Revista Brasileira de Economia (Impresso), Rio de Janeiro, v. 51, n. 3, pp. 325-346, 1997.

David Mengle, ISDA research notes – The importance of close-out netting. 2010. https://www.isda.org/a/USiDE/netting-isdaresearchnotes-1-2010.pdf.

Davies, Glyn. A history of money: from ancient times to the present day / Glyn Davies. Cardiff: University of Wales Press, 1994 Umfang xix, 715 p. MLE: QK 100: 04.

De Soto, Jesús Huerta. Money, Bank Credit, and Economic Cycle. Ludwig von Mises Institute; 2nd edition (14 April 2009).

Debt Maturity and the Deadweight Cost of Leverage: Optimally Financing Banking Firms. Author(s): Mark J. Flannery. Source: The American Economic Review, Vol. 84, No. 1 (March., 1994), pp. 320-331 Published.

Decision to take resolution action in respect of Banco Popular Español, S.A.(2017/C 222/05). Available at – https://eur-lex.europa.eu/legal-content/EN/TXT/?uri=uriserv%3AOJ.C_.2017.222.01.0003.01.ENG.

DeGrauwe Paul. The New Bail-in Doctrine: A recipe for banking crises and depression in the eurozone. CEPS Commentary 4 April 2013.

Deutsche Bundesbank. Bank recovery and resolution – the new TLAC and MREL minimum requirements. July 2016. https://www.bundesbank.de/resource/blob/654532/7046f093197a1e4ab2e1f2446aff8934/mL/2016-07-minimum-requirements-tlac-mrel-data.pdf.

Deutsche Bundesbank. Fundamental features of the German Bank Restructuring Act. June 2011. https://www.bundesbank.de/resource/blob/707210/d60f5843069da07d666b02f2e8706c8f/mL/2011-06-fundamental-features-german-bank-restructuring-act-data.pdf.

Deutsche Bundesbank. The European banking package – revised rules in EU banking regulation. June 2019. https://www.bundesbank.de/resource/blob/800764/d87f4df7102744e5b52f284fc03d186d/mL/2019-06-bankenpaket-data.pdf.

Dewatripont, Jean-Charles Rochet & Jean Tirole. Balancing the Banks: Global Lessons from the Financial Crisis. Princeton University Press (9 May 2010).

Dewatripont, Mathias / Nguyen, Gregory / Praet, Peter / Sapir, André. The role of state aid Control in improving Bank resolution in Europe. Bruegel Policy Contribution. Issue 2010/04 May 2010.

DG Internal Market. 'Discussion paper on the debt write-down tool – bail-in'. 2011 http://www.feelingeurope.eu/Pages/bail_in_en.pdf.

Die Deutsche Kreditwirtschaft. Comments on the Commission's proposal for amendments to the BRRD/CRR in conjunction with the MREL/TLAC-requirements. 17 March 2017. Available at – https://bankenverband.de/media/files/20170317_DK-Papier_MRELVorgaben_in_CRRuBRRD_englisch.pdf.

Directive (EU) 2017/2399 of the European Parliament and of the Council of 12 December 2017 amending Directive 2014/59/EU as regards the ranking of unsecured debt instruments in insolvency hierarchy.

Directive (EU) 2019/878 of the European Parliament and of the Council of 20 May 2019 amending Directive 2013/36/EU as regards exempted entities, financial holding companies, mixed financial holding companies, remuneration, supervisory measures and powers and capital conservation measures.

Directive (EU) 2019/879 of the European Parliament and of the Council of 20 May 2019 amending Directive 2014/59/EU as regards the loss-absorbing and recapitalisation capacity of credit institutions and investment firms and Directive 98/26/EC.

Directive 2001/24/EC of the European Parliament and of the Council of 4 April 2001 on the reorganisation and winding up of credit institutions.

Directive 2002/47/EC of the European Parliament and of the Council of 6 June 2002 on financial collateral arrangements.

Directive 2013/36/EU of the European Parliament and of the Council of 26 June 2013 on access to the activity of credit institutions and the prudential supervision of credit institutions and investment firms, amending Directive 2002/87/EC and repealing Directives 2006/48/EC and 2006/49/EC.

Directive 2014/49/EU of the European Parliament and of the Council of 16 April 2014 on deposit guarantee schemes.

Directive 94/19/EC of the European Parliament and of the Council of 30 May 1994 on deposit-guarantee schemes.

Directive 97/9/EC of the European Parliament and of the Council of 3 March 1997 on investor-compensation schemes.

Directive 98/26/EC of the European Parliament and of the Council of 19 May 1998 on settlement finality in payment and securities settlement systems.

Dodd-Frank Wall Street Reform and Consumer Protection Act. PUBLIC LAW 111-203 – JULY 21, 2010. https://www.congress.gov/111/plaws/publ203/PLAW-111publ 203.pdf.

Dombalagian, Onnig H. The Expressive Synergies of the Volcker Rule. Boston College Law Review March, 2013.

Dombret, Andreas [et al.] Thomas Huertas. The Bank Recovery and Resolution Directive (The Case for Bail-ins). De Gruyter – Berlin, 2013.

Dombret, Andreas [et al.]. Titel Stability of the financial system: illusion or feasible concept?. Impressum Cheltenham: Edward Elgar, 2013 Umfang 537 S.: Ill. – Bibliothek HSG Erdgeschoss QK 600 D667.

Dougherty, Carter. Stopping a Financial Crisis, the Swedish Way. The New York Times. 22 September 2008. http://www.nytimes.com/2008/09/23/business/worldbusiness/23krona.html.

Dragomir, Larisa. European prudential banking regulation and supervision – the legal dimension. Ort, Verlag, Jahr: London: Routledge, 2010.

DZ Bank Group. Financial reports 2019. Key figures. https://www.halfyearreport.dzbank.com/financial-report/key-figures.

E. Liikanen. Final Report by the High-level Expert Group on Reforming the Structure of the EU Banking Sector dated October 2012.

EBA. Consultation Paper. Draft Implementing Technical Standards on disclosure and reporting of MREL and TLAC. 22 November 2019. https://eba.europa.eu/sites/default/documents/files/document_library/Publications/Consultations/2020/CP%20on%20ITS%20on%20disclosure%20and%20reporting%20of%20MREL%20and%20TLAC/Consultation%20paper%20on%20the%20ITS%20on%20disclosure%20and%20reporting%20of%20MREL%20and%20TLAC.pdf.

EBA. Consultation Paper. Draft Regulatory Technical Standards. On the assessment of recovery plans under the draft directive establishing a framework for the recovery and resolution of credit institutions and investment firms. 20 May 2013. http://www.eba.europa.eu/documents/10180/204980/EBA-CP-2013-08---CP-on-Draft-RTS-on-Assessment-of-Recovery-Plans.pdf.

EBA. Consultation Paper: Contributions of institutions to resolution financing arrangements. June 2014.

EBA. Consultation Paper: Draft Regulatory Technical Standards on the contractual recognition of stay powers under Article 71a(5) of Directive 2014/59/EU May 2020.

EBA. Decision concerning establishment of the Standing Committee on Resolution (ResCo). 22 January 2020. https://eba.europa.eu/sites/default/documents/files/document_library/About%20Us/Legal%20Framework/Updated%20Files%2026022019/854483/2020%2001%2022%20BoS%20ESAs%20Review%20-%20ResCo%20RoP.pdf.

EBA. Discussion Paper on Defining Liquid Assets in LCR under the draft CRR. 21 February 2013. https://eba.europa.eu/documents/10180/42030/DP-on-defining-liquid-assets-in-the-LCR.pdf.

EBA. Discussion Paper: Application of early intervention measures in the European Union according to Articles 27-29 of the BRRD (EBA/DP/2020/02) June 2020.

EBA. Draft final report: Draft Implementing Standards on the provision of information for the purpose of resolution plans under Article 11(3) of Directive 2014/59/EU (EBA/ITS/2018/02). April 2018.

EBA. Draft Regulatory Technical Standards on criteria for determining the minimum requirement for own funds and eligible liabilities under Directive 2014/59/EU. 28 November 2014. https://eba.europa.eu/sites/default/documents/files/documents/10180/911034/1871eff7-5515-4db8-b422-caff4a10d535/EBA%20CP%202014%2041%20%28CP%20on%20draft%20RTS%20on%20MREL%29.pdf?retry=1.

EBA. EBA final draft Regulatory Technical Standards on prudent valuation under Article 105(14) of Regulation (EU) No 575/2013 (Capital Requirements Regulation – CRR). 23 January 2015. https://www.eba.europa.eu/documents/10180/642449/EBA-RTS-2014-06+RTS+on+Prudent+Valuation.pdf.

EBA. EBA: Final report: Guidelines on the provision of information in summary or collective form the purposes of Article 84(3) of Directive 2014/59/EU (EBA/GL/2016/03) April 2016.

EBA. EU-wide stress testing. https://eba.europa.eu/risk-analysis-and-data/eu-wide-stress-testing.

EBA. Final draft Implementing Technical Standards amending Commission Implementing Regulation (EU) No 680/2014 (ITS on supervisory reporting) with regard to the Leverage Ratio (LR) following the EC's Delegated Act on the LR. 15 June 2015. https://eba.europa.eu/sites/default/documents/files/documents/10180/1113844/dd6cd991-2620-4c58-886a-de4dcf75b20d/EBA-ITS-2015-03%20Final%20Draft%20ITS%20amending%20ITS%20on%20LR%20Reporting.pdf?retry=1.

EBA. Final draft implementing technical standards on the form and content of disclosure of financial support agreements under Article 26 of Directive 2014/59/EU (EBA/ITS/2015/07) July 2015.

EBA. Final draft regulatory technical standards on procedures and contents of notifications referred to in Article 81(1), (2) and (3) and the notice of suspension referred to in Article 83 of Directive 2014/59/EU (EBA/RTS/2015/04) July 2015.

EBA. Final draft regulatory technical standards on resolution colleges under Article 88(7) of Directive 2014/59/EU (EBA/RTS/2015/03) July 2015.

EBA. Final draft regulatory technical standards on the assessment of recovery plans under Article 6(8) of Directive 2014/59/EU (Bank Recovery and Resolution Directive BRRD) (EBA/RTS/2014/12). July 2014.

EBA. Final Draft Regulatory Technical Standards on the content of resolution plans and the assessment of resolvability (EBA/RTS/2014/15). December 2014.

EBA. Final draft Regulatory Technical Standards on the content of recovery plans under Article 5(10) of Directive 2014/59/EU establishing a framework for the recovery and resolution of credit institutions and investment firms (EBA/RTS/2014/11). July 2014.

EBA. Final draft regulatory technical standards specifying the conditions for group financial support under Article 23 of Directive 2014/59/EU (EBA/RTS/2015/08) July 2015.

EBA. Final Draft Technical Standards and Guidelines on Recovery Plans, and Guidelines on the range of scenarios to be used in recovery plans. July 2014. https://eba.europa.eu/regulation-and-policy/recovery-and-resolution/guidelines-on-the-range-of-scenarios-to-be-used-in-recovery-plans#pane-289.

EBA. Final guidance: Guidelines on the minimum list of qualitative and quantitative recovery plan indicators (EBA/GL/2015/02). May 2015.

EBA. Final Guidelines on the rate of conversion of debt to equity in bail-in. 5 April 2017. https://eba.europa.eu/sites/default/documents/files/documents/10180/1807514/c9f9a3e2-37d0-4643-a1ad-8503d827a3bd/Guidelines%20on%20the%20rate%20of%20conversion%20of%20debt%20to%20equity%20in%20bail-in%20(EBA-GL-2017-03).pdf.

EBA. Final guidelines: on the minimum list of services or facilities that are necessary to enable a recipient to operate a business transferred to it under Article 65(5) of Directive 2014/59/EU (EBA/GL/2015/06) May 2015.

EBA. Final Report Draft Implementing Technical Standards on procedures and templates for the identification and transmission of information by resolution authorities to the EBA, on minimum requirements for own funds and eligible liabilities under Article 45(17) of Directive 2014/59/EU (EBA/ITS/2017/06) September 2017.

EBA. Final Report on Draft Regulatory Technical Standards on the valuation of derivatives pursuant to Article 49(4) BRRD. https://eba.europa.eu/sites/default/documents/files/documents/10180/1312572/6d9950e7-47ce-49f8-aa35-0690b7740678/EBA-RTS-2015-11%20RTS%20on%20the%20valuation%20of%20derivatives.pdf.

EBA. Final Report on Draft Regulatory Technical Standards on the contractual recognition of write-down and conversion powers under Article 55(3) of Directive 2014/59/EU. 03 July 2015. https://eba.europa.eu/sites/default/documents/files/documents/10180/1132911/c66aa9cb-e2ff-4896-85e6-dca7ba5cba65/EBA-RTS-2015-06%20RTS%20on%20Contractual%20Recognition%20of%20Bail-in.pdf.

EBA. Final report. Draft RTS on simplified obligations under Article 4(6) of Directive 2014/59/EU. EBA/RTS/2017/11. December 2017.

EBA. Final report: Draft implementing technical standards on procedures, forms and templates for the provision of information for resolution plans under Article 11(3) of Directive 2014/59/EU of the European Parliament and the Council (EBA/ITS/2015/06). July 2015.

EBA. Final Report: Draft Implementing Technical Standards on the uniform formats, templates and definitions for the identification and transmission of information by competent authorities and resolution authorities to the EBA for the purposes of Article 4(7) of Directive 2014/59/EU (EBA/ITS/2015/05). July 2015.

EBA. Final report: Draft Regulatory Technical Standards on a minimum set of the information on financial contracts that should be contained in the detailed records and the circumstances in which the requirement should be imposed (Article 71(8) BRRD) (EBA/RTS/2015/13) December 2015.

EBA. Final report: Draft regulatory technical standards on independent valuers under Article 36(14) of Directive 2014/59/EU (EBA/RTS/2015/07) July 2015.

EBA. Final report: Guidelines on the interpretation of the different circumstances when an institution shall be considered as failing or likely to fail under Article 32(6) of Directive 2014/59/EU (EBA/GL/2015/07) May 2015.

EBA. Final report: Guidelines on triggers for use of early intervention measures pursuant to Article 27(4) of Directive 2014/59/EU (EBA/GL/2015/03) May 2015.

EBA. Final report: Recommendation on the coverage of entities in a group recovery plan (EBA/Rec/2017/02). November 2017.

EBA. Final Report: Report on the implementation and design of the MREL framework (EBA-Op-2016-21) December 2016.

EBA. Guidelines on stress tests of deposit guarantee schemes under Directive 2014/49/EU. 24 May 2016. https://eba.europa.eu/sites/default/documents/files/documents/10180/1472555/dea33e8f-d902-433a-ab85-7b95c0b4d6b3/EBA-GL-2016-04%20(Final%20report%20on%20GL%20on%20DGS%20stress%20tests).pdf.

EBA. Guidelines in failing or likely to fail (EBA/GL/2015/07). https://eba.europa.eu/regulation-and-policy/recovery-and-resolution/guidelines-on-failing-or-likely-to-fail.

EBA. Guidelines on factual circumstances amounting to a material threat to financial stability and on the elements related to the effectiveness of the sale of business tool under Article 39(4) of Directive 2014/59/EU. https://eba.europa.eu/sites/default/documents/files/documents/10180/1080767/79c49d39-bd8e-44ae-9e23-d3cf04cc0609/EBA-GL-2015-04%20Guidelines%20on%20the%20sale%20of%20business%20tool.pdf.

EBA. Guidelines on the application of simplified obligations under Article 4(5) of Directive 2014/59/EU. EBA/GL2015/16. July 2015.

EBA. Guidelines on the determination of when the liquidation of assets or liabilities under normal insolvency proceedings could have an adverse effect on one or more financial markets under Article 42(14) of Directive 2014/59/EU. https://eba.europa.eu/sites/default/documents/files/documents/10180/1080779/6441452a-d464-4618-9296-d71549a4f2c2/EBA-GL-2015-05%20Guidelines%20on%20the%20asset%20separation%20tool.pdf.

EBA. Guidelines on the range of scenarios to be used in recovery plans (EBA/GL/2014/06). July 2014.

EBA. Guidelines on the sale of business tool. Available at https://eba.europa.eu/regulation-and-policy/recovery-and-resolution/guidelines-on-the-sale-of-business-tool.

EBA. Guidelines on the specification of measures to reduce or remove impediments to resolvability and the circumstances in which each measure may be applied under Directive 2014/59/EU (EBA/GL/2014/11). December 2014.

EBA. Guidelines on the types of tests, review or exercises that may lead to extraordinary public support measures for institutions under Article 32(4)(d)(iii) of the Bank Recovery and Resolution Directive (EBA/GL/2014/09) September 2014.

EBA. Guidelines on treatment of liabilities and shareholders in bail-in. https://eba.europa.eu/regulation-and-policy/recovery-and-resolution/guidelines-on-the-treatment-of-shareholders-in-bail-in and https://eba.europa.eu/regulation-and-policy/recovery-and-resolution/guidelines-on-treatment-of-liabilities-in-bail-in.

EBA. Guidelines: Concerning the interrelationship between the BRRD sequence of write-down and conversion and CRR/CRD (EBA/GL/2017/02) April 2017.

EBA. Handbook on Valuation for purposes of Resolution. 22 February 2019. Vanjhttps://eba.europa.eu/sites/default/documents/files/documents/10180/2613666/9f0772ea-a052-49e5-86ce-64c157adff10/Valuation%20Handbook.pdf.

EBA. Implementing Technical Standards (ITS) amending ITS on additional liquidity monitoring metrics. https://eba.europa.eu/regulation-and-policy/liquidity-risk/implementing-technical-standards-its-amending-its-on-additional-liquidity-monitoring-metrics.

EBA. Letter to Commission. June 2020. https://eba.europa.eu/sites/default/documents/files/document_library/About%20Us/Missions%20and%20tasks/Correspondence%20with%20EU%20institutions/2020/885560/2020%2006%2012%20Letter%20to%20Mr%20Berrigan%20re%20Request%20for%20new%20deadlines%20under%20the%20RRM_rev.pdf.

EBA. Opinion of the European Banking Authority on the Commission's Intention to Amend the Draft Regulatory Technical Standards Specifying Criteria Relating to the Methodology for Setting Minimum Requirement for Own Funds and Eligible

Liabilities According to Article 45(2) of Directive 2014/59/EU (EBA/Op/2016/02) February 2016.

EBA. Opinion on the perimeter of credit institutions. 27 November 2014. http://www.eba.europa.eu/-/eba-publishes-an-opinion-on-the-perimeter-of-credit-institutions.

EBA. Recovery, resolution and DGS. https://eba.europa.eu/regulation-and-policy/recovery-and-resolution.

EBA. Regulatory Technical Standards and Guidelines on business reorganization plans under Directive 2014/59/EU. https://eba.europa.eu/sites/default/documents/files/documents/10180/1312804/9ecf6b00-dbcf-493d-9ff4-016d7442e410/EBA-RTS-2015-12%20RTS%20and%20EBA-GL-2015-21%20GLs%20on%20Business%20Reorganisation%20Plans.pdf?retry=1.

EBA. Regulatory Technical Standards on valuation for the purposes of resolution and on valuation to determine difference in treatment following resolution under Directive 2014/59/EU on recovery and resolution of credit institutions and investment firms. https://eba.europa.eu/sites/default/documents/files/documents/10180/1853532/88566587-ff6f-4116-a08e-282eb4ea2f78/Final%20draft%20RTSs%20on%20valuation%20in%20resolution%20(EBA-RTS-2017-05%20&%20EBA-RTS-2017-06).pdf.

EBA. Report on impact of differences in leverage ratio definitions - Leverage ratio exposure measure under Basel III and the CRR. 4 March 2014 https://www.eba.europa.eu/documents/10180/534414/EBA+-+Leverage+ratio+analytical+report.pdf.

EBA. Report on Net Stable Funding requirements under Article 510 of the CRR. 15 December 2015. https://eba.europa.eu/sites/default/documents/files/documents/10180/983359/bb66d52d-4eb1-43c9-8924-5054d46c125f/EBA-Op-2015-22%20NSFR%20Report.pdf?retry=1.

EBA. Report on the appropriate target level basis for resolution financing arrangements (EBA-OP-2016-18) October 2016.

EBA. Results of 2014 EU-wide stress test - Aggregate results. 26 October 2014. https://eba.europa.eu/sites/default/documents/files/documents/10180/669262/5e16daf5-30a3-4684-b2cc-d60916ff2eaa/2014%20EU-wide%20ST-aggregate%20results.pdf?retry=1.

EBA. Risk Reduction Package Roadmaps. November 2019. https://eba.europa.eu/sites/default/documents/files/document_library/EBA%20Risk%20Reduction%20Package%20Roadmaps.docx.pdf.

EBA. Single Rulebook Q&A. https://eba.europa.eu/single-rule-book-qa.

EBA. Technical advice by the European Banking Authority on classes of arrangements to be protected in a partial property transfer (EBA/Op/2015/15) August 2015.

EBA. Technical advice on delegated acts on the deferral of extraordinary ex-post contributions to financial arrangements (EBA/Op/2015/06) March 2015.

EBA. Technical advice on the delegated acts on critical functions and core business lines. EBA/Op/2015/05. March 2015.

EBA. Technical advice on the delegated acts on the circumstances when exclusions from the bail-in tool are necessary (EBA/Op/2015/07) March 2015.

EBA. The Single Rulebook. http://www.eba.europa.eu/regulation-and-policy/single-rulebook.

ECB The Implementation of Monetary Policy in the euro Area, – http://www.ecb.europa.eu/pub/pdf/other/gendoc2011en.pdf.

ECB. Aggregate report on the Greek comprehensive assessment 2015. https://www.bankingsupervision.europa.eu/ecb/pub/pdf/aggregatereportonthecomprehensiveassessmentexsum201510.en.pdf.

ECB. Comprehensive Assessment. https://www.bankingsupervision.europa.eu/banking/comprehensive/html/index.en.html.

ECB. ELA Procedures – underlying the Governing Council's role pursuant to Article 14.4 of the Statute of the European System of Central Banks and of the European Central Bank with regard to the provision of ELA to individual credit institutions. 17 October 2013.

ECB. Euro short-term rate statistics. https://www.ecb.europa.eu/stats/financial_markets_and_interest_rates/euro_short-term_rate/html/index.en.html.

ECB. List of Supervised entities. Dated 1 February 2020. https://www.bankingsupervision.europa.eu/ecb/pub/pdf/ssm.listofsupervisedentities202003.en.pdf?afd073a65797209ba3dd55ad4bc84251.

ECB. List of Supervised entities. Dated 1 May 2020. https://www.bankingsupervision.europa.eu/ecb/pub/pdf/ssm.listofsupervisedentities202006.en.pdf.

ECB. Sensitivity Analysis of Liquidity Risk – Stress Test 2019 Final Results. 7 October 2019. https://www.bankingsupervision.europa.eu/press/pr/date/2019/html/ssm.pr191007_annex~537c259b6d.en.pdf.

ECB. Supervisory Practices Comprehensive Assessment. https://www.ecb.europa.eu/ssm/assessment/html/index.en.html.

ECBC. Australian Covered Bonds. http://www.ecbc.eu/framework/98/Australian_Covered_Bonds.

Economist Article – German banks – http://www.economist.com/news/finance-and-economics/21566013-defending-three-pillars-old-fashioned-favour.

EconoTimes. Moody's: European legislative developments and global resolution framework implementation impact creditor hierarchies, increase complexity. 5 May 2016. https://www.econotimes.com/Moodys-European-legislative-developments-and-global-resolution-framework-implementation-impact-creditor-hierarchies-increase-complexity-204766.

Ed. Douglas W. Arner et al., 'Systemic Risk in the Financial Sector – 10 years after the great crash'. 2019. CIGI Press.

Editors – Giovannini, Alberto. Mayer, Collin. European Financial Integration. Cambridge University Press. 1996.

Editors Simon Grima. Pierpaolo Marano. Governance and Regulations' Contemporary Issues. 2018. Vol 99. Emerald Group Publishing.

Elsas, Ralf. Preemptive distress resolution through bank mergers. Erschienen: Frankfurt am Main: Univ., Fachbereich Wirtschaftswiss., 2004 – Umfang: 40 S. Serie: Working paper series: Finance & accounting; 137.

Emilios Avgouleas and Charles Goodheart. Critical Reflections on Bank Bail-ins. March 2015. Journal of Financial Regulation Vol 1 Issue 1.

English law Banking Act of 2009

Entwurf Bankeninsolvenzverordnung-FINMA – Kernpunkte, published by the Swiss Financial Market Supervisory Authority on 16 January 2012, available at: https://www.finma.ch/de/~/media/finma/importiertedokumente/regulierung/anhoerungen/17-biv-finma/kp-biv-finma.pdf?la=de.

Erkens, David H. Corporate governance in the 2007-2008 financial crisis: Evidence from financial institutions worldwide. Mingyi Hung, Pedro Matos. Journal of Corporate Finance 18 (2012) 389-411.

European Agreement on a Voluntary Code of Conduct on Pre-Contractual Information for Home Loans. Available at – https://www.mnb.hu/letoltes/agreement-en-1.pdf.

European Banking Authority. Regulatory Technical Standards on criteria for determining the minimum requirement for own funds and eligible liabilities under Directive 2014/59/EU. https://eba.europa.eu/sites/default/documents/files/documents/10180/1132900/a0fc8387-e98e-4c3f-ae9d-11fb75511662/EBA-RTS-2015-05%20RTS%20on%20MREL%20Criteria.pdf?retry=1.

European Commission – MEMO/14/294

European Commission – MEMO/14/296

European Commission – MEMO/14/297

European Commission Services. Working paper 'Bail – in tool: a comparative analysis of the institutions' approaches'. 18 October 2013.

European Commission. A European Deposit Insurance Scheme (EDIS) – Frequently Asked Questions. 24 November 2015. https://ec.europa.eu/commission/presscorner/detail/en/MEMO_15_6153.

European Commission. Agreement on terms for the phasing-out of State guarantees for Austrian banks. 2 April 2003. https://ec.europa.eu/commission/presscorner/detail/en/IP_03_476.

European Commission. Bank recovery and resolution. https://ec.europa.eu/info/business-economy-euro/banking-and-finance/financial-supervision-and-risk-management/managing-risks-banks-and-financial-institutions/bank-recovery-and-resolution_en#documents.

European Commission. Commission Staff Working Document Impact Assessment Accompanying the Document Proposal for a Directive of the European Parliament and of the Council. 2012.

European Commission. Commission's services' report on asset transferability. 14 November 2008. https://ec.europa.eu/info/sites/info/files/rep-14112008_en.pdf.

European Commission. Communication from the Commission on Application of State aid rules to support measures in favour of banks in the context of the financial crisis. 1 August 2013.

European Commission. Communication from the Commission on Temporary Framework for State aid measures to support the economy in the current COVID-19 outbreak. 8 May 2020. https://ec.europa.eu/competition/state_aid/what_is_new/sa_covid19_2nd_amendment_temporary_framework_en.pdf.

European Commission. Deposit Guarantee Scheme – Frequently Asked Questions 15 April 2015. http://europa.eu/rapid/press-release_MEMO-14-296_en.htm?locale=en.

European Commission. DG Internal Market and Services Working Document – Technical Details of a Possible EU Framework for Bank Recovery and Resolution. January 2011.

European Commission. DG Internal Market and Services Working Document – Technical Details of a Possible EU Framework for Bank Recovery and Resolution. January 2011. https://ec.europa.eu/finance/consultations/2011/crisis-management/docs/consultation_paper_en.pdf.

European Commission. Effects Analysis on the European Deposit Insurance Scheme (EDIS). 11 October 2016. https://ec.europa.eu/info/sites/info/files/161011-edis-effect-analysis_en.pdf.

European Commission. EU Bank Recovery and Resolution Directive (BRRD): Frequently Asked Questions. Brussels, 15 April 2014.

European Commission. Memorandum: State aid: Overview of decisions and on-going in-depth investigations in the context of the financial crisis. December 2013 – MEMO/13/1147 – http://europa.eu/rapid/press-release_MEMO-13-1147_en.doc.

European Commission. Precautionary recapitalisations under the Bank Recovery and Resolution Directive: conditionality and case practice. 5 July 2017. https://www.europarl.europa.eu/RegData/etudes/BRIE/2017/602084/IPOL_BRI%282017%29602084_EN.pdf.

European Commission. Press release – State aid: Commission approves amended restructuring plans for Alpha Bank and Eurobank at: https://ec.europa.eu/commission/presscorner/detail/en/ip_15_6184.

European Commission. Report on the application and review of Directive 2014/59/EU (Bank Recovery and Resolution Directive) and Regulation 806/2014 (Single Resolution Mechanism Regulation) at: https://ec.europa.eu/info/sites/info/files/business_economy_euro/banking_and_finance/documents/190430-report-bank-recovery-resolution_en.pdf.

European Commission. State Aid Register as of April 2019.

European Commission. State aid SA.35382 (2013/N) – The Netherlands Rescue SNS REAAL 2013. Brussels. https://ec.europa.eu/competition/state_aid/cases/247614/247614_1415897_100_2.pdf.

European Commission. Structural reform of the EU banking sector. 2018. https://ec.europa.eu/info/business-economy-euro/banking-and-finance/financial-supervision-and-risk-management/managing-risks-banks-and-financial-institutions/structural-reform-eu-banking-sector_en.

European Commission. Study on the differences between bank insolvency laws and on their potential harmonization – Final report. November 2019. Available at https://ec.europa.eu/info/sites/info/files/business_economy_euro/banking_and_finance/documents/191106-study-bank-insolvency_en.pdf.

European Commission. Treaty establishing the European Stability Mechanism Signed. 29 July 2015. https://ec.europa.eu/economy_finance/articles/financial_operations/2011-07-11-esm-treaty_en.htm.

European Parliament. Briefing on The precautionary recapitalisation of Monte dei Paschi di Siena. 4 July 2017. https://www.europarl.europa.eu/RegData/etudes/BRIE/2017/587392/IPOL_BRI(2017)587392_EN.pdf.

European Stability Mechanism. ESM Treaty Reform – Explainer. https://www.esm.europa.eu/about-esm/esm-treaty-reform-explainer.

European Stability Mechanism. Explainer on ESM Reform and Revisions to the ESM Treaty. 24 June 2019. https://www.esm.europa.eu/press-releases/explainer-esm-reform-and-revisions-esm-treaty.

European Stability Mechanism. Explainers. https://www.esm.europa.eu/explainers.

European Stability Mechanism. Frequently Asked Questions on the European Stability Mechanism (ESM). 2014. https://www.esm.europa.eu/sites/default/files/2014-07-28_faq_esm_archived.pdf.

European Stability Mechanism. Guideline on Financial Assistance for the Recapitalisation of Financial Institutions. https://www.esm.europa.eu/sites/default/files/20141208_guideline_on_financial_assistance_for_the_direct_recapitalisation_of_institutions.pdf 2013.

European Stability Mechanism. Guideline on Financial Assistance for the Direct Recapitalisation of Institutions. 8 December 2014. https://www.esm.europa.eu/sites/default/files/20141208_guideline_on_financial_assistance_for_the_direct_recapitalisation_of_institutions.pdf.

European Union. Withdrawal of Commission proposals (2018/C 233/05). Available at https://eur-lex.europa.eu/legal-content/en/TXT/?uri=CELEX:52018XC0704(03).

Explanatory Memorandum to the Proposal for a regulation of the European Parliament and of the Council on structural measures improving the resilience of EU credit institutions / COM/2014/043 final – 2014/0020 (COD).

Federal Act on Financial Institutions (Financial Institutions Act, FinIA) consolidated as of 18 February 2020, available at https://www.admin.ch/opc/en/classified-compilation/20152662/index.html.

Federal Act on the Amendment of the Swiss Civil Code (Part Five: The Code of Obligations) dated 30 March 1911 (consolidated as of 1 January 2020), available at https://www.admin.ch/opc/en/classified-compilation/19110009/202004010000/220.pdf.

Federal Deposit Insurance Corporation. Bank of America Corporation Resolution Plan. Bank of America, N.A. Resolution Plan. FIA Card Services, N.A. Resolution Plan. Public Executive Summary. 1 July 2014 https://www.fdic.gov/regulations/reform/resplans/plans/boa-fia-idi-7114.pdf.

Federal Deposit Insurance Corporation. Failed Bank List. https://www.fdic.gov/bank/individual/failed/banklist.html.

Federal Deposit Insurance Corporation. JPMorgan Chase Acquires Banking Operations of Washington Mutual. 25 September 2008. https://www.fdic.gov/news/news/press/2008/pr08085.html.

Federal Deposit Insurance Corporation. Managing the Crisis. https://www.fdic.gov/bank/historical/managing/documents/history-consolidated.pdf.

Federal Deposit Insurance Corporation. Purchase and Assumption Agreement. 31 May 2019. https://www.fdic.gov/bank/individual/failed/enloe-p-and-a.pdf.

Federal Deposit Insurance Corporation. The Banking Crises of the 1980s and Early 1990s: Summary and Implications. 1997. http://www.fdic.gov/bank/historical/history/vol1.html.

Federal Register. Notices. 18 December 2013. Vol 78 No 243. https://www.fdic.gov/news/board/2013/2013-12-10_notice_dis-b_fr.pdf.

Federal Register. Rules and Regulations. 14 November 2019. Vol. 84. No. 220. Available at https://www.occ.treas.gov/news-issuances/federal-register/2019/84fr61974.pdf.

Federal Reserve Bank of New York. ARRC Consultation on Spread Adjustment Methodologies for Fallbacks in Cash Products referencing USD LIBOR. 21 January 2020. https://www.newyorkfed.org/medialibrary/Microsites/arrc/files/2020/ARRC_Spread_Adjustment_Consultation.pdf.

Federal Reserve Bank of New York. Statement introducing the SOFR averages and index. 2 March 2020. https://www.newyorkfed.org/markets/opolicy/operating_policy_200302.

Federal Reserve Bank of New York. Statement Regarding Publication of SOFR Averages and a SOFR Index. 12 February 2020. https://www.newyorkfed.org/markets/opolicy/operating_policy_200212.

Federal Reserve Board. Transaction Data: Bear Stearns, JPMorgan Chase, and Maiden Lane LLC. 2 August 2013. http://www.federalreserve.gov/newsevents/reform_bearstearns.htm.

Fehr, Marc. Genossenschaftsbanken: Brüsseler Bürokraten gefährden Volksbanken. 31 July 2013. https://www.wiwo.de/unternehmen/banken/genossenschaftsbanken-bruesseler-buerokraten-gefaehrden-volksbanken/8551312.html.

Feibelman, Adam. Living Wills and Pre-Commitment (17 November 2011). American University Business Law Review, Vol. 1, No. 1, 2011; Tulane Public Law Research Paper No. 11-8.

Financial Institutions Ordinance (Finanzinstitutsverordnung, FINIV, consolidated as pf 1 January 2020) available at: https://www.admin.ch/opc/en/classified-compilation/20192376/index.html.

Financial Services Authority. Living Wills: How Can the Concept be Implemented?. Speech by Thomas F. Huertas, Director, Banking Sector, FSA and Vice Chairman, CEBS. Wharton School of Management, University of Pennsylvania Philadelphia.

Financial Services Authority; 12 February 2010. https://a-teaminsight.com/uk-fsas-huertas-talks-up-practical-implications-of-living-wills-legislation-including-counterparty-data-requirements/?brand = ati.

Financial Services Regulation in Europe. Second Edition. Edited by Etay Katz.

Financial Times Fannie Mae and Freddie Mac state payouts reach $185bn. http://www.ft.com/intl/cms/s/0/ea648d00-47ba-11e3-b1c4-00144feabdc0.html#axzz3FaLmgDyV.

Financial Times. AIG Bailout. http://www.ft.com/intl/cms/s/0/b649ff9a-97e0-11e1-83f3-00144feabdc0.html#axzz3FaLmgDyV.

Financial Times. http://lexicon.ft.com/Term?term = investment-bank.

Financial Times. http://lexicon.ft.com/Term?term = market-maker.

Financial Times. http://lexicon.ft.com/Term?term = toxic-assets.

Financial Times. UK building society mergers forecast. 28 August 2011. http://www.ft.com/cms/s/0/a905ff18-d18a-11e0-89c0-00144feab49a.html#axzz3JyitCaOP.

Building Society Association. Mergers and Conversion. 1 October 2018. https://www.bsa.org.uk/information/consumer-factsheets/general/mergers-and-conversions-(1).

Financial Times. Wirecard collapses into insolvency. 25 June 2020. https://www.ft.com/content/ac949729-6167-4b6c-ac3f-f0aa71aca193.

Financial Times. Wirecard: the downfall of Germany's fintech star. 26 June 2020. https://www.ft.com/content/8569779b-64e5-4008-a634-0a97a7cf9eb5.

Finanzmarktstabilisierungsgesetz. 2009 C.H. Beck. https://beckassets.blob.core.windows.net/product/toc/26703/jaletzke-finanzmarktstabilisierungsgesetz-fmstg-9783406587603.pdf.

Finch, Vanessa. Corporate Insolvency Law. Cambridge University Press Second Edition 2009.

Fitch Ratings. Impact of European Banking Union on Banks More to Gain Than Lose. Special Report September 2013.

Flannery, Mark J., Maintaining Adequate Bank Capital (1 April 2013). Forthcoming, Journal of Money, Credit and Banking. Available at SSRN: http://ssrn.com/abstract = 2258181.

Francesco Guerrera. Peter Thal Larsen. Gone by the board? Why bank directors did not spot credit risks. Financial Times. 25 June 2008. http://www.ft.com/intl/cms/s/0/6e66fe18-42e8-11dd-81d0-0000779fd2ac.html#axzz3GhyS212G.

Frege, Michael / C. Keller, Ulrich. Riedel, Ernst. Insolvenzrecht. 19 June 2015. C.H. Beck.

French Code monétaire et financier

French Monetary and Financial Code

FSB. 2019 list of global systemically important banks (G-SIBs). 22 November 2019. https://www.fsb.org/wp-content/uploads/P221119-1.pdf.

FSB. Adequacy of loss-absorbing capacity of global systemically important banks in resolution. Consultative Document. 10 November 2014. https://www.fsb.org/wp-content/uploads/TLAC-Condoc-6-Nov-2014-FINAL.pdf.

FSB. Consultative Document on Cross-border recognition of resolution action. 29 September 2015. https://www.fsb.org/wp-content/uploads/c_140929.pdf?page_moved = 1.

FSB. Consultative Document: Assessment Methodology for the Key Attributes of Effective Resolution Regimes for Financial Institutions. 'August 2013 https://www.fsb.org/wp-content/uploads/r_130828.pdf'.

FSB. Guidance on Developing Effective Resolution Strategies regarding Recovery and Resolution Planning for Systemically Important Financial. 16 July 2013. http://www.financialstabilityboard.org/publications/r_130716b.pdf.

FSB. Guiding Principles on the Internal Total Loss-absorbing Capacity of G-SIBs ('Internal TLAC'). 6 July 2017. https://www.fsb.org/wp-content/uploads/P060717-1.pdf.

FSB. Key Attributes of Effective Resolution Regimes for Financial Institutions. 'October 2011 https://www.financialstabilityboard.org/publications/r_111104cc.pdf' and 'October 2014 update https://www.fsb.org/2014/10/key-attributes-of-effective-resolution-regimes-for-financial-institutions-2/'.

FSB. Overview of Responses to the Public Consultation by the Financial Stability Board. 03 November 2015. https://www.fsb.org/wp-content/uploads/Cross-Border-Recognition-of-Resolution-Actions.pdf.

FSB. Policy Measures to Address Systemically Important Financial Institutions. 04 November 2011. Available at: http://www.financialstabilityboard.org/publications/r_111104bb.pdf.

FSB. Principles on Bail in Execution. 21 June 2018. https://www.fsb.org/wp-content/uploads/P210618-1.pdf.

FSB. Recovery and Resolution Planning for Systemically Important Financial Institutions: Guidance on Developing Effective Resolution Strategies. 16 July 2013. https://www.fsb.org/wp-content/uploads/r_130716b.pdf.

FSB. Recovery and Resolution Planning: Making the Key Attributes Requirements Operational – Consultative Document. 'November 2012 – http://www.financialstabilityboard.org/publications/r_121102.pdf'.

FSB. TLAC Term Sheet. 9 November 2015. https://www.fsb.org/wp-content/uploads/TLAC-Principles-and-Term-Sheet-for-publication-final.pdf.

FSB. Towards full implementation of the FSB Key Attributes of Effective Resolution Regimes for Financial Institutions. 12 November 2014. Available at: http://www.financialstabilityboard.org/wp-content/uploads/Resolution-Progress-Report-to-G20.pdf.

G20. https://g20.org/en/Pages/home.aspx.

Garcia, Gillian. Failing prompt corrective action. Journal of Banking Regulation, 171-190 (2010). http://www.palgrave-journals.com/jbr/journal/v11/n3/pdf/jbr201011a.pdf.

Gebhardt, Günther and Reichardt, Rolf and Wittenbrink, Carsten,. Financial Instruments Fair Value Accounting for (not against) the Banking Industry (June 2003). CFS Working Paper No. 2003/21. Available at SSRN: http://ssrn.com/abstract=430260 or http://dx.doi.org/10.2139/ssrn.430260.

Gerhard Picot. Franz Aleth. Unternehmenskrise und Insolvenz: Vorbeugung, Turnaround, Sanierung. 1999 C.H. Beck.

German Kreditwesengesetz

Gesetz zur Abschirmung von Risiken und zur Planung der Sanierung und Abwicklung von Kreditinstituten und Finanzgruppen dated May 2013. Available at: http://dipbt.bundestag.de/extrakt/ba/WP17/508/50871.html.

Gesetz zur Änderung der Insolvenzordnung und anderer Gesetze vom 26.10.2001.

Gesetz zur Errichtung eines Finanzmarkt – und eines Wirtschaftsstabilisierungsfonds. Available at http://www.gesetze-im-internet.de/fmstfg/.

Gesetz zur Fortentwicklung der Finanzmarktstabilisierung vom 17 Juli. 2009 https://www.buzer.de/gesetz/8888/index.htm.

Gesetz zur Reorganisation von Kreditinstituten available at http://www.gesetze-im-internet.de/kredreorgg/index.html.

Gesetz zur Umsetzung eines Maßnahmenpakets zur Stabilisierung des Finanzmarktes (Finanzmarktstabilisierungsgesetz - FMStG) vom 17 October 2008.

Giovanoli Mario. [et al.]. International bank insolvencies: a central bank perspective. The Hague: Kluwer Law International, 1999 Reihe (International banking, finance and economic law; Vol. 12) Gehe zu International banking, finance and economic law Bibliothek.

Giovanoli, Mario Devos, Diego. International Monetary and Financial Law: The Global Crisis / The Editors and Contributors. Impressum New York: Oxford University Press, 2010.

Goodhart, Charles & Segoviano, Miguel A. 'Basel and procyclicality: a comparison of the standardised and IRB approaches to an improved credit risk method,' LSE Research Online Documents on Economics 24821, London School of Economics and Political Science, LSE Library 2004.

Grant Kirkpatrick. The Corporate Governance Lessons from the Financial Crisis. OECD. http://www.oecd.org/finance/financial-markets/42229620.pdf.

Gros, Daniel / Schoenmaker, Dirk. Cleaning up the mess: Bank resolution in a systemic crisis. Centre for European Policy Studies June 2012 - https://www.files.ethz.ch/isn/144177/DG%20&%20DS%20Bank%20Resolution%20in%20a%20Systemic%20Crisis.pdf.

Grünewald, Seraina. Rechtliche Rahmenbedingungen der Bankenabwicklung. In: von der Crone, Hans Caspar. Schweizer Schriften zum Finanzmarkrecht - Finanzstabilität: Status und Perspektiven. Volume 112. Schulthess Juristische Medien AG, 2013.

Grünewald, Seraina; Weber, Rolf H. Bail-in: Zaubertrank oder Pandorabüchse der Bankensanierung? Schweizerische Zeitschrift für Wirtschafts - und Finanzmarktrecht, 2013.

Gstädtner, Thomas, Dr. Asset Quality Review der Europäischen Zentralbank. Recht der Finanzinstrumente, Aufsatz, 01/2014, 24 February 2014.

Gstädtner, Thomas, Dr. Das Bankenrestrukturierungsrecht als Grundbestandteil der europäischen Bankenunion. Recht der Finanzinstrumente, Aufsatz, März 2013.

Hans-Peter Siebenhaar. Austria cuts a deal with Heta creditors. Handelsblatt Today. 19 May 2016. https://www.handelsblatt.com/today/finance/debt-relief-austria-cuts-a-deal-with-heta-creditors/23538004.html.

Hans-Peter Siebenhaar. The lasting legacy of Austria's bad bank. Handelsblatt Today.14 March 2016. https://www.handelsblatt.com/today/finance/failed-state-the-lasting-legacy-of-austrias-bad-bank/23536570.html?ticket=ST-3321637-py3fKrgZmVIOkvxSqKaP-ap4.

Henkel, Christoph. Harmonizing European Union Bank Resolution: Central Clearing Of Otc Derivative Contracts Maintaining The Status Quo Of Safe Harbors. Transnational Law & Contemporary Problems - Spring 2013.

Henning Schoppman et all. European Banking and Financial Services Law. 2nd edition. 2006. Kluwer Law International.

Heta Asset Resolution. 28 July 2015. https://www.heta-asset-resolution.com/en/old_attachments/ad_hoc_haasang_28072015_final_engl.pdf.

HFSF. Report for the period January – June 2016. http://www.hfsf.gr/files/act_report_Jan_Jun_2016_en.pdf.

HFSF. Report of the Fund's activities for the period of January – June 2014. http://www.hfsf.gr/files/HFSF_Activities_Report_January_June_2014_en.pdf.

HFSF. Report of the Fund's activities for the period of January – June 2013. http://www.hfsf.gr/files/HFSF_activities_Jan_2013_Jun_2013_en.pdf.

HFSF. Report of the HFSF for the period July – December 2015 at: http://www.hfsf.gr/files/announcement_20160406_en.pdf.

Hirsch, Jr., Frank A. and Dowdy, Joseph S. Whither Wachovia? Wells Fargo Wins the Battle for the Storied North Carolina Banking Institution. Volume 13 – Citation: 13 N.C. Banking Inst. (2009).

HM Treasury, Banking reform: delivering stability and supporting a sustainable economy, dated June 2012. Available at: https://www.gov.uk/government/uploads/system/uploads/attachment_data/file/32556/whitepaper_banking_reform_140512.pdf.

Hoelscher David. Bank Restructuring and Resolution. International Monetary Fund, 1 October 2006 – Business & Economics.

Hofmann, Christian. A Legal Analysis of the Euro Zone Crisis. 18 Fordham J. Corp. & Fin. L. 519 2013.

Horn, Norbert. German Banking Law and Practice in International Perspective. Impressum Berlin: De Gruyter, 1999 – Umfang Online-Ressource – Uni St Gallen.

Hüfner, Felix. The German Banking System: Lessons from the Financial Crisis. Economics Department – Working Papers, No. 788, OECD Publishing – http://dx.doi.org/10.1787/5kmbm80pjkd6-en.

Hüpkes, Eva H. G. The legal aspects of bank insolvency: a comparative analysis of Western Europe, the United States and Canada. The Hague: Kluwer Law International, 2000 Reihe (Studies in comparative corporate and financial law; vol. 10) Gehe zu Studies in comparative corporate and financial law Bibliothek HSG Obergeschoss PU 1560 H887.

Hüpkes, Eva. 'Form Follows Function' – A New Architecture for Regulating and Resolving Global Financial institutions. European Business Organization Law Review / Volume 10 / Issue 03 / September 2009. Published online: 28 September 2009.

Hupkes, Eva. Insolvency – why a special regime for banks?. 21 January 2003. International Monetary Fund. https://www.imf.org/external/np/leg/sem/2002/cdmfl/eng/hupkes.pdf.

Ian F. Fletcher. Insolvency in Private International Law. 2nd edition. 2007. OUP.

Ian F. Fletcher. Law of Insolvency. 5th edition. 2017. Sweet & Maxwell.

IFRS https://www.ifrs.org/.

Independent Commission on Banking. The Final Report. Dated September 2011. Available at: https://researchbriefings.files.parliament.uk/documents/SN06171/SN06171.pdf.

Institut für Städtebau, Wohnungswirtschaft und Bausparwesen e.V. in Berlin Volume 73 and 74.

Institute of International Finance. 'Making Resolution Robust-Completing The Legal And Institutional Frameworks for Effective Cross-Border Resolution of Financial Institutions'. IFF 2012.

International Monetary Fund and the World Bank. 'An Overview of the Legal, Institutional, and Regulatory Framework for Bank Insolvency'. Dated 17 April 2009 Available at https://www.imf.org/external/np/pp/eng/2009/041709.pdf.

International Monetary Fund. Chapter 25 Insolvency: Why a Special Regime for Banks?. Current Developments in Monetary and Financial Law. Vol 3. 2005. https://www.elibrary.imf.org/view/IMF072/01499-9781589063341/01499-9781589063341/ch25.xml?language = en&redirect = true.

International Monetary Fund. Country Report No. 19/189 Switzerland: Financial Sector Assessment Program; Technical Note-Stress Testing the Banking Sector dated June 2019, available at: https://www.imf.org/ ~ /media/Files/Publications/CR/2019/1CHEEA2019009.ashx.

International Monetary Fund. European Commission Consultation – An EU Framework for Cross-border Crisis Management in the Banking Sector. 29 January 2010. https://www.imf.org/external/np/eur/2010/pdf/012910.pdf.

International Monetary Fund. FACTSHEET – Where the IMF Gets Its Money. 19 November 2013. http://www.imf.org/external/np/exr/facts/finfac.htm.

International Monetary Fund. Press Release: IMF Executive Board Concludes 2014 Article IV Consultation with Austria. 15 September 2014. https://www.imf.org/en/News/Articles/2015/09/14/01/49/pr14423#P18_327.

International Monetary Fund. Spain: Financial Sector Reform – Third Progress Report. IMF Country Report No. 13/205 July 2013.

International Monetary Fund. Spain: The Reform of Spanish Savings Banks Technical Notes. June 2012. Country Report No. 12/141. https://www.imf.org/external/pubs/ft/scr/2012/cr12141.pdf.

International Monetary Fund. Subsidiaries or Branches: Does One Size Fit All?. Discussion Note of the International Monetary Fund Staff: dated 7 March 2011, prepared by Jonathan Fiechter, İnci Ötker-Robe, Anna Ilyina, Michael Hsu, André Santos, and Jay Surti.

International Swaps and Derivatives Association. Position Paper on Challenges with Expanding BRRD Moratoria Powers. August 2017. https://www.isda.org/a/IkiDE/brrd-position-paper-final.pdf.

ISDA. 2002 Master Agreement. https://www.isda.org/traditional-protocol/2002-isda-master-agreement-protocol/.

ISDA. Bail-in Article 55 BRRD Protocol. 2016. https://www.isda.org/protocol/isda-2016-bail-in-art-55-brrd-protocol-dutchfrenchgermanirishitalianluxembourgspanishuk-entity-in-resolution-version/.

ISDA. Resolution Stay Jurisdictional Modular Protocol. 3 May 2016. https://www.isda.org/protocol/isda-resolution-stay-jurisdictional-modular-protocol/.

ISDA. Universal Resolution Stay Protocol. 2015. https://www.isda.org/protocol/isda-2015-universal-resolution-stay-protocol/.

J, Deslandes. M, Magnus. Further harmonizing EU insolvency law from a banking resolution perspective? April 2018. Economic Governance Support Unit. https://www.europarl.europa.eu/RegData/etudes/BRIE/2018/614514/IPOL_BRI(2018)614514_EN.pdf.

James McAndrews et al. What Makes Large Banks Failures So Messy and What to Do about It? 2014. FRBNY Econ Pol Rev 229. 236 – 240.

Jaschinski, Siegfried: Das deutsche Finanzsystem: Achillesferse der Wirtschaft? / Siegfried Jaschinski. Stuttgart Schäffer-Poeschel 2011.

Javier Aríztegui. Savings bank restructuring and institutional protection schemes. Speech at conference organized by Caja Granada. Granada. 17 December 2010. https://www.bis.org/review/r101222e.pdf.

Jianping Zhou and others. From Bail-out to Bail-in: Mandatory Debt Restructuring of Systemic Financial Institutions. International Monetary Fund. Monetary and Capital Market Department and Legal Department. 24 April 2012. https://www.imf.org/external/pubs/ft/sdn/2012/sdn1203.pdf.

Jo Hoje; Durairaj, Vivek; Driscoll, Tim; Enomoto, Andrew; Ku, Joseph. Bank mergers: Bank of America-Merrill Lynch vs. Wells Fargo-Wachovia acquisitions. Journal of Case Research in Business & Economics. June 2010, Vol. 3, p1-9. 9p. 1 Chart, 2 Graphs.

John Hawkins and Philip Turner – BANK FOR INTERNATIONAL SETTLEMENTS. Bank restructuring in practice: an overview. Bank for International Settlements, Monetary and Economic Department, 1999 – Bank management – 221 pages.

Josef Urschitz. Wir hatten noch ein paar Fragen. 12 February 2014. https://www.diepresse.com/1561946/wir-hatten-noch-ein-paar-fragen.

Jukernheinrich, Martin and Korioth, Stefan and Lenk, Thomas and Scheller, Henrik and Woisin, Matthias. Jahrbuch für öffentliche Finanzen 2010. Berliner Wissenschafts-Verlag, Band 218.

Kaal Wulf A. Initial Reflections On The Possible Application Of Contingent Capital In Corporate Governance. Notre Dame Journal of Law, Ethics & Public Policy 2012.

Kähr, Michael. Die Voraussetzungen für die Ergreifung von Massnahmen bei Insolvenzgefahr nach Article 25 BankG. Schweizerische Zeitschrift für Wirtschafts – und Finanzmarktrecht, 2013.

Kähr, Michael. Sanierungsrecht für Banken. Der Schweizer Treuhänder, 2014, Issue 3.

Kane, Edward and Luc Laeven. Deposit Insurance around the World – Issues of Design and Implementation. The MIT Press – Cambridge, Massachusetts – 2008.

Kerlin, Jakub. The Role of Deposit Guarantee Schemes as a Financial Safety Net in the European Union. 2017. Palgrave Macmillan. 1st edition.

Kersting, Christian. Combating the Financial Crisis: European and German Corporate and Securities Laws and the Case for Abolishing Sovereign Debtors' Privileges. Texas International Law Journal, Vol. 48, No. 2, 2013. Available at SSRN: http://ssrn.com/abstract=2268475.

Kindleberger Charles P. (Author), Robert Aliber (Author). Manias, Panics, and Crashes: A History of Financial Crises. Wiley; 5 edition (4 October 2005).

Klein, Maury. The Panic of 2008 + Snowden, Kenneth. The anatomy. Both in The Panic of 2008 by Mitchell and Wilmarth.

Klimek et alt. To bail-out or to bail-in? Answers from an agent-based model. 6 March 2014.

Koller, Robert and Wolfgang, Kotzur, Dr. Bail-in und Folgefragen. Recht der Finanzinstrumente, Zivilrecht, Nr. 2/2014, 26 May 2014.

Korte, Josef. Catharsis - The real effects of bank insolvency and resolution. Discussion Paper - Deutsche Bundesbank - No 21/2013.

Krahnen, Jan Pieter, Prof. Dr. Bail-In-Anleihen: ein effektives Instrument zur Wiederherstellung der privaten Haftung im Bankenmarkt. Betriebs-Berater, BB 42.2013, 14 October 2013.

Kunz, Peter V. Kreuzfahrt durch's schweizerische Finanzmarktrecht. KSR - Kleine Schriften zum Recht. Stämpfli Verlag AG: 2014, Bern.

Labonte, Marc. Systemically Important or 'Too Big to Fail' Financial Institutions. Congressional Research Service July 2013.

Labrosse, John Raymond [Hrsg.]. Financial crisis management and bank resolution. London: Informa, 2009 XXXVII, 338 S.

Labrosse, John Raymond. Financial crisis containment and government guarantees. Ort, Verlag, Jahr: Northampton, MA: Edward Elgar Pub, 2013.

Lastra, Rosa M. [Hrsg.]. Bank failures and bank insolvency law in economies in transition. The Hague [u.a.]: Kluwer Law Internat, 1999 XVI, International economic development law.

Lastra, Rosa M. and several contributors. Cross-Border Bank Insolvency. Impressum New York: Oxford University Press, 2011.

Lastra, Rosa Maria. Central banking and banking regulation. London School of Economics and Political Science, 1996 Notiz Am Kopf des Einbandes: Financial Markets Group. London School of Economics Bibliogr. Literaturverz.

Lastra, Rosa. Banking Union and Single Market: Conflict or Companionship?. Volume 36 - Issue 5 Fordham International Law Journal.

Law on transparency, anti-corruption and modernisation of economy ('Sapin 2 Law').

Leckow, Ross. Operational issues. In: Lastra. Cross Border Bank Insolvency.

Leitao, Miriam. A Saga Brasileira: A Longa Luta De Um Povo Por Sua Moeda. São Paulo: Record, 2011.

Lüdenbach/Hoffmann. IFRS Kommentar. 11. Auflage.

Lundberg, Eduardo. Rede De Proteção e Saneamento Do Sistema Bancário. In: SADDI, Jairo (org.). Intervenção e liquidação extrajudicial no Sistema Financeiro Nacional: 25 anos da lei 6.024/74. Texto Novo, São Paulo, 1999.

Lundberg, Eduardo. Saneamento do Sistema Financeiro - A Experiência Brasileira dos Últimos 25 Anos. In: SADDI, Jairo (org.). Intervenção e liquidação extrajudicial no Sistema Financeiro Nacional: 25 anos da lei 6.024/74. Texto Novo, São Paulo, 1999.

MacNeil, Iain. Bail-in protocol: When, who and how?. 'Law and Financial Markets Review' Volume 7 Issue 4 (August 2013).

MacNeil, Iain. Editorial - Bail-in protocol: when, who and how?. Law and Financial Markets Review, DOI: 10.5235/17521440.

Martina Miskova. Lucia Országhovál. Národná banka Slovenska., 'MREL: Gone Concern Loss Absorption Capacity.' 2015. Available at https://www.nbs.sk/_img/Documents/_PUBLIK_NBS_FSR/Biatec/Rok2015/03-2015/06_biatec_3-15_miskova-orszaghova.pdf.

Mastroeni, Orazio. ECB. Pfandbrief - style products in Europe. http://www.bis.org/publ/bppdf/bispap05b.pdf.

Matej Marinč and Razvan Vlahu. The Economics of Bank Bankruptcy Law. Springer-Verlag Berlin Heidelberg 2012.

Matej Marinc. Razvan Vlahu. The Economic Perspective of Bank Bankruptcy Law. 2011. https://papers.ssrn.com/sol3/papers.cfm?abstract_id=1822682.

Matej Tomec and Timotej Jagric. Does the Amount and Time of Recapitalization Affect the Profitability of Commercial Banks? 2017. Czech Journal of Economics and Finance (67, number 4). https://journal.fsv.cuni.cz/storage/1390_318-341_jagric_final_issue_4_2017.pdf.

Mathias Dewatripont/Jean Tirole,. The Prudential Regulation of Banks. MIT Press 1994.

McCormick, Roger. Legal Risk in the Financial Markets. New York: Oxford University Press, 2010.

McCoy, Patricia A. and Pavlov, Andrey D. and Wachter, Susan M. Systemic Risk through Securitization: The Result of Deregulation and Regulatory Failure. Connecticut Law Review, Vol. 41, p. 493, May 2009.

McGuire Claire. Simple Tools to Assist in the Resolution of Troubled Banks. The World Bank January 2012.

Menichetti, M. J. (1999). Außenhandelsabwicklung. In: Enzyklopädisches Lexikon des Geld-, Bank - und Börsenwesens, 4. Aufl., Verlag Fritz Knapp, Frankfurt/M. 1999, S. 63-73.

Michael J. Fleming and Asani Sarkar. The Failure Resolution of Lehman Brothers. 3 April 2014. Liberty Street Economics. https://libertystreeteconomics.newyorkfed.org/2014/04/the-failure-resolution-of-lehman-brothers-.html.

Michael Schillig. Bank Resolution Regimes in Europe I - Recovery and Resolution Planning, Early Intervention. 25 August 2012. https://papers.ssrn.com/sol3/papers.cfm?abstract_id=2136101.

Mishkin, Frederic S. The economics of money, banking, and financial markets. Boston: Pearson Addison Wesley, 2010 MLE: QC 300: 24.

Moulton, Rob and Nicola Higgs. Corporate governance in financial institutions. C.O.B. 2013, 109(Sep), Compliance Officer Bulletin - 2013.

Müssig, Karlheinz. Bank-Lexikon: Handwörterbuch für das Geld-, Bank - und Börsenwesen. Wiesbaden: Gabler, 1988.

Neue Zürcher Zeitung. Kein Stress für Schweizer Banken. 27 October 2014. http://www.nzz.ch/wirtschaft/kein-stress-fuer-schweizer-banken-1.18412651.

Nobel, Peter. Das Finanzmarktaufsichtsrecht Mitte 2011 bis Mitte 2012. Schweizerische Zeitschrift für Wirtschafts - und Finanzmarktrecht, 2012.

Ono, Fabio Hideki. O Acordo de Basiléia, a Adequação de Capital e A Implementação no Sistema Bancário Brasileiro. Monografia. Instituto de Economia, Unicamp, Campinas, 2002.

Ordonnance portant diverses dispositions d'adaptation de la legislation au droit de l'Union européenne en matière financière 2015.

Panagiotis Delimatsis, Nils Herger. 'Financial regulation at the crossroads implications for supervision, institutional design and trade'. ':Alphen aan den Rijn' Wolters Kluwer Law & Business, 2011

Parker, David. Closing a Failed Bank: Resolution Practices and Procedures. International Monetary Fund, 1 April 2011 - Business & Economics - 236 pages.

Patrick S. Kenadjian (Ed.). Too Big to Fail - Do we need a special insolvency law for Banks? 2012 Institute for Law and Finance Series 9. https://www.degruyter.com/view/title/122850?tab_body=toc.

Patrick S. Kenadjian (Herausgeber) Ritter, Lawrence S.; Silber, William L.; Udell, Gregory F. Principles of money, banking & financial markets. 12. ed. Harlow: Pearson Ed., 2014.

Perotti, Enrico C. The Political Economy of Finance (22 February 2013). Available at SSRN: http://ssrn.com/abstract=2222630 or http://dx.doi.org/10.2139/ssrn.2222630.

Petitjean, Mikael. Bank failures and regulation: a critical review. Journal of Financial Regulation and Compliance 2013.

Pfandbriefgesetz (PfG) dated 25 June 1930 (consolidated as of 1 January 2015).

Philipp Bagus, Juan R. Rallo Juliány and Miguel A. Alonso Neira. Bail-in or Bail-out: The Case of Spain. CESifo Economic Studies, Vol. 60, 1/2014, 89-106 doi:10.1093/cesifo/ifu009. Advance Access publication 18 February 2014.

Pistor, Katharina. A Legal Theory of Finance. Journal of Comparative Economics, Vol. 41, No. 2, 2013. Columbia Public Law Research Paper No. 13-348.

President of the Eurogroup. Statement on ESM direct recapitalization instrument. 10 June 2014. https://www.consilium.europa.eu/media/28065/143163.pdf.

Prof. Dr. Christos V. Gortsos. A poisonous (?) mix: Bail-out of credit institutions combined with bail-in of their liabilities under BRRD - The use of 'government financial stabilisation tools' presented at the Workshop of the Financial and Monetary Law Working Group of the European University Institute (EUI. Florence. 12 October 2016). https://papers.ssrn.com/sol3/papers.cfm?abstract_id=2876508.

Proposal for a Directive of the European Parliament and of the Council establishing a framework for the recovery and resolution of credit institutions and investment firms and amending Council Directives 77/91/EEC and 82/891/EC, Directives 2001/24/EC, 2002/47/EC, 2004/25/EC, 2005/56/EC, 2007/36/EC and 2011/35/EC and Regulation (EU) No 1093/2010. COM/2012/0280 final - 2012/0150 (COD).

Proposal for a regulation of the European Parliament and of the Council amending Regulation (EU) 806/2014 in order to establish a European Deposit Insurance Scheme (COM/2015/0586 final- 2015/0270 (COD)).

Proposal for a regulation of the European Parliament and of the Council on structural measures improving the resilience of EU credit institutions / COM/2014/043 final - 2014/0020 (COD).

Puga, Fernando Pimentel. Sistema Financeiro Brasileiro: Reestruturação Recente, Comparações Internacionais e Vulnerabilidade à Crise Cambial. Banco Central do Brasil. Data: 03/1999.

Pulver, Urs. Zahlungs - und Effektenabwicklungssysteme sowie Vereinbarungen zur Risikoreduktion - Abschirmung in der Insolvenz / I.-III. In: Sprecher, Thomas. Sanierung und Insolvenz von Unternehmen III Schwerpunkt: Das neue Bankeninsolvenzrecht. Schulthess Juristische Medien AG, 2013.

PwC. Lehman Brothers International (Europe) in Administration. Joint Administrators' progress report for the period 15 September 2008 to 14 March 2009. 14 April 2009. https://www.pwc.co.uk/assets/pdf/lbie-progress-report-140409.pdf.

Randell, Charles. Triggers for Bank Resolution. 'In: Too Big To Fail - Brauchen wir ein Sonderinsolvenzrecht für Banken?' (Institute for Law and Finance Series) [Gebundene Ausgabe].

Rayroux, François, Conti, Christelle. New Ordinance of FINMA on the Insolvency of Banks: A Critical Assessment. Swiss Capital Markets Law. Issue 31, 2012.

Regulation (EU) 2019/876 of the European Parliament and of the Council of 20 May 2019 amending Regulation (EU) No 575/2013 as regards the leverage ratio, the net stable funding ratio, requirements for own funds and eligible liabilities, counterparty credit risk, market risk, exposures to central counterparties, exposures to collective investment undertakings, large exposures, reporting and disclosure requirements, and Regulation (EU) No 648/20.

Regulation (EU) 2019/877 of the European Parliament and of the Council of 20 May 2019 amending Regulation (EU) No 806/2014 as regards the loss-absorbing and recapitalization capacity of credit institutions and investment firms.

Regulation (EU) No 1093/2010 of the European Parliament and of the Council of 24 November 2010 establishing a European Supervisory Authority (European Banking Authority), amending Decision No 716/2009/EC and repealing Commission Decision 2009/78/EC.

Regulation (EU) No 806/2014 of the European Parliament and of the Council of 15 July 2014 establishing uniform rules and a uniform procedure for the resolution of credit institutions and certain investment firms in the framework of a Single Resolution Mechanism and a Single Resolution Fund and amending Regulation (EU) No 1093/2010.

Reiser, Nina. Deposit Insurance and its Contribution to System Stability. Schweizerische Zeitschrift für Wirtschafts - und Finanzmarktrecht, 2014.

Rene Smits. Is my money safe at European banks? Reflections on the 'bail-in' provisions in recent EU legal texts. Capital Markets Law Journal, Vol. 9, No. 2.

Republik Osterreich Parliament. Löschung der BMF-Informationsseite zur Hypo Alpe Adria. https://www.parlament.gv.at/PAKT/VHG/XXV/J/J_09441/index.shtml.

Repullo, Rafael and Jesús Saurina. The Countercyclical Capital Buffer of Basel III: A Critical Assessment 45. In: The Crisis Aftermath: New Regulatory Paradigms Centre for Economic Policy Research London 2012.

Rosato, John F. Down The Road To Perdition: How The Flaws Of Basel Ii Led To The Collapse Of Bear Stearns And Lehman Brothers. 17 Conn. Ins. L.J. 475 2011.

Rumersdorfer, Birgit. Financial crisis - A challenge for the European Union. August 2013 https://www.pravo.unizg.hr/_download/repository/Birgit_Rumersdorfer.doc.

Rundschreiben 2015/2 - Liquiditätsrisiken, consolidated as of 7 December 2017. Available in German at: https://www.finma.ch/de/ ~ /media/finma/dokumente /rundschreiben-archiv/2015/rs-15-02/rs-15-02-02-20171207.pdf?la = de.

Salviano Junior, Cleofas. Bancos estaduais: dos problemas crônicas ao Proes. Publisher, Banco Central do Brasil, 2004.

Sampford, Charles. Adam Smith's Dinner. In Macneil, Iain & O'Brien, Justin (Eds.) The Future of Financial Regulation. Hart Publishing, Oxford U.K. (2010).

SAREB (Sociedad de Gestión de Activos Procedentes de la Reestructuración Bancaria). https://www.sareb.es/.

SAREB. Who are we. https://www.sareb.es/en_US/about-us/who-we-are.

Scharpf, Paul Schaber, Mathias. Handbuch Bankbilanz. Publisher: IDW, Pub date: 2013.

Schelo, Sven /Andreas Steck. 'Das Trennbankengesetz: Prävention durch Bankentestamente und Risikoabschirmung'. ZBB 2013, 227.

Schelo, Sven. 'Die Vorschläge der Bundesregierung zur Bankenregulierung'. NJW, Editorial Heft 21/2010.

Schelo, Sven. 'Neue Restrukturierungsregeln für Banken'. NJW 2011, 186.

Schelo, Sven. 'Reform der Unternehmenssanierung'. DB 2010, 2209.

Schelo, Sven. 'Wenn Banken wanken - Ist das Bankenmoratorium ein geeignetes Mittel?'. NJW, Editorial Heft 42/2008.

Schich. Financial Turbulence: Some Lessons Regarding Deposit Insurance. Financial Market Trends OECD 2008.

Schiltknecht, Reto. Das neue schweizerische Bankeninsolvenzrecht. Sonderdruck aus Europa Institut Zürich, Band 138. In: Sprecher, Thomas. Sanierung und Insolvenz von Unternehmen III. Schulthess, available at: https://www.finma.ch/d/finma/publikationen/Documents/europa-institut-artikel-schildknecht-bankeninsolvenzrecht-d.pdf.

Schiltknecht, Reto. New FINMA Banking Insolvency Ordinance. A key element in the effective restructuring and orderly market exit of banks. FINMA, 2012. Available at: https://www.finma.ch/en/ ~ /media/finma/dokumente/dokumentencenter /anhoerungen/abgeschlossene-anhoerungen/17-bankeninsolvenzverordnung/fb-biv-finma-d.pdf?la = en.

Schiltknecht, Reto. Stabilität und Instabilität des schweizerischen Bankensystems. Schweizerische Zeitschrift für Wirtschafts - und Finanzmarktrecht, 2013.

Schiltknecht, Reto; McHale, Christopher. Erste Erfahrungen mit dem bedingten Wandlungskapital (CoCos). Gesellschafts - und Kapitalmarktrecht, 2012.

Schoenmaker, Dirk. Internationalisation of banking supervision and deposit insurance. Journal of International Banking Law 1993, 8(3), 106-112.

Schooner, Michael W. Taylor; Heidi Mandanis. Global Bank Regulation Principles and Policies. 2010 ELSEVIER.

Schwob, Renate; Müller, Artikel 37g. In: Zobl, Dieter; Schwob, Renate; Geiger, Hans; Winzeler, Christoph; Kaufmann, Christine; Weber, Rolf H. Thomas S.; Kramer, Stefan. Kommentar zum Bundesgesetz über die Banken und Sparkassen - Stand: 22. Schulthess Juristische Medien AG, 2014. .

Securities and Exchange Commission. 17 CFR Parts 200, 240, and 249. Release No. 34-87005; File No. S7-05-14. RIN 3235-AL45. https://www.sec.gov/rules/final/2019/34-87005.pdf.

Sester, Peter. Cross-Border Bank Insolvency Regulation in the G20 context. 'Nobel, Peter (Hrsg.); Krehan, Katrin (Hrsg.); Tanner, Anne-Cathrine (Hrsg.) Law and Economics of Global Financial Institutions. Third International Conference on Law and Economics at the University of St.Gallen. June 4, 2010 St. Gallen, Switzerland'.

Seventh Council Directive 83/349/EEC of 13 June 1983 based on Article 54 (3) (g) of the Treaty on consolidated accounts.

Silvia Merler. Bank liquidation in the European Union: clarification needed. January 2017. https://bruegel.org/wp-content/uploads/2018/01/PC-01_2018.pdf.

Simon Gleeson. International Regulation of Banking. 3rd edition. 2018.

Simon Gleeson. Legal aspect of bank bail-ins. January 2021. LSE Financial Markets Group Paper Series. http://www.lse.ac.uk/fmg/assets/documents/papers/special-papers/SP205.pdf.

Simon Gleeson. The Single Resolution Mechanism and the EU crisis management tools. 2016 in The European Banking Union and the Role of Law. 2019. Edited by Gianni Lo Schiavo.

Siqueira, Francisco José de. Instituições financeiras: regimes especiais no direito brasileiro. Revista de Direito Bancario e do Mercado de Capitais, São Paulo: Revista dos Tribunais, v. 4, n. 12, p. 44-71, ABR/JUN/2001.

Smits, Rene. 'Is my money safe at European banks? Reflections on the "bail-in" provisions in recent EU legal texts'. Capital Markets Law Journal, 2014 Standard & Poors. 'How A Bail-In Tool Could Affect Our Ratings On EU Banks'. 2012.

Spiegel International. EU Deal Protects Taxpayers in Bank Bailouts. 27 June 2013. https://www.spiegel.de/international/business/eu-deal-would-require-bail-ins-in-future-bank-rescue-plans-a-908175.html.

SRB. ABLV. https://srb.europa.eu/en/content/ablv.

SRB. Banca Popolare di Vicenza and Veneto Banca https://srb.europa.eu/en/content/banca-popolare-di-vicenza-veneto-banca.

SRB. Banco Popular. https://srb.europa.eu/en/content/banco-popular.

SRB. Banking Industry Dialogue Meeting. 18 June 2019. https://srb.europa.eu/sites/srbsite/files/presentation_on_srb_resolution_planning.pdf.

SRB. Banking Industry Dialogue Meeting. The Banking Package and the next SRB MREL policy. 16 December 2019. https://srb.europa.eu/sites/srbsite/files/industry_dialogue_16_december_2019_-_srb_-_the_banking_package_and_the_next_srb_mrel_policy_1.pdf.

SRB. Critical functions approach. 2017. https://srb.europa.eu/sites/srbsite/files/critical_functions_final.pdf.

SRB. Critical Functions. https://srb.europa.eu/en/content/critical-functions.

SRB. Decision of 17 March 2020. determining whether compensation needs to be granted to the shareholders and creditors in respect of which the resolution actions concerning Banco Popular Español S.A. have been effected (SRB/EES/2020/52) https://srb.europa.eu/sites/srbsite/files/srb_ees_2020_52_final_decision_en.pdf.

SRB. Expectations for Banks 2019. https://srb.europa.eu/sites/srbsite/files/srb_expectations_for_banks_2019.pdf.

SRB. Expectations for Banks. March 2020. https://srb.europa.eu/sites/srbsite/files/efb_main_doc_final_web_0.pdf.

SRB. Framework for Valuation February 2019. https://srb.europa.eu/sites/srbsite/files/framework_for_valuation_feb_2019_web_0.pdf.

SRB. Minimum Requirement for Own Funds and Eligible Liabilities (MREL). Addendum to the SRB 2018 MREL policy on new CRR requirements. 25 June 2019.

SRB. Minimum Requirement for Own Funds and Eligible Liabilities (MREL) 2018 SRB Policy for the second wave of resolution plans. 16 January 2019. https://srb.europa.eu/sites/srbsite/files/public_mrel_policy_2018_-_second_wave_of_plans.pdf.

SRB. Minimum Requirements for own funds and eligible liabilities (MREL). SRB Policy under the Banking Package. 20 May 2020. https://srb.europa.eu/sites/srbsite/files/srb_mrel_policy_2020.pdf.

SRB. MREL: Approach taken in 2016 and next steps. https://srb.europa.eu/sites/srbsite/files/srb_mrel_approach_2016_post_final.pdf.

SRB. Notice of the Single Resolution Board of 2 August 2018 regarding its preliminary decision on whether compensation needs to be granted to the shareholders and creditors in respect of which the resolution actions concerning Banco Popular Español S.A. have been effected and the launching of the right to be heard process (SRB/EES/2018/132) https://srb.europa.eu/sites/srbsite/files/srb_ees_2018_132_notice_of_the_srb_final.pdf.

SRB. Public Interest Assessment: SRB Approach. https://srb.europa.eu/sites/srbsite/files/2019-06-28_draft_pia_paper_v12.pdf.

SRB. Resolution Cases. https://srb.europa.eu/en/content/resolution-cases.

SRB. Resolution Q&A. https://srb.europa.eu/en/content/resolution-qa.

SRB. SRF grows to €33 billion after latest round of transfers. 17 July 2019. https://srb.europa.eu/en/node/804.

SRB. The SRB will not take resolution action in relation to Banca Popolare di Vicenza and Veneto Banca. 12 December 2017. https://srb.europa.eu/en/node/341.

SRB. What is the Single Resolution Fund?. https://srb.europa.eu/en/content/single-resolution-fund.

Stefano Micossi, Ginevra Bruzzone and Miriam Cassella. Bail-in Provisions in State Aid and Resolution Procedures: Are they consistent with systemic stability?. CEPS Policy Brief No. 318, 21 May 2014.

Steinglass, Matt. Netherlands may need to compensate SNS Reaal shareholders. Financial Times. 12 July 2013. http://www.ft.com/intl/cms/s/0/3d826730-eae8-11e2-bfdb-00144feabdc0.html#axzz2o1x5IoNL.

Steve Schifferes. Can Banking regulation be global?. BBC. 18 March 2009. http://news.bbc.co.uk/2/mobile/business/7950758.stm.

Stone, Douglas. William, Ziemba. Land and Stock Prices in Japan. http://pubs.aeaweb.org/doi/pdfplus/10.1257/jep.7.3.149.

Subramanian, Guhan and Sharm, Nithyasri. Citigroup - Wachovia - Wells Fargo Case. Harvard Law School. Product Number: 10-03. Publication Date: Rev. 23 September 2010.

Swiss Debt Enforcement and Bankruptcy Law

Swiss Federal Banking Act

Swiss Financial Market Supervisory Authority. Banking Insolvency Ordinance comes into force. 22 October 2012. https://www.finma.ch/en/news/2012/10/mm-inkraftsetzung-bankeninsolvenzverordnung-finma-20121022/.

Swiss National Bank - Bezeichnung von systemrelevanten Banken, available at: https://www.snb.ch/de/iabout/finstab/finstab_pub/id/finstab_pub_banksector.

Swiss National Bank. Banks in Switzerland. 2019. https://www.snb.ch/en/mmr/reference/banks_2019/source/banks_2019.en.pdf.

Swiss National Bank. Determination of Systemically Important Banks. https://www.snb.ch/de/iabout/finstab/finstab_pub/id/finstab_pub_banksector.

Swiss National Bank. Publikationen: Bankensektor. 2019. https://www.snb.ch/de/iabout/finstab/finstab_pub/id/finstab_pub_banksector.

Symes, Christopher F. 'Statutory Priorities in Corporate Insolvency Law An Analysis of Preferred Creditor Status'. Imprint: Ashgate Published: December 2008.

Tarullo, Daniel. Banking on Basel: The Future of International Financial Regulation. Peterson Institute; 1 New edition (30 September 2008).

The Economist. Too much of a good thing. 10 October 2013. https://www.economist.com/special-report/2013/10/10/too-much-of-a-good-thing.

The Financial Market Stabilisation Fund Act (Finanzmarktstabilisierungsfondsgesetz) 17 October 2008.

Thießen, Friedrich Cramer, Jörg E. / Albrecht Dietz. The Oxford Handbook of Banking (Oxford Handbooks) Paperback - 2 March 2012.

Thole; Christoph. Gläubigerschutz in einem Sonderinsolvenzrecht für Banken. 'In: Too Big To Fail - Brauchen wir ein Sonderinsolvenzrecht für Banken?"' (Institute for Law and Finance Series) [Gebundene Ausgabe] Patrick S. Kenadjian (Herausgeber).

Thomas Conlon, John Cotter. Anatomy of a Bail-In. March 2014 http://papers.ssrn.com/sol3/papers.cfm?abstract_id=2294100.

Thomson Reuters. Austria to turn Volksbanken into 'bad bank'. 2 October 2014. https://uk.reuters.com/article/uk-austria-volksbanken-idUKKCN0HR1RI20141002.

Tobias H. Tröger. Why MREL won't help much. 2017. Page 7. https://www.imfs-frankfurt.de/fileadmin/user_upload/IMFS_WP_117.pdf.

Treaty establishing the European Stability Mechanism between The Kingdom of Belgium, The Federal Republic of Germany, The Republic of Estonia, Ireland, The Hellenic Republic, The Kingdom of Spain, The French Republic, The Italian

Republic, The Republic of Cyprus, The Republic of Latvia, The Republic of Lithuania, The Grand Duchy of Luxembourg, Malta, The Kingdom of Netherlands, The Republic of Austria, The Portuguese Republic, The Republic of Slovenia, The Slovak Republic and The Republic of Finland. 2 February 2012. https://www.esm.europa.eu/sites/default/files/20150203_-_esm_treaty_-_en_1.pdf.

Tully, Shawn. Sheila Bair: 'I'm sure Vikram still blames me'. CNN Money. 16 October 2012. https://fortune.com/2012/10/16/sheila-bair-im-sure-vikram-still-blames-me/.

Uchida, H. and G. Udell, 'Banking in Japan', in A. Berger, P. Molyneux, and J. Wilson eds., Oxford Handbook of Banking, Ch. 35, Oxford University Press, 2010.

Ulrich van Suntum. Cordelius Ilgmann. Bad banks: a proposal based on German financial history. Eur J Law Econ (2013) 35:367-384.

UNCITRAL. Legislative Guide on Insolvency Law. 2005. Available at https://www.uncitral.org/pdf/english/texts/insolven/05-80722_Ebook.pdf.

Uhndritz, Sven-Holger: Die doppelnützige Treuhand in der Restrukturierungspraxis. In: Bauer, Michael; Kantowsky, Jan; Schulte, Axel (Hrsg.): Stakeholder Management in der Restrukturierung. Wiesbaden, 2012, S. 269-285.

United Nations Commission on International Trade Law. Model Law on Cross-Border Insolvency Law with Guide to Enactment and Interpretation. http://www.uncitral.org/pdf/english/texts/insolven/1997-Model-Law-Insol-2013-Guide-Enactment-e.pdf.

US Code of Federal Regulations.

Varriale, Gemma. A definitive guide to CoCos. International Financial Law Review January 2013.

Verordnung der Eidgenössischen Finanzmarktaufsicht über den Konkurs von Banken und Effektenhändlern (Bankenkonkursverordnung-FINMA, BKV-FINMA). 30 June 2005. Available at: http://www.admin.ch/opc/de/classified-compilation/20051042/index.html.

Verordnung der Eidgenössischen Finanzmarktaufsicht über die Insolvenz von Banken und Effektenhändlern (Bankeninsolvenzverordnung-FINMA, BIV-FINMA). 30 August 2012 (consolidated as of 1 April 2017). Translation for information purposes only published by the Swiss Federal Council, available at: https://www.admin.ch/opc/en/classified-compilation/20112977/index.html.

Verordnung über die Banken und Sparkassen (Bankenverordnung, BankV1). 17 May 1972 (consolidated as of 1 January 2020). Available at: https://www.admin.ch/opc/de/classified-compilation/20131795/202001010000/952.02.pdf.

Verordnung über die Börsen und den Effektenhandel (Börsenverordnung, BEHV) dated 2 December 1996 (consolidated as of 1 May 2013), available at: http://www.admin.ch/opc/de/classified-compilation/19960659/index.html.

Verordnung über die Eigenmittel und Risikoverteilung für Banken und Effektenhändler (Eigenmittelverordnung, ERV) vom 1. Juni 2012 (Stand am 28 Marz 2020), available at: https://www.admin.ch/opc/de/official-compilation/2020/1105.pdf.

Vliet, Lars Van. The German grundschuld. Edinburgh Law Review 2012.

Voigtländer, Michael / Demary, Markus / Schindler, Felix / Westerheide, Peter / Köndgen, Johannes. A European Internal Market for Housing Finance. https://www.zew.de/de/publikationen/a-european-internal-market-for-housing-finance/.

von der Crone, Hans Caspar; Monferrini, Isabelle. Kapital und Notfallplanung - Standortbestimmung zur Regulierung systemrelevanter Finanzinstitute. Schweizerische Zeitschrift für Wirtschafts - und Finanzmarktrecht, 2012.

Walter, John R. Depression-Era Bank Failures: The Great Contagion or the Great Shakeout?. Federal Reserve Bank of Richmond Economic Quarterly Volume 91/1 Winter 2005.

Webel, Baird / Labonte, Marc. Government Interventions in Response to Financial Turmoil. Congressional Research Service Feb 2010 Diane Publishing.

Wehling, Axel and Ockenga, Tim. Finanzmarktregulierung nimmt Fahrt auf. Versicherungswirtschaft Verlag, Fundstelle 2014.

World Bank Group. Understanding Bank Recovery and Resolution in the EU: A Guidebook to the BRRD. April 2017. http://pubdocs.worldbank.org/en/609571482207234996/FinSAC-BRRD-Guidebook.pdf.

World Bank. Principles for Effective Insolvency and Creditor Rights Systems (Revised) 2016. http://pubdocs.worldbank.org/en/919511468425523509/ICR-Principles-Insolvency-Creditor-Debtor-Regimes-2016.pdf.

Wulfken, Jörg. EU-Komission: Die EU-Richtlinie für die Sanierung und Abwicklung und ihre Auswirkung auf die Refinanzierung von Banken. Kreditwesen 20/2012, Nr. 1054, Seite 28-31.

Wünsch, Oliver. Die Quadratur des Kreises: Rechtliche und ökonomische Aspekte der Abwicklung von Banken. Schweizerische Zeitschrift für Wirtschafts - und Finanzmarktrecht, 2012.

Zentralbibliothek Zürich; Beschreibung:XXV, 418 S, 24 cm Zentralbibliothek ZRH.

Zimmermann, Marc-Daniel. Capital Markets, Fair Value Accounting and Regulatory Capital Evidence from the U.S. and the European Banking Industry during the Financial Crisis of 2007-2009. Impressum St. Gallen, 2013 Umfang Online-Ressource Reihe (Dissertationen / Universität St. Gallen; No. 4195).

Index

INTERNATIONAL BANKING AND FINANCE LAW SERIES

1. Jan Job de Vries Robbe, *Innovations in Securitisation. Yearbook 2006,* 2006 (ISBN 90-11-2533-7).
2. Jim Bartos, *United States Securities Law: A Practical Guide,* Third edition, 2006 (ISBN 90-411-2362-8).
3. Hui Huang, *International Securities Markets: Insider Trading Law in China,* 2006 (ISBN 90-411-2557-4).
4. Barth et al., *Financial Restructuring and Reform in Post-WTO China,* 2007 (ISBN 90-411-2573-6).
5. Zhongfei Zhou, *Banking Laws in China,* 2007 (ISBN 978-90-411-2519-4).
6. Jan Job de Vries Robbe & Paul Ali, *Expansion and Diversification in Securitization Yearbook 2007,* 2007 (ISBN 978-90-411-2661-0).
7. Ross Buckley, *International Financial System. Policy and Regulation,* 2008 (ISBN 978-90-411-2746-4).
8. Jan Job de Vries Robbe, *Securitization Law and Practice: In the Face of the Credit Crunch,* 2008 (ISBN 978-90-411-2715-0).
9. Phoebus Athanassiou, *Hedge Fund Regulation in the European Union: Current Trends and Future Prospects,* 2009 (ISBN 978-90-411-2856-0).
10. Jan Job de Vries Robbe, *Structured Finance: On from the Credit Crunch: The Road to Recovery,* 2009 (ISBN 978-90-411-2787-7).
11. Gaetane Schaeken Willemaers, *The EU Issuer-Disclosure Regime: Objectives and Proposals for Reform,* 2011 (ISBN 978-90-411-3394-6).
12. Panagiotis Delimatsis & Nils Herger (eds), *Financial Regulation at the Crossroads: Implications for Supervision, Institutional Design and Trade,* 2011 (ISBN 978-90-411-3355-7).
13. Raffaele Scalcione, *The Derivatives Revolution: A Trapped Innovation and a Blueprint for Regulatory Reform,* 2011 (ISBN 978-90-411-3430-1).
14. Douglas Arner & Ross Buckley, *From Crisis to Crisis: The Global Financial System and Regulatory Failure,* 2011 (ISBN 978-90-411-3354-0).
15. Anton P. Trichardt, *Letters of Comfort: A Trans-Systemic Analysis,* 2012 (ISBN 978-90-411-3600-8).
16. Eddy Wymeersch, *Alternative Investment Fund Regulation,* 2012 (ISBN 978-90-411-3690-9).
17. Asif H. Qureshi & Xuan Gao (eds), *International Economic Organizations and Law: The Perspective and Role of the Legal Counsel,* 2012 (ISBN 97890-411-3427-1).
18. Rhys Bollen, *The Law and Regulation of Payment Services: A Comparative Study,* 2012 (ISBN 978-90-411-3818-7).
19. Ramandeep Kaur Chhina, *Standby Letters of Credit in International Trade,* 2012 (ISBN 978-90-411-4560-4).

20. Dirk Zetzsche (ed.), *The Alternative Investment Fund Managers Directive*, Third Edition, 2020 (ISBN 978-94-035-0910-5).
21. Lorenzo Sasso, *Capital Structure and Corporate Governance: The Role of Hybrid Financial Instruments*, 2013 (ISBN 978-90-411-4843-8).
22. Pablo Iglesias-Rodríguez, *The Accountability of Financial Regulators: A European and International Perspective*, 2013 (ISBN 978-90-411-3874-3).
23. Seraina Neva Grünewald, *The Resolution of Cross-Border Banking Crises in the European Union: A Legal Study from the Perspective of Burden Sharing*, 2014 (ISBN 978-90-411-4909-1).
24. Megan Bowman, *Banking on Climate Change: How Finance Actors and Transnational Regulatory Regimes are Responding*, 2015 (ISBN 978-90-411-5223-7).
25. Jin Sheng, *China's Listed Companies: Conflicts, Governance and Regulation*, 2015 (ISBN 978-90-411-5925-0).
26. Sven Schelo, *Bank Recovery and Resolution*, Second Edition, 2020 (ISBN 978-94-035-1881-7).
27. Luis M. Hinojosa-Martínez & José María Beneyto (eds), *European Banking Union: The New Regime*, 2015 (ISBN 978-90-411-5263-3).
28. Gill North, *Effective Company Disclosure in the Digital Age*, 2015 (ISBN 978-90-411-3815-6).
29. Hanneke Wegman, *Investor Protection: Towards Additional EU Regulation of Investment Funds?*, 2016 (ISBN 978-90-411-5252-7).
30. Ruth Plato-Shinar, *Banking Regulation in Israel: Prudential Regulation versus Consumer Protection*, 2016 (ISBN 978-90-411-6791-0).
31. Bader Alkhaldi, *Saudi Capital Market: Developments and Challenges*, 2017 (ISBN 978-90-411-8351-4).
32. Yves Mauchle, *Bail-In and Total Loss-Absorbing Capacity (TLAC): Legal and Economic Perspectives on Bank Resolution with Functional Comparisons of Swiss and EU Law*, 2017 (ISBN 978-90-411-8998-1).
33. Uzma Ashraf Barton, *Rethinking Regulation of International Finance: Law, Policy and Institutions*, 2018 (ISBN 978-90-411-8838-0).
34. Phoebus L. Athanassiou, *Digital Innovation in Financial Services: Legal Challenges and Regulatory Policy Issues*, 2018 (ISBN 978-90-411-8781-9).
35. Gu Bin, *The Law and Governance of the Asian Infrastructure Investment Bank*, 2019 (ISBN 978-94-035-0631-9).
36. Gerald Nels Olson, *Money, Morality and Law: A Case for Financial Crisis Accountability*, 2019 (ISBN 978-94-035-0941-9).

www.ingramcontent.com/pod-product-compliance
Lightning Source LLC
Chambersburg PA
CBHW071240230926
51849CB00001B/171
* 9 7 8 9 4 0 3 5 1 8 8 1 7 *